The Corpse : A History

THE CORPSE,
A History

by
CHRISTINE QUIGLEY

McFarland & Company, Inc., Publishers
Jefferson, North Carolina, and London

British Library Cataloguing-in-Publication data are available

Library of Congress Cataloguing-in-Publication Data

Quigley, Christine, 1963–
   The corpse: a history / by Christine Quigley
      p.   cm.
   Includes bibliographical references and index.
   ISBN 0-7864-0170-2 (library binding : 50# alk. paper) ∞
      1. Dead—Social aspects.   2. Dead—History.   3. Funeral
rites and ceremonies.   4. Cryonics.   5. Donation of organs,
tissues, etc.   I. Title.
GT3150.Q55   1996
393—dc20   96-30366
                                                     CIP

Manufactured in the United States of America

*McFarland & Company, Inc., Publishers
   Box 611, Jefferson, North Carolina 28640*

For you, Cris

Contents

viii   Contents

Introduction

Although civil and legal institutions do not agree on
exactly when life ends, most people are able to recognize
a corpse without referring to a dictionary.
　　—Kim Long and Terry Reim, *Fatal Facts: A Lively
　　Look at Common and Curious Ways People Have Died*[1]

Overview

Death. The word conveys a threat to each of us. One day our heart will
cease to beat. One day the electrical activity in our brain will draw to a close.
One day we will no longer think, work, play. We won't even relax as we know
it now. Each of us will become a corpse. We will make the transition from
animate to inanimate. As a corpse, we will not require food, we will not require
water, and we will not require air. We will, however, require disposal or preservative treatment, or we will contaminate the environment of those who continue to live. We trust the living to package our body and deposit it in the
ground, incinerate it, or apply whatever method prevails in our culture. We
may make some decisions in advance—pay for a plot or complete an organ
donor card—but many processes to which our remains will be subject are
beyond our control before and after death. Will we be autopsied? Exhumed?
Unless we are cremated or mummified, we will surely decay. Unless we make
other arrangements, we will most likely be embalmed. If we die in the wrong
place at the wrong time, our body might be cannibalized, get scavenged by
animals, or remain unidentified. If we die at the wrong hands, our body may
be violated, dismembered, and discarded. Be assured that our corpse will not
feel any of these things. The satisfaction, grief, or outrage lie with our survivors.

Opposite: Dead person, New York. Photo by Berenice Abbot, 1930. Reprinted with permission from Berenice Abbot/Commerce Graphics Ltd., Inc.

1

Corpses may be used for everything from personal pleasure to prolonging the life of a stranger. They have been ransomed and sold, exposed to public ridicule and public adoration. Their parts have been preserved in jars and in churches. And, like the living, some corpses have been discriminated against. Because where there are humans, there are (or will be) human remains, a history of the corpse spans time and place. The fact of death injects the corpse into both art and religion, as well as occasionally into our daily lives, where it can be symbolic of our own mortality or a focus for our grief over the death of the person who used to inhabit it. Either way, the dead can repulse or attract. Their pervasive presence and elusive nature, in addition to sheer volume, make corpses a worthy study. This book will document the roles that corpses have played in our history and will at the same time bring to light the techniques to which we have subjected them.

Certification of Death

A corpse becomes official when a death certificate is completed by the attending physician, coroner, or medical examiner and filed with the local government. In the U.S., a death certificate is required for all deaths except those of fetuses weighing less than 500 grams, which are considered medical specimens. A special fetal death certificate is usually required for stillbirths. The regular death certificate, which is rejected if not filled out in black ink, varies from state to state but usually requires the following information about the deceased: name, sex, race, and citizenship; date and place of death or date and place the body was found; date and place of birth (if known), age or approximation, and Social Security number; marital status, name of surviving spouse, and parents' names; occupation and residence; cause of death and contributing factors, manner of death (natural, accident, suicide, homicide, or undetermined), and time of death; whether an autopsy was performed; method of bodily disposition; name and address of funeral home and cemetery or crematory; and signature of the certifier.

The legal time of death is the moment at which death is pronounced, whether it follows the failure of resuscitative efforts or the discovery of a body. Except in cases of legal execution and people dead on arrival at the hospital, death may be *pronounced* and the time recorded by a paramedic, nurse, or police officer. In international waters, pronouncement may be made by the captain of the ship. The death must be *certified*, however, by the coroner or medical examiner, or under specified circumstances by the attending physician. A physician may complete the death certificate when a person dies of a known terminal illness, under hospice or nursing home care, or in the hospital (though not during treatment or surgery). If the cause of death is questionable or the results of the autopsy or other tests are not yet available, the cause may be listed as "pending" until it can be determined. If a U.S. citizen dies outside the United States, as approximately 8,000 Americans do each year, the next of kin is furnished by the nearest American consular office with a "report of death," which has the legal status of a death certificate. Until the death certificate is filed and a certificate of disposition (a burial or cremation permit) issued by local authorities, the corpse may not legally be disposed of. In the U.S., disposal is the responsibility of next-of-kin in the order specified by state law (usually surviving spouse, adult children, parents, siblings).

Death Rates and Causes

It is from death certificates that annual statistics are compiled by the U.S. Center for Health Statistics, allowing us to calculate our nationwide death rate at more than 2 million per year and the worldwide death rate at some 50 million annually. In 1989, it was calculated that three people in the world died every two seconds. In 1990, a total of 49,936,000 people died, 13.1 million of them children under the age of five, and 9.4 million of these under one year of age. In 1991, a total of 50,289,000 people died, the majority (38,888,000) in developing countries. In the same year, 718,000 Americans died of heart disease, 514,000 died of cancer, 144,070 died of cerebrovascular disease, 91,700 died accidental deaths, 30,200 took their own lives, 29,850 died of AIDS, 27,440 were murdered or killed by legal intervention, and 14 of the 2,482 men and women on death row in the U.S. were executed. Of the 43,500 motor vehicle fatalities recorded in the U.S. in 1991, 18,500 resulted from the collision of two or more cars and 7,000 were pedestrians struck and killed. In 1992, there were 2,183,000 deaths in the U.S., 1,129,600 of them males and 1,053,590 of them females. Of this number, more than 1,000,000 were age 75 or older. Estimates in the same year put the number of abortions worldwide at 150,000 per day.

Five years ago it was calculated that an American dies every 16 seconds, a total of 5,400 a day. Fifteen years from now, the rate is expected to rise to 7,200 a day, 300 an hour, 5 a minute.[2] The American Board of Funeral Service Education has expressed its doubts that the graduating classes of morticians, which are currently shrinking, will be able to keep pace. And yet, despite the numbers, a large percentage of us have never had a one-on-one confrontation with a dead human body. Other than the initiated medical student and those whose business it is to remove, examine, or treat the corpse, few have stumbled across a dead stranger or have had to identify a loved one at the morgue. The bodies we have seen have been clothed and masked by cosmetics. We have not been privy to the bloating of a body pulled from a river, the rosy complexion of a victim of carbon monoxide poisoning, or any of the other sights and smells of death "in the raw."

Physical Properties of a Dead Body

In some ways, it is lucky that most deaths now occur in the hospital, since death is occasionally less than self-evident. A dead body is supposed to be cold, but in the case of a violent or painful death the body temperature may continue to rise for up to an hour after death. Even under normal conditions, a body may take ten hours to cool completely. A corpse is supposed to be stiff, but rigor mortis is dependent on air temperature, cause of death, and condition and age of the body. Rigor usually begins two to six hours after death, starting in the eyelids, neck, and jaw, and spreading through the face, down both arms, and into the chest, abdomen, and legs. It is usually complete within twelve hours of death, although it can be "broken" by applying sufficient force. And it subsides in twelve to forty-eight hours, starting in the jaw and proceeding in the same order. Rigor mortis, also called cadaveric spasm, is a stiffening of the muscles that occurs when adenosine triphosphate (ATP, the energy source that allows muscles to contract) disappears some four hours after death. The rigor softens only after the muscle fibers begin to decompose. It will begin more quickly and last longer in a strong body than a weak or emaciated one. An obese person may not develop rigor mortis, but a thin person may develop it rapidly. It will end more quickly in the bodies of infants and convulsive people. In the heat, it will begin and end faster, and in the cold it will begin quickly and end slowly. Violent exercise or struggle before death may hasten its onset, and a slow death may prevent it from occurring at all.

A corpse may not be cold or stiff, but in most cases death will be recognized. In his book *How We Die*, Sherwin B. Nuland writes: "The appearance of a newly lifeless face cannot be mistaken for unconsciousness. Within a minute after the heart stops beating, the face begins to take on the unmistakable gray-white pallor of death; in an uncanny way, the features very soon appear corpse-like, even to those who have never before seen a dead body. A man's corpse looks as though his essence has left him, and it has."[3]

Traditionally, cessation of heartbeat and breathing have betrayed the corpse. When American painter Charles Willson Peale (d. 1827) asked his daughter to take his pulse, she replied that she couldn't feel any. "I thought not," were Peale's last words. Other classic signs indicating death are the relaxation of sphincter muscles and changes in the eyes which are still looked to by resuscitation teams deciding whether to continue their attempts. The eyes very quickly become dulled and the pupils dilated; then the eyes become covered with a cloudy film and flatten just enough to be noticed. To these observances have been added increasingly sensitive tests to ascertain the death of the body and later the brain (brain death is now the legal definition of death): no moisture on a mirror held over nostrils and mouth, no swelling or discoloration upon tying off the end of a finger, absence of reflexes, insensitivity to electrical stimuli, acid reaction to litmus paper placed under the eyelid, reddening of the conjunctival sac when a drop of ether is instilled in it, the bursting of an air-filled blister when a flame is applied to the skin, no reaction to noxious stimulation, and absence of blinking and ocular movement upon turning the head and irrigating the ears with ice water. Today legal brain death is evidenced by lack of brain activity (verified with an electroencephalograph), cornea sensitivity, pupil reaction to light, cough reflex, and spontaneous breathing. The criteria for brain death differ around the world, meaning that a person declared dead in one country may not be considered dead in another.

Simply put, a corpse will not respond. Its muscles are flaccid (although the penis may appear to be erect), its face is expressionless, and the lips are parted, formless, and pale. The skin becomes waxy, blue on the extremities and purplish where the blood has settled. "The color disappeared from both eyelid and cheek, leaving a wanness even more than that of marble," wrote Edgar Allan Poe.[4] A dead body will not bleed, except through the action of gravity. Neither will it have a blood pressure, a fact that alerted one student nurse that her patient had just suffered cardiac arrest. Although machines have aided in the diagnosis of death, from the suggested use of X rays (to which dead flesh offers more resistance) in 1896 to the later development of the electroencephalograph, intuition and observation play major roles: "A living being feels alive; a dead person feels like a pack of meat under plastic," says a police officer,[5] a fact which Nuland backs up: "The surrounding muscles, if they are not still in an element of spasm, have begun to assume the flaccid consistency of meat slabbed in a butcher's display case. The skin has lost its elasticity."[6] Still, as an award-winning Dr. Maze pointed out in 1890, the only sure sign of death is putrefaction, a topic that will be covered in a later chapter.

THE CORPSE AS AN OBJECT OF GRIEF

The Symbol

The skeleton need not be whole in order to play its role.
It may be dismantled and divided into small pieces; each
of its bones possesses the same symbolic value.
—Philippe Ariès, *The Hour of Our Death*[1]

Reminders of Mortality

Human remains, in the form of a body or a skeleton, rarely fail to evoke a passing thought about death. For those in the death professions, a corpse may represent making a living. For those in the health professions, a lifeless body may represent failure. For the rest of us, the symbolism of the dead lies somewhere in between. We see in the corpse our own fate and the fate of those we love. We equate the vanishing of flesh which results in the skeleton with the vanishing of our memory in the minds of the living. "All the corpses in the world are chemically identical, but living individuals are not," wrote Carl Jung.[2] When we die, we relinquish our individuality. Void of personality, the corpse joins the masses. Once the skin, muscles, and organs have fled their frame, the bones attest only to the fact that a life was lived. Except to the scientist, they do not offer the who, what, where, and when. The skeleton is the halfway point to not having existed at all.

In the medical school, science lab, or figure drawing classroom, the skeleton is a generic teaching device, full-scale models of which are now available in neon colors. The pelvic bones easily indicate whether the previous owner was male or female, but beyond that little is known even about how the skeleton, which may be decades old, was acquired by the school. In a museum, a skeleton, which may be centuries old, is usually better identified, but often causes viewers to question if resting in a glass case is resting in peace.

Part I title page: **Dead child. Nineteenth-century tintype. Collection of the author.**

Homicide detectives and forensic anthropologists strive to identify the disarticulated skeleton occasionally found in the woods. But who remembers or has recorded the names once attached to the neatly arranged skulls in the Parisian catacombs?

Our own bones outlive us, but in anonymity. Cemeteries promise perpetual care, but there is no guarantee against the graves eventually being moved and the markers mixed up, if not discarded. Even so, the gravestone or plaque bears little more than a name, dates of birth and death, and relationship ("Beloved Wife and Mother") to the living who will soon follow. The dead may live in human memory for two or three generations, but their descendants follow them to the grave and are subject to the same extinction. Although in life, bones are living tissue that bleed when cut and heal when broken, after death they are reminders of the fate of our bodies and our personalities. Before the advent of the X ray, CT scan, and MRI, the skeleton was invisible until after the body had died and decayed. Today the grinning skull that mocks our earthly endeavors may be our own.

While the skeleton conveys the constant threat of death, the sight of a corpse may raise even more immediate concerns about health and longevity, particularly if the body is our own gender and age. *What if this were my funeral?* If the color and style of the hair or other superficial characteristics match someone we know, it may also force a comparison. *What would I do without my husband (or wife)?* The circumstances of death witnessed on the evening news may apply to anyone. The sheet-wrapped body being carried down the steps of a suburban townhouse might be the next-door neighbor. The body being freed from a wrecked car with the jaws of life might be your son or daughter. The next innocent victim caught in the crossfire of a drive-by shooting might be you.

The symbolism that a corpse has for the living has much to do with context. The sightless eyes of a relative who has finally been released from a terminal illness may stir feelings of attachment to the physical remains, though they are only a vestige of the once-healthy individual. The patient now sleeping in repose hints that some day, some way, we too will never wake up. On the other hand, the withered body of a cadaver, minus clothing and eyeglasses, provokes the distancing necessary to cut it up. This direct confrontation with the meat that remains after the spirit is gone ruthlessly weeds out those would-be doctors who equate the corpse too wholly with their own mortality: "During the first year of medical school, when we began dissecting a human body, the first depressions in the class showed up. One kid hung himself in his garage; another had a psychotic break. I am convinced it is a more difficult and dramatic period for medical students than is generally acknowledged."[3]

Some of those who go on to become practicing physicians are accused of treating their patients in the same cold, businesslike way they treated their cadaver, regarding death as inevitable.[4] Others who mingle thoughts of the living with the dead include not only murderers during premeditation, but anyone who has viewed an embalmed corpse. Despite its artful preparation, we compare the casketed body with the living individual and of course find it lacking. There is silence and serenity where a few days before there was conversation and cantankerousness. The body we pay our respects to also reinforces the often overlooked idea that death does not only occur to strangers.

To some, the corpse symbolizes the promise of a future existence. In ancient Egypt, the integrity of the mummy ensured entry into the next world. For practitioners of cryonics, the frozen body is a chance at reentry into this world at a future time. Among believers in the Last Judgment, the corpse, while initially an empty shell, holds the promise of being reunited with the soul and resurrected in an incorruptible form. In cases shaded slightly with guilt, the brain-dead body means continued life to those awaiting organ transplant, and unfortunate victims may equal sustenance—and therefore survival—to those in extreme circumstances. In other situations, the corpse has been made to signal the living, to warn them against doing wrong or to shock them out of their complacency. The corpse of a suicide may herald to society an injustice or a neglect that has taken place, even without a note to confirm it. Historically, the corpses of kings have been disentombed and used as scapegoats to ridicule the previous regime. And perhaps most obviously, the bodies hanging from the gallows at public executions, and disputably those put to death behind prison walls, symbolize the wages of societal sins.

In ways both revered and reviled, the corpse, or parts of it, is kept in remembrance. An urn on the mantel containing cremated remains is a beacon of grief and remembrance in a more three-dimensional way than a photograph. A portion of the body of a saint, enshrined for public veneration by the faithful, becomes a symbol of piety and inspires the same quality in those who pray to the saint for guidance and protection. By means of a twisted private worship, murderers have been known to hoard body parts from their victims and use them as mnemonic devices to relive the details of their crime again and again. In cases just as frightening, the entire body is coveted by the necrophile who equates it with pleasure and love and practices his or her affections on it. In contrast, specimens from the bodies of murder victims may serve as the evidence which convicts their attackers.

There are also corpses that are not kept in remembrance, but are at their death "larger than life." These include the body of a newborn or stillborn, in which death has occurred before life has begun; the unidentified body, which lays bare our fears of anonymity in death; and the body of a leader or celebrity which, despite the honors their remains may receive, symbolizes the democracy of death. The dissected body offers knowledge and practice to those in the anatomy lab long after it would otherwise have wasted away. The bodies of dead soldiers and civilian casualties speak to opposing nations about the inhumanity of war. And the volumes of corpses resulting from accident or disaster call human frailty urgently to mind.

In ancient Egypt, a mummy was conveyed to the banquet hall after a feast to sober the guests and remind them of their mortality. Bombarded as we are with the icon of the skull and the outline of the sheet-draped body, both at times cause us to ponder our death and wonder how and when it will come. The powdered face of an embalmed elderly relative may imply that death is painless. The bruised face of a beating victim may suggest the opposite. A Halloween skeleton may be only a caricature of bones bleached by the sun, but it offers us the gentle chance once a year to reassess our lives with regard to our assumed longevity. The empty eye sockets of a specimen at the natural history museum or the depiction of a skull and crossbones on a dangerous household chemical are both warnings. The poison label warns against eating or drinking the contents, and the skull warns us to "Eat, drink, and be merry ... for tomorrow we die."

Fear and Fascination

When faced with the dead, the living cover their eyes and then peek through their fingers. In one way or another, the dead are shielded from view to protect them and us from our natural curiosity. The closed casket forces mourners to rely on their memories, but denies them the opportunity to witness death, if after the fact. Bodies that are exposed in the funeral home are sanitized and don't reveal the real effects of death. This usual distancing from death may help explain why most of us crane our necks at the site of a gory accident. In his book *Disaster*, Allen Troy theorizes: "The variety of motives that make up this impulse to gather at the scene of a disaster cover a range that perhaps begins with a desire for a vicarious taste of violence at a glimpse of a crushed body or severed limb and extends into an enthusiastic self-congratulations of having missed the consequences of disaster oneself."[5]

When a body has been torn by the force of a tornado, crushed by a steering wheel, or split by a fall, all available forces are marshaled to repair the human damage. From the care of the emergency crew at the site to that of the trauma team at the hospital, the clinically dead are worked over by many hands that try to restore life. Once death is irreversible, "In the center of the devastation lies a corpse, and it has lost all interest for those who, moments earlier, were straining to be the deliverers of the man whose spirit occupied it," as Nuland tells us.[6] Those who are interested at that point are civilians— those who don't see death on a daily basis, who wonder at the devastation required to silence the human body, but are restricted from the emergency room. What they see is on the street, and they, like paramedics, face it together.

To stand shoulder to shoulder and watch as an unfortunate victim of accident is declared dead at the scene is to share the possibilities and the probabilities. "This could happen to any of us" is easier to accept than "This could happen to me." Emotionally, there seems to be safety in numbers. We can relax our guard to some extent and examine the external symptoms of death: the blood, the mutilation, the contortions. Over 100,000 people came to gawk at the blood-stained field where French mass murderer Jean-Baptiste Troppmann had disposed of six of his eight victims in 1869. A vengeance-driven curiosity caused thousands to board a train to Palmetto, Georgia, in 1899 to see a black man lynched and buy a slice from his body as a souvenir. And a smaller crowd to whom John Dillinger had become almost a hero dipped handkerchiefs in his blood after federal agents brought the gangster down in Chicago in 1934.

Even when a body has not been disfigured, it is still more easily gazed at when we band together. Certain rites, by custom or necessity, have always been social events. While sharing their mutual grief, relatives and friends cushion the sight of the deceased by their collective presence at the wake. The presence of three or more other students blunts the shock of unveiling the cadaver in the gross anatomy lab. Executions, though no longer public, are still witnessed by an invited crowd that includes not only journalists and average citizens, but often the family members of the condemned. Exhumations are carried out by the collected representatives of several agencies. In many places the indigent are buried by work crews. And even nineteenth-century bodysnatchers often worked in teams of two or three.

This fraternity among coworkers and complete strangers functions as a shield, sometimes allowing a false sense of security. The "it-won't-happen to me" mindset is evident as drivers speed off once through the bottleneck caused by a collision. *Miami Herald* crime reporter Edna Buchanan illustrates the point with swimmers warned of dangerous rip currents: "One was told personally by lifeguards that it was too dangerous to venture into the water. He insisted that he had gone swimming every morning for ten days and had no intention of disrupting his routine. His body washed up a short time later.... You would think that that would scare the rest of the swimmers out of the water. Not in Miami. Determined to have fun or die, they ran like lemmings into the sea, many within sight of the blanket-draped corpse on the beach."[7]

When a person is one-on-one with a dead body, he or she is rarely as carefree. If the first to encounter the body, an individual is more likely to run to a telephone to contact the authorities than to ignore the corpse or inspect it for damage. Alone one is on equal ground with the corpse, face to face with one's fate. Few but necrophiles are devoid of the natural revulsion the rest of us feel. Others—morticians and coroners among them—have dulled their fear by repetition.

Experience with death lessens its mystery, at least physically. The fear and awe of death (and if we extrapolate, the fear and awe of the corpse) seems to diminish with age. The older one becomes, the more friends one has buried, and therefore the more accustomed one becomes to death. Again Edna Buchanan provides an example:

> Young people ... are drawn morbidly to death. They even carry babies and lead small children by the hand to come quick and see this awful something, anything that has happened. But the elderly won't go out of their way to see a dead body. They won't go out of their way to avoid one, either. Elderly bathers will slip surreptitiously under yellow police lines protecting a body found in an alley and drag their beach chairs down that alleyway, carefully skirting the corpse, of course, simply because it is the most direct route to their destination. Why detour for death?[8]

The elderly seem to have made their peace with death. They do not overly identify with the corpse, nor do they run from it.

Such peace comes with contemplation. Forced as it may be through the deaths of one's contemporaries or sought after as it was in times past, facing death brings a reconciliation with it and a renewed appreciation for life. The Greeks and Romans slept in tombs to dream of, question, and receive inspiration from the dead. St. Ignatius Loyola meditated on a skeleton as a spiritual exercise in the sixteenth century. A common form of meditation among Buddhist monks is the "recollection of death" in which a monk sits in the graveyard or crematorium and contemplates corrupt bodies or the ashes of bodies that have been incinerated. The meditation often specifically includes the comparison of the monk's own body with that of the corpses. This provokes a profound awareness of life's brevity and instability and the inevitability of death.[9]

In other ways, the contemplation and acceptance of death manifest themselves as a rehearsal in which the living play the part of their own corpse. French actress Sarah Bernhardt (d. 1923) liked to receive friends while lying in a coffin which she had insisted her mother buy her during a bout with consumption as a teenager. Immortal teenager James Dean recorded monologues about how it would feel to lie in the grave, drew pictures of himself as a corpse surrounded by candles, and had himself photographed in a casket at the local funeral establishment. When poet John Donne (d. 1631) arranged to be sketched before his death, he posed in a winding sheet with his eyes closed. Charles V (d. 1658), Holy Roman Emperor and king of Spain, was known to rehearse his own funeral. And among the lesser-known to practice being a corpse is a woman cataloged in *Mad and Magnificent Yankees* who had a $30,000 casket specially designed and built over a period of years in the late 1800s: "Mrs. Hiller was so proud of it she had it set up in the front parlor. When her friends came to call, she would climb in and lie down so they could see 'just how splendid she would look when she was all laid out.' She even had a wax model of herself made, attired in her fabulous burial robes, and she placed the model in the casket in the parlor."[10] Through what is perceived as eccentricity, Mrs. Hiller and her more famous counterparts may have conquered their fear by joining in what cannot be beaten.

On the opposite end of the spectrum, death is impersonalized as a means of distancing ourselves from it. The wake is no longer held in the parlor of the home; the parlor has become the living room and the funeral parlor has become the funeral *home*. The face of death is covered not only after the last breath has been exhaled in the hospital room, but when it is forced out by the electric chair or noose. The execution hood is intended to protect the sensitivities of onlookers from the grimaces of strangulation and the gore of electrocution. What it also does is provide a screen separating life and death from each other. When the dead are separated by six feet of earth, they also lose much of their individuality and most of their immediacy. Thus laypersons can traverse a cemetery with much more ease than they can a crowded morgue. The same effect may be achieved by the display of specimens in a medical museum, labeled only anatomically and stored in the safety of corked or capped jars. Similarly, the skeleton that has been denuded of its facial features has less impact than the preserved head of a mummy, which in turn has less impact that the face of an intact corpse. In skeletal form in museums and cemeteries, the dead temper our curiosity by somehow sanctifying their surroundings, suggesting that we are to learn from them, not ogle at them. In bodily form in a medical setting, the dead so closely resemble us that we offer respect almost subconsciously, lowering our voices in their presence.

Some people—necrophobics—develop physical symptoms including nausea, dizziness, and chills when they even think about corpses. For the rest of us, fear of the dead may be fear of the unknown future they represent, despite the fact that Elisabeth Kübler-Ross has determined that even those with faith in a promising afterlife fear death. Fascination with the dead may be evidence of an innate death drive, in spite of the fact that John Hinton has found fear of death to be biologically necessary lest the human race die out through the taking of unnecessary risks.[11] Fear of the dead may stem from the fear that their bodies are contagious, as indeed they were in times of plague and still are where typhoid and dysentery have strongholds. Yet the dead are looked to as a means to "pre-experience" death. At the same time that we hesitate to touch them, we may examine them closely for cause of death, signs of pain, and indications that the soul has in fact taken flight.

These observations are undertaken only with certain defenses—a professional detachment, a physical barrier or the distance allowed by television or photography, or (as mentioned above) the company of others. Unless we are in these ways separated from the dead, we rarely allow them to outnumber us. We arrive in droves as the bodies of murder victims are removed from the yard of a rural home, partly out of morbid fascination and partly to steel ourselves and each other against the mounting horror. When exponential horrors are discovered—the hundreds of followers of Peoples Temple founder Jim Jones arrayed on the ground in Guyana and the victims of Adolf Hitler stacked by the thousands in the concentration camps—the mere photographs leave us awestruck and overcome despite the passage of years.

Time does not erase the fear and awe we have in the presence of death and its victims. Fear of the dead goes back much further than the horror movies that have conditioned us to beware that the eyes of a corpse may spring open at the same time it grabs our wrist to prevent us from running. Modern concerns are less about the walking dead and more about death's causes and postponement, but few today would be comfortable touring the catacombs on their own. We are less preoccupied with premature burial and more with premature death. The corpse of a child is fearful not because it was doomed by supernatural powers to an early death, but because current preventative and curative techniques were not advanced enough to save the child's life. We may look at a corpse to discern differences between it and us. If the body is that of a seventy-year-old man or woman, the young may relax their guard a little, considering the death to be in the natural order of things. If the body belongs to a twenty-year-old man who was struck by a car or a thirty-year-old woman stalked and killed by a serial murderer, the tables are turned with the realization that we have little control over death at best. Fear of the dead is now fear of the failings of contemporary medicine, but it has always been fear that we could be next. In our heavily populated society, it is easy to hide behind the statistics, to keep death both out of sight and out of mind. When we catch sight of a dead body, whether we shy away or are drawn in for a closer look, it reminds us of the facts of life, of which death is arguably the most important. When corpses are presented to us in numbers, we are even more profoundly prompted about our obligation to join the great majority.

Superstitions

The universal fear of death that the corpse represents has led to numerous superstitions which govern the actions of the living toward it. The seemingly inert remains of a human life are endowed with both positive and negative power: they can harm a child in the womb and blight crops, but they can also heal the sick. As the byproduct of a soul that has entered another dimension, the corpse inspires fear of retribution by its ghost and the possibility that it has some influence over who will follow it to the grave. The living waver between protecting the corpse against evil spirits and fearing its own recently released ghost.

In deference to the power of the spirit of the recently deceased, several customs have arisen involving touching or kissing the body. Such acts allow the living to make peace with the dead and, in some ways, with the idea of death. According to European superstition, touching a corpse as it lays in a coffin before burial ensures good fortune for the living and allows the dead to rest in peace. The gesture of touching or kissing the corpse indicates that one bears no ill will toward the deceased and prevents the spirit from haunting. Touching the forehead of a corpse protects one against dreaming of the dead person or seeing his or her ghost. According to Kentucky folklore, touching a corpse is said to remove all fear of death. The spirit is often thought to be affected by the way the living treat or mistreat the corpse. The Hebrews believed that if a corpse was hurt in any way, the soul suffered. In Chinese folklore, if a cat were allowed to jump over a corpse, the spirit would haunt the area. In Haiti, a child whose parent has died is urged to kiss and step over the corpse as a means of keeping the spirit away. The Assyrians believed that failure to perform burial and other rites of the dead would cause their spirits to haunt the family. Omitting a pillow from the casket ensures that the stay in purgatory will be short. Placing a coin under the head of a corpse prevents it from stealing from the living. The threat of haunting by the ghost even guides the treatment of bodies of strangers: passing a dead body lying on the ground is said to be a bad omen.

Certain preventive measures may also reduce the risk of unleashing a harmful spirit or render the newly dead less vulnerable to evil spirits that may snatch away the soul or take possession of the body. The washing of the body and the vigil kept over the corpse are customs that arose to guard it from demons. If knots of any kind are allowed to remain in the clothing, the spirit will never rest in peace. The procession to the grave is carried out without stopping or hindrance lest the dissatisfied spirit escape from the body and haunt the survivors. The corpse should be conveyed feet first so the ghost will not return. It was suggested that those who attend a funeral return by a different route to confuse the ghost that may try to follow them. English superstition warns against a corpse being carried to the church by a new road. Although a corpse is said to be blessed if rain falls on it, letting one's tears fall on the body will cause its spirit to be restless. For the same reason, one should never allow a corpse to be reflected in a mirror. The hair of the corpse often has special significance. Some pygmy peoples cut off the hair to rob the corpse of magical strength that would allow it to walk again. A Mississippi superstition holds that a woman's hair should never be plaited for burial or the devil will send his demons to unbraid it even before the body is in the grave. Burial face down was intended to prevent a witch or vampire from causing further trouble.

Through a superstitious contagion by which the dead are ensured proper treatment, the performance or neglect of certain tasks is believed to cause additional deaths. A traditional belief states that if a corpse remains unburied over a Sunday, another village resident will die within a week. Another claims that if a corpse remains in the house longer than usual, another death in the family will follow shortly. Exhuming a body is also said to provoke a death or calamity among the surviving family members. And moving a body from one parish to another is sure to cause sickness and death in the new location. The qualities of a corpse may also be indicators of a death to follow. A corpse remaining warm long after it should be cold is an omen of a death in the family. If rigor mortis fails to set in, it indicates that another death will follow quickly. A corpse with open eyes is waiting for the next person to die. It is said that the tradition of placing pennies on the eyes of a corpse was originally intended to remove the reflection of death upon the living, thereby preventing the dead from passing on their condition. Greek villagers believed that exhumed remains which are yellow-brown show that the deceased lived a good life, while blackened remains indicate that the deceased lived badly, thus providing physical evidence of a benevolent or malevolent spirit.

Corpses are traditionally believed to be harmful to unborn or newborn children, and the two extremes are life are often isolated from one another. Touching a cadaver was formerly believed to halt menstruation. Pregnant women were urged not to attend funerals, and women were discouraged from carrying their babies in a funeral procession. If a pregnant woman closed the eyes of the dead, superstition dictated that unless she crossed herself on her stomach, she might give birth to a blind infant. In Kentucky, it was believed that if a pregnant woman merely looked at a dead person, her baby would die. If an infant was buried face down it was thought to prevent the birth of other children in the family.

The corpse was believed to be imbued with otherworldly powers which, if harnessed, could be put to good use. Necromancy, or communication with the dead, traditionally required the presence of the corpse, but the body could also be put to less esoteric uses. According to wide belief, the touch of a corpse's hand was thought to cure warts and other ills—as the body decays, so will the warts. Perspiration from a corpse was applied while still warm to goiters, birthmarks, tumors, or hemorrhoids to heal them. The hand of a person who had died an early death was believed to cure scrofula. Grinding the bone of a long-dead corpse into powder and applying it to cancer or sores was said to effect their relief. Ground skull or water drunk from the crown of a skull was given to epileptics to prevent seizures. According to one recipe, nine pieces of the skull are ground into powder and ingested; if all nine pieces are not used, the dead man will come looking for them. In the Scottish highlands, the skull of a suicide was used, and those cured were never again permitted to touch a dead body or view a funeral. Toothache was said to be relieved by drinking water out of a skull, especially of a hanged man, or biting the tooth out of a skull. Pills made from the ground skull of a hanged man were thought to be effective against the bite of a mad dog. Touching a dead body was used to cure swollen glands, tumors, and even the hunchback of a child. Rubbing the afflicted part of one's body against that of a hanged criminal was a sought-after privilege that ensured a most powerful cure. In Jordan, the corpses of murdered men were said to have remarkable healing power if their blood was drunk or their bodies were stepped over. Sometimes cure was affected merely by touching the affected part of the body to the same part on the corpse. The curative powers of the dead even extended to their shrouds, which were believed to soothe headache and swelling, and the water in which they were washed, which would calm fits. Chewing a plant which grew in a skull caused aching teeth to come out and moss from a skull was believed to staunch blood, cure headaches, and relieve symptoms of plague.

In some ways, the corpse may become a sacrificial victim after the fact, aiding in human endeavors and protecting against harm. In other ways the corpse spreads its lifelessness to its surroundings. Fishermen once believed that fishing was good in waters where a drowning had occurred. Drenching an exhumed body during a drought is thought to bring rain. Yet if a corpse is carried over a field, the field will thereafter yield poor crops or become barren. It was said that nothing would grow on the spot where a violent death took place, but the grass where the saintly were slain appeared greener. A corpse carried on board a ship will cause bad weather sufficient to threaten life. In contrast, fire is said to be extinguished where a corpse is kept.

Although most of these superstitions are no longer taken literally, we still honor them in many timeless customs. We still close the eyes of a corpse and maintain the continuity of the funeral cortege. We no longer look to the corpse as a cure for disease, but many do offer the kiss of peace as a sign of respect. In less obvious ways, the ancient beliefs continue their hold over us. We still find something distasteful, beyond mere physical disgust, about exhuming the dead. To this day, sailors consider a corpse on board bad luck. And, while we would not exclude her, we may be jarred by the juxtaposition of life and death when we see a pregnant woman at a wake. In *The Space of Death*, Michel Ragon points out, "The dead are no longer feared, but we continue to shut them away in coffins, which have been nailed down or (even more securely) screwed down, and which are then enclosed in sealed, concrete burial vaults, under a very heavy stone. And all this is further enclosed in a cemetery surrounded by high walls, the gates of which are kept locked."[12]

When they were heeded, these folklorish injunctions about the corpse served to allay our fears: *If we bury the body promptly, no harm will come to us. If we touch it, it will rest in peace.* In their current diluted manifestations, or camouflaged as signs of respect, superstitions still betray a nervousness in the presence of the dead, a silent acknowledgment of their power over the living.

Speaking of Corpses

From the clinical to the cynical, the language of death is ruled by dichotomy. A person is either *deceased* or *food for worms*. In its presence, the body is referred to by name or as *the loved one*; behind its back, it is described by its worst qualities. "Speak nothing but good of the dead" is a commandment broken by fear which manifests itself as ridicule. While respect for the dead is sometimes mandated, mocking death is like whistling in the dark and bolsters us against our mutual fate.

The inactivity of the dead is a popular theme in our speech. Once he *hands in his dinner pail* and *lays down his knife and fork*, a corpse is *down for the long count* with *belly up* and *toes up*. Before her death is declared, a woman may be termed an *unconscious person*, and she is a *silent passenger* if she rides the rails to get to her final destination. The corpse is without energy or will. Life has *winked out* and the body is *deanimated*. All must be done for it: it is *salted away*, *sewn in a blanket*, and put *in cold storage* or *on ice* until it can be buried *six feet under*. Once *put to bed with a shovel*, the dead can do nothing but *take a dirt nap* in a *bed of clay*.

Although they can't initiate action, dead bodies are almost always the object of actions not only by their survivors, but by insects, animals, and the natural processes of decay. The minute the heart stops beating and the brain's electricity flickers out, the body becomes *meat*. Depending on how well it is sheltered, it is shortly thereafter *dog meat*, *crow bait*, or *flybait*. Whether or not rigor has set it, it is called a *stiff*. If there is a delay in the discovery of a body, it may deserve to be called a *stinker* by the employees at the medical examiner's office or a *floater* if found in the water. If unclaimed, the body will soon be *morgue-aged property* and may be nicknamed *John R. Corpse* rather than John Doe.

At the mercy of the living, physically and linguistically, the dead body has given its name to a verb. *To corpse* is to kill, and murder has its own consequences for the dead. They are *X'd out*, *blotted off the map*. To be *stopped in one's tracks* may be the dark side of *dying with one's boots on*. Slang sometimes bypasses the act of homicide and looks forward to the laying out of the body. To murder is to *put a lily in one's hand* or to *put on a slab*. Autopsy will reveal the bullet wounds that indicate death *by lead poisoning*. Other causes of death yield other synonyms. *Megacorpses* was coined as a unit of 1 million corpses in reference to the casualties of atomic warfare. Even conventional warfare may result in soldiers becoming *cannon fodder* and *going home in a box*. While war casualties are said to have *bought the farm*, anyone who is buried becomes a *landowner*. Those who choose cremation as a means of disposition will end up as *cremains* rather than a *carcass*. One who plans for cryonic suspension will be a *corpsicle* instead of *filling a casket*.

In the world of the living, the dead can only fill up a box, a morgue drawer, or a hole in the ground. They assault the senses of the living. When the living dull their own senses, for instance with drink, the language of death is borrowed to describe their condition. An inebriated person is often described as *dead drunk* and may characterize his or her condition the next morning as *death warmed over*. One in a deep sleep may be *dead to the world* or *dead as a doornail*, while *deadpan* describes an expressionless face. Someone in a threatened position may be *dead meat* and someone in a hopeless situation a *dead duck*. Death and disturbing the dead are both used as threats in our figures of speech. "Drop dead," we answer to someone who insults us. "Over my dead body," we respond to a proposal we strongly dislike. Either an enemy or an idea may be *better off dead*. When the volume on the stereo is too high, we complain that the music is *loud enough to wake the dead*. If we do something a dead friend or relative would have objected to, we suggest that the body would *roll over in the grave*.

With these idioms, we restore some life to the dead to coerce our own actions. When we give life to the idea of death—offering it a skeletal body we make it even more fearsome and powerful. It is awe-inspiring: the *Great Leveller* or the *Great Whipper*. It has the wisdom of age and the strength of immortality: *Old Man Mose* or the *Old Floorer*. And it is rarely benevolent: the *Grim Reaper* or *Grim Monarch*. We allow ourselves the hypocrisy of making fun of the individual dead, while showing respect to death's personification. At the same time that the dead are rotting in their graves, Death stands upright above them and the living, wielding his merciless scythe. In Mexico, where an annual celebration (El día de los muertos) is given over to Death and his victims, the reaper is much more approachable. As Octavio Paz explains: "The word death is not pronounced in New York, in Paris, in London, because it burns the lips. The Mexican, in contrast, is familiar with death, jokes about it, caresses it, sleeps with it, celebrates it; it is one of his favorite toys and his most steadfast love."[13] To them, Death is the *bald, bucktoothed*, and *bony one*. He is the *equalizer*, but he is also *skinny* and *shaky*. He is the *bold one*, but has *rooster's feet*. The *clean and peeled one* is *frugal* and *grave*, but is also known as *smiley*. Our Grim Reaper is mysterious and cloaked. That of the Mexicans is exposed, befriended, and teased about his boniness. Through his image and their many nicknames, Mexicans make a caricature of Death, allowing even children to become familiar with the idea of death and to face their mortality. Unlike Americans, who euphemize the newly deceased (or *departed* or *defunct*) but mock the buried and use morbid analogies but dread the reaper, the people of Mexico prefer to fraternize with the enemy and thereby steal away some of his symbolic power.

The Visual Image
2

We think we know how to look at death because we've
looked at paintings: the dead Patroclus, the dead Ajax,
the dead Christ, the dead Marat, dire tableaux of
butchered limbs in baroque versions of antiquity.
Photography allows less of a remove, but maybe it is
possible to inure oneself to Alexander Gardner's Civil
War battlefields full of corpses or the trophy or memorial
images of propped-up dead Communards or Dalton Gang
members. Those bodies become historical or symbolic,
and their flesh is thus transubstantiated mentally into
some odorless and enduring substance like marble or wax.
    —Luc Sante, *Evidence*[1]

The Depicted Corpse

Death looms large in the art of the ages. If a corpse featured in a painting retains its identity over time, as does that of a king or a saint, the canvas
becomes a historical document as well as a message-bearing icon. When a
corpse loses its individual identity, as does the central figure in a family
deathbed scene after several generations, it gains generality and a broader rel-
evance. Or the corpse may be intended as a symbol from the start, the tran-
sitoriness of life represented by a decayed figure or the triumph of death
signified by an active, skeletized form. While a depicted corpse need not be
nameless to be symbolic, certain of the perennial themes of death—inevitability and democracy among them—lend themselves to generic representation.
Other themes, such as the capriciousness and universality of death, may be
inferred from a recognized body sculpted as a visual record or a death scene
painted to record a moment in history. Whether the intent is historic or
metaphoric (or both), the presence of a corpse in a painting or sculpture is
rarely incidental, and the focus on it raises the questions and hopes that we
have about our individual and collective end.

22

Before the advent of photography or in situations where photography was considered to be in ill taste, artists recorded scenes of death. In 1515, Jean Perréal documents *The Arrival of the Queen's Body and Its Reception by Cardinal Jean de Luxembourg*, a presentation in keeping with her royalty, but lonely nonetheless: the panoply does not hide the fact that death, even for kings and queens, is a solitary venture. Sir Hubert von Herkomer's posthumous portrait of *Queen Victoria After Death* softens the sight of the queen on her bier, while at the same time allowing her to lie in state for posterity. The painting may call forth the idea that the mighty must fall, but it also captures facial features which can be seen in her descendants. Such pictures continue to portray the deaths of the past as if they had just taken place, allowing the viewer to be present as Napoleon expires and the Duke of Wellington is laid to rest.

In a more important role, the dead body of Jesus still attached to the cross provides a detailed image on which Christians can focus thoughts of his sacrifice. Shown as he is removed from the cross, the pain of his crucifixion and the grief over his death can be imagined with more immediacy. The Christ portrayed by Rogier van der Weyden in his mid-fifteenth-century *Descent from the Cross* has been painstakingly detached from the cross and is held by loving arms as his head falls to one shoulder. Hugo van der Goes details the bleeding wounds in Jesus' side and on his forehead in his *Descent from the Cross*. When Jesus is sculpted lying across his mother's knees in Michelangelo's *Pietà*, his death becomes palpable to the viewer. His uncomfortable positioning in Van Dyck's 1634 pietà reminds one that the dead do not sense. In his painting of the entombment, Michelangelo focuses on the weight of the lifeless body of Christ as it is conveyed to the tomb from which he will rise. In Caravaggio's painting on the same theme, Christ's arm drags on the ground as his body is carried and his shroud falls away to reveal the human musculature. Unconventional viewpoints taken by Mantegna during the Renaissance, in which the body of Christ is foreshortened from below, and taken by Salvador Dali in the mid-twentieth century, in which the crucifixion is seen from above, render the details of human life and human death: the feet with holes where the nails pierced them and the tortured shoulders of the fixed, outstretched arms.

In paintings of the death of Jesus and the saints, their suffering is made all the more profound by emphasizing that the death was truly *felt* by the victim and his or her contemporaries. The Virgin Mary's body is tended to by respectful Christians who are grief-stricken and sorrowful despite the promise of life after death; her holy corpse, prior to its assumption, is reacted to and attended by those who shared her life and survived her. In Rubens' *Entombment of Saint Stephen*, the limp body of the martyr is treated tenderly as if mourners are unwilling to part with it; while he is now a patron, he was once a living, breathing human being. In Giotto's *Death of St. Francis*, the saint is surrounded by his brethren as he is surrounded by his faith. Even though they are not painted or sculpted from life, images of the deaths of Christ and the saints give an imagined face and a projected reality to their suffering. Often realistic portrayal is used to achieve this end, but stylized paintings of the Passion offer equally poignant images. *The Yellow Christ* by Paul Gauguin in 1889 exaggerates the length of Christ's arms to heighten the sense of agony as he is stretched across the cross. Max Beckmann's painting *Descent of the Cross* in 1917 presents the body of Jesus not in the limp pose of the Renaissance, but in a gesture as stiff and cumbersome as the ladder with which he was taken down.

When the death of a monarch or a peasant has just transpired, the deceased is portrayed as just out of reach, not literally but figuratively. The deathbed is often the scene of a last goodbye, as survivors lean closer for the whisper of a last word or the sound of a last breath. In *Poor Folk*, a 1908 painting by Léonie Humbert-Vignot, a woman's face evidences her surprise and distress at finding dead in bed a mother who has been denied the company of her loved ones in her agony. The familiar image of the family gathered around the recently deceased shows death as a peaceful process for the dying, but an agonizing separation for those left behind. The living sometimes throw themselves upon the dead in their grief. In *The Dead Wife*, a late nineteenth-century painting by George Cochran Lambdin, a husband clutches his wife's clasped hands and buries his face in her shoulder, unwilling to let her go. With the body still intact and the appearance of sleep, there is a strong tendency to deny the death, a subject taken to extremes in the nineteenth century. In an Austrian print of 1897, a man retrieves his fiancée from the tomb in what is titled *The Madness of Love*. In *Young and His Daughter* of 1804, P. A. Vafflard depicts a father carrying the body of his daughter and the spade he has used to "rescue" her from the grave.

When death is accepted, the objective of the artist is to capture the likeness of the newly dead and the details of death. For centuries, the recumbent figures of kings, knights, and bishops carved to lie atop their tombs indicated by the clasp of their hands in prayer, the often open eyes, and the vertical draping of their garments that they were not intended as images of death, but as figures in repose awaiting the Last Judgment. But toward the end of the Middle Ages, artists closed the eyes of the dead, swapping symbols of status—the scepter and the crozier—for signs, such as a rosary in hand, that the body had been laid out for burial. The facial expressions begin to show the pain associated with dying or to compare death with sleep, but they also aim at resemblance and were many times modeled after a drawing of the deceased or a death mask. Although crowned, the recumbent figures of King of Navarre Charles III, who died in 1425, and his wife, Eleanor of Castile, who died nine years earlier, are human rather than idealized.

As they strove to achieve a good likeness, artists shortened full-length figures to busts, concentrating on the face as the seat of the personality. Funerary portraits of the sixteenth century show the closed eyes and slightly parted mouths of highly individualized faces, with upper bodies lying hidden beneath carefully arranged bedclothes. Portraits of the dead, while they never lost favor, regained popularity in the nineteenth century and were the specialty of American painters William Sydney Mount and Shepard Alonzo Mount, whose images capture the calm and release in the faces of the dead. With high death rates and short lifespans, drawings and paintings of the loved one—as well as sculptures on the tomb—assisted the family in revisiting and remembering them.

The theme of premature death is a by-product of the paintings and sculptures of dead children commissioned by their parents to preserve their memory. Realistic paintings of children at death began to appear in the seventeenth century. They are sometimes alone in the image and other times accompanied by a grieving mother, who in Charles Willson Peale's *Rachel Weeping* from the 1770s has her eyes raised heavenward in a mute appeal. In the 1840s, Jarvis Hanks recorded in *Death Scene* the three-fold grief of a man who has just become a widower: on the fringes of the painting, he closes his eyes to the main subject of his wife, dead and open-eyed, and the two still-born children in her lap. Whether just born or of a young age, the dead body is displayed gently, as if it has been put down for a nap. An 1886 tomb in Milan includes a sculpture of a baby being "tucked in" by an angel who very much resembles him.

In contrast to the solitary figure, young or old, the deathbed scene in some cases becomes a family portrait, preserving the memory of the living along with the moment of death. When this tableau is sculpted for the tomb, it remains suspended in time and allows strollers in the cemetery to take their place around the bed among the life-sized statuary. Journalistic images of the dead also allow the modern viewer to see inside the scene as if looking through a window and to compare the ways corpses have been treated over the centuries. Whether the names survive or the bodies become representative of an era, the pictures and statuary speak of (or speak out for) respect for the dead. A fifteenth-century painting of a burial details the careful lowering of a body wrapped in a winding sheet while tonsured clergy carry out the ceremony of absolution and a sober party of black-draped mourners looks on. The drawings of the 1873 excavations in Paris which revealed the Meringovian cemetery show drab workers unearthing boxed skeletons under the watchful eyes of their top-hatted overseers and the eager eyes of the restrained crowds. Fifty years earlier, Marlet took as his subject the sightseers who toured the Paris morgue regularly, hoping to sate their curiosity for the morbid. Paintings and prints of murder and execution often appeal to the same instincts in the contemporary and the modern viewer.

In many works of art, however, the use of the corpse is not gratuitous. It is deftly executed as a purposeful means of conveying the extremes of the human condition. Eugene Delacroix borrowed corpses and human limbs from a nearby hospital to use as models for his vision of *The Raft of the Medusa*, painted two years after the horrific event in which the 30 survivors of the hastily prepared raft resorted to cannibalism of the bodies of the 120 who died. Jacques-Louis David recorded the 1793 death of revolutionary Jean-Paul Marat, slumped over in his bath still holding his pen after being stabbed in the chest by his assassin Charlotte Corday. Many artists have depicted the horrors of war in answer to the politics of the period. The illustrations in the twelfth-century Huntingfield psalter show rivulets of blood issuing from the severed heads and legs of knights killed in battle, while Picasso's famous *Guernica*, inspired by the Spanish civil war, graphically illustrates the screams and contortions of trampled victims. Jacques Callot produced a series of three etchings entitled *Les Misères et les Malheures de la Guerre* in 1633, showing mass hanging, burning at the stake, and death by firing squad. Francisco José de Goya took up the theme in the early 1800s after Napoleonic troops invaded Spain. His etchings of the dead being stripped of their clothes, tipped into a common grave, and left dismembered and beheaded are scenes which he saw or which were described to him by others who lived through them. French artist Georges Roualt's series *Miséréré et Guerre*, etched between 1916 and 1927, conveys a lasting impression of World War I. Such images have become propaganda in the quest for peace. As eyewitness accounts of the cruelties humans inflict on one another, they all the more strongly represent the ordeals of war as a personal experience rather than an abstract concept.

Death and dismemberment of another sort were popular in the sixteenth and seventeenth centuries. The subjects of dissection record and sometimes mock the curiosity of the living. The paintings commissioned in the seventeenth century by Dutchmen lucky enough to attend an anatomy lesson show their fascination with death; they gesture toward an articulated skeleton or are grouped intimately around an open cadaver in scenes that parallel later photographs of medical students. An eighteenth-century painting shows surgeon William Cheselden dissecting a bald, naked corpse for the benefit of a small audience of wigged, well-dressed men. The bearded cadaver in Rembrandt's 1632 painting of *Doctor Tulp's Anatomy Lesson* resembles the spectators, but only one appears to be looking at the skinned arm. The men in the paintings don't seem to connect the cadaver with their own mortality, but the proximity reinforces the viewer's tendency to compare life and death. This idea is made plain in *The "Theatrum Anatomicum" of the University of Leyden, with a Crowd of Curious Spectators*, of the University of Leyden, with a Crowd of Curious Spectators," an early seventeenth-century engraving by Bartolomeus Dolendo (after J. C. Woudanus) in which skeletons caper over the auditorium crowd bearing placards that remind the oglers to remember their own deaths, the brevity of life, and the possibility of a similar fate.

In many images the adjacent placement of the living and the dead is an intentional device warning of the constant presence and possibility of death. An illustration intended to serve the purposes of the nineteenth-century sanitary movement, *Enon-Chapel Cemetery, and Dancing Saloon*, contrasts the merry-making of the revelers above in the dance hall with the boxed and loose bones below in the crypt, arguing the dangers of possible contamination. A water-color by Sir John Gardner Wilkinson shows a peasant woman searching for antiquities in a Theban tomb, watched only by the dead. Beyond illustrating the obvious idea of robbing the dead, the mummies hint that she will one day be as incapable of protecting their treasures as they are and that even attempts at preservation of the body will eventually result in dust.

Comparison in a single image of the intact corpse and the corrupt or skeletonized corpse further emphasizes the devaluation of the physical. Life abandons the body quickly; flesh soon follows. An illumination from the *Heures de Neville* (c. 1435) allows comparison between the unclothed corpse, the corpse sewn into its shroud, and the bones that scatter the churchyard long after the shroud has disintegrated. This theme became even more explicit in the tomb sculpture of the fourteenth, fifteenth, and sixteenth centuries. The monuments compare the body as it looks in life with an example of its appearance after decomposition. Costly robes have been replaced with a scant shroud that allows visual access to the disfigurement brought on by decom-position. Dried flesh reveals the rib cage and evokes the image of the naked skeleton it soon will be. On the sixteenth-century tomb of René of Challons, the "transi," as the partially decayed body is called, indicates what the corpse will look like three years after death. The transi may recline on the tomb, allowing a glimpse of what is taking place within or it may stand up to deliver its message with the visual aids of timepieces or vermin.

The decomposed body is offered to the audience in hopes that the sight of decay and the predators of the flesh will provoke its members to be mind-ful of pride and preoccupation with the body. In a fifteenth-century sculp-ture, *The Seducer*, Satan in the guise of a handsome young man is caught in the act of offering an apple to Eve, while from the back he is feasted on by toads, snakes, and lizards. In the early sixteenth-century painting *Lovers*, attributed to Grünewald, a man and woman still exhibit a bit of modesty as their upright but withered bodies are run through with snakes and dotted with insects. After the scavengers have finished their task, only the bones remain. Like the transi, these may remain an immobile symbol, or they may take on a life of their own.

The skeleton figures in many paintings are known collectively as "van-ities." In portraits and still lifes, the skeleton—or its most important compo-nent, the skull—signifies at a glance the mortality that we must all lay claim to. The seventeenth-century artist of *The Mirror of Life and Death* halves the model vertically: the flowing hair, eye, smile, and breast on the left all dis-appear in the "x-ray" image on the right. James Ensor made an etching of a reclining skeleton in 1886 and called it *My Portrait in 1960*. In *The Burgk-maier Spouses* by Lucas Furtenagel in 1529, the faces of a couple stare out at the viewer, while at the same time a mirror held by the wife reflects not flesh, but bone. By including the skull in a still life along with things of transience (cut flowers, music, games, and soap bubbles), the artist allows the skull's integrity to defy the life within that is long gone. The skull, even in disguise, is used as a "memento mori." The oblong shape in the foreground of Hans Holbein the Younger's *Ambassadors Jean de Dinterville and Georges de Salve* of 1533 is an anamorphosis of a skull, recognizable only at an angle. In a popular nineteenth-century image, an optical illusion is created when the image of a seated woman and her reflection in a mirror combine to reveal a skull. The featureless face and immediate symbolism of the skull remind the audience that death can and will come to anyone and everyone.

Predating the vanity painting is the Dance of Death, in which everyone is coerced into joining hands with Death. The motif began early in the fifteenth century in France (where it was called the *Danse Macabre*), then spread to Germany (where it was the *Totentanz*), Italy, Switzerland, and Spain. In its first manifestations in chapels, churchyards, and charnel houses, it was a mural in which living people of all ranks alternated with skeletons or corpses in a dance or procession. It soon appeared in books of hours, paintings, and tapestries. The name has come to include any representation in which Death presides over a group of people of all ages and conditions, exemplifying the original themes of universality and democracy.

In his *Dance of Death* series of 41 woodcuts in the sixteenth century, Hans Holbein the Younger represents Death demanding his due without an invitation; his subjects are not called to a dance but are instead interrupted at their daily tasks. He invites himself to the banquet of the king and toys with the crown of the emperor as he sits on the throne. He grabs the bishop by the arm and pulls the monk by his cowl. He mocks the nobleman who raises his sword to defend himself, raises his hand to strike an old woman leaning on her cane, and runs a knight through with his own lance. He even pulls a child away from his mother. The prints alone and in combination explain today, as they did to the illiterate of the time, that there is no protection from Death.

While the traditional Dance of Death represents skeletons making off with people of all occupations, some artists merge the two images. Mexican iconography blends the victor with the victim, resulting in skeletons of all professions: revolutionaries, musicians, soldiers, cowboys, bicyclists. Other examples include the sixteenth-century sculpture in the Velez chapel in the Cathedral of Murcia, Spain, which depicts a skeleton preaching from a pulpit, and the eighteenth-century funeral medallion in the Church of Tuntange, Luxembourg, which shows the skeletons of a man and wife clasping each other in a belated attempt to comfort and allay fear. In a modern Dance of Death series by Fritz Eichenberg, wood engravings personify death as a seller of guns and drugs, a pimp, and a warmonger. Good or bad, the living must die. Whether they assist Death in his mission or push him away when he arrives, they still have to pay his price for life.

Often the single images of death taking his due show him as a seducer of women. Edvard Munch took up the theme in a 1864 etching *Maiden and Death*. He is depicted as approaching from the rear, allowing his victim no advance notice of his presence. In *The Young Woman and Death*, painted by Hans Baldung Grien in the sixteenth century, the leering skeleton sneaks up behind a young woman who bears her child in her arms. The specter, obvious to the viewer but unseen by his victim, reinforces the constant potential of death of which we are often unaware. In Gustav Klimt's painting *Death and Life* from the early 1900s, Death is eagerly awaiting the opportunity to strike at a member of the family depicted as a cluster of all generations. Death is almost always presented as enjoying his occupation. In Nicolas Manual Deutsch's 1517 image of *Death and the Young Woman*, a skeleton still wearing tatters of flesh couples his kiss of death with a grope beneath the woman's skirt.

Death's victims, as portrayed by some artists, do not try to fight him off. In 1515, Hans Baldung Grien sketched *Death and the Maiden* in which an eyeless skeleton grabs a woman from behind and kisses her with his lipless mouth; his victim is surprised, but not panicked, and closes her eyes to his embrace. Grien seems to delight in separating lovers. In another of his paintings, Death forcibly vies for a woman's attention by biting at the hem of her gown as a knight attempts to carry her away on horseback. Occasionally, the roles are reversed, and a female skeleton does the tempting. In Felicien Rops' 1893 painting *Death at the Ball*, the skeleton is costumed in a colorful gown, with dainty bones revealed at head and toe, and leans back as if swung around the dance floor or dipped by her partner, who is not depicted. Thomas Cooper Gotch uses a similar theme in his early twentieth-century painting *Death the Bride*. As a symbol of our "marriage" to death, the skeleton is an adaptable image.

Death is equipped to kidnap and to kill. He is sometimes given wings with which to carry off the living. In a tomb sculpture by Bernini in the seventeenth century, patron Alexandro Valtrino is being flown away by a skeleton whose birdlike wings liken him to an angel. In a 1792 engraving by Daniel Chodowiecki, *Totantanz*, a skeleton snatches up a baby from its cradle and carries it away with batlike wings that give it a more sinister connotation. While tamer skeletons are depicted minding the time and kissing young women, the Grim Reaper is shown wielding weapons with which to carry out his duties. These include spears, bows and arrows, and the proverbial scythe. In paintings of the Triumph of Death, the skeleton is no longer lecherous, but still insatiable. In scenes of the plague, men are succumbing to the dread disease even as they carry the dead to the grave; in scenes of Death on horseback or in his chariot, no one survives. The mere skeleton and his minions have become agents of the Apocalypse. Everyone must die before they can be resurrected from the dead. The reaper mows them down and, as fearful as he is, provides the means to immortality. After he has done his work, the dead can be judged.

Visual descriptions of particular judgment from Ars Moriendi manuals caution the dying person to make a good death by presenting angels and devils fighting over his or her soul, sometimes symbolized by a small child. In the illustration *Individual Judgment* from a late nineteenth-century catechism, a "split-screen" contrasts the soul in bodily form being wafted up to heaven by the angels with the sight of it being dragged down to hell with chains by a demon.

A mass-produced lithograph from the nineteenth century combines many themes: a dying man's choice is made plain by a priest who points to vignettes of heaven and hell, while a skeleton holding an hourglass urges him to be quick with his decision. Paintings of the Last Judgment show the dead in large groups as they emerge from the ground or await their turn at the scales. In *Resurrection of the Flesh* painted by Luca Signorelli at the turn of the sixteenth century, bodies come to life, climb out of their graves, and reunite with their loved ones. Bas reliefs in many churches depict the dead first pushing the lids off their coffins and climbing out, then submitting to a weighing of their sins by Christ, and lastly standing with the righteous to await the pleasures of heaven or being led with the rest of the damned to the torments of hell.

The visual arts record our ambivalence about death. Painters and sculptors have used the subject of the corpse to raise themes of condemnation of, resignation to, and even sympathy with, death. The skeletal personification of death sometimes ransacks and other times seduces. The dead body is portrayed in sleep and in decay. The multitudes of the dead are shown piled in war and awakening at the Last Judgment. Within the sculpture or painting, the living often rail against death. Those looking at the image may reassure themselves that the death depicted is remote, but they may also be compelled to compare themselves with the dead or their survivors. In some works, viewers mourn the victims of war, share the bereavement of a mother or lover, and grieve along with the family at a deathbed or with an entire country at a state funeral. In others, the audience faces the decay of the body, its partial preservation as skeleton or mummy, and its sometime dissection as a teaching device or conversation piece. Except through killing ourselves or others, we can't choose the circumstances of death; we can, however, manipulate how it is presented or represented. To suit the purpose of artist or audience, a corpse may be portrayed as ideal or real, but either way the artist provides a context in which to contemplate the dead and death in general.

The Poetic Corpse

Poets have taken the commonplaces of death and illustrated them, through imagination or personal tragedy, with corpses of power and subtlety, corpses to pity and to fear. The bodies they conjure up express the themes of democracy as vividly as the Dance of Death. They evoke the threat of death as easily as a vanity painting and convey the fate of the flesh as obviously as a transi on a tomb. Poets paint with words death's horrors and its promise. They use the corpse as a vehicle to advance themes of abandonment, grief, and denial, and the skeleton to suggest death's triumph and universality. While a long poem may serve as a meditation on death—a thanatopsis—a short poem or a selected verse may serve as a memento mori.

Death, despite its being raged against, is the price we all must pay for having lived. Edna St. Vincent Millay (d. 1950) states in "Dirge Without Music" that she is not resigned to the common fate of the intelligent, the brave, the beautiful, and the kind, all of whom go "Down, down, down into the darkness of the grave." While dying may be a social event, death is shared only in theory and rarely in practice. The individual dead join the great majority after the fact, according to an anonymous poet of the late nineteenth century:

> So, deadest, now thy brows are cold,
> I see thee what thou art, and know
> Thy likeness to the wise below,
> Thy kindred with the great of old.

Wealth and status do not exclude anyone, as John Dryden (d. 1700) notes: "All human things are subject to decay, / And when fate summons, monarchs must obey." James Shirley (d. 1666) personifies Death as laying his icy hand on kings. Even attempts at preservation of the flesh are ultimately in vain: death and decay are both inevitable. "The winds of Luxor fiercely blow / Against my cheeks the dust of kings," writes Robert Cary, illustrating that even the painstakingly embalmed bodies of the pharaohs crumble.

Before decomposition has caused profound changes to the body, its resemblance to the living in almost all respects causes a yearning in the forlorn survivors to hold the body again, to have one more embrace. Oliver Wendell Holmes (d. 1894) in *The Last Leaf* speaks of mossy marbles resting on the lips that he has pressed in their bloom. Robert Burns (d. 1796) resents the grave stealing his "Highland Mary" and imagines how her once rosy lips have turned pale: "And mouldering now in silent dust / That heart that loved me dearly." Two hearts that may at times have beat as one have been separated. Occasionally, a poet finds comfort in the fact that he and his beloved will rest together after death:

> Oh! that we two lay sleeping
> In our nest in the churchyard sod,
> With our limbs at rest on the quiet earth's breast,
> And our souls at home with God.

A more likely fate, however, is to share the cemetery with strangers. A poem in *Poor Richard's Almanack* makes light of the disdain of the common grave:

> Syl. dreamt that bury'd in his fellow clay,
> Close by a common beggar's side he lay:
> And, as so mean a neighbor shock'd his pride,
> Thus, like a corpse of consequence, he cry'd;
> Scoundrel, begone; and hence forth touch me not:
> More manners learn; and, at a distance, rot.
> How, scoundrel, in a haughtier tone cry'd he;
> Proud lump of dirt, I scorn thy words and thee:
> Here all are equal; nor thy case is mine;
> This is my rotting place, and that is thine.

During its transformation to dust, the corpse will probably merge with the surrounding soil and will eventually become indistinguishable from its fellows. In *Measure for Measure*, William Shakespeare (d. 1616) contrasts the warm, living body with the cold, inanimate corpse:

> To lie in cold obstruction and to rot;
> This sensible warm motion to become
> A kneaded clod.

The work of flesh-eating insects occurs prior to complete dissolution, and is in fact an aid in it. It is a lesson in humility that the body should be an incubator for flies, food for scavengers. Voltaire (d. 1778) makes plain the dreaded image:

> To numerous insects shall my corpse give birth,
> When once it mixes with its mother earth:
> Small comfort 'tis that when Death's ruthless power
> Closes my life, worms shall my flesh devour.

The soul may ascend to heaven, but the corpse is subject to processes that are at the same time natural and revolting. Edgar Allan Poe (d. 1849) points out the disparity between the heavenly body and the earthly body in *The Conquerer Worm*: "seraphs sob at vermin fangs / In human gore imbued." The resulting "dust," though it is more likely to be mud, still holds the promise of an afterlife. George Herbert (d. 1633) looks forward to the resurrection and the subsequent reunion of the dead:

> Summon all the dust to rise,
> Till it stir, and rub the eyes;
> While this member jogs the other,
> Each one whisp'ring, *"Live you, brother?"*

Although family, friends, and lovers may one day find each other again in heaven, they remain parted until the Last Judgment. The dead are still with us in bodily form, but are soon put away in caskets and into tombs. In "We Are Seven," William Wordsworth (d. 1850) tells of Sister Jane moaning in bed until God released her of her pain, "And then she went away." Where there were living beings, there are now only empty spaces. They remain only in memory, and Mathilde Blind muses in "The Dead" that "their invisible hands these hands yet hold." Andrew Marvell (d. 1678) urges his paramour to live while she can, lamenting in "To His Coy Mistress" that worms will try her long-preserved virginity: "The grave's a fine and private place, / But none, I think, do there embrace."

Robert Louis Stevenson (d. 1894) reminds the reader that the dead are simply a few steps ahead and that we will soon enough catch up with them. But until that time, once the beloved has died, the love may remain centered on the precious face and body. In "The Unquiet Grave," an anonymous poet uses the voice of the dead to warn the living against too fond a remembrance, lest they pine away:

> You crave one kiss of my clay-cold lips,
> But my breath smells earthy strong;
> If you have one kiss of my clay-cold lips
> Your time will not be long.

Only a lock of hair is allowed as a remembrance, as suggested in a nineteenth-century poem by Annie R. Blount:

> Clip one soft and silken ringlet
> From the forehead cold;
> For the graveyard now is claiming
> All those threads of gold.

Occasionally, unrequited love may become unnoticed death, as illustrated in "The Sorrows of Werther," by William Makepeace Thackeray (d. 1863):

> Charlotte, having seen his body
> Borne before her on a shutter,
> Like a well-conducted person,
> Went on cutting bread and butter.

For most poets, however, the sight of the corpse of a lover is an abomination. The reality is denied or fought against and rarely accepted without bitterness toward death itself, perhaps a disguised rage at God.

For some poets, it is the grave or the graveyard making claim to the corpse. For others, Death himself covets the beautiful and the young for his own bed. A Victorian epitaph muses:

> Father, do not strive to save her,
> She is mine and I must have her;
> The coffin must be her bridal bed,
> The winding sheet must wrap her head;
> The whisp'ring winds must o'er her sigh,
> For soon in the grave the maid must lie;
> The worm it will riot on heavenly diet,
> When death has deflowered her eye.[2]

Ralph Cheney speaks of a female Death in need of a lover, remarking that "all who sleep with her lie curiously still." Death is not always lustful, but is very often portrayed as ruthless and insatiable. An English epitaph paints Death as a fisherman who toys with his victims as he takes them away one by one: he is never satisfied with his catch. Ralph Waldo Emerson (d. 1882) describes him as covetous. Henry Wadsworth Longfellow (d. 1882) characterizes him as a reaper who cuts down the useful and the beautiful: "He reaps the bearded grain at a breath, / And the flowers that grow between."

There are times, however, when Death is given a gentle personality. In a verse ascribed to Ann Boleyn (d. 1536), the poet asks Death to rock her asleep. Speaking from Death's point of view, twentieth-century poet Margaret Widdemer in "The Dark Cavalier" promises, "My arms shall welcome you when other arms are tired." Death sometimes allows his victims to doze off and to take their leave without pain. Thomas Hood (d. 1845) writes:

> Our very hopes belied our fears,
> Our fears our hopes belied—
> We thought her dying when she slept.
> And sleeping when she died.

Death is omnipresent, as Percy Shelley (d. 1822) points out in singsong rhyme: "Death is here and death is there, Death is busy everywhere." In poetry, death forcibly takes possession of bodies or gently rocks the dying to sleep. Death lays his victims in a mouldering grave or stores them intact for their rising. He is a youthful rival of living men or an old and tyrannical charioteer. He is the center of attention at the deathbed or a silent and skeletal stealer of souls. Graveyard poet Edward Young (d. 1765) makes apologies for the divergent portraits of death, commenting in "Night Thoughts" that no one who has met Death has lived to tell about it: "Who can take / Death's portrait true? The tyrant never sat."

The Photographed Corpse

Since its development, photography has been used to materially immortalize the dead long past their bodily dissolution. In the mid-nineteenth century, parents carried the corpses of their children into the photographer's studio to have them memorialized in a daguerreotype; in the twentieth century, corpses are photographed at the scene and again after transport to the morgue to document them for police and autopsy files. In the 1860s, the cartes de visite, small prints produced from a single negative, allowed the visage of the deceased to be shared with distant relatives; today, a funeral home in Washington state and a photographer in California videotape funerals for the benefit of family members too far away to attend. In the 1870s, postmortem photographs of Jesse James and other outlaws were reproduced as stereo cards to be viewed in the parlor of the home; in 1928, a reporter used a hidden camera to photograph the electrocution of murderess Ruth Snyder for the front page of the *New York Daily News*. Images of the dead on film are fixed in time and serve memory, history, the law, and curiosity.

Photography, though not at first inexpensive, gave families who could not afford a painted portrait the opportunity to save and savor the image of a loved one who would soon pass out of their lives forever. Prior to the late 1800s, the sentiment toward the image was not dulled by the visible signs of death. There was no attempt to beautify the corpse before tripping the shutter, even though the long exposure times that were demanded (and possible with an unmoving subject) produced images of high quality and detail. Rigor in the limbs, blood on the face, and darkened nails all point to the obvious, despite the deliberate positioning described by Albert Southworth, a daguerreotype artist, to an 1873 audience: "You may do just as you please so far as the handling and bending of corpses is concerned. You can bend them till the joints are pliable, and make them assume a natural and easy position."[3] Babies were posed in their carriages, children on their mothers' laps or with their favorite toys, and adults seated or in their coffins. The dead body, a willing model for photographers and a treasured image for their clients, was accepted at face value with or without props.

By the turn of the century, the larger size of the popular 5"×7" cabinet card allowed the photographer to touch up the negative. This technique and the makeup applied after embalming came into use led to a more prepared and less obvious presentation of the dead. In some cases, an artist was employed to paint eyes over the corpse's lids in a photo. Michael Lesy researched just such an instance dating from 1898 for his *Wisconsin Death Trip*: "Mrs. Friedel had a picture taken of her little baby in its coffin. Then when a fellow came up the road who did enlargements, she had just the baby's face blown up to a two foot picture. But, since the baby's eyes were closed, she had an artist paint them open so she could hang it in the parlor."[4] After he opened his Harlem studio in 1916, James Van Der Zee collaged comforting images of angels and the afterlife around the upholstery of the caskets in which his African-American subjects lay to soften the remembrance of their deaths.

The names of the dead, which occasionally appear in the wreaths surrounding the casket, are usually lost once the heirs of the photograph die. But in the case of notable deaths, a photograph becomes the property of history and offers up a true memory, rather than an artistic interpretation, to generations who could not otherwise have witnessed it. Contemporaries captured the image of Abraham Lincoln lying in state (1865), Emperor Maximilian in his coffin (1867), and the body of Patriarch Joachin enthroned for veneration (1912). What are now historical images were often journalistic verifications of death at the time. Before photojournalism was an established genre, Alexander Gardner preserved on film the sequence of the execution of Lincoln's conspirators, from the reading of the sentence to the hanging bodies after they had stopped swinging. Train robbers and other outlaws were propped up in their coffins for pictures in which the lethal bullet holes are prominent. In 1934, postmortem photographs verified the deaths of George "Baby Face" Nelson and John Dillinger. The following year, a photograph of Freddie and Ma Barker in the morgue reported that they were no longer a threat.

Photographed scenes of carnage take their place in the history books alongside written accounts, fixing the words to the reality that the image reinforces. The lost lives of the soldiers in the Civil War were and are made real by seeing the corpse-strewn battlefields photographed by Gardner, Matthew Brady, and Timothy O'Sullivan. A critic wrote in the *New York Times* in 1862 that Gardner in effect had brought bodies from Antietem and Gettysburg and laid them on our doorsteps. Mafia violence earlier this century is made plain in photos of acts of revenge and mob retaliation: the bloodied face of Ben "Bugsy" Siegel killed in his girlfriend's living room; the prone body of Albert Anastasia, head of Murder, Inc., next to the barber's chair in which he had sat, and the members of "Bugs" Moran's gang machine-gunned in Chicago's St. Valentine's Day massacre. The barbarism of the Nazis is given undeniable form in landscapes of shaved and emaciated bodies. And the accounts by survivors of the 1973 plane crash portrayed in the movie *Alive* become especially chilling when coupled with the photographs of cannibalized human limbs taken upon their rescue.

Whether or not they were intended to, many depictions of death cater to the taste for vicarious violence. Some, however, are not shared but hoarded for this purpose. Serial killers often photograph their victims after they rape and murder them—the details of the crime, in living color, are etched more vividly on paper than on their minds and serve as catalysts to relive the event. Douglas Ubelaker and Henry Scammell explain in *Bones: A Forensic Detective's Casebook*: "They take pictures of their killings, as happens frequently in such cases, not in an impulse to flirt with danger or flaunt their crimes to others, but rather because murder is such an ephemeral event, they hope to preserve the moment and make it endlessly retrievable for future reverie.[5]

This need for personal evidence can also lead to their capture. In fact, one killer was caught when he went back to the photo store to have enlargements made. Morbid curiosity, more than evidence of social or vigilante justice, lies behind popular images of the bodies of those killed by lynch mobs. After the lynching of Leo Frank, a Jewish man being held as a suspect in the murder of schoolgirl Mary Phagan in 1913, hundreds of photos and licensed postcards of the body were sold in the few days before the Atlanta City Council made it unlawful to sell photographs of a person hanged illegally.

Corpses have been used as both prop and propaganda in photographs. Pictures of garbage cans filled with bloody fetuses are distributed by those opposed to abortion, while artist Joel-Peter Witkin makes stillborn fetuses the unlikely objects of interest in his disturbing photographs. A picture of stacked skulls and longbones in a catacomb is a photographic memento mori, less anecdotal than the portraits of anatomy lessons which often include a skeleton arm in arm with poker-faced students gathered around the cadaver with scalpels and manuals in hand. A skull may be placed under the hand of a man in a life portrait to suggest the contemplation of death, or it may be photographed with a cigarette between its teeth to remind us of the dangers of smoking. The dead can be introduced into a photograph with levity or sobriety. They can overwhelm the viewer in their sheer numbers, or a single body can touch upon individual mortality. Photographs allow the viewer to accept the message conveyed or to reject it, but do not allow him or her to deny that the picture—or at least its components—is real.

With the use of photography, we can get as close as we want to death and yet still remain distant from it. A photograph allows us to satisfy our curiosity in private, with prolonged stares that would be rude at a wake. We can observe deaths that are distant in time, examining the disfigurement of the victims of Jack the Ripper or the parents of Lizzie Borden. We can give free rein to our inclination to speculate about the nature of death, all the more pronounced when it is taken with force. In *Rough Justice: Days and Nights of a Young D.A.*, David Heilbroner remarks on viewing the 8"×10" black and white prints in a homicide file: "At first I found the photographs a little disappointing. There were no gaping wounds in the body or pools of blood. ... If you didn't know he had been murdered, you might have thought he was daydreaming, but knowing that the man in the picture was dead—or, as I soon found out, stabbed to death—transformed the otherwise unremarkable image into an object of fascination."[6] A 1989 photo essay by Rudolf Schäfer[7] makes the point that we are most afraid of—that the dead are most often just like us, minus life: the people in his posthumous portraits are young and old, ugly and beautiful, peaceful and pained.

Barring any "trick shots," photographs provide objective proof of the circumstances of death, even when they defy logic. A photograph by William Dyviniak taken ca. 1940 and entitled "Hangman's Holiday" verifies the unlikely result of a car crash in which the propelled driver was found suspended from a telephone pole. A photograph was made as a lasting visual description of a forty-five-year-old woman found dead standing upright in the corner of a timber yard in Germany. Police photographers back up the written descriptions of a murder scene, which can be disputed, with a photographic record that cannot. Police in Wisconsin made a photographic record of the grisly relics that Ed Gein had fashioned from the skin and bones of his victims in the 1950s before interring them. Among the photos in Luc Sante's book *Evidence*,[8] chosen from 1,400 images taken by the New York Police Department from 1914 to 1918, are murdered corpses open-mouthed and sometimes open-eyed in surprise, corpses framed by the shapes of their own blood, and corpses stuffed into a barrel or discarded in the woods. Such evidence is so persuasive that prosecutors almost always face an argument over the admissibility of showing photos of the murder victim to the jury; though they are allowed more often than not, smelling salts have been kept at the ready.

Beyond their power to educate or inflame a jury, forensic photographs can be used to identify the dead by broadcast to the public. When the head and partial body of a woman were found in the Seine in 1876, photographs of her face were sold in the newspaper and tobacco kiosks of Paris. Although police received 183 false leads and located dozens of other missing women, the dead woman was finally identified and her husband was executed after he confessed. More recently, forensic anthropologists have developed techniques of superimposing the photo of a skull against a photograph from life to prove identity. Other scientists have photographed the body at different stages of decay for use in determining how long ago a newly discovered body or skeleton died.

Photography has always had a hand in bringing killers to justice. But today, except in laboratories and law enforcement agencies, the victims are presented less as individuals and more as symbols of the violence of the age. Both evidential and commemorative value has been overshadowed by shock value, and photographs of the dead are rarely shown except for sensational purposes. While in the nineteenth and early twentieth centuries, memorial portraits were worn in lockets and hung on the wall, photographs from life are now considered more appropriate to represent the deceased. They may be printed next to the obituary, attached permanently to the gravestone, or provided to the embalmer to ensure lifelike restoration. Early this century, a funeral provided the opportunity for a family portrait which included the casketed relative. Now Kodaks and Polaroids of parents and grandparents laid out for burial are considered vulgar and have no place in the family album.

Views of the dead are either snapped reverently and looked at in private, like the body of a premature baby that has perished, or are obtained through bribery, like the picture purchased by the *National Enquirer* of Elvis Presley in his casket and published in questionable taste on their front cover. They are, however, still taken. A woman appalled that her cousin had photographed a deceased relative lying in a coffin received support from Ann Landers in 1991, but drew criticism from more than 1,000 of the columnist's readers.[9]

At the turn of our century, we are having another look at the images which we have hoarded, forgotten about, or been protected from. In defense of her book, *Looking at Death*, Barbara Norfleet notes: "There are many ... photographs of death that we never see. We see the site of a murder, but never the victim. We see the twisted metal of a car wreck or plane crash, but only after the bodies have been removed. We read of a suicide, but we do not see the body. People still die of disease, but their obituary photographs portray them at an earlier age when they were healthy."[10] Surveys of death photography, such as Norfleet's, include images of the especially macabre—bodyless heads of executed Japanese and the headless body of a victim of Ifugao headhunters—in the interest of completeness. The images are not meant to be gawked at, like a traffic accident, but to be used to reach an understanding of our relationship with death of the past and present, and thereby the future. Gallery exhibits such as "Taken: Photography and Death" at the Tartt Gallery in Washington, D.C., in 1989 and "The Interrupted Life" at New York's New Museum of Contemporary Art in 1991 offer their share of gore, but also provide a respectful forum for examining the realities of and reasons for photographing the dead. Photographs in books or art collections allow a physically nonthreatening glimpse or an exhaustive contemplation of the various ways in which the body and its life are parted, naturally or forcibly, and the events that follow.

The Televised Corpse

To photography, film adds the elements of motion and sequence. The imprint on the still negative is multiplied to become a story—acted, reenacted, or taken from life. Stories of death abound in the movies and on television, but the screen often blurs the distinction between fact and fantasy. We are given an occasional firsthand look at the corpse in news footage and documentaries, but the pictures of the dead offered even in shows "based on true stories" are at best an approximation. The faked corpse is doctored for dramatic effect or toned down for primetime viewing. It is a prop in plots that cater to the vicarious thrill of watching others being killed. As a device, it may overshadow actual death by suggesting to children that the dead can get up and resume their activities after a scene is completed or by masking from adults the physical realities of brutal deaths. A professor who became a police officer was astonished at the difference between simulated death and the real thing: "Violent death. So still. So much blood from such a small wound.... How many people had I seen shot to death on television shows and in movies over the years? I wondered. It had never looked anything like this before. I felt a chill and stepped back from the body."[11]

The controversy over violence on television usually centers on the action rather than the aftermath, so corpses—though plentiful—are rarely realistic. The result of the estimated 18,000 fictional murders a child sees by his or her high school graduation are bodies shot, stabbed, and poisoned in amounts ten times those of the admittedly high national crime rate. They provide clues that allow fictional medical examiners and amateur detectives to solve their murders, but they do not give the public an accurate picture of the destruction that can be wrought on the body by a single bullet or the grimace left on the face of a poison victim. The violence on TV is sometimes defended as having a cathartic effect, but others suggest that those most sensitive to it are the same people who are unable to control their tempers. While television is said to strengthen perceptions of the effectiveness of the police, it may also provoke anxiety about becoming one of the victims so often portrayed. Rarely, though, is the viewer allowed to identify with the body, murdered or otherwise.[12] Along with the lack of accuracy, the corpse is portrayed unsympathetically. In the movies and on television, we never see the corpse of the hero; but we see the corpse of the "bad guy" who has received poetic justice for his or her antisocial act. Dramas proffer accounts of death which are idealized and uninformed. Death is neither democratic nor messy. A person pushed out a window of the tenth floor inevitably falls through the roof of a convertible or an awning, breaking the fall but never the body. Executions, correctly depicted as painful, are mistakenly portrayed as swift; electrocution, for instance, rarely requires a second jolt and almost never makes reference to the immediate autopsy which often follows. Bodies are invariably discovered while still intact or after they have been skeletonized, never during the particularly distasteful intermediate stages. And just as anachronisms are apparent to those who look for them in historical movies, the drama or action film often contains a "corpse" whose chest can be seen rising and falling.

Some films, however, contain a genuine death in which a living body stops breathing before our eyes. The makers of "snuff films" abuse the medium to this end by drafting a victim for the purpose of recording his or her torture and death for replay or distribution. Others accidentally catch death in the act and record what becomes part of the historical record. Abraham Zapruder's film of John F. Kennedy being shot in 1963 provides a narrative of a national tragedy and its aftermath. Recorded as a souvenir of the president's visit to Dallas, it became, with the images of the president's caisson, a visual focus for the country's grief, replayed again and again to break through the barrier of disbelief and to ascertain exactly what happened. The killing that followed of Kennedy's alleged assassin Lee Harvey Oswald was also documented accidentally on film, and the surprise and pain on his face remains archived for posterity.

Television allows a surreal combination of closeness to the dead visually and distance from them physically. We witness Kennedy's assassination and his wife's anguish, but do not feel the warmth of his blood on our clothes as she does. The corpse is placed right in front of the viewer, recognizable but not palpable. This quality is taken advantage of in the Los Angeles Medical Examiner's office, where a closed-circuit television picture gives next of kin the opportunity to make an identification while remaining insulated from the sights and smells of the morgue itself. The new procedure is believed to soften the emotionally wrenching experience of standing next to the body of a loved one as the face is uncovered. The cover is occasionally removed from the faces of the unclaimed dead and their photographs broadcast to the public in hope of an identification, but more often than not, the truly dead that we see on TV retain their anonymity by being quickly tucked into body bags. Even so, television news reporters find the sequence of wheeling the gurney to the ambulance or morgue wagon an almost imperative backdrop to a breaking story about the murder that happened last night or the crime scene that has just been discovered. To accommodate them, law enforcement has had to bow to stage direction. When sheriff's officers carried a body from the Chicago residence of John Wayne Gacy, Jr., in 1979 and were told by a member of the TV crew that the crew wasn't ready yet, the officers carried the victim back inside the house and came out on cue a few minutes later.[13]

Death on film has been taken to extremes. It is molded to fit the screenwriter's image instead of serving as evidence of the realities of death. The corpse is couched within the rigid parameters of a one-hour murder mystery or a neatly wrapped-up detective drama, serving merely as a reason for the principal characters to gather. Horror movies are peopled with the stinking and grabbing dead to play on our fears, and the television watcher is bombarded with corpse after corpse of no real substance. It is ironic that we no longer witness the deaths of our loved ones in their beds, but watch the contrived deaths of actors from our own beds via network or cable television, as the editors of a textbook chapter on death education point out, "Within a matter of decades, fictional death has moved into the home as a form of entertainment while actual death has moved *out* of the home, into the lonely, impersonal atmosphere of a hospital ward.[14] The deaths which we are privy to through the television medium are often so bizarre that they tell us nothing about death as it will occur in our own lives, in home, hospital, or hospice.[15] But if recent television programming is any indication, we are becoming more interested in the realities of death, at least of strangers. Public television aired the four-part series "Death: The Trip of a Lifetime," a survey hosted by Greg Palmer examining death and burial customs around the world. And Home Box Office piloted a documentary program called "Autopsy," which reveals the secrets of homicide investigation. Alas, video rentals of the less redeeming "Faces of Death," the sensational film clips of human tragedy too graphic for the eleven o'clock news, are more accessible.

The Death Mask

Although the eyes are said to be the windows of the soul, when they are closed in death the entire face becomes a mirror of the life it once housed. Preserving its image has been a sacred duty over the centuries. The ancient Egyptians painted a portrait of the deceased and attached it to the head of the mummy so that the soul would recognize it upon its return. In the Middle Ages, artists strove for a true likeness in the wood or wax representations of the dead carried on the bier in place of the "vulgar" corpse; in doing so, they focused on the face and the making of a mask soon became standard practice. As Philippe Ariès points out. "There is an impulse to save from destruction a few things that express an incorruptible individuality, particularly the face, which contains the secret of the personality."[16]

The death mask combines the accuracy of a photograph, which it predates, with the additional spatial dimension of a sculpture. It does not have to *evoke* the dead, it *is* the dead. The facial characteristics that identified a person in life and the expression that characterized him or her in death—ideally one of serenity, like that of Felix Mendelssohn-Bartholdy (d. 1847)—are preserved forever. The classic death mask is made by oiling the face, ears, and neck and pouring on plaster to make a mold. The casts made from it can be painted, have glass eyes set in the holes, and have hair added for a lifelike effect. The original mold can be used over and over again to reproduce the exact image of the deceased for homage in the home and patronage in the museum.

The death mask is an entity that lends itself to display. Collections of death masks are housed at Princeton, Edinburgh University, the Castle Museum in Norwich, England, and the Black Museum at Scotland Yard. They satisfy those who were too far away in place or time to pay their last respects to a great man or who require visual aids to bring the pages of history to life. Castings of the death mask of Napoleon Bonaparte, from the original plaster of paris mold taken by Francis Burton, M.D., after the emperor's death in 1821, are still on view in the museums of Europe. In the nineteenth century, the death mask of Ludwig van Beethoven (d. 1827) often graced the decor of the drawing rooms of the middle class. Casts of the death masks of Napoleon, Beethoven, sculptor Antonio Canova (d. 1822), musician and composer Franz Liszt (d. 1886), and President Abraham Lincoln (d. 1865) are currently available by mail order from the historical molds.

Death masks also satisfy the curiosity of those who are eager to stare safely into the face of a killer or those who routinely make it their business. The face of William Burke, the man who gave his name to bodysnatching, was molded after his hanging and possibly before his public dissection in 1829; his accomplice William Hare had a life mask made during the trial. The entrance to the crime lab of the Chicago Police Department contains the death masks of public enemies John Dillinger and "Baby Face" Nelson, both of whom were killed in 1934. The death masks of convicted murderers Nicola Sacco and Bartolomeo Vanzetti were put on display in New York City after their controversial execution in 1927 and were viewed by hundreds of people.

Both art and science have had a stake in the creation of death masks. Robert Wilkins, author of *The Bedside Book of Death*, attributes the number of death masks of criminals made in the nineteenth century to the study of phrenology and postmortem research into criminality.[17] The tradition of having the death mask prepared by a qualified sculpture artist continues well into the twentieth century. The death mask of Jefferson Davis (d. 1889) was prepared by Atlanta sculptor Orion Frazee. Grover Cleveland's death mask was cast by Princeton sculptor Edwin Wilson after the president's death in 1908. The masks of Sacco and Vanzetti were made by artist William Gropper. And the death mask of musician and composer William C. Handy (d. 1958) was done by Isaac S. Hathaway, curator of the ceramics department at Alabama State College.

Because the image has such exact detail and because the masks were usually made immediately after death, it is sometimes difficult to distinguish a death mask from a life mask. While her successors work from life photographs, Madame Tussaud was compelled by revolutionaries and the government during the French Revolution to make lifelike wax reproductions from freshly guillotined heads. In the first third of this century, nearly every European student had a plaster cast of the face of an unidentified woman, the "Inconnue de la Seine," who had been discovered dead in the river; her slight smile and peaceful expression make it seem as if she modeled purposely for the portrait. Some masks, however, leave no question that death has occurred. Death spasms are visible in the masks of playwright Richard Brinsley Sheridan (d. 1816) and poet Samuel Taylor Coleridge (d. 1834), and a slight grimace is evident in that of philosopher and mathematician Blaise Pascal (d. 1662). Author Sir Walter Scott's 1832 death mask shows evidence of the stroke from which he died and the scar left when the skull was removed to examine the brain at autopsy.

Unlike the anonymous and fleshless skull, the death mask is not a lesson in mortality, but a mnemonic device for recalling an individual life, career, or reputation. Its value lies in the authenticity of reproduction; a death mask may in fact fetch high prices, as did a Dillinger death mask which was auctioned off in Chicago in 1991 for $10,000. Although death masks are not often cast today, the practice was known in Egypt's Fourth Dynasty, common in the fifteenth and sixteenth centuries, and widespread in Victorian times. The reasons vary, but the power of the image remains constant. F. Gonzalez-Crussi explains our fascination in *The Day of the Dead and Other Mortal Reflections*:

> When wax or a malleable substance is used, the impression is obtained by intimate contact between the moldable material and the object reproduced. There is no space, no discontinuity between the two. In a certain sense it may be said that the wax becomes, during the imprinting, a physical extension of the dead person's face; and therefore the wax imprint is thought to contain an element of the objective reality of the model that a sculpture or a painting cannot seize.... Modern photography, being two-dimensional, also falls short of the power of the wax impression, which brings back something of the physical presence of the departed into the world of the living.[18]

The death mask leaves us something we can hold on to, literally and figuratively.

The Memory Picture

Scientists have convinced us that the eyes of the dead do not retain the image they last saw, but many believe that the last look at a corpse produces an indelible image in the minds of the living which may haunt in some circumstances, but will help in others. The proof that this offers to mourners disallows denial of the death and assists them in their bereavement. The "memory picture" spoken of by funeral directors is not merely a self-serving concept, but a positive image of the deceased on which to focus our grief. We have an emotional attachment to the body from which we must be weaned. This is said to be the purpose of the funeral, a forum designed to acknowledge the passing of a unique life by confronting the individual corpse.

Seeing the face of a loved one that has undergone the practiced restoration of a professional embalmer does not so much cushion the blow as provide a picture of the deceased that the mind can refer to side by side with memories of the person while he or she was alive. Although restoration has been criticized as merely a tribute to the embalmer's skill, at its best the features are given a look of serenity which compares favorably with our expectations that they now rest in peace. Indications of pain and suffering, even on the faces of those who die violently, are smoothed away. An observer of Abraham Lincoln in his casket reported: "I saw him in his coffin. The face was the same as in life. Death had not changed the kindly countenance in any line. There was upon it the same sad look that it had worn always, though not so intensely sad as it had been in life... . It was the look of a worn man suddenly relieved."[19] A Dr. Heim remarked in 1895 that the facial expressions of those who "die in their boots" are far more tranquil and hopeful that those of people who anticipated and were resigned to their fate.[20] When this is not the case, the embalmer's art may compensate.

In contrast, seeing the body before it has been prepared for viewing is sometimes excruciating and may leave permanent psychological scars. Two years after he was asked to identify her body, the father of a victim of the Yorkshire Ripper died of what his wife considers a broken heart. She says, "He couldn't forget seeing her in the mortuary when he had to identify her.... All he could say was there was blood all over her beautiful hair."[21] After a woman saw a morgue photograph of her mother, who had given her up for adoption at birth and was killed a year later, she told Edna Buchanan, "I had never seen a dead person before ... especially my mother. It was horrible. I think my life stopped for a while... . I was having trouble sleeping, having nightmares."[22] A person who discovers a dead body may have to contend with post-traumatic stress disorder in which the image is replayed in horrific detail. But even before the cosmetics have been applied, there is often a value in observing the dead body. Harry Singletary of the Florida Department of Corrections maintains that witnessing the execution of a relative completes the family's grief cycle; it may for a policeman mark the end of a case.[23] Being allowed to see and touch the dead allows the reality to sink in. If we cannot make sense of the death, we can at least part with the remains. After her mother died of a terminal illness, Simone de Beauvoir wrote: "It was so expected and so unimaginable, that dead body lying on the bed in Maman's place. Her hand was cold; so was her forehead. It was still Maman, and it was her absence for ever."[24]

When the body of a loved one is missing, survivors are robbed of the opportunity to bid it a last farewell and often experience a lack of closure with regard to the death. Robert Yount, an embalming instructor and mortician, explains: "Psychologists, grief counselors, health care professionals, mental health people have pretty much consistently come to the conclusion that part of the grieving process can be accomplished through a physical viewing of the body. A finality. A period at the end of a sentence."[25]

Survivors may find it difficult to believe that the death has occurred without visual proof, particularly if a family member dies away from home or tragically. A closed casket that hides the body of an accident victim provokes speculation about the remains inside, but in sparing mourners the anxiety of seeing the mutilation, it does not give them the concrete proof they may need to accept the premature death. In some cases, friends who have given emotional support to a person who dies of AIDS in the absence of family feel cheated of an important social and personal means of parting with their companion when the same family removes the body for distant burial. A memorial service often makes use of photographs of the deceased in life, preferring mourners to create their own composite memory picture. Because it is often held after the body has been cremated or donated, the service purposely avoids drawing attention to the physical remains: "When we think about the death of someone dear to us, the 'body image' is involved—we identify emotionally. We tend to feel sensations that the deceased is now incapable of feeling. For example, we tend to cringe a bit at the thought of a corpse being dissected, or of burning, or of intolerable injury."[26] In cases where a person is presumed dead after he or she has been missing for a number of years, survivors do not have the luxury of choice. The lack of a body precludes viewing, and the slim hope that the person escaped death is never entirely put to rest.

A last look at the deceased is believed to be therapeutic for adults and children alike. It is urged on the bereaved not only by funeral directors, but by nurses giving patients a chance to come to terms with their miscarried pregnancy. The memory of a body discovered or a family member in the morgue may be framed in blood, but it is as permanent as the death itself. The picture of a family member posed in the casket may be powdered and rouged to hide the ravages of age or disease, but it does not camouflage the fact that death has occurred. Paraphrasing Erich Lindemann, professor of psychiatry at Harvard, Dr. Edgar N. Jackson writes: "Nothing helps people face reality like the moments of truth when the living confront the dead. This has in most cultures and in most times been central in the funeral process. To avoid confronting death is to pervert the purpose of the funeral and reduce its efficiency. The change of status death brings can best be faced through recognizing physical death as the basic step toward honest and healthful mourning."[27]

Viewing the body in the hospital, morgue, or funeral home gives death reality and finality. Whether the sight is sad or scary, bland or beautified, it closes our physical relationship with the dead while allowing the emotional tie to continue through remembrance. The memory picture paints a lifelike—but not a living—image that can be called up both in grief and after the acceptance of the death.

THE LAST RITES
OF A CORPSE

The Preparation

And so much *handling* of corpses. To this day, it is the
part of dying that I resent the most. This making free
with the body, washing it, combing its hair, flipping it
over to do the backside. Dragging it upstairs by its heels,
perhaps, or kissing it.
—Richard Selzer, *Confessions of a Knife*[1]

The Anointing

To be ready for their last journey, the dead must be cleansed physically
and spiritually. The washing of the body was the duty of the family and
neighbors before this function was handed over to professional caretakers. The
cleansing of the soul common in many cultures is usually a priestly function.
Up until the early nineteenth century, bereaved families had the option of
employing a "sin eater," a social outcast who would take on the moral tres-
passes of the newly dead for a small fee. More often they chose to summon
the Roman Catholic priest, whose actions and the oil he applied were swathed
in ritual and performed not for money, but to save one of his flock from purgatory and allow admittance directly into heaven. In the Bible, anointing is
documented by St. James: "Is any sick among you? Let him call for the elders
of the church, and let them pray over him, anointing him with oil in the
name of the Lord: And the prayer of the faithful shall save the sick, and the
Lord shall raise him up; and if he have committed sins, they shall be forgiven
him." (James 5:14-15)

In the fifth and sixth centuries, the faithful had oil blessed by the bishop
and brought it home to cure the sick. It was given orally or rubbed on the
affected part or on the head, breast, and shoulders to affect a more general
relief. After the twelfth century, the oil became the exclusive preserve of the

Part II title page: Woman on a canopied bier. Early twentieth century. Collection of the author.

priest, who carried it with him to the home and enlisted the laity only in recit-ing prayers and psalms during the rite.

The names historically bestowed on the last rite shroud it in mystery: "I was captivated by the words 'extreme unction.' The words themselves were oily and rich, just like the exotic oils I imagined being rubbed into the pale wrinkled flesh of a dying person."[2] The Greeks referred to it as the "oil of prayers." The oil used in the sacrament is in fact olive oil. It is blessed by pro-nouncing a form of exorcism over it in a Chrismal Mass said on Holy Thurs-day. The blessing is performed by a bishop or a priest authorized by the Holy See. The oil, *oleum infirmorum*, is then distributed by the diocese to the parishes and is supposed to be kept in a vessel of silver or gold, although one of lead or tin may be used. In Eastern Orthodox rites, water or wine is some-times added to the oil. If the supply dwindles during the year, unblessed oil may be added in quantities smaller than the blessed oil; any remaining at the end of the year is burned.

The procedure used for anointing allows for the many conditions the priest may encounter. He is to use the flesh of his right thumb to apply the oil, but may use an instrument, or *virgula*, if there is risk of infection or con-tagion. The anointing is most often in the form of a cross made on each of the organs of sense, although anointing the loins was discontinued in 1925. The eyes, if closed, are anointed on the lids or if open, on the brows. The ears are anointed on the lobes and the nose on its tip or on each nostril. The mouth should be anointed over both lips if closed, or near the lips if open. The back of the hands and the palms are both anointed. The feet may also be anointed on the soles and insteps, but this may be omitted if they are covered or have not been washed. If any of the body parts are missing or bandaged, anointing should be done closest to them. If a body has been beheaded, the head and trunk should be anointed simultaneously. After anointing, the unctions should be wiped off with cotton. If life is uncertain, or there is a danger to the priest or a physical obstacle preventing his access, a short form of the sacrament allows him to anoint the sense organs of the head with the cheeks representing the sense of touch. In extreme cases, a sin-gle anointing of any of the sense organs, but preferably the forehead, is con-sidered valid.

Anointing and the recitation of prescribed prayers are intended to give the soul strength to resist the horror of death and to prepare it for entrance into heaven. Last rites are not intended to give a blanket forgiveness of all sins, and recipients must at least show proper attrition. Erasmus condemned the idea of allowing the dying a last-minute repentance. The Venerable Bede was of the opinion that the sacrament would not have effect unless penance had first been performed. Among those rendered unconscious in an act of sin, distinctions were made between persons shot in adultery or wounded in a duel, who may have had time to make an act of contrition, and those who died in a drunken state and should not be anointed. The sacrament is not bestowed on children until they have attained the age of reason and can make confessions of their sins.

Although it is an attempt to restore health to the body if necessary for the salvation of the soul, extreme unction has traditionally been allowed only when the dying were beyond the capability of sinning. After the twelfth century, the church clarified that the sacrament was to be given when a person is dying or at the point of death, not just in danger of death, since the recipient should not have the chance to repeat sins which have been thus cleansed. In the Middle Ages, it was a common belief that if a person who had been anointed subsequently recovered, he or she had to abstain from dancing, eating meat, marital relations, and other pleasures of the flesh; summoning the priest was therefore postponed until the very last minute. Well into the nineteenth century, the priest was one of the players in the public event that surrounded the deathbed, but after the turn of the century, the family hesitated to call the priest until the person was unconscious or dead for fear that his presence would upset the dying individual.

In the early 1900s, the consensus of theological opinion held that a person was alive for up to a half an hour after apparent death due to lingering illness and at least an hour after a sudden accident. The soul was thought to adhere to the body for some time after the cessation of circulation and respiration. This period of latent life was thought to vary from shortly after the pronouncement of death until putrefaction, which contradicted previous instructions that the priest should discontinue the anointing if the person dies during the rite. A 1927 volume offers this guidance: "Priests will find a practical application of these opinions not only in the many accidental deaths which occur daily, but in the executions of criminals by hanging, electrocution or shooting. In every instance the priest should endeavor to administer as quickly as possible the sacraments of Penance and Extreme Unction to the unfortunate man."[3] The priest and chaplain were therefore justified in anointing the body of Private Eddie Slovik after his execution by firing squad in 1945. Later, however, Pope Pius XII deemed that the separation of the soul from the body renders the body no longer human and thus unfit for the reception of the sacraments. He explained in an address to an international congress of anesthesiologists that extreme unction would not be valid after blood circulation had stopped, for instance after the removal of artificial respiration apparatus.[4] With Vatican II in 1963, the name of the sacrament was changed to "The Anointing of the Sick" to complete its dissociation from the dead, and "Last Rites" was eliminated from liturgical language. The decree declares that the faithful should receive anointing as often as they become ill and whenever a threat to life is present because of sickness. In addition, the sacrament may be administered to several people at once, such as in a home for the aged. If a person has already died by the time he arrives, the priest should not anoint, but should pray, asking God to forgive the deceased's sins and receive him or her into his kingdom.[5]

Laying Out

In ancient Egypt and modern America, preparation of the dead for burial has been carried out by professionals. In ancient Rome and in the Victorian era, only city-dwellers or the well-to-do had the means to hire someone to lay out their dead. In other times and places, the duties of washing and arranging the body have been performed by family, friends, and neighbors. The task of laying out the dead most often fell to the women of the household. Greek and Roman women were charged with closing the eyes and mouth of the dead. The ancient Greeks considered the laying out of the dead a sacred duty of female relatives, who were allowed the space of one day to wash, dress, and anoint it with oils, perfumes, and spices. In some parts of China, only women are allowed to handle corpses because they are considered immune to the pollution of death and because female hair is believed to absorb it. In early New England, female neighbors with experience in laying out the dead offered their assistance to the bereaved and later advertised their services as "layers out of the dead."

Washing the dead was both a practical and symbolic gesture. In ancient Greece and Rome, the eldest son washed the corpse with warm water to guarantee that life was extinct. Hebrew women cleansed the corpse to purify it, a task which priests were not allowed to undertake. Unlike the Jews, Christians considered the body sacred rather than a contaminant and washed the corpse even during times of plague to allow the deceased to appear to best advantage in the afterlife. Although they did not believe the corpse to be contagious, ancient Greeks offered water from an outside source to anyone who touched the body. The ancient custom of disposing of all standing water in a house in which a person has died is believed to have grown out of the necessity of discarding the water which was used to bathe a corpse.

Once the body has been cleaned, it is dressed in its best clothing or special burial garments. In rural areas and small towns in the nineteenth century, if a person died away from home, the body was quickly returned to the house and placed in bed; the corpse was washed, dressed in his best suit or her favorite dress, and moved from the bedroom to the parlor where it would reside until the burial. An oral history taken from a gravedigger points out the irony of burying the dead in their finery: "There ain't no sense in puttin' brand new clothes on a corpse. When you're dead you're dead; you go down under the ground, and that's all there is to it. It just ain't right, givin' new clothes to the worms to eat, when there's plenty of folks walkin' around that could use 'em."[6] Nevertheless, it is important to the family that the body be suitably attired for the viewing. The ancient Greeks dressed the body of an unmarried or recently married person in wedding attire and laid soldiers out in their uniforms. The ancient Romans dressed the dead in a white toga with the insignia of rank for display on a funeral couch. In some cultures, the body was not clothed, but placed in a shroud. After washing the corpse, the early Christians wrapped the limbs and body in a linen sheet along with preservative oils and spices such as myrrh and aloe, the use of which was borrowed from the Hebrews and continued in commemoration of Jesus.

In many cultures, special care was taken to prevent the soul from being hindered in its exit. Knots were untied in clothing or ribbons. The hair of the corpse was unbraided and sometimes cut off. The feet were stretched out to facilitate movement of the soul through the body and out the mouth. For primarily superstitious reasons, the eyes of the dead were closed. Although conceived as a means to prevent the death stare, placing coins on the eyes of the dead had the practical advantage of keeping them shut after the body became stiff. Family members learned by experience several techniques for keeping the body presentable. American colonists restrained putrefaction by wrapping the body in an alum-soaked cloth, immersing it in alcohol, or filling the disemboweled body cavity with charcoal. In the nineteenth century, those who laid out the dead positioned the body on a sheet-draped board between two chairs and often propped a forked stick underneath the chin to keep the mouth shut. They plugged the orifices and straightened the limbs. And they placed ice beneath and around the body or covered the face with a wet cloth to retard the decomposition that ensued rapidly in warm weather.

The tasks associated with the laying out of the dead were assumed by professional embalmers in the late 1800s. Today family members may still choose a dress or suit for the deceased, but no longer have to clean and clothe the corpse. The body is often removed from the home by ambulance and pronounced dead on arrival at the hospital. The nursing staff has a roster of duties only vaguely reminiscent of the community "layers out of the dead": they are required to close the mouth and eyes, clip off all intravenous lines and catheters, clean the soiled body and pack the orifices, wrap the wrists in gauze and tie them together, wrap the face to protect it during transit to the morgue or funeral home, and cover the body with a sheet or paper drape. Instead of hanging a lock of hair on the door to warn of a corpse within, the modern nurse attaches a mortuary tag and list of personal effects to the finger or toe to insure against loss of identity or property. Less is done by emergency department nurses, who remove only nondisposable medical equipment and cover the body to avoid tainting the autopsy findings. Corpses are now handled with efficiency by strangers where they were once cared for by loved ones. Between the hour of death and the appointment for the family visitation, they are artfully and scientifically prepared by morticians who have been trained in schools prior to being schooled by experience.

Embalming

Embalming was embraced by Americans during the Civil War when it was introduced to allow the return of dead soldiers to their families for burial. The embalming of Abraham Lincoln set a precedent which has been followed ever since without much question. Although it is rarely mandatory or permanent, preservation of the body by chemical means has become ingrained in our society and increasingly accepted in others, most notably Japan and New Zealand. By prolonging and improving the appearance of the dead, embalmers create an aesthetically pleasing centerpiece for the funeral. By postponing the effects of decomposition, they put the physical fate of the body out of sight and therefore out of mind. Like their forerunners, the mummifiers of ancient Egypt and the barber-surgeons of seventeenth-century Europe, modern embalmers can upon request provide a durable and lasting corpse for dissection or indefinite display. But the majority of their clients are not intended for a dissecting table or a glass casket. They need only withstand a few days at room temperature to give family members time to gather around them and say their goodbyes.

The means to preserve the dead, mainly for transport, have been sought in both ancient and modern times. The ancient Greeks perfumed and spiced the dead to mask the odor of putrefaction. According to Homer, the body of Patrocles was preserved by the injection of nectar and ambrosia through his nostrils. The ancient Scythians disemboweled their kings, filled their bodies with cypress, frankincense, anise, and parsley seed, and covered the body in wax. The bodies of Agesipolis, king of Sparta, and Emperor Justin II were each embalmed in honey. The body of Alexander the Great was preserved in honey and wax for conveyance to Memphis, where it was exhibited in a glass coffin. The ancient Egyptians, discussed in a later chapter, mummified the body to provide a house for the soul by dehydrating it with salt. The Egyptian techniques were adopted in some measure by Europeans after 500 A.D. and practiced on Charlemagne (d. 814) and William the Conqueror (d. 1087), whose bodies were washed internally and externally after their organs were removed. In 1550, Ambroise Paré embalmed the dead by disemboweling them and removing the heart and brain, inserting aromatic powders in incisions made in the limbs, washing with aqua vitae and vinegar, anointing with turpentine, sprinkling with powders, and wrapping in linen and cerecloth. In the seventeenth-century settlement of New France (today's Quebec), those who could afford it had the bodies of their loved ones preserved in alcohol and shipped back to the motherland. Admiral Horatio Nelson's body was brought to London in 1805 in a barrel of brandy. When Nancy Martin died at sea in 1857, her father had her body immersed in a cask of alcohol for the rest of the trip so that she could be buried (still in the cask) in North Carolina. And in 1895, the body of Prince Henry of Battenberg, who died of malaria in West Africa, was returned to England for a royal burial in an improvised tank made of biscuit tins and filled with navy rum.

It was in the 1800s that experiments with embalming for purposes of funeralization began. The chemical preservation of bodies for anatomical dissection had been carried out since the seventeenth century, when Dutch physicians injected a wine-based solution into the body, replaced the organs that had been removed, and allowed the corpse to dry. In England, barber-surgeons were charged with embalming the dead. They opened the abdomen and chest, removed the organs, washed the cavity, filled it with spices, and closed it. In the following century, physicians William (d. 1783) and John Hunter (d. 1793) injected into the arteries a solution of turpentine, vermilion, lavender, and rosemary that did not require evisceration. The body was then massaged to work the chemicals into the tissues. But the 1840 translation of the French text *History of Embalming* by Philadelphia professor Dr. Richard Harlan provided interested Americans with actual instructions. By the nineteenth century, states started to require licensing of competent embalmers. At the same time, the apparatus required for the procedure made it impractical to embalm in the home and therefore led to the establishment of the funeral home. Although a patent for a corpse preserver (an ice-filled box) was issued in 1843, the first patent for embalming primarily by the injection of a chemical compound was granted in 1856.

During the Civil War, Thomas H. Holmes popularized the technique of arterial embalming that allowed the bodies of soldiers to be returned home for burial. It is estimated that between thirty and forty thousand Civil War dead were embalmed. The prodigious "Doctor" Holmes claimed to have embalmed 4,028 men, charging $100 each for officers and $25 for enlisted men. After the war he was said to have accumulated specimens of his work in his Brooklyn home: "There were bodies in hall closets and under the basement floor, preserved heads on living room tables. Bottles of embalming fluid and homemade root beer stood side by side in the window of his pharmacy."[7]

Holmes' method of injecting a solution of bichloride of mercury into the body was soon followed by others, among them W. R. Cornelius: "I shipped colonels, majors, captains and privates by the carload some days. I had no trouble with embalming by the Holmes process, using the femoral artery. The only trouble was that the subject would become discolored, but would keep any length of time.... Both armies treated me properly and paid me promptly."[8]

Embalmers also began to apply restorative techniques to the disfigured dead. Before the Civil War had ended, the first formal organization of morticians, the Undertakers Mutual Protective Association of Philadelphia, was formed and an "Order Concerning Embalmers"—a system for licensing embalmers of the war dead and for establishing uniform fees—had been put in place by the War Department. Embalming found favor after the body of military hero Colonel Ellsworth was embalmed by Dr. Holmes in 1861 and put on display in Washington, New York, and Albany. Embalming gained even more acceptance after President Lincoln was assassinated in 1865, when hundreds of thousands of mourners viewed his embalmed body on its many stops between Washington, D.C., and Springfield, Illinois, and found its presentation more appealing than that of the unembalmed relatives and friends they had seen. Cavity embalming was added to the regimen in the 1870s with the development of the trocar. The hardening action of formaldehyde, which both preserves and disinfects, was discovered in 1893 and replaced the poisonous mercury and arsenic solutions that had been used.

The increased demand for embalming in the latter part of the century led to the first schools for morticians, the Cincinnati School of Embalming established by C. M. Lukins in 1882 and the Rochester School of Embalming opened by Dr. August Renouard the same year. (Today there are 41 embalming schools approved by the American Board of Funeral Service Education.) At the end of the 1800s, states began passing legislation requiring the licensing of embalmers. By the turn of the twentieth century, embalming had become the standard of professionalism in the United States for shipping, sanitizing, and improving the appearance of the dead. Embalming was done in the home as recently as the 1950s, but now routinely takes place in funeral homes in the United States, Canada, and Australia and increasingly in England.

Embalming has since been criticized as a dishonest process that masks the realities of death. Rabbi Maurice Lamm and Naftali Eskreis contend in the *Journal of Religion and Health* that making a display of the flesh minus the mind demonstrates the lifelong emphasis on appearance over value and causes viewers to remark that the deceased "looks good" rather than reflecting that he or she "was good."[9] In *The Facts of Death*, Michael A. Simpson compares the function of the mortician to that of a beautician, modifying the uncomfortable realities of the body.[10] The embalmer repairs any disfigurement to achieve an ideal memory picture for the benefit of bereaved relatives: "He does the physical work of taking the ritually unclean, usually diseased, corpse with its unpleasant appearance and transforming it from a lifeless object to the sculptured image of a living human being who is resting in sleep."[11] Although it is obvious to the mourners that the deceased will not be waking up, it is important to them that the body look its best. To this end, makeup experts and hair stylists from the studio accompany the body of a film star to the funeral home for preparation. The dead without celebrity status are made up to match as closely as possible photographs from life provided by the family, although some embalmers have complained that the family would not recognize the difference between a masterpiece and a mediocre job.[12] The embalmer uses the tricks of his or her trade to ready the sight of the deceased for tear-filled, yet critical, eyes.

Morticians, who now require up to 5,000 hours of training to be licensed, have traditionally been proud of their work. In *Dracula*, Bram Stoker puts words of self-congratulation in the mouth of the undertaker who prepares Lucy's body: "She makes a very beautiful corpse, sir. It's quite a privilege to attend on her. It's not too much to say that she will do credit to our establishment!"[13] As embalming gained acceptance, some practitioners took sample corpses on tour and exhibited them in barbershops, country fairs, and public halls to solicit new business. An 1885 contest in the trade journal *Sunnyside* offered $1,000 to the funeral director who exhibited the best-looking corpse 60 days after it had been embalmed.[14] Barbara Norfleet writes in *Looking at Death* that by the turn of this century the embalmer had become so adept at his job that the subjects of postmortem photographs of the period are many times only recognizable as corpses by their crossed arms.[15] Not only can they smooth away the effects of pain and violence, embalmers can enhance a person's natural beauty and remove some of the indicators of age. In *The American Way of Death*, Jessica Mitford claims that the W. W. Chambers mortuary issued a calendar containing nude photographs of a sampling of the women they had embalmed, with the legend "Beautiful Bodies by Chambers."[16] Laurieanne Sconce, former co-owner of the Lamb Funeral Home in Pasadena, bragged: "I would do the cosmetics and hair.... I had a God-given talent. I had so many people say, 'She never looked so good.'"[17]

There are many products on the market to assist professional embalmers in the restoration of the dead: "There are hundreds of arterial and cavity fluids, eyecaps, tissue-builders ... sure-closes, feature-forms, electricinjectors, creams, waxes, surface restorers, sealers, emolient dyes, and liquid cream cosmetics in a long range of colors from suntan through beige to moonlit blonde, so that every subject of care can look twenty years younger."[18] The tools of the trade also include the hardware necessary for external and internal preparation. Mechanical or electrical lifts assist in moving the body, and special tables with gutters and drains are used during the embalming and restoration. The procedure, which ideally should be done within eight hours of death, takes approximately two to three hours and may be preceded by massage and manipulation to break rigor mortis, if present. The body is first undressed, washed with disinfectant soap, and towel-dried. It may also be sprayed with a disinfectant. It is then arranged on a table using a head rest and limb emollient so that the head is above the chest and the body is tilted slightly to the right. It may be washed a second time with soap or bleach, and solvents may be used to remove any stains on the skin. Orifices are swabbed and packed with cotton to prevent leakage, and cream may be applied to the hands and face. The mouth is swabbed, and dentures are removed, disinfected, and replaced. Fluids may be drained or suctioned, and the trachea and esophagus are sometimes tied off internally to prevent further secretions. The mouth is stitched manually with mandibular sutures at the gum line and through the nasal septum, wired closed, or pinned with a needle injector. Tissue builder may be injected into the lips to give them fullness if they have flattened. The throat is packed with gauze. The mouth is padded with mortuary putty or cotton (or a plastic or metal mouth-former), if necessary, and given a pleasing expression. The face may be shaved with an electric razor. The eyeballs may be injected with cavity fluid to restore their roundness and knobbed plastic caps are often placed beneath the lids so that they do not appear sunken. The lids may be sealed shut with vaseline or eye cement, or the lower ones may be tucked underneath the upper lids to rid the eyes of wrinkles.

To commence with arterial embalming, one or two small incisions are made at the clavicle, upper arm, or groin, and then the carotid, axillary, or femoral arteries and a major vein are brought to the surface. A tube is inserted into the vein for drainage of the blood as it is pushed out of the body during the embalming process. Three to four gallons of embalming fluid consisting of formaldehyde (a hardener), glycerine (to counteract dehydration), borax (to keep the blood fluid and prevent clots), germicide, dye (to give the skin a natural color), and other agents are injected into the arteries under a steady or pulsating pressure by hand, gravity drainage, or a centrifugal pump. Since the right side is more visible during the viewing, the left side is embalmed first if any problems are anticipated. The embalmer strives to reach a happy medium between underembalming, which could result in rapid deterioration of the body, and overembalming, which could cause dehydration and lip and eye separation to occur. The injection is carefully monitored and the body is massaged toward the extremities (or alternatively, toward the heart) to assist in the distribution of fluid throughout the circulatory system. Blood clots are sometimes loosened by rocking the table or lifting the feet. Occasionally, a pre-injection solution is introduced into the blood vessels first to prevent the embalming fluid from coming into contact with the blood and causing discoloration.

After the arterial embalming, cavity embalming is done by repeatedly piercing the stomach, intestines, liver, bladder, and rectum with a long, wide-bore needle called a trocar, which suctions out tissue, food, blood, gases, urine, and feces. A smaller trocar is then used to inject concentrated preservative fluid into the chest and diaphragm, and directly into the tissues where necessary. The holes made by the trocar are sealed with plastic buttons. If the nails are still discolored, an instrument may be used to raise the fingernail from its bed to allow the application of cosmetics. The incisions at the injection sites are covered with dry incision seal, sutured, and smoothed with putty. Any wounds are disinfected and sewn closed. The body is positioned with the left hand over the right hand and left for several hours while the tissues become firm and dry. Any swelling is reduced by removing tissue from beneath the skin. Bruises or burns are removed with bleach or covered with opaque paint. Rough skin is sandpapered. Missing body parts are formed with plaster casts or modeled from restorative wax or other materials. The body is shaved, rewashed, and dressed; the hair is shampooed, set, and combed; and the hands are manicured. Cosmetics in oil, liquid, cream, and powder form are then applied to the hands and face, eyebrows and eyelashes are finished with an eyebrow pencil and mascara, the body is transferred to the casket, and the hands are arranged with the help of positioning blocks and glue. Several tricks are used to fit larger corpses into a standard casket, including turning the body slightly and flexing the legs.

Bodies that are difficult to embalm include those that have been autopsied, which may have been disfigured when their wrists were tied or may have faces which are stained with pooled blood and noses which are flattened after being covered too tightly with a sheet. To prepare an autopsied body, the abdominal cavity is dried and dusted with embalming powder and embalming fluid is injected through the abdominal arteries. The organs are soaked in embalming fluid, replaced in the body, and dusted. The Y-incision is resewn and coated with a liquid sealant. The bodies of the chronically ill are also difficult to embalm, although there are now computer programs to determine which preservative chemicals to use based on the medical history of the deceased. Fluorescent dyes may also be added to embalming fluid so that ultraviolet light can be used to reveal whether the fluid has reached all areas of the body. Other difficulties are encountered in embalming bodies that have been frozen, have marked rigor mortis, have dried out, are swollen, are badly damaged, or are decomposing. Heads that have been decapitated are sewn back on with dental floss, and splints are used to prevent the head from sagging. Bodies that are mangled or crushed may simply be immersed in embalming fluid. Embalmers may only be able to disinfect bodies that have decayed in order to eliminate vermin and odor.[19]

Although it is not mandated as a public health measure unless the body is being transported by common carrier, embalming does take steps toward sanitizing the corpse. In performing their tasks, embalmers must take care to avoid contamination from the body fluids of those with hepatitis, herpes, AIDS, and other contagious conditions. The preparation room should have an exhaust system to rid the air of harmful gases that may be released from the body. Other precautions embalmers are encouraged to take include having preventive globulin injections regularly to protect against hepatitis, using disposable sheets and body pouches when the body is being removed to the funeral home, and wearing double gloves and covers on their hair, eyes, and shoes. In addition, the body should be moved gently to prevent releasing microbes into the air. After it is drained, the blood from a contagious corpse is disinfected before disposal. And the entire preparation area is cleaned with a disinfectant (corgolic acid, lysol, iodine, or ethyl alcohol are common) or household bleach. In fact, embalmers are more at risk from the chemicals they use—which can cause cancer, kidney failure, heart disease, cirrhosis of the liver, and chromosomal damage—than from the bodies they prepare.

The result of such elaborate ministrations is a body that will remain life-like for a matter of days until funeral services can be held. Modern embalmers do not pretend to mummify the dead indefinitely, although they rarely go out of their way to inform their clients of the limitations of their art: "There are still many people who think that embalming, like a diamond, is forever, and go for it even if they aren't planning to view."[20] Medical embalming requires special techniques such as full immersion to preserve a body for dissection over several months, whereas standard embalming methods merely delay decomposition. But at least one embalmer has made the promise of physical immortality and has gained hundreds of clients as a result: John Chew, director of funeral services at Lynn University in Boca Raton, Florida, professed in 1992 to have solved the secret of Egyptian mummification and offered to preserve bodies for thousands of years.[21]

According to Philippe Ariès, the mystique of embalming has Christian as well as pagan origins: "The old embalming procedures were used mainly to pass on a little of the incorruptibility of saints to illustrious, respected men who had died. Since one of the miracles that proves the saintliness of a man is the extraordinary incorruptibility of his corpse, by helping to make a body incorruptible one was setting it on the road to sainthood, participating in the sanctification."[22]

When Eva (Evita) Perón, wife of exiled dictator Juan Perón, died in 1952, she was elevated to the level of a saint by the Argentinian people and her body was prepared as if it were a holy relic. It took Spanish pathologist Dr. Pedro Ara six months to complete the task, which began with immediate embalming. An American publication claimed that he began his preparation at her deathbed, preventing her doctors from administering any drugs that would counteract the embalming chemicals.[23] Dr. Ara's first challenge was to ready the body for a sustained viewing by the public. After replacing the blood with glycerine, he placed her body in the glass-topped casket along with some detoxicant tablets to counteract microbes or insects. During the thirteen days in which she lay in state, the only problem encountered was a mist which developed on the glass and had to be cleaned off several times.

Evita's body was removed to Dr. Ara's laboratory and drained of the glycerine through incisions made in the heels and neck. For a year it was repeatedly submerged in a bath of 150 liters of acetate and potassium nitrate and injected many times with mixtures of formol, thymol, and alcohol. Afterward, it was coated with a thin, hard layer of transparent plastic and put on display for Juan Perón, Evita's family, and her close friends. Perón, who came to see the body three times, wrote: "I was under the impression that she was asleep. I could not take my eyes away from her breast because I hoped at any moment to see her arise and the miracle of life repeat itself.... Her face was as if of wax, clear and transparent, her eyes closed as if she was dreaming. Her hair had been beautifully dressed and she shone with a special radiance."[24] The body was at this time photographed and x-rayed from all angles. After the Argentinian Revolution, officers contended that the body was a fake. One observer reported that when the body was tapped, it rang hollow, like a mannequin. It required another x-ray session, a series of examinations, and the excision of a finger from the body to convince them that it was authentic. To avoid a cult developing around the body of the beloved Evita, a junta—after confirming with Dr. Ara that the body would never decompose and being denied a special request made to the Catholic church for cremation—hid the body for 15 years. It was located in 1970 and transported the following year to Juan Perón in exile in Madrid. There Dr. Ara was summoned and unpacked the body to find it in almost perfect condition. An ear had been bent, the forehead scarred, a fingertip had broken, and the exterior of the body showed a crack at the throat, but it was otherwise intact. In 1974, after lying in state again, this time alongside the body of her husband, Eva Perón's body was at last handed over to the family and is now entombed.

Several other bodies over the years have been treated to withstand the ravages of time. The body of Emperor Charlemagne (d. 814) was embalmed, dressed in his royal robes, and seated with crown and scepter on the throne, where he remained for 400 years until buried by Frederick II. James II's body was embalmed after his death in 1701 and left to the care of English Benedictines in Paris; when the lead coffin was confiscated during the French Revolution, a witness reported that the body was perfectly preserved, with hair, fingernails, and teeth intact, and the fingers pliant.[25] The will of Utilitarian philosophor Jeremy Bentham (d. 1832) directed that his body be dissected and the clothed skeleton and embalmed head be brought out to attend board meetings at University College Hospital in London. Bentham believed that the preserved body, which he termed an *auto-icon*, was a person's finest memorial and would spare survivors the necessity of commissioning stone sculptures. He still sits in the hallway of the university, although a wax model has been substituted for the mummified head. The wife of English eccentric Martin van Butchell had the distinction of being "the preserved lady" from her death in 1775 to the destruction of her body in a 1941 bomb raid. To comply with his wife's will, which stated that her annuity would continue only as long as she remained above ground, Butchell had her corpse embalmed and exhibited it in a glass-lidded coffin in his home until his second wife insisted that he donate it to the Royal College of Surgeons. The body of Enrico Caruso was put on display for six years after his death in 1921 and given an annual change of clothes. After Anderson McCrew's death in 1913, the unclaimed body of the one-legged African-American hobo circulated in the carnival circuit as "The Amazing Petrified Man." He was not buried until 60 years after his accidental death. As recently as 1982, the heavily embalmed body of

Charles "Speedy" Atkins could be seen in the corner of the mortuary where he worked and acquired his nickname. And in Plymouth, England, in 1984, a local artist fought for the right to embalm the dead body of a friend and keep it as a memento.[26] Most people, however, are ready to consign the dead to the ground after the funeral.

While it doesn't always promise permanence, embalming protects mourners from the sights, smells, and sounds of the decay of their loved ones. The use of a combination of art and science to make the dead presentable is intriguing in its defiance of the laws of nature. Men from Benjamin Franklin, who speculated about the possibility of embalming drowning victims for future reanimation, to Elvis Presley, who often visited the Memphis Funeral Home late at night, have been fascinated by embalming. Its purposes have been debated by individual thinkers, including advocates of cremation, and by the major religions, several of which (Sikh, Islam, Judaism, Buddhism, and Hinduism) discourage its use. Even the motives of embalmers, beyond the financial, have been called into question by women including Annie Oakley, who specified that she should have a female embalmer. Embalming is not, however, a hotly contested issue. The decision to embalm is dependent on the necessity of transport or the desire for a wake, and the decision to view or not to view is made on a case by case basis.

The Display

Separation is a bilateral process requiring vigorous and
determined efforts on both sides: as the body must leave
the group, so the group must leave the body.
　　—Robert Garland, *The Greek Way of Death*[1]

The Wake

After its rather elaborate preparation, the corpse is ready to play a passive role in the first stage of the funeral. The visitation, or initial viewing by the immediate family, reacquaints the living with the member they have lost to death. The wake, which often follows, allows friends to view the deceased and to comfort the bereaved in the body's presence. While a watch over the dead has in the past had many purposes, its modern function is to offer a less-than-shocking focus and a neutral forum for survivors to confront the dead. They may vent their feelings of denial and anger if necessary or simply share their sadness and memories with others gathered for the same purpose. In the "slumber room" of the funeral home, the memory picture—framed in the casket of choice—is ready for a final prayer, a kiss of peace, or another parting gesture. Even those who choose cremation have the option, where regulations permit, of renting a casket so that the body can be displayed at a visitation service before it is transferred to a cremation container.

The practice of watching the dead arose from the fear of being buried alive. The ancient Greeks waited three days before burying the dead and viewed the body to guarantee that death had actually transpired and the corpse did not suffer violence. The ancient Hebrews held a vigil as a precaution against premature burial, an act of piety and occasion for prayer, and a chance to rule out suspicion of foul play and to ensure property was distributed fairly."[2] Early Christians allowed relatives and intimates to view the face of the deceased and borrowed the Jewish custom of leaving the sepulchre unsealed for three days so that the corpse could be prayed for and scrutinized

63

for signs of life. From the grave, the watch moved to the home. In the sixteenth, seventeenth, and eighteenth centuries, the body was displayed outside the door of the house. Years ago in Japan, the corpse was relegated to the yard after death, necessitating a watch over it to protect it from wild animals. In nineteenth-century America, the body was exhibited in the bedroom where death had occurred and viewing the remains replaced the custom of visiting before or during death.[3] Today the body reposes in the funeral home, and guarding the deceased through the night is left to its director. Because airplanes have reduced the travel time necessary for mourners to convene, the modern wake lasts hours rather than days.

Now a solemn affair, the wake used to be an occasion for rowdiness and rivalry. In Scandinavia, it was often an opportunity for courtship. In medieval Europe, most notably in Ireland, mourners engaged in drinking, smoking, storytelling, song and dance, and mockery. They played games of dexterity and endurance and staged contests of strength and agility. The corpse was sometimes involved in both the pranks and the games. After the limbs of an arthritic body were tied down to straighten them for the wake, a practical joker would sometimes cut the ropes, causing the corpse to move or sit up. Others might cause the body to move by surreptitiously shaking the bed or table, while roughhousing sometimes overturned the table and caused the corpse to fall to the floor. If a game of cards were played, the deceased was given a hand or served as the gaming table. The body was sometimes outfitted with a pipeful of tobacco or taken onto the dance floor. Such pastimes, repeatedly condemned by local bishops and priests, kept the watchers over the dead occupied through the night and assured the deceased of his or her continued presence among the living.

While the wake is a common rite of the dead today as in the past, the living often eschew it for their loved ones and for themselves in advance of their own deaths. In a 1971 study of 30,000 people, Edwin Shneidman found that only 6 percent approved of lying in state at the funeral and 70 percent did not wish their bodies to lie in an open casket. Women, especially, were against the practice. In *The Widower*, a daughter of co-author Willard K. Kohn commented, "Mother wouldn't have wanted anyone to see her looking like that, and we didn't need to go through that wake to realize she was dead."[4] Many death educators also find disfavor with the general practice of viewing the dead, but opinion is divided among religious leaders: it is believed helpful by Eastern Orthodox and Roman Catholic clergy and a majority of Protestant ministers, but is believed to have no value by most Jewish rabbis. The opinion of Elisabeth Kübler-Ross is that viewing is only necessary if the family has not been prepared for the death, as in the case of a sudden unexpected death.[5] Catholic and Protestant clergy discourage an open-casket service, suggesting that viewing take place before the wake and be confined to close family members. Less conservatively, Methodist minister Edward Bauman writes: "The body, in our experience, is frequently the key to opening the door to the expression of honest and real feelings. The body, when properly used, is particularly helpful as a tool to getting the grief work well started and to doing it promptly."[6] Display of the body may be thought of as vulgar by some and sentimental by others, but it is a tradition with both long roots and a long list of supporters. In the United States, 65 percent of funerals are still conducted with open caskets.

Several psychological reasons have been put forth to defend the custom of the wake. Author Bertram S. Puckle maintained that a delay between death and burial gradually conditioned friends and relatives to the changed condition of the deceased and allowed them to observe the corpse to quell hopes that it might return to consciousness.[7] The open-casket wake, which occurs in about nine out of ten funerals, is often used as evidence of denial, but researchers T. Parsons and V. M. Lidz interpret it as the tendency to want the deceased to appear in a manner that makes former capacities recognizable and as an extension of control over death.[8] Funeral director and sociologist Vanderlyn Pine finds value in the wake as representing the end of activity for the deceased. Psychology professor Dr. Judith Morton Stillion agrees that seeing the dead person assists grieving by showing that there is no return. According to Howard C. Raether of the National Funeral Directors Association, the presence of the body provides an immediate and proper climate for mourning, making it natural to talk about the deceased, when it may otherwise be hard to express oneself.[9] While the benefits of the wake may be argued, it seems to do more than simply provide a justification for embalming.

Lying in State

When the grieving party is an entire nation, arrangements must be made for the public to pay their respects in person to a body they may have known in life only via the television, radio, or written word. Hundreds and sometimes thousands of people line up to file past the open casket of a political leader or popular entertainer. When a king or "The King" dies, the display of the body is part of the panoply of a state or celebrity funeral. National mourning results in large numbers of people who are often in need of crowd control. The idolatry of supporters or fans makes the switch from life to death, sometimes with grave consequences. When the body is displayed temporarily, mourners share their shock and pain and take advantage of the last opportunity to see for themselves the famous face. When the body is exhibited indefinitely, it becomes an icon to a cause, a lasting symbol rather than a fleeting grief object.

After the breakup of the Soviet Union, the lines of people waiting to view the body of Vladimir Lenin grew shorter, but he remained a popular tourist attraction. Since death, his body has been kept at 61 degrees Fahrenheit and 70 percent relative humidity and the exposed head and hands have been bathed with embalming fluids and checked for bacteria twice a week.[10] In October of 1993, Russian President Boris Yeltsin took the first step in eradicating the bodily symbol of Communism by removing from Lenin's tomb the honor guard that had been established five days after his death in 1924. Even without the honor guard, however, a certain decorum was still respected at the tomb, and visitors, who waited in line for three hours, were not allowed to bring cameras, wear hats, or keep their hands in their pockets. The fate of the remains is now uncertain. Lenin's own wish was to lie next to his mother and sister in St. Petersburg's Volkov Cemetery, but officials of the Russian Orthodox Church have objected to his burial on sanctified ground because of his atheism. Even the family is in disagreement. Although Lenin's wife had begged the Communist leaders to bury rather than enshrine the body, his niece Olga Ulyanova believes the body should be preserved. Lenin's corpse, like that of Eva Perón, has elicited accusations that it is a wax imitation, and it may one day rest, like hers, in a private tomb. Lenin may, on the other hand, be buried behind the mausoleum like Joseph Stalin was in 1961 after an extended display within the mausoleum. Others who do not have the luxury of privacy in death include Chinese Chairman Mao Tse-Tung, preserved in Beijing, and Vietnamese leader Ho Chi Minh, who lies in state in a refrigerated tomb in Hanoi, guarded by four soldiers at attention and visited by more than 15,000 people each week, many of them schoolchildren. Such shrines to the body, more so than the memory, will continue to attract pilgrims and possibly create new ones.

Lying in state permanently is the exception to the rule. Only a brief display of the body of French revolutionary Jean-Paul Marat, assassinated in 1793, was possible. He lay in state only until the premature putrefaction caused by his skin disease made a quick burial necessary, but afterward, thousands lined up to view his heart, which was exhibited by a radical group. Queen Anne of Denmark lay in state for ten weeks until the money for an elaborate funeral could be raised, but the bodies of many famous people are put on display only for the time it takes to allow the massive crowds to file past. The 25,000 mourners viewing the remains of Buffalo Bill Cody in the Colorado State Capitol rotunda in 1917 were hurried along by a master of ceremonies equipped with a top hat and cane, who urged them, "Step lively please, a big crowd's behind. Hurry up folks."[11] Often the emotion of the event, in combination with a long wait and the crush of the crowd, has disastrous consequences. When President Ulysses S. Grant lay in state in New York's City Hall in 1885, over 300 policemen fought to control the crowd of 300,000 mourners. When Stalin's body was put on display after his death in 1953, dozens of men and women were trampled to death by the huge crowd that came to view it. Most recently, several Iranians were crushed to death during a stampede to view the body of Ayatolla Khomeini at his death in 1989.

The crowds and injuries connected with the lying in state of Eva Perón's body in 1952 were innumerable. Eight people were killed in the crush as the corpse was removed from the ambulance for display at the Ministry, and over 2,000 were treated for injuries during the next 24 hours. There were said to be at least 20 deaths and 4,500 injured in all. What was intended to be a three-day event was extended to thirteen days as some two to three million Argentines waited four to six abreast in lines more than 30 blocks long to file past the glass-topped casket. After their wait of up to 16 hours, mourners touched the casket, kissed the glass, crossed themselves, or broke down uncontrollably.[12]

The tragic death of silent film star Rudolph Valentino in 1926 was followed by widespread grief and more than a few suicides. During the first two days in which his body lay in state in New York, the crowd of 30,000 stripped Frank Campbell's Funeral Chapel in search of souvenirs, since the casket had been sealed to thwart them. As the mourners packed the streets, the police lost control, and windows were smashed, cars were overturned, and hundreds of people were trampled. Eventually, 90,000 people filed past Valentino's body to view his profile through a glass plate in the casket.

At his death in 1977, Elvis Presley's fans converged in Memphis. In *They Went That-A-Way*, Malcolm Forbes writes: "Within an hour of the announcement of his death that afternoon, more than 1,000 people crowded around the gates of Graceland. By the next day, when Elvis's reconstructed, post-autopsied body was laid out in his mansion, some 80,000 had made the pilgrimage. Hundreds fainted, one man had a heart attack, a woman went into labor, and the National Guard was called out."[13] By the twentieth century, the stars of screen and stage had assumed the place of royalty in American culture, particularly after their deaths.

Despite its hazards, the practice of allowing the public to view the body of a deceased notable has a long history. Beginning with the funeral of Henry II in 1189, it became customary for the body of the king to be displayed during the funeral procession. In the centuries that followed, if the corpse were not fit for display it was obscured with a shroud or a wax or wooden effigy was substituted. Many English kings and statesmen have reposed temporarily in London's Westminster Hall. In 1910, the body of Edward VII lay in state for three days as a half million people viewed his body. In 1936, over 800,000 people came to see the body of George V over a four-day period. Sir Winston Churchill lay in state in Westminster Hall for three days after his death in 1965. St. George's Chapel at Windsor Castle provided a setting for 57,000 people to file past the coffin containing the Duke of Windsor (d. 1972), who had abdicated the throne in 1936. American presidents usually lie in state in the capitol rotunda in Washington. The body of President James A. Garfield drew a crowd of 150,000 mourners who took two days to file past the bier after his assassination in 1881. In 1923, Warren Harding was viewed by 20,000 people. As Herbert Hoover lay in state at 1964, viewers were calculated at 2,500 an hour. After President John F. Kennedy was assassinated in 1963, 250,000 mourners filed past his closed casket.

The popularity of those who lie in state mirrors—and in some cases may appear to exceed—their popularity during life. Crowds attracted by authors have numbered from 3,000 (Mark Twain, d. 1910) to 50,000 (Will Rogers, d. 1935). Victor Hugo was viewed by thousands as he lay in state under the Arc de Triomphe in 1884, and his coffin was followed to the Pantheon by two million readers, some waving placards bearing the titles of their favorite books. Religious leaders who have many followers in life also have a large following in death. The body of Brigham Young (d. 1877) was viewed by 25,000 people and that of Henry Ward Beecher by 30,000 ten years later. Thousands turn out to pay their respects to the remains of a beautiful voice, a unique acting ability, a talented musical performance, or a crowd-pleasing swing of the bat. When Judy Garland's body was placed on view in New York, her fans waited in line eight abreast to see her in her casket. A total of 20,000 viewed the body of Louis Armstrong in 1971. The body of Billie Holiday (d. 1959) drew a crowd of 10,000, that of Hank Williams (d. 1953) drew 20,000, and that of Mahalia Jackson (d. 1972) drew 50,000 in Chicago and 70,000 in New Orleans. Babe Ruth's remains were viewed by 40,000 at his death in 1948. The crowds that have lined up to view the bodies of American inventors also evidence their respect. Although only employees having 30 or more years of employment with Eastman-Kodak were invited to attend George Eastman's visitation service in 1932, thousands of people had flocked to view the body of Thomas Edison the year before. Wilbur Wright had 25,000 mourners in 1912 and Henry Ford had 75,000 in 1947. Social reformers have had their share of support: 10,000 for Susan B. Anthony (d. 1906) and 22,000 for Malcolm X (assassinated 1965). The crowds gathered at the biers of political leaders numbered 25,000 for William Jennings Bryan in 1925 and Richard Daley in 1976, thousands for Adlai Stevenson in 1965, and 40,000 for Hubert Humphrey in 1978. Confederate President Jefferson Davis drew 150,000 at his death in 1889, and Bobby Kennedy drew 100,000 after his 1968 assassination.

Although the Russians were thought to have held the record for the number of viewers of a body lying in state, the estimated 5 million people who viewed Stalin's corpse could only have done so, according to a mathematician, if they had been marshaled by in two lines at 22 miles an hour.[14] The United States, then, may hold the record in the person of Abraham Lincoln. It is estimated that over 7 million Americans viewed the body of the assassinated president during its 14-day journey to Springfield, Illinois, in 1865. In Washington, D.C., 25,000 viewed the body and at each stop of the funeral train—Baltimore, Harrisburg, Philadelphia, New York, Albany, Buffalo, Cleveland, Columbus, Indianapolis, and Chicago—the coffin was brought out and opened to display the president's face. Once the train reached its destination, the body lay in state for 24 hours to allow an additional 75,000 a glimpse of the famous face. With the famous as well as with family, seeing is believing. The urge to view the body of a renowned man or woman who lies in state seems to be made up of equal parts of star-struck curiosity and heartfelt grief.

The Funeral

After it is viewed privately or publicly and before it is buried or cremated, the corpse is subject to a ritualized ceremony in which the life of the individual is commemorated and his or her death lamented. Funerals offer survivors the chance to outfit the dead for their final journey and accustom themselves to their absence. The executive director of the National Funeral Directors Association calls the funeral "an organized, purposeful, time-limited, flexible, group-centered response to death." It is organized in a planning session with the funeral director and may or may not include a committal service. It is purposeful, although the focus has slowly shifted from the needs of the dead to those of the living. It may last minutes or days, but its beginning and end are marked symbolically. It may be altered to accommodate situations in which the body is not present or when circumstances dictate that it be held in two separate geographic locations. But it is always a social event during which grief and memories are shared with others.

In nineteenth-century England, memorial gloves and rings were distributed as invitations to the funeral. In the United States, funeral invitations were delivered or an inviter dispatched to friends and neighbors. In the late nineteenth century, many Americans still held the funeral in the home. Although few funerals were carried out in the funeral parlor, the undertaker took charge of the event and took pains to arrange a beautiful setting for the deceased. Except in rural areas, where the casket was built by the local cabinet-maker, it was ordered from a catalog and adult funerals were postponed several days, depending on the time of year, to allow for the travel time of distant relatives. Today preparations for a funeral begin with a telephone call to the funeral director, followed by a meeting in which the arrangements are made and a casket selected from the many on display in the showroom. The funeral director places a death notice in the local newspapers, schedules the removal of the body to his or her facility for preparation, takes care of much of the paperwork involved in the death, and counsels the bereaved when necessary. With the director's help, the viewing or wake, funeral rite, procession, and committal service are planned and carried out over two to four days. The extent of the funeral services is dictated by the age, race, religion, social class, and economic status of the deceased and the surviving family. Home funerals have become a rarity, and planning one's funeral in advance has become increasingly common.

Funeral and committal services have most often been religious in nature but have often also been grand affairs surpassing what many people can afford. When a Roman of high status died, the funeral was held during the day and an oration was made in the forum. Early Christians held funeral rites in the home, in the church, and at the cemetery. The rituals were carried out under the direction of the clergy. Ostentation marked the funerals of wealthy Englishmen during the Middle Ages, which included the prolonged tolling of bells, hundreds of candles, and rites up to a week in length. Funerals from the later feudal period through the Renaissance were lavish and expensive, but by joining burial clubs or guilds, commoners were also assured of a large turnout at their funeral because it was a requirement of membership. Although Puritans in the American colonies at first did not utilize the clergy for funeral services, by the end of the seventeeth century a sermon was preached over the body and sometimes printed and distributed. In France, a decree of 1794 stated that funerals were no longer religious ceremonies and must be held at midnight in private and without ceremony. Ecclesiologists in Victorian England criticized showy funerals and opposed the adornment of coffins with worldly emblems. They favored the use of tapers and the clasping of the hands of the deceased in an attitude of prayer.[15] The religious tenets of Judaism and Roman Catholicism dictate that the service be conducted with the casket closed, and most Protestant churches discourage their followers from having an open-casket service. The service consists of eulogies, prayers, and many times hymns, and often includes a brief biography of the deceased.

In a 1971 study of 30,000 people, Edwin Shneidman found that 47 percent think rituals are important for survivors, but 33 percent want no funeral at all.[16] The memorial service, without the presence of the casket, may serve as a happy medium. Held by choice, as with cremation, or by necessity, as when a person has been presumed dead or is being buried elsewhere, the memorial service claims to place the emphasis on the life of the deceased rather than on his or her earthly remains. A rite which includes an open-casket visitation period is purported to force grieving family members and friends to accept a death on an emotional level as well as an intellectual level. But whether a memorial service or traditional rite is held, the funeral is a finite event whose purpose is to assist the bereaved in accepting the death and mark the beginning of their lives without the deceased, as noted by Howard C. Raether and Robert C. Slater: "The funeral is an experience in which a person can face the reality of the death, let memory become a part of the process of grieving, express honest feelings, accept community support, and attempt to place the death in a context of meaning."[17]

It is important to some to include a secular rite in the service. Sometimes the profession of the deceased calls for a special observance, such as the breaking of the wand of a professional magician over the casket by a colleague. Rites analogous to a "moment of silence" have been carried out to mark the passing of a widely mourned individual. When Alexander Graham Bell died in 1922, telephone service was suspended for one minute as a tribute. Although a proposal to turn off all electric power for a few minutes was turned down by Congress, lights nationwide were dimmed at 9:59 P.M. on the evening of Thomas Edison's funeral in 1931. During the funeral of Henry Ford in 1947, all industry within the state of Michigan halted production for one minute, while at the same time all buses and cabs and most private vehicles parked at the curb. Wailing over the dead has in the past followed prescribed patterns and served specific purposes. Among the Mandinko, wailing was a means of reminding the corpse of the sorrow it has caused the community. In Africa and in Europe, keeners were hired to wail at the wake or funeral. Lamenting the dead by wailing was practiced by the ancient Greeks and Hebrews and was performed by the family or by hired mourners. Greeks included in their lamentations deliberate touching of the body to indicate that the corpse was not held in complete abhorrence.[18] The early Christians showed more restraint, reciting psalms, saying prayers, and singing hymns for the soul of the departed.

The somber respect which traditionally characterized funeral ceremonies continues in some cases, but has given way to levity in others. Edward Bauman reports, "At the same funeral, I have seen different persons react with hysterical involvement or passive rejection to the fact of death."[19] Warren Shibles concurs, "Practices vary from feeding children popcorn at funerals, and yelling, kicking and jumping in the grave, to completely silent ceremonies."[20] In a special report of 1843, Edwin Chadwick noted the disrespect shown to the corpse among the lower classes: While with the upper classes a corpse excited feelings of awe and respect, with the lower orders "it is often treated with as little respect as the carcass in a butcher's shop. Nothing can exceed their desire for an imposing funeral; nothing can surpass their efforts to obtain it; but the deceased's remains share none of the reverence.... It [the corpse] was pulled about by the children, things were rested on it, it was even used as a hiding place for the beer or gin bottle."[21]

The violent reaction of Iranians to death, in which the bereaved tear their clothing, pull out their hair, and scratch themselves contrasts with the Malagasy funeral that becomes a bawdy and drunken revel to amuse and entertain the corpse. Grief is expressed in numerous ways, some of which seem to deny the loss, but displays of emotion are an expected and socially accepted part of the funeral ritual. Michael Lesy quotes an American funeral director expressing his preference: "Personally, I prefer Italian funerals. Weeping, screaming, women throwing themselves about, men kissing the lips and hands of the dead, people trying to jump into the grave, embracing the coffin, having to be restrained and carried away in a swoon. Then everyone returns home; they eat; they drink; they weep; they feast on food, they drink their tears; they acknowledge the death and then—they resume their lives."[22] The funeral is a forum at which the anguish about a death can be expressed and acknowledged and after which life can continue without the deceased.

The committal, or graveside, service begins with the conveyance of the deceased to the burial site. The ancient Greek procession began an hour before dawn and was attended by men regardless of age, any women over age sixty, and blood relatives of the deceased over sixteen years of age. In ancient Rome, the poor were buried at night by torchlight, but well-to-do Romans were able to hire professional undertakers, whose staff included funeral criers, musicians, singers of dirges, jesters and actors, and torchbearers, all of whom made for a grand procession. The numbers of carriages, palls, hatchments, mourning clothes, and black draperies used in feudal funerals and provided from the late sixteenth century by an undertaker were a drain on the estate of the deceased. In many cultures, including Chinese, Tibetan, and Korean, a representation of the dead person replaced the corpse in procession. Royal or episcopal funerals of the Middle Ages often displayed a wax or wooden effigy of the body already encased in the coffin, which was draped in a pall. The processions of those in the burial guilds included a cross bearer, eight monks, and three acolytes. In the early Christian funeral procession, the body was borne not by hired bearers, but by volunteers as an act of mercy. Today pall bearers are usually family members and close friends of the deceased, and they transfer the casket from the funeral home to the hearse and then from hearse to graveside. In the early 1980s, approximately 75 percent of funerals in the United States included both a funeral and graveside service.

In ancient Rome, burial, rather than cremation, allowed for greater display during which the site was consecrated and earth was cast upon the remains. At the gravesite it was customary for early Christians to give alms of food and money to the poor. After the Reformation, the English also gave alms to the poor rather than spending money on pageantry at the funeral. After the service it became fashionable for those of many faiths to provide food and gifts for those attending the funeral. American colonists offered participants food and drink on the occasion of a death, although the Revolutionary War necessitated simplicity. Victorians gave away locks of hair to the mourners as keepsakes. The modern funeral customarily includes a brief committal service after which mourners symbolically throw a handful of dirt into the grave or lay a flower on the casket. This is followed by an informal and intimate gathering after the return home in which the immediate family shares in food prepared by neighbors and relatives. Ongoing observances of the death may include saying requiem masses for the dead at regular intervals.

Funeral rituals have changed since they first developed over 50,000 years ago. They are no longer held in the home and only sometimes in the church, but are most often conducted in the funeral home's chapel. While they still arrange for all the practical requirements of the wake and funeral, funeral directors are now also trained to assist the living in their time of grief. Funerals lasting several days have given way to services only 20 minutes in length. The hearse is now motorized, rather than horse-drawn, and the casket is lowered into the grave mechanically, rather than with ropes. Yet the gathering of the family for the wake, the assembly at the funeral, and the mourners in procession remain an important part of our culture symbolically and emotionally. That each funeral can be tailored to suit the celebration of an individual life is a function of the rite's versatility. That a single funeral can be reacted to uniquely by each mourner is an indication of our own individuality. It is sometimes the presence of loved ones, sometimes the words spoken in the funeral sermon, and sometimes the freedom to express one's grief in public that make the funeral as valuable today as it has been in the past. As Avery D. Weisman in *On Dying and Denying* writes, "Even among skeptics, today's funeral is an efficient format for parting company with the dead."[23]

The State Funeral

Most often preceded by lying in state, the state funeral is a momentous occasion in which the body of a military or political leader is honored before being laid to rest. The death of a king or president is met with widespread sorrow and long-lasting symbols. Throughout the nation and sometimes the world, bells toll, guns are fired, and flags are flown at half-staff. The state funeral is the focus for all who are touched by the death to participate in acknowledging it, if only by observing the ceremony. While attendance at the funeral is usually limited, the procession through the streets gives access to everyone who is able to gather, and the services are broadcast on television to a worldwide audience. The state funeral has always been a carefully prepared and highly choreographed rite. It remains so today and retains the symbolism used to mark the passing of historical heroes by their contemporaries.

The funerals of kings often include a lengthy and solemn procession in which the poor are invited to participate. When Henri IV died in 1413, his body was accompanied by a procession of 2,000 people, including 224 Franciscans, 200 gentlemen in waiting, 192 Dominicans, 172 archers, 160 officers of the king's household, 100 Augustinians, 83 Capuchins, 50 Carmelites, 35 Bernardins, 24 criers, 17 bishops and archbishops, and 500 poor. After the body of Louis XVIII lay in state in 1824, the departure of his procession was announced by 101 bursts of cannon and the ringing of all the church bells in the city. The cortege included the royal guard, gendarmes, high command of the city, first military division, national guard, infantry, light cavalry, artillerymen, lifeguards, pages, and 400 poor. Until the nineteenth century, citizens of the same gender as a deceased British monarch were selected to walk in the procession, for which they were given a coveted suit of warm black clothing.

The state funeral of Admiral Nelson in London in 1806 set the stage for those that followed. After he lay in state, his body was carried atop a hearse designed for the occasion. The procession culminated in a four-hour service. The funeral of the Duke of Wellington in London in 1852 was also a grand occasion. His coffin was surrounded by a guard of honor at Walmer Castle until the funeral—which was held two months after his death—could be arranged. The Duke's medals and orders lay at the foot of the coffin as it was viewed at Chelsea Hospital by 10,000 mourners over a three-day period. The body was then borne on an 18-ton hearse—17 feet high, 22 feet long, and 10 feet wide—that took three weeks to make and cost £11,000. The enormous funeral car was drawn by 12 plumed black horses and followed by 40 mourning coaches past crowds that numbered more than a million. The procession included representatives from each regiment of the army and a riderless horse with boots reversed in the stirrups to signify the loss of a great leader. All parish churches tolled their bells simultaneously, and tower guns marked the end of the ceremony, although sales of poetic memorials and other souvenirs continued at a brisk pace. Queen Victoria planned her military funeral in advance of her death in 1901. Her body was returned from the Isle of Wight to Portsmouth on the royal yacht *Alberta* accompanied by 38 Royal Navy battleships, cruisers, and destroyers, five German ships, and ships from Portugal, France, and Japan. The vessels formed a double line between which the yacht passed as they fired their guns, and bands played the funeral marches of Chopin and Beethoven. The queen was then transported to London by train, across the city on a gun carriage, and from Paddington to Windsor on another train.

Winston Churchill (d. 1965) also laid out the details of his funeral in advance of death, dictating the order in which the British regimental guard marched, the music they played, the route to St. Paul's Cathedral, the flyover by Royal Air Force pilots, and the path to Chartwell Cemetery.[24] Charles Dickens (d. 1870), on the other hand, directed that he be buried privately, unostentatiously, and inexpensively. Although not a national leader, he was highly admired and heavily mourned. His funeral was—against his wishes—a public event with a lengthy cortege and numerous spectators in full mourning which culminated in his burial in Westminster Abbey. Thirty thousand spectators gathered to watch the procession of Napoleon's body when it was returned from St. Helena. The hearse was pulled by 16 horses through the city of Paris, which had been decorated for the occasion, including the erection of a Greek-style temple at the dock.

Traditional symbols of mourning and an outpouring of sympathy have also accompanied the funerals of American presidents and military men. The funeral of William Henry Harrison in 1841 was attended by 40 clergymen and included a viewing in the East Room of the White House. A military parade included the traditional riderless horse, several cannons, and a funeral carriage drawn by six pairs of white horses. After the death of Zachary Taylor in 1850, bells tolled from the time of the announcement through the following day. A contemporary newspaper account described the 1865 procession which carried Abraham Lincoln's body to the Capitol: "The avenue was cleared the whole length.... The sound of muffled drums was heard, and the procession, with a slow and measured tread, moved from the home of mourning on its mission with the remains of the illustrious dead. Despite the enormous crowd the silence was profound."[25] As the body was returned to his hometown by train, draperies were hung and bonfires lit at each station stop. The 1889 funeral of president of the Confederacy Jefferson Davis, was attended by delegations from many states and clergy of all faiths. The body of William Howard Taft (d. 1930) was carried on a caisson led by eight gray horses and followed by military units of soldiers, sailors, and marines. When Franklin D. Roosevelt died in New York in 1945, his body was returned to Washington by train. A caisson pulled by six white horses brought the casket to the East Room of the White House, and a cortege later that evening brought the casket to Union Station to be returned for a funeral at Hyde Park during which 600 cadets from West Point stood in formation. At his death in 1964, Douglas MacArthur received 19-gun salutes at American military posts around the world. In 1969, Dwight Eisenhower was dressed in full army regalia and given a military funeral complete with taps and a 21-gun salute. The many contributions of Richard Nixon were honored at his 1994 funeral with the firing of rifles and cannons and the presence of all the living American presidents.

Several American presidents and their families have preferred at least some of the funeral rites to remain private. At Grover Cleveland's death in 1908, the burial service of the Presbyterian church was read over his body after President Theodore Roosevelt arrived at the home. The president, family, and a few close friends offered a prayer at the cemetery as members of the National Guard kept the crowd at a distance. When Theodore Roosevelt died in 1919, his simple service was attended by 500 mourners, but the graveside service was restricted to the family and close friends. After Warren Harding lay in state in Washington and in his hometown of Marion, Ohio, in 1923, a private funeral was held in his father's house. When Herbert Hoover died in 1964, he lay in state in New York, where a private funeral was held, and in Washington. The body was then flown to his birthplace of West Branch, Iowa, where 75,000 attended the graveside ceremony. Harry Truman's funeral in 1972 was held at the Truman Library in Independence, Missouri, and attended only by his hometown friends. Since Truman was one of the few presidents who did not lie in state at the Capitol, a memorial service was held at Washington National Cathedral.

John F. Kennedy's funeral after his assassination in 1963 is a profound memory in the lives of millions who watched in person or on television. After his body was returned to Washington, a vigil was kept by a military honor guard and two priests as his casket lay in repose in the East Room of the White House. After lying in state in the Capitol rotunda, the casket was removed as the Navy Band played "Hail to the Chief." Six gray-white horses, three of them riderless, drew the casket from the Capitol to St. Matthew's Cathedral as Chopin's "Funeral March" was played. The caisson was followed by the president's horse Black Jack, with boots reversed in the stirrups, and dignitaries from 92 nations, who were protected by Secret Service agents and bodyguards. Heads of state, prime ministers, and royalty from Austria, Belgium, Canada, Denmark, Ethiopia, France, Great Britain, Greece, Israel, Japan, Korea, Norway, the Philippines, Sweden, Turkey, and West Germany attended the pontifical requiem mass celebrated by Richard Cardinal Cushing. The casket was blessed by Cardinal Cushing and saluted by Kennedy's three-year-old son John Jr. outside the cathedral. The procession resumed with the muffled beating of drums and crossed Arlington Memorial Bridge. After the procession reached Arlington National Cemetery, the National Anthem was played and 50 jet planes—one for each state—flew overhead in formation; Air Force One flew over alone. Cardinal Cushing said a prayer at the gravesite, Kennedy was given a 21-gun salute and three additional volleys of gunfire, and taps was played. The flag that had covered the casket was folded and presented to his widow, who later lit the eternal flame over his grave.

The death of a head of state often causes the nation to stand still in its grief and his or her successor to proclaim a national day of mourning. Philippe Ariès points out: "Except for the death of statesmen, society has banished death. In the towns, there is no way of knowing that something has happened: the old black and silver hearse has become an ordinary gray limousine, indistinguishable from the flow of traffic. Society no longer observes a pause; the disappearance of an individual no longer affects its continuity. Everything in town goes on as if nobody died anymore."[26] In contrast, mourners from far and wide gather to pay tribute to a public life in rites both public and private. Lines form to file past the open or closed casket as citizens pay their respects to a fallen leader, and crowds gather to watch or follow the funeral procession through the capital city. The grief is more poignant when that leader has been the victim of assassination. A patriotic people rally around the body of a president killed by one of their own or a foreign national. Local vigils are held around the country, commemorative souvenirs are sold, eulogies are published in the newspapers, and prayers are offered at dining room tables. For members of the armed forces, the military funeral offers some of the symbolic elements used to honor men who have given their lives—at least in part—to their country, including the playing of taps, the 21-gun salute, and the presentation of the American flag to the widow. For the commander in chief, the timeless addition of drums and cannons, companies in formation from each branch of the military, peers drawn to the funeral from around the world, and countless mourners in the streets demonstrate the impact of the death nationally and internationally. As the one who led the country is now led by the country to his grave, everyone shares in the leavetaking of a man or woman who has passed into history.

The Disposition

Getting rid of the body is the only thing a death ritual *has* to do for the public good. Everything else is an elective.

       —Greg Palmer, *Death: The Trip of a Lifetime*[1]

Storage and Transport

Besides being carried in the casket from the church or chapel to the hearse for the procession to the cemetery, the corpse undergoes many journeys less ritualized. It may be removed from the place of death in an ambulance, rolled down hospital hallways in a cart, taken to the morgue or funeral home in a van or wagon, and manipulated once there by specially designed lifts. Like its mourners, the body may have to travel by train or plane to reach the site of the funeral and burial. Between rites and rides, the corpse must sometimes be stored: it may await its turn at autopsy, await identification, await the planning of the funeral, or await the spring thaw for burial. The storage and transport of the body allow the opportunity for mishaps. Corpses have been mixed up, misplaced, or otherwise misused. They have been posthumous victims of air or rail disasters. And they have been offered as an excuse by mortuary drivers using high-occupancy vehicle (HOV) traffic lanes.

Bodies must sometimes be kept fresh until the funeral or burial can be scheduled (next-of-kin usually has 24 hours in which to bury, cremate, embalm, or refrigerate a body). In his television program "Death: The Trip of a Lifetime," Greg Palmer introduces us to Dr. K. A. Boiteng, the chief medical examiner of Kumasi, Ghana, who stores bodies in a large freezer equipped with a backup generator. After a family has raised enough money for a proper funeral, which may take more than a year, they give him a week's notice so that he can thaw the body of their loved one. The corpse of J. Paul Getty was embalmed and kept under refrigeration at Forest Lawn Memorial Park in Glendale, California, for almost three years until permission was obtained to bury him on the property of the museum he founded. In China, a body may be stored until the spouse of the deceased dies so that husband and wife can be buried together. Mass accidents and disasters often necessitate the designation of a temporary morgue where the dead can be placed until identification can be made by relatives or scientists. Crime waves may sometimes cause city morgues to run out of storage space. When murder in Miami broke records in the early 1980s, the Dade County medical examiner, Joseph H. Davis, leased a large refrigerated trailer from Burger King to handle the overflow of bodies.[2] Storage of bodies, except in tombs or mausoleums, is usually temporary, but may become permanent through habit or neglect. The owner of the Lewis J. Howell Mortuary in Jacksonville, Florida, claimed that paperwork had caused a delay in disposing of the 44 decomposing bodies stacked like cordwood in a closet. Investigators disagreed after dating one of the bodies to 1978.[3]

With exceptions that vary according to state law, bodies may only be transported by mortuary personnel. When a body is removed from a home, the family are asked to leave the room to allow the funeral director to perform his or her duties privately and efficiently. When a corpse is removed from a public place, it is handled much more gently than it may otherwise be. "To swing the body violently onto the stretcher, to yank the straps across the chest and legs, and then to bounce it downstairs probably would draw considerable attention," explains Vanderlyn Pine.[4] Such attention is unavoidable when special arrangements must be made, sometimes with the local fire department, to remove the bodies of obese people from their homes.

When a person dies in a health care facility, the next of kin will be asked to sign a release to permit the hospital to remove the body from the room and prepare it for release to a funeral home. Within the hospital, the body is moved on a wheeled tray designed to keep it concealed from visitors. The gurney has a hidden shelf for the body, so that it appears empty when covered with a sheet, but it is not very effective according to a morgue room supervisor: "We've got a cart with a special white shroud that goes almost down to the floor. The transporters are supposed to keep it private when they go down in an elevator and not let anyone else on. But people end up riding down with the bodies all the time and I don't think there's any doubt in anyone's mind what's under there."[5] The body is removed from the room with such speed, however, that it is often the staff who fail to notice. Dead bodies are spoken of by David Dempsey in *The Way We Die* as being spirited down the freight elevator; Elisabeth Kubler-Ross speaks of "the remarkable disappearing act that occurs as the body is cleverly whisked out of sight."[6] In some states, a body donated to science may be picked up by the medical school after the death certificate has been signed. Some states also allow crematory workers to remove the body from the hospital. Depending on state requirements governing the time lapse between death and disposition and the proper containment of the body (including embalming or the use of dry ice), the family may apply for a transit permit from the health department to take it to the crematory themselves.

During the funeral, the corpse is most often transported by hearse, once drawn by horses and later powered by gasoline. Earlier this century, several variations on this theme were tried in the U.S.: a funeral car built to hold a casket and 36 people in Cleveland in 1910; a funeral bus manufactured by Packard in 1916 that held the casket, the flowers, and 20 mourners; funeral trains that conveyed caskets and funeral parties to suburban cemeteries; and a flying hearse, a seaplane built in 1921 to carry a casket and 12 passengers. In other countries, the dead were often still transported by hand. In Scotland, bearers worked in rotation to carry the body 70 or more miles for burial near his or her ancestors. Early African and South American peoples transported the remains of their dead long distances to bury them in their traditional homeland. Today's motorized procession often includes a police motorcycle escort, a hearse containing the casket, a limousine in which the immediate family is chauffeured, and a long cortege of cars driven by mourners which other drivers are prohibited from interrupting.

Many people die far from home and are returned to their loved ones intact, despite the expense. The reasons, as Tom Weil theorizes in *The Cemetery Book*, are often sentimental: "Death and burial at home, snug in one's native soil, seems so much cozier than reposing in some far land. The enfolding sod and clods of familiar earth coddle us more than can any alien terrain."[7]

Others consider a foreign land their homeland, even if the deceased never lived there. The descendants of Spanish conquistadors sent bodies to Spain for burial centuries after the conquest of South America and many modern Jews return their dead to Israel for burial. When a corpse requires shipment to its final destination by common carrier, it must be packaged in a casket or fiberboard shipping container, which is then enclosed in a wooden case equipped with six handles, a canvas receptacle, or a water-repellent shipping tray with six-inch sidewalls and a protective cover. The remains must be placed on a full-length absorbent pad, secured to prevent shifting, and if they are contagious or disinterred, they must be embalmed and hermetically and permanently sealed. Paperwork accompanying the body must be attached to the outside of the container, and its head end must be clearly marked. If the remains are being shipped internationally, they may require a burial permit, transit permit, certified copy of the death certificate (translated into English if being imported), a letter verifying that the body has no contagious disease, an affidavit from the embalmer, a letter from the funeral home stating that the casket contains only the remains of the deceased, and an export permit. Airlines may require that someone accompany the corpse. If there is not enough room in the cargo bay, the body may be strapped across two first-class seats. Special arrangements may be made, depending on the status of the deceased. After the death of Vice President Hubert Humphrey in 1978, President Jimmy Carter dispatched Air Force One to Minnesota to fly the body to Washington, D.C., for services. The president asked that the seats in the jet be removed so that the body would not have to be put in the baggage compartment.

Moving the body is subject to the vagaries of the weather and the limits of modern transportation. During the 1888 blizzard in the northeastern United States, several funeral processions were stalled and the coffins (and in some cases the hearses) were stored in nearby barns until the procession could resume. One hearse overturned in the snow, spilling the body from the casket. After Green-Wood Cemetery was established in Brooklyn in 1838, funeral parties were ferried across New York's East River. The horse-drawn carts were loaded onto a flat barge, and coffins occasionally slipped into the river. The horrified funeral party sometimes attempted to have the box retrieved and reloaded, but there is no accurate record of the number of unintentional water burials that occurred before the erection of the Brooklyn Bridge in 1883.[8] When the body of American composer Stephen Collins Foster was taken from New York to Pittsburgh after his death in 1864, the train in which it was carried had an accident on a Pennsylvania bridge. Although several cars were thrown into the river, the baggage car containing Foster's body escaped harm. Hearse-driver Jack Volkering was not so lucky in 1989, when he was hit head-on and crushed to death by the casket he was transporting as it broke loose and hurtled forward. Passengers on an Eastern Airlines flight lost not their lives, but only their luggage when an airtray containing a human corpse leaked into the baggage compartment. The body of a man found frozen in the wilderness in 1987 was itself lost when it fell off the struts of a helicopter to which it was attached for transport. The unidentified body was not located a second time.

The removal of bodies leaves room for abuse, usually by those entrusted with their care. In 1797, the administrator of the department of the Seine made the following accusation: "When a body is being transported to its place of burial, I have seen our porters go into a bar. Throwing by the door the pitiful remains that have been entrusted to them, they quench their thirst with copious libations of spirits."[9] Undertakers carrying away the lynched body of Leo Frank, who had been in custody as a suspect in a 1913 child-murder, were stopped by a frenzied man who caused them to drop the body and then began to grind his heel into the dead man's face. In a sadistic scheme, one serial killer left the bodies of his rape and murder victims partially concealed, reported their location anonymously to police, and rushed back to the hospital where, as an ambulance driver, he was called upon to pick up the bodies.[10] Others have used the corpse to smuggle secret documents, jewels, and drugs across international borders.

Those who transport the casket by hand may receive welcome fringe benefits. "I get my exercise acting as a pallbearer to my friends who exercise," said American politician Chauncey Depew (d. 1928).[11] Children were once selected as pall-bearers so that the event would leave them with an everlasting impression of human mortality. When sixteenth-century farmer Matthew Wall died, the bearers dropped the coffin, which woke up its occupant. Wall banged on the lid until they released him and lived many more years. On the other hand, pall-bearing may be deadly. A letter written from plague-ridden Danzic in 1709 reported the following sight: "Not far from my lodgings a stout woman who had died was being carried away, and, perhaps, because the bearers were too weak, they stumbled with the coffin, which flew from their shoulders and broke to pieces, so that the naked corpse fell out, revealing such a fearful sight that it so frightened one of the bearers that he immediately sank dead to the ground."[12] After Henry II of England died at Chinon in 1189, his body was transported only ten miles before the fetor forced the procession to stop and a hasty burial was arranged at the nearby Abbey of Fontevrault.[13]

The difficulties of transporting the body were acknowedged by the Crusaders, who boiled the corpse to separate flesh and bone. The flesh was buried at the place of death, and the bones were carried home to Europe for Christian burial. After the body of Philip III was boiled in wine and water, his bones and heart were sent to St. Denis Cemetery for interment. The disarticulated skeleton became a concentrated version of the body and was considered its noblest part.[14] Others, including Pope Boniface VIII, disapproved of the mutilation. To discourage the practice, a papal bull in 1300 declared that anyone who cut up or boiled a human body would be excommunicated. After the fourteenth century, the bodies of many important people were dismembered for remote burial or dissemination to several tombs. The bowels of William the Conqueror were buried in Châlus, his body in Caen, and his heart in Rouen. King Charles V (d. 1380) also had three tombs, and his high constable Bernard Du Guesclin had four: one each for the flesh, heart, bowels, and bones. The heart was often singled out for special treatment: sent to Jerusalem for burial, conserved as a relic, or enshrined in cathedrals. All three uses led the Catholic church to reverse its policy and condone the practice. Among the French nobility of the seventeenth century, it was taken for granted that there would be a separate tomb for the heart. Others since then have continued the practice. The heart and entrails of David Livingstone, for instance, were buried in Zambia, Africa, after his death in 1873, while the rest of his body was sent back to England for burial in Westminster Abbey.

While each grave is usually marked, the path over which the corpse was conveyed is not. Certain structures were made and reused, such as the lich stone in some cemeteries on which the coffin was rested to await the clergyman. King Edward I of England provided the exception. When the body of his wife, Eleanor of Castile, was brought from Lincolnshire to Westminster, he had memorial crosses erected at each stopping place. Many of these still survive, but the last one—Charing Cross—is a copy made to replace the destroyed original. The transport of the body is also usually a finite procedure. The Celestis Corporation of Florida, however, formulated a plan to keep the dead in perpetual motion. Although opposed by several astronomers, the company received approval from the U.S. Department of Transportation to launch orbiting mausoleums that would each contain the cremated remains of more than 10,000 people in tiny pill-shaped containers. The service would cost $3,900, and survivors could see the craft through telescopes. A remarkable precursor called the Navohi was proposed early in this century by James O'Kelly of New York. A coffin would be placed upright in the elliptical structure, and acid allowed to seep over the body would produce gas which would be ignited by a series of levers. The inrush of air to replace the burning gas would cause the Navohi to speed like a rocket into the sky. Neither the Navohi nor the orbiting mausoleum has yet gotten off the ground, nor has a plan by a Tokyo funeral home to have bodies transported to the moon for burial.

The storage and transport of bodies has typically been carried out surreptitiously. Cemeteries do not publicize the facility in which they keep the "winter bodies" until the weather warms. Airlines do not highlight the fact that some of their passengers are in the baggage compartment. Hospitals do not route vehicles from the medical examiner's office or the funeral home through the main entrance. A grand funeral procession is an expected rite of the honored, but the common cortege is a nuisance that halts one's progress on the road. A lone hearse or morgue wagon is an unwelcome reminder of what lays inside. At the occasional funerals one may attend, the mourners are distracted from watching the attendants situate the casket in the rear of the funeral car after the service and lower it into the grave at the cemetery before or following the committal rite. The corpse and the casket are perceived as static entities within the changes of scene, when in fact they both require much manipulation.

Earth Burial

Dead bodies have been buried, with some variation, for thousands upon thousands of years. They have been inhumed in gardens, churches, and family plots. They have been placed in the grave lying down, standing up, and seated. They have been entombed in caves, vaults, and charnel houses. In some cases, the heart and the body or the flesh and the bones have been buried separately. Burial has been opposed as polluting the earth and defended as fertilizing it. At the same time that burial removes the body from sight, it results in a small piece of real estate that allows the grave to be revisited.

Cemeteries are both sacred ground and tourist attractions, and as burial continues to rival cremation, Forest Lawn and Père Lachaise continue to vie for their share of permanent residents and temporary visitors.

Burial is today the most prevalent method of disposal among Christians, Jews, and Muslims, but it has a long history. Humans first began burying the dead between 100,000 and 40,000 years ago, possibly to conceal the corpse from scavengers or cannibals. Burial is intended to protect the dead, and they have often been provided with at least one layer of material between their bodies and the earth, even if their families are impoverished. Early Christians buried the lower classes naked in winding sheets. In medieval times, the body was usually wrapped in a cloth shroud tied at the head and foot and the bodies of royalty and aristocrats were wrapped in leather envelopes. In the nineteenth century, the unclothed corpses of the poor were wrapped in paper for burial. Today corpses are buried in everything from their best suits of clothes to pajamas, graduation gowns, wedding dresses, or clown suits. As Jeffrey Iserson points out, "Except as demanded by religion or tradition, there is no dress code for the dead."[15]

Coffins and caskets were crafted to house the body safely and permanently in its own compartment. The containers in which the dead have been placed vary from culture to culture, time to time, and person to person. The Myceneans often entombed the dead in earthen storage vessels otherwise used to store grain. Celts sometimes carved coffins from trees planted at the birth of the deceased. Greek children were buried in household receptacles. Wooden, stone, and lead coffins were occasionally employed in medieval times. Magician Harry Houdini (d. 1926) was buried in a bronze coffin he had purchased for one of his escape routines, and a Swedish candy salesman was buried in 1993 in a coffin made entirely of chocolate. The Sekapans of Borneo entomb the corpse in the hollow trunk of a tree, while Benjamin Sowah carves coffins in the shape of automobiles, rockets, and power boats for the dead of Accra, Ghana. Of the myriad varieties of caskets available today, F. Gonzalez-Crussi writes: "Let the skeptical philosopher inveigh against the futility of the effort behind the superb craftsmanship; and let his dyspeptic followers rail against the uselessness, the vanity of shaping these beautiful vessels that are to crumble, unseen, carrying their putrefying cargo to the bowels of the earth. The fact remains that they are beautiful."[16]

In the nineteenth century, a variety of caskets were designed for the presentation, preservation, and protection of the corpse. The English experimented with stone, marble, granite, slate, porcelain, earthenware, bitumen, asphalt, paper, peat, India rubber, iron, and glass in search of the ideal coffin. Before embalming was common, newly interred airtight coffins were often "tapped" by boring a hole in them to prevent the gases of decomposition from causing an explosion. In 1848, the Fisk coffin—metal, mummiform, and airtight—was promoted to prevent grave-robbing. Other deterrent devices followed, including the mortsafe, an iron grid buried over or around the coffin. In the 1860s, a rectangular casket with a glass viewing panel on top was introduced in the U.S. Although caskets today are mass-produced, they have occasionally been specially made. When Robert Earl Hughes, the heaviest human on record, died in 1958, his 1,069-pound body was buried in a casket the size of a piano case and lowered into the ground by crane.[17]

The dead of some cultures were provided with their own burial chamber. At the end of the Neolithic age, funerary chambers were lined with mud or wood to prevent sand from caving in and destroying the body; a lid of wood and clay was fashioned over the grave so the corpse would not get crushed.[18] When they did not cremate their dead, the ancient Greeks deposited coffined bodies in shaft tombs, columns, square-cut tombs, or temple like structures. Early Hebrews who could afford to do so laid their loved ones to rest in tombs or in caves; the body of Jesus was placed in a cave. Romans carved galleries, chambers, and passages for the burial of their relatives, but often allowed fellow Christians to use them. William "Tender" Russ, a 61-year-old gravedigger, prefers above-ground burial to the grave: "Vaults are sweet places. Everybody lies in lead first, then wood, so there's no smell."[19] Today a metal or concrete grave liner or burial vault into which the casket is placed is a requirement in most cemeteries. The wealthy have granite and marble structures designed and built to house their own body and those of their spouse and offspring. Indoor and outdoor mausoleums standing several stories high include niches for caskets and vases for flowers.

Although caskets and tombs have often been promoted or perceived as a means to preserve the corpse, several methods have been purposely undertaken to accelerate the decomposition of the body under and above ground. The ancient Greeks procured stone coffins from a limestone quarry in ancient Troy, believing them to dissolve corpses placed inside within 40 days. They called the coffins "sarcophagi" from their words for flesh-eating. From the fifth century, they drilled holes in the bottom to allow the liquid from decomposition to drain away. The soil of the French cemeteries les Innocents in Paris and Alyscamps in Arles was said to have the miraculous property of consuming a buried body in several hours or days. When a bishop could not be buried in either one, a little soil from them was conveyed to his grave.[20] In the nineteenth century, permeable coffins of lattice-work and wicker that allowed the corpse to return to the earth were patented and sold. Because of their rich soil, churchyards yielded rich grass which was trimmed by allowing animals to graze on it; clergymen also planted crops among the graves. In 1972, Malcolm Wells renewed the advocacy of the organic burial of the body in simple cloths, to return the body to the life cycle. "The body again becomes part of trees, flowers, soil.... . One's blood pulses through the earth. The cemetery would be a garden of life, filled with growth and animals instead of metal, plastic, and concrete," he writes in the journal *Environmental Quality*.[21]

For some, the corpse is meant to remain intact. Burial is not considered complete unless it contains the entire body, even those parts discarded during life. Some Orthodox Jews save nail clippings and any organs removed from their bodies for burial after death. In Chenahlo, Mexico, hair that has fallen out in combing and fingernails cut off in laying out the dead are buried with the corpse.[22] Others remove pieces of the corpse before burial as keepsakes or for superstitious reasons. One aboriginal tribe was reputed to remove the fingernails and tie the hands of the dead, and tie or amputate the feet, to prevent them from digging out of the grave.[23] The Dyaks of Borneo cut a lock of the dead person's hair and some fingernail clippings and placed them in a wooden box to allow the soul to pass into the first level of heaven. Saints have been subjected to minor mutilations in order to preserve relics for veneration before their bodies are lowered into the crypt. And Victorians often clipped some hair from the head of the deceased to weave into a memorial or place in a locket.

Since antiquity, flowers have been a staple in the rituals and superstitions surrounding the disposal of the dead. The life that the blossoms represent is thought to counter the death that is being acknowledged. A prehistoric grave discovered in Shanidar, Iraq, contains the pollen of eight different flowers. In ancient Greece, female relatives crowned the head of the deceased with flowers and wove them into wreaths. The Romans blanketed the couch of the dead with leaves and blossoms and burned incense. In Nepal, a flower also serves as food for the dead: leaves of the tulasi are placed on the tongue and an infusion of the flower is given as a drink. Today's funerals often require a separate car to bring the flowers and wreaths from the funeral chapel or church to the gravesite. In addition to flowers, food was often provided to sustain the dead on their journey to the next life. The ancient Egyptians offered cakes, oils, and beer to the dead, which were sometimes passed into the corpse's mouth by means of a tube. The ancient Greeks and Romans made offerings of food and drink. In Middle Gaul, mourners invited the corpse to take part in the meal of honey, eggs, bread, milk, and wine which was eaten as the cortege made its way to the grave. During the funeral party, members of the Lobi tribe of Africa push food into the mouth of the deceased. A Chinese funeral observance includes cooking a chicken as the last meal for the deceased; it is placed near the casket and buried with the body. In certain parts of the country, Russians buried food with the corpse to soothe any hunger pangs, a custom which survived in the scattering of grains of corn or rice on the grave.[24] In most modern Muslim burials, offerings of food and drink are brought to the graveside. Mexicans provide food for the dead during their celebrations, but believe the dead only digest its essence, leaving it intact but flavorless.

Many cultures, including our own, have thought it fitting to provide their dead with gifts both useful and symbolic. A belief in an afterlife is surmised from the food, weapons, and charcoal included in the 40 or so Neandertal burials which have been uncovered. In Le Moustier, France, a skeleton was found face down with its forearms under the head and a hand ax near the left arm. In the French Dordogne, remains have been found in a crouching position, often on an east-west axis, with gifts and traces of feasts.[25] Other prehistoric graves contain evidence of torches and bodily adornments such as headdresses and bracelets. In ancient Greece, a coin was placed in the mouth of the corpse as payment for Charon and a honey cake was placed next to the body to appease Cerberus. The coin was later replaced by medieval Christians with a communion wafer. The Maoris and others have buried their dead with an egg, a symbol of rebirth. Mycenaeans buried the dead with the tools of their trade, though they sometimes took them back after a decent interval. Swedes customarily bury an unmarried woman with a mirror so that she can arrange her hair on Resurrection Day.

Gift giving continues today as bereaved Americans tuck special items in the casket of a loved one. Friends of police officer Richard Miller, who was killed in the line of duty in 1986, provided him with a supply of Hershey's Kisses and his favorite beer. Friends of a Hell's Angel equipped the deceased with brass knuckles, switchblades, and marijuana. A Charleston funeral director was touched by the friends of a 17-year-old accident victim who participated in laying out the body and paid their respects at the open-casket service held at her school: "And, at the end of it, all her friends filed by and tossed in mementos, little things that reminded them of her: candles, records, roach clips, books, beer cans, whatever. Then we closed the coffin and we buried her.... It was so moving! It was perfect."[26]

Preparing in advance, Queen Victoria made a list of keepsakes she wanted to accompany her in the grave. Among them were one of Prince Albert's dressing gowns, a plaster cast of his hand, numerous photographs, several articles of jewelry, and some shawls and handkerchiefs. She also instructed that a lock of hair and a photograph of her devoted attendant and friend John Brown be placed in her left hand. The items were included in her casket and hidden from view by a cushion and a posy of flowers.[27]

Fashion, religious tradition, and idiosyncrasy have all at times dictated special positioning of the body within the grave. According to his own instructions, a man of Brazoria County, Texas, was buried standing up on his own property in 1832, so that no one would be able to say "Here lies Britt Bailey." Clement Spelman (d. 1672) of Norfolk, England, was also buried upright. Richard Hull of Leith Hill, England, was buried astride his horse upside down in the belief that the world will be inverted on Judgment Day. Willard Aldrich (d. 1882) of Mishawaka, Indiana, made provision to be buried sitting at a table holding a deck of playing cards, a bottle of whiskey, and his pipe, with his boots and shotgun at the ready underneath. At the request of Reuben Smith (d. 1899) of Amesbury, Massachusetts, his body was buried seated in a reclining chair next to a table on which lay his favorite pipe, a newspaper, and a checkerboard. According to another account, the table also contained matches, candles, and a key to the tomb door. Also in 1899, Mrs. George S. Norton of Pawling, New York, was buried sitting upright in her rocking chair, and Monsieur Halloin of Caen was buried in the bed in which he died, having been tucked in snugly by his relatives. John "Mad Jack" Fuller, an eccentric member of Parliament, was said to have been buried sitting up wearing a silk tophat and holding a bottle of claret.[28] In *Death: An Interdisciplinary Analysis*, Warren Shibles reports that one man in Missouri asked to be buried on his side because he always slept that way and another was buried with his rifle and Colt revolver loaded and cocked.[29] For some people, positioning is not as important as location. Hebrews believed that family members buried together remained together in Sheol. Spouses can now purchase companion spaces in which they will lie one above the other. Foregoing the family plot, many animal lovers choose to be laid to rest near their pets. In 1978, Lillian Kopp became the first person to be interred in Chicago's Paw Print Gardens, where she now rests near her German shepherd, "Rinty," who died in 1972.[30] Pulitzer Prize–winning author Ellen Glasgow left instructions for several of her dogs to be disinterred from her garden and Richmond's Pet Memorial Park so that they could be buried with her in 1945.

Special outfitting or placement indicated status in the Middle Ages, when the bodies of the wealthy and powerful were buried in a sitting position and knights were buried in their armor. Others were driven by space considerations or supernatural beliefs. Before his death, Ben Jonson (d. 1637) asked for 18 inches of ground in Westminster Abbey, so he was buried upright in the north aisle. The Chiriguonos of South America, on the other hand, buried corpses with their heads downward to prevent their escape from the grave. Burial was often done with resurrection in mind. Neandertals bound the body in a prenatal position, and Cro-Magnons colored it with red ochre, rituals which suggest to some that paleolithic humans believed in the rebirth or reanimation of the dead. In Babylon and Sumer, sacrificed servants were interred in a crouching posture so they could spring forth and serve on command. Muslims are laid with the right side facing Mecca, while Buddhists are laid with the head to the north. Grave orientation among Christians is dictated by revelations of the Last Judgment and the words of St. Paul, who likened the corpse to a planted seed which will rise to grow again. The faithful were traditionally interred so that when they sit up, they will face the east. Priests were buried facing west so they could watch over their congregation.

Even when cemeteries are not connected to a church, most peoples have considered them sacred places. Once they began burying their dead, hunter-gatherers returned to the site to honor them, which resulted in the development of villages and cities around burial sites.[31] Roman tombs were protected by law, and burial within a given spot rendered it inviolable.[32] In 752 A.D.,

St. Cuthbert obtained permission from the pope to use land adjacent to churches as burial ground. In 1225, fifty ships returned to Pisa laden with earth from Jerusalem so that believers could be buried in truly holy ground.[33] Beginning in the eighteenth century, the burial plot became protected by virtue of being owned. "The burial concession became a certain form of property, protected from commerce, but assured in perpetuity," writes Ariès.[34] In addition to being sanctified and protected, the cemetery has at times been considered exclusive. The unfaithful and the unbaptized were refused posthumous access to the church graveyard. When a woman died during pregnancy in the Middle Ages, the fetus would sometimes be cut from the womb and buried outside the churchyard.[35] In the more charitable parishes of England, sinners, stillborns, and suicides were allowed the privilege of burial within the churchyard, but their graves were placed north of the church, their bodies were oriented north to south, and their headstones were reversed. In general the north side of the church was reserved for suicides and murderers, the east for ecclesiastics, south for the upper classes, and west for the lower classes. In America, African-Americans were formerly not allowed to bury their dead in white cemeteries. Until 1958, Forest Lawn restricted its occupancy to Caucasians. The choice of cemetery had become a social decision. Père Lachaise became known as Paris's best postmortem address, where those who could afford it may "rub mouldering shoulders with the elites."[36] The undertakers of the nineteenth century promised that the purchase of a hermetically sealed coffin would protect the body from the dust of less eminent corpses.[37] Jews who wish to be buried near a noted rabbi in Israel's cemetery on the Mount of Olives may pay upwards of $20,000 for the privilege. Graveyards of all kinds collect the bodies of those of many different social strata. A New York City physician explains: "If you struggle all your life to get good jobs and the best apartments and to send your children to Harvard, why the hell should you want to spend 3,000 years lying under a highway in Queens? You might be poor while you're breathing, but if you care enough to scrimp for a few years, most people can still manage to reach new heights in death. Money might not get you into Harvard anymore, but it can still get you buried next to its alumni."[38] A site overlooking a river will command a higher price than one near an expressway. In addition to its location, the tomb has become in some cases a blatant display of wealth, not only in appearance but in the ways in which it is outfitted for the comfort of the deceased.

Preparations made in advance of death or by surviving relatives seem to suggest the imposition of living needs on the lifeless corpse. The tomb of a wine merchant in a Rochechouart cemetery is wired for electricity and telephone service. Art collector Joseph Hirshhorn was buried with three phones in his casket, but rumors that the graves of Mary Baker Eddy, founder of Christian Science, and radio evangelist Aimee Semple McPherson contain telephones are false. Forest Lawn Memorial Park in California offers the options of air conditioning and music, as well as earthquake- and bomb-proof vaults. A tombstone in Anking, China, was built as a stove to warm the grave of a tycoon plagued by colds all his life. A tomb in Madagascar contains a clock wound regularly for the deceased by his family. There have been instances, however, where the furnishings of the tomb are simply intended to prevent boredom. A woman laid to rest in a California mortuary asked to be interred with a portable television tuned to her favorite soap operas. Pretending a consciousness in the grave, Greg Palmer muses:

> I know it's a completely irrational perception, but being dead sounds like the most boring thing you could possibly be. Lying there with no books, no magazines, no television, nobody to talk to, nothing... . No appointments on the horizon, no crypt-side book, no disintegrating companions. And what if your feet start to itch? It would be agony. No, unless you speak fluent worm, you're stuck with itchy feet and no one to talk to, just staring forever at the underside of a coffin lid. I've seen quite a few coffin lid undersides in the last two years, and not one held my interest for more than a few seconds, much less ten zillion years.[39]

Whether they need them or not, the dead are sometimes provided—through their own foresight or the thoughtfulness of survivors—with all the comforts of home.

Although the hackneyed phrase "You can't take it with you" remains true, many people have tried. Willie M. Stokes, Jr., was buried as he wished in a coffin shaped like a Cadillac Seville with head and tail lights, steering wheel and chrome grille, wearing a red velvet suit and fedora, and clutching fistfuls of money with diamond-ring-filled fingers.[40] Numerous other people have been buried in their cars: Corvettes, Cadillacs, and Thunderbird convertibles. In Manila's Chinese cemetery, which contains 5,000 mausoleums, those along "Millionaires' Row" have ornate furnishings, marble walls and floors, paintings, stained glass windows, bathrooms, kitchens, staircases, and other embellishments. At least one boasts a stocked bar for visiting relatives[41] and another sports mail slots on the door.[42] The advice of Colonel Sanders, founder of Kentucky Fried Chicken, should perhaps be heeded: "There's no reason to be the richest man in the cemetery. You can't do any business from there."[43]

In contrast to these lavish offerings and accommodations, the dead have sometimes been inhumed in collective graves or chambers to save money, time, or space. Ancient Romans buried their slaves in a common pit. Noble Romans often built mausoleums for themselves, their family members, and their servants that housed several hundred bodies. Philippe Ariès quotes a French gravedigger about the communal grave in use in Minot since the nineteenth century: "To reuse a tomb, I reopen it. If the old coffin is intact, I leave it as it is and put the new one on top of it. But usually I find bones and pieces of metal and wood. I remove all this debris and put it aside in a little pile, and then, when the new coffin has been lowered into the grave, I put everything on top of it."[44]

Space has often been at a premium, with estimates that American graveyards will be full by 2020, and throughout the world the dead are occasionally or regularly evicted from their resting places and their graves reused. Overcrowding of cemeteries became a familiar problem in Victorian England. One source from 1880 reported that the "commonses" were dug up every twelve years and any remains burnt. Several graveyards were said to contain implements for chopping up and burning bodies buried less than a week to make room for new graves.[45] Earlier this century, an interview with gravedigger William "Tender" Russ yielded the following statement: "Village folk have been buried over and over again in the same little bits of churchyard. You have to throw somebody out to get somebody in—three or four sometimes. I always put all the bones back so that they lie tidy-like just under the new person. They're all soon one."[46]

Today graves are recycled in Berlin every 50 years and in Denmark every 15 years. In London, graves at prestigious cemeteries have 99-year leases. In Vancouver, British Columbia, a 30-year renewable lease is signed. Vaults in New Orleans are swept clear of bones regularly. In Moslem countries, remains are removed to a common grave after several years so that burial grounds can be refilled. In some cultures, burial is intended to be temporary. Bodies are buried until the flesh decays, then the bones are exhumed, cleaned, and reburied or preserved.

Many peoples have had to tackle the problems posed by the decay of bodies in their midst. The ancient Greeks buried the dead under the stone floors of their houses until the practice was forbidden for reasons of hygiene. Romans prohibited burial inside the city walls. The bodies of Christians were long held to be holy relics meriting burial within the confines of the church itself. Medieval Christians preferred their bodies to remain near the saints or the altar. In England and Europe, corpses were typically buried under the church floor. But by the sixth century, burial vaults within churches were filled with cracked and rotted wooden coffins, which presented a direct source of disease to worshipers.[47] When the crypts were full, the bones were disinterred and piled up in attics and galleries and under the eaves of the church. In the fourteenth century, the French created charnel houses to store the accumulated bones of the dead. Despite the smell, they were visited, decorated, and used to hold catechism classes and conduct special services on feast days. But even these grew full and led to storage in the Parisian catacombs.

When burial within the church became physically impossible, parishioners had to be content with graves in the churchyard or "God's Acre," as it was called. Beginning in the fifteenth century, testators began requesting burial in the church cemetery so they could lie near the graves of their family members.[48] But like churches, churchyards became overcrowded and began to offend the public. In the mid-seventeenth century, it was common for graves to be left open for several days and for the earth piled to the side to contain bones and skulls from earlier burials. In the eighteenth century, a shortage of space in the churchyards necessitated the stacking of coffins, which commonly raised the ground level several feet above that of the church.[49] St. Dennis Parish Church in Cornwall, England, was surrounded by a retaining wall for this reason. Bodies from the French Cimetière des Innocents burst through the wall of an adjacent apartment house and spewed into its basement, causing a scandal.[50] America, too, was having its share of problems. After frequent complaints, the Boston selectmen ordered in 1786 that coffins be placed a minimum of three feet underground, that no tombs or graves be left open, and that no bones remain on the surface.

By the nineteenth century, graveyards were considered to be a principal source of poisonous fumes, believed to be immediately noxious and to cause lingering illnesses. G. A. Walker protested that saturated burial grounds were emitting "pestiferous exhalations" in his 1839 book, *Gatherings from Graveyards*.[51] J. C. Loudon stated his opinion in *On the Laying Out, Planning and Managing of Cemeteries and on the Improvement of Churchyards* published four years later: "To inhale this gas, undiluted with atmospheric air, is instant death; and even when much diluted, it is productive of disease which commonly ends in death."[52] Loudon suggested hastening the destruction of corpses with quicklime. Queen Victoria's postmaster general, Dr. Lyon Playfair, estimated that in 1849, 2,572,580 cubic feet of noxious gases were emitted from 52,000 metropolitan burials.[53] French architect Paul Coupry made the following statement in an 1887 memorandum: "No site is naturally good for the creation of a cemetery.... We do not understand how, to this day, river water or spring water has been allowed to bathe or simply wash the corpses, so that all the putrefaction of those corpses, diluted and carried off by those waters, outside the cemetery, later come and poison our food and infect the air."[54]

As reformers convinced the public of the hazards posed by the proximity of the dead, they often used the infamous example of the Enon Chapel, which opened for worship in London in 1823 and in 1847 began double duty as a rented dance hall. By 1842, an estimated 12,000 bodies had been interred in the basement at the rate of 30 per week by a preacher motivated by burial fees and sales to anatomical schools. The odor which rose through the floorboards caused women to faint during church services, and the black flies which crawled out of the caskets tormented children during Sunday school.

The result of attempts at reform were restrictions on churchyard burials and the creation of planned cemeteries, often outside urban areas. After the Civil War, burial within American city limits was often prohibited. And special care is taken today with regard to polluting natural resources. For instance, the bodies of victims of the explosion of the nuclear power plant at Chernobyl in 1986 were buried in lead coffins that were soldered shut to prevent radiation from seeping into the water table. Sanitary precautions are now taken, but overcrowding remains a common problem in cemeteries in several parts of the world. There is a six-week wait to be buried in any of the 116 cemeteries in Berlin, and the Japanese conduct a lottery semiannually to determine whose ashes will be buried and whose will be kept in underground cellars.[55]

While the disposal of the body and its attendant rites have been carried out over the ages for the benefit of the soul or spirit of the deceased, Adolf Holl points out that the special attention is in some sense coerced:

> All the wrapping up and coffining and burying; the heavy stones on the grave; the sealed urns; the dead laid under the floor of the house (as in ancient Mesopotamia) or inside the precincts of a cemetery; the carefully piled up bones in prehistoric and medieval ossuaries; the provision of food, vessels, jewelry, and (as in Sumerian Ur) the slaying and burial with the dead man of wives, servants, and war-horses, so that he may be more comfortable and live according to his proper state in the other world; the repeated gifts of food brought to the grave; the endless prayers and litanies for the dead—all the funeral customs that are as old as mankind have their origin, according to Dr. Freud, in a very simple and well concealed impulse: fear of the dead.[56]

To avoid their return, we ensure that the dead are buried in ceremony—equipped with food, household goods, and sometimes human company and furnished with grave markers that pay homage to their lives and at the same time keep them in their graves. Those to whom luxury is a necessity in life are buried extravagantly, and those who are renowned are buried with honors.

But even wealth cannot prevent the mishaps and mismanagement that occasionally accompany the disposal of the dead. A court awarded compensation for mental anguish to the descendants of people buried in a Louisiana cemetery after the owner allowed the property to be drilled for oil. When unionized gravediggers in Cook County, Illinois, went on strike, cemeteries were ordered to supply relatives with the tools and equipment to bury their own dead. In Washington in 1989, a widow sued a funeral home after the death of her spouse when she saw one of her relatives wearing the Stetson cowboy hat that her husband was supposed to be buried wearing. In addition to human failures, burial equipment also breaks down. Funeral homes have been taken to court when caskets have not been closed properly, have leaked, have fallen apart, or have had handles come loose and injure pallbearers. Today most large casket companies carry multimillion dollar liability insurance policies for claims against the performance of their caskets.[57]

After interment or entombment, graves are marked fittingly and holidays are set aside to visit and decorate them, but some still get lost or overlooked.

In *The Cemetery Book*, Tom Weil characterizes his visits to the world's grave-yards as serendipitous discoveries of the famous and the infamous as well as all the rest of us:

> Here and there and everywhere I came across the dead—long-gone, just gone, young, old, hardly started, ripe departed, Christian and Jew, Muslim and Mormon, saints and sinners, losers and winners, outlaws and in-laws, black and white and red all over, rich and poor, top dogs and fat cats, big shots and small fry, the once healthy and wealthy and wise and foolish and poor, the dead in all their rich variety, scattered about the earth in capital cities, small towns, remote corners, crowded burial grounds, empty fields, lying in the earth remembered, forgotten, adored, ignored, commemorated, nameless, all, all claimed by the great democracy of death.[58]

The two million acres of cemetery land in the U.S. contain an average of 2,000 or more bodies per acre. Many are buried, but only a fraction are remembered. As Memorial Day traditions wane, graves are maintained in modern cemeteries through "perpetual care" and in historic graveyards by strangers who restore and care for them as outdoor museums. Burial sites containing many famous people in close proximity get the most attention and draw the largest crowds. Cemeteries planned as parks and museums, in addition to their function as graveyards, have become places of pilgrimage for those who wish to visit the graves of the famous and the heroic. More than 1.5 million tourists visit Forest Lawn in Glendale, California, each year to see, among the sculptural attractions, the resting places of Hollywood legends. Père Lachaise in Paris, which became famous for the celebrities within by 1850, welcomes 800,000 visitors annually. The gravesite of John F. Kennedy and many others at Arlington National Cemetery draw crowds of two million a year.

Water Burial

Corpses have been consigned to a watery grave for reasons both super-stitious and practical. Bodies on board have been buried at sea to avoid slowing the ship, and they have been jettisoned, along with other cargo, to lighten the load. The dead have been propped up in their vessel and pushed out to sea for their last journey, and they have been thrown into the sea as a hasty and inexpensive means of disposal or as a way to avoid posthumous mutilation. To avoid the fate of Davey Jones' Locker, bodies have been disguised or misleadingly labeled. Conversely, many seafarers request sea burial, accompanied by a brief committal service. Committing bodies to the sea is sometimes a tradition, sometimes a necessity, and other times a personal preference. The underwater grave is not usually visited by surviving family members, but may be rediscovered by marine archaeologists. The bodies may be skeletized by fish or preserved by certain chemicals in the water. They may remain attached to their weights, or they may float free and wash up on shore. But as with earth burial, neither fresh nor salt water can guarantee against eventual dissolution.

Seafaring superstition holds that a corpse on board a ship will draw bad weather down on it or slow its progress and should be tossed overboard if this occurs. According to an apocryphal story, even royal bodies are not safe. When the body of Henry IV (d. 1413) was transported from London to Feversham down the Thames, the crew was said to have jettisoned their cargo when the ship got into difficulty. When the tomb at Canterbury was opened in 1832, however, it did contain the king's remains. To conceal from the superstitious crew the fact that a corpse was on board, one captain, shouldered with the responsibility of transporting the bishop of Derry, packed the body in a crate labeled "antique statue."[59] The belief that bad luck will attach itself to any ship on which a dead person is carried, along with the health hazards of harboring a decaying corpse, is said to have prompted the committal of the body of a dead sailor to the waves. When this was carried out, the remaining sailors avoided watching the corpse sink for fear that they would soon follow. If a man killed another man at sea during the reign of Richard I, his punishment was to be bound to the dead body and thrown into the sea.

Burial at sea has also been practiced to protect not only ships' crews, but the coastline. In a form of foundation sacrifice, Teutons inserted the bodies of children into the dykes on the sea coast to protect the structures from the waves. Sea burial has also been undertaken to avoid certain fates to which the corpse might otherwise be subjected. One was described by Charles Kightly in *The Perpetual Almanack of Folklore*: "On May the 20th 1736 the corpse of Samuel Baldwin was immersed in the sea off the Needles, on the New Hampshire coast. This was performed in consequence of an earnest wish the deceased had expressed, in order to disappoint the intention of his wife: She had repeatedly assured him in their domestic squabbles (which were very frequent) that if she survived him she would revenge her conjugal sufferings by dancing on his grave."[60]

The bodies of both the rich and the poor have been consigned to the sea. Those of Norse chiefs and heroes were set adrift in death ships on rivers and oceans, a tradition which reached its peak in the seventh and eighth centuries. Viking kings were seated under a tent on a ship. A slave girl and the king's favorite horse were sacrificed to accompany him, and the ship was set aflame and pushed out to sea. In modern times, when a man who had captained a $60,000 yacht for a multimillionaire's daughter for 40 years died in her service, she had his body propped in his cabin and then had the yacht towed several miles off the Florida coast and sunk.[61] In Tibet, the corpses of poor people, lepers, and babies are often thrown into streams and rivers as a quick and inexpensive way to dispose of them.

When a person died at sea, those with him or her often attempted to bring the body home for burial. The bodies of Spanish and French sailors who died at sea in the eighteenth and nineteenth centuries were kept in the ship's hold rather than being buried at sea so that they could be interred in a church cemetery. An epitaph in South Dennis, Massachusetts, tells the story of a recovery from the sea:

> Of seven sons the Lord his father gave,
> He was the fourth who found a watery grave.
> Fifteen days had passed since the circumstance occurred,
> When his body was found and decently interred.[62]

In some cases this did not prove possible and a cenotaph was erected in memory of the deceased. Vikings buried a rune rod containing the dead man's name in place of the body. A paradoxical epitaph in Winslow, Maine, is carved on what is probably a cenotaph: "Here lies the body of John Mound, / Lost at sea and never found."[63] In a few cases, the remains did not constitute enough to bury in a grave. Explorer Captain James Cook had a disagreement with Hawaiian natives and was killed by them in 1779. After stabbing and drowning him, they cut the body up and presented pieces of it—his scalp, bones, and hands—to his crew, who buried the remains at sea.

If no special precautions have been taken, the dead will eventually rise to the surface of the water or wash up on shore. In some island cultures, the bodies of the dead are wrapped in cloth and weighted with stones before being dropped into the ocean.[64] In the British navy in the nineteenth century, the dead were sewn in their hammocks with shot at their feet before being launched overboard. In at least one instance, bodies at sea were purposefully resurrected. The bodies of 66 men killed when the U.S. *Maine* was bombed and sunk in Havana Harbor in 1898 were brought up 12 years later and interred at Arlington National Cemetery.

Today military sea burial takes place when death occurs on the high seas and there are no facilities to refrigerate the body until the ship reaches port, when military personnel are killed on board a ship during war, or by specific testamentary request of active or retired navy personnel.[65] In other branches of the service, those eligible for a military burial may choose burial at sea if the U.S. Navy has a ship and personnel available when and where the burial is to take place. The U.S. Coast Guard performs the same service for their retirees and their spouses.[66] Sea burial is also a means of disposal in dire circumstances. Thirteen days after his plane went down in the Pacific Ocean, Captain Eddie Rickenbacker and his six companions were forced to abandon the body of the seventh, who had died on board the life raft. The zippers of Sergeant Alex Kaczmarczyk's flying suit were fastened, the men said the Lord's Prayer, and the body was pushed into the water, where it remained visible for some time.[67] Civilians are more often cremated and their ashes scattered at sea, but can be buried at sea bodily through a handful of private companies. The corpse is sewn up in canvas or enclosed in a rough plank coffin, weighted, and slid into the sea. The Environmental Protection Agency requires a description of the exact location of the disposal so that the body can be identified if it is later recovered.

The total number of bodies buried at sea has been estimated at more than one million.[68] These include the victims of foul play dumped in the ocean as a means of execution or disposal and victims of cannibalism thrown off the ship to hide the evidence of such desperate means of survival. They include wartime casualties or victims of marine disasters whose bodies were never recovered. They include Norse kings ensconced in special boats, navy personnel in crates, and impoverished island natives wrapped only in a shroud. Some remains have been committed to the sea intact and others after they have been cremated. The graves cannot be marked, except in memory or by latitude and longitude, but the oceans—like the land—contain the remains of countless numbers of our predecessors.

Cremation

There are many reasons and many precedents for burning a body rather than burying it. Cremation saves money and space. It also saves time. The incineration of a corpse over a matter of hours saves years of slow dissolution underground and yields a few pounds of bone fragments that can be kept in the home, sent through the mail, or scattered. Cremation, however, has had its share of bad publicity. While the cautious have carried it out to prevent bodysnatching, it has been practiced by the superstitious to prevent vampirism and used by killers to dispose of their victims. It was also used as a posthumous punishment before it was socially accepted. And it has been exploited as an efficient means of disposal for large numbers of bodies, as it was in the German concentration camps. Despite some of its history, cremation continues to gain popularity in countries where land is scarce and where the tradition of burial is losing its stronghold.

Cremation was practiced by Stone Age Europeans, ancient Australians, Iron Age Palestinians, and ancient Babylonians.[69] Scandinavians began to cremate their dead during the Middle Bronze Age and persisted through the tenth century, when the establishment of Christianity led them back to burial. The ancient Greeks began to cremate rather than bury their dead in about 1,000 B.C. Fire was associated with purification. According to Homer, the Greeks doused the ashes of funeral pyres with wine, after which the closest relative placed them in an urn. Greek warriors cremated their dead on the battlefield and brought the bones or ashes home for entombment with honors. Cremation was practiced on all but infants before they had reached the teething stage, suicides, and those who had been struck by lightning. Romans borrowed the custom of cremation from the Greeks around 750 B.C. but later returned to the practice of earth burial. A curious practice flourished in the interim in which the finger of a corpse was cut off and buried, while the rest of the body was burned. When a Roman was cremated in the first century, the bones were washed with milk and placed in an urn.

Cremation has been widely thought to free the spirit from the dead body. In Asia, however, cremation is delayed a day to allow the spirit to free itself from the corpse before it is burned. Although human ashes are believed by some to retain a protective influence over the living when scattered, the reduction of the corpse to ashes leaves nothing large enough for the ghost to return to and reanimate, so it has been taken as a preventative measure by the superstitious. It also serves the purpose of doing away with the body and therefore with the raw material for mutilation by animals or collection by humans as relics and souvenirs. Sir Thomas Browne, an advocate of cremation, described the alternatives in the seventeenth century: "To be knaved out of our graves, to have our skulls made drinking-bowls, and our bones turned into Pipes, to delight and Sport our Enemies are Tragical abominations escaped in burning Burials."[70] Although bones may sometimes be recovered, there is no body to ravage. In the only Old Testament example, Saul and his sons are cremated to prevent further mutilation of their bodies by the Philistines.

As burial grounds became overcrowded and unsanitary in nineteenth-century Europe, cremation was promoted as hygienic and space-saving and slowly began to regain popularity. Queen Victoria's surgeon Sir Henry Thompson and others formed the Cremation Society of England in 1874 and built the country's first crematorium at Woking in 1878, although they were not permitted by the home secretary to use it. Meanwhile, Dr. Julius Lemoyne built the first crematorium in the United States in 1876, and although it was constructed for his own disposal, he allowed others to use it. Cremation gained advocates in America, where a number of cremation societies were organized in the early 1880s and began campaigns to educate the public. The British public took heart in the decisions of the court. When one Englishman requested permission to cremate his wife and mother in 1882, it was refused, but no action was taken when he built a private crematorium on his estate and cremated them anyway. The next year a Welshman was acquitted after burning the body of his five-month-old son, following which the first human cremation at Woking was carried out in 1885 and cremation was soon opted for by the majority. By the turn of the century, 24 crematories were operating in the U.S. and over 13,000 Americans had been cremated. In 1913, the first national association, the Cremation Association of America, was established. Despite its reputation as a "clean" method of disposal, cremation does pose some environmental hazards, from the release of mercury from cremated tooth fillings to the burning of bodies containing diagnostic or therapeutic radioactive isotopes.

Cremation has long been practiced in the East by Hindus and Buddhists and is now required in some large Japanese cities. In India, Hindus immerse the body in holy water, lay it on a pyre, conduct a brief ceremony, cut the winding sheet, and rub the corpse with ghee, clarified butter. The chief mourner, usually the oldest son, lights the pyre—that of a man at the head and that of a woman at the foot—with fire kindled in the home of the deceased. Mourners march around the fire without looking into it. The bursting of the skull indicates that the soul has been released from the body. If the skull does not burst, it is shattered. After the ceremony, the family gathers the bones and casts them into the Ganges to ensure passage into the next world.[71] In certain parts of India, the custom of suttee prevailed through the nineteenth century. When a man died, his wife (or sometimes his mother or sister) was obligated to join him on the funeral pyre. The woman climbed onto the pyre and sat amidst the flames with his head in her lap until they were both reduced to bones. While some lit the fire themselves, others were tied to their husbands' bodies to prevent them from jumping off. Scholars believe that suttee was guided by a misinterpretation of Hindu scripture and by the examples set by the wives of Krishna and Vasudeva. Even after suttee was outlawed in 1829, it continued as a religious and cultural tradition which spared the widow the desolation brought on by her condition and removed the financial burden she would become on her son.[72]

Cremations in the West follow a different pattern. The cremation process is accomplished in a furnace or retort fired by oil, propane, natural gas, coke, or electricity that recirculates hot gases. Before the body is placed in the retort, it is stripped of all clothing, jewelry, dental bridges, prostheses, and other devices such as pacemakers. The body may then be wrapped in a paper sheet or container of combustible material. If a metal casket is used, the top must be removed or left open and there may be an additional charge for its disposal after burning. If a temperature of 1800 to 2500 degrees Fahrenheit is maintained, an adult body weighing approximately 160 pounds can be reduced to ash in about an hour, but most cremations take two and a half to three hours to complete. During the process, skin and hair burn first, muscles contract, the abdomen swells and splits, soft tissue is destroyed, the bones are exposed, the viscera disappears, the bones glow, and the skeleton falls apart. Cremation is mainly a process of evaporation and leaves six to twelve pounds of ashes and bone fragments that may vary in color from gray to white. These "cremains" are retrieved after the retort has cooled—and after any pieces of metal from the casket or body have been removed with a magnet—and may be pulverized by hand or in a grinding machine to a fine powder. They are returned to the family in a temporary container of cardboard, metal, or plastic and later enshrined or buried in urns ranging from sports trophies to priceless Ming vases.

Amateurs have found cremation a difficult task. Murderers who attempt to dispose of a victim's body by burning are rarely successful. The difficulty is pointed out in a biography about London pathologist Francis Camps (d. 1972): "A body is not particularly combustible material and most people, including the ignorant, know that crematoria work at extremely high temperatures. A few sticks of wood and bits of paper, even when soaked with paraffin, would hardly generate enough heat in the open air to completely destroy a body."[73] Funeral pyres are not always entirely successful. In the seventeenth century, Sir Thomas Browne wrote an ode of sorts to the toe of King Pyrrhus which refused to burn on his funeral pyre.[74] After the body of poet Percy Shelley washed ashore near Viareggio two weeks after he had drowned in 1822, Italian authorities required that the body be cremated. Shelley's friends Edward Trelawny, Lord Byron, and Leigh Hunt burned the corpse on the beach after dousing it with wine and oil. The skull fell apart, and the brains could be seen bubbling. As salt and frankincense were added to the flames, the body was almost entirely consumed, but the heart had remained intact. After burning his hand to retrieve it, Trelawny presented it as a relic to Shelley's wife.

Because they are dry and compact, cremated remains can be divided or combined easily. Some couples request that their ashes be mixed in a single urn after their deaths. Other people put different portions of the cremains to different uses, storing some in an urn, a handful in the garden, and a pinch in a locket.[75] The ashes of many people have been scattered over the places they loved to visit while alive. The ashes of labor leader Joe Hill (d. 1915) were disseminated to all the local chapters of the Industrial Workers of the World, except that of Utah, and to unions on every continent. Once John Lennon's body was cremated in Hartsdale in mid-December of 1980, the ashes were disguised as a Christmas package so that they could be returned to his widow Yoko Ono in New York City without being stolen by one of his grief-stricken fans. Cremated remains can be delivered in small packages, but not by United Parcel Service or Federal Express, which will not transport anything they cannot replace if lost or damaged. They can also be stored in small compartments. An urn requires only a sixteen-inch plot, so eight urns can be buried in the space taken up by one body. According to a French report in 1973, the United Kingdom saved through cremation in a single year an area of ground equivalent to 607 football fields.[76]

A number of creative means of dispersing or using human ashes have been suggested or carried out. The ashes of Cazimir Liszinski, who was burned as a heretic in Poland in 1689, were put into a cannon and shot into the air. In modern times, ashes have been loaded into cartridges or fireworks and fired into the sky. In the early nineteenth century, Abbé François-Valentine proposed that human bones be vitrified to produce glass from which medallion portraits and busts could be produced for mourners. A famous artist had his ashes mixed with oil paints and used to paint a portrait for his family.

Tibetan medals are crafted from red clay and the crushed bones of holy men. The wife of a mortician has asked that her ashes be tossed from a hot air balloon because she was afraid to ride in one while alive.[77] The Ghia Gallery of San Francisco sells jewelry in which cremated remains can be worn. The ashes of the dead have even been consumed by the living. When the king of Caria in Asia Minor died in 353 B.C., his wife added a portion of his ashes to her drink every day until her death two years later. More recently, Florida widower Joe Cannon had his wife's head cryonically preserved and her body cremated. He put Terry Cannon's ashes in capsules and swallows one with each meal.

The members of a San Diego cremation society have asked that no pains be taken with the disposal of their remains. Although it is against the law, they would prefer to have their ashes thrown out with the garbage or flushed down the toilet. While the disposal of a corpse is rigidly prescribed, there are fewer restrictions on the disposition of ashes. But as with whole bodies, accidental or deliberate mishandling has also occurred with cremains. The body of D. H. Lawrence was disinterred and cremated in 1935. His ashes were shipped from France to New York and sent by rail to New Mexico, where his wife lived. She mistakenly left the urn on the platform at the station, noticed they were missing after she was 20 miles away, and successfully retrieved them for burial in her yard. When the ashes of American journalist Alexander Woollcott (d. 1943) were sent to Hamilton College for burial, they were delivered instead to Colgate University. After being rerouted, they arrived at Hamilton College with 67 cents postage due.

A preneed request for cremation may not be honored by one's survivors, as the following epitaph from Cardington, Ohio, testifies:

> My husband promised me
> That my body should be
> Cremated but other
> Influences prevailed.

Even those hired to perform the service or carry out the disposal may shirk their duties or take advantage of their position. Pilot B. J. Elkin contracted with more than 100 funeral homes and crematoriums to scatter the ashes of their clients over the ocean or the mountains. The Pacific-bound remains reached their destination; the remains of over 5,300 people meant for the Sierras were simply dumped on some land Elkin owned. There have also been several news reports over the years of crematoria personnel who harvested the gold dental work from the mouths of the dead and burned several bodies at once, afterward dividing up the ashes. A mortuary in Costa Mesa, California, settled a suit for $14 million after 25,000 clients claimed that their relatives had been cremated en masse. Others have sued crematoriums after receiving misidentified ashes. The Neptune Society of Los Angeles returned cremated remains to a widow whose husband's body was found four months later in a mortuary refrigerator. A Florida woman discovered a set of dentures (which her husband did not wear) when scattering his ashes. When it was discovered that his remains had already been scattered at sea, against his explicit wishes, the woman was awarded $500,000 in compensatory and punitive damages.

Disposing of the body by burning has been disapproved of by many religions for reasons ranging from its pagan associations to its deliberate breakup of the body. Cremation is forbidden in Islam, which teaches that the dead body is fully conscious of pain. It was resisted by the ancient Jews and is still forbidden in Orthodox and conservative Judaism. It is also forbidden in Shintoism and Zoroastrianism and disapproved of by Mormons and the Russian Orthodox church. Roman Catholics resisted the practice for centuries as inconsistent with bodily resurrection and allowed it only to prevent the spread of disease. It was sometimes used on the bodies of dead Christians by their enemies as a punishment, but was officially approved for the faithful in 1964, except when its desire is based on denial of Christian dogma. Christian fundamentalists continue to oppose it as unsanctioned by the Bible, historically anti–Christian, and defeating the literal bodily resurrection.[78] But Brigham Young and others confirmed for their followers the fact that although particles of the body may be in different locations, they will all be brought together for the Last Judgment.

Some object to cremation because of its association with the Nazis during World War II. With diabolical efficiency, the Germans under the leadership of Adolf Hitler built cremation ovens which they then used to dispose of the bodies of millions of Jews and others. They carried out experiments at Auschwitz in 1943 to determine which combination of bodies required the least amount of fuel and found it to be a well-nourished adult, and emaciated adult, and a child. The prisoners forced to carry out mass cremations of their fellows became very familiar with the properties of the human corpse, as reported by a prisoner on the death brigade in Janowska Camp in Poland: "The length of time required to burn the bodies depends on whether the bodies are clothed or naked, fresh or putrid. Clothed bodies burn more slowly, as do those in an advanced state of decay. The difference in time of burning between fresh and putrid bodies is a matter of one day. Children and women burn faster. But success in our work depends on how much experience we have. In the beginning it took us one week, using much oil to burn the same sized pyre that took only two days using one quarter the amount of oil later on. It's a matter of 'know-how.'"[79] Under the guidance of the SS, female bodies were arranged on the bottom layer to feed the fire with their additional subcutaneous fat. Sergeant Major Otto Moll, overseer of crematoriums, forced laborers to dig drainage channels in the sloped cremation pits so that the fat from the burning bodies would run down and collect in pans; it was then poured back onto the fire to make it burn faster.[80] The ashes of the dead were used to surface roads or were sold as fertilizer. Later the bodies of Goering and ten other Nazi leaders were themselves cremated and the ashes thrown into a muddy gulch outside Munich. The location was kept secret to prevent the later establishment of a shrine.

Although it is giving way, there has been American aversion to cremation. In *The Bedside Book of Death*, Robert Wilkins summarizes the theories put forward to explain this attitude: consumers believe that embalming preserves the body indefinitely, funeral directors have a financial stake in elaborate burials and memorials, and cremation necessarily involves shortened recall by the bereaved.[81] A memorial service even with the urn present lacks the "memory picture" said to be so important in accepting a death. And yet the memory of the dead is often invoked in defense of cremation by those who choose to remember their loved one in life through photographs rather than laid out in death. Even though a traditional funeral may be held before cremation, many believe that the decision to cremate does not allow the release of grief, that the reduction of the body is equivalent to the denial of the death. After the service, the small container of ashes is too easily forgotten in a closet rather than visited at the gravesite. Michael Marchal writes in *Parish Funerals*: "For far too many people in the death-denying culture of America, cremation is the easy way out. This is corroborated by funeral directors. As one said, she has hundreds of unclaimed urns in storage awaiting final disposition."[82] For others, however, cremation does not preclude a viewing of the embalmed body before it is reduced. The choice to cremate is not made for merely economic reasons. And the ashes are sometimes interred in columbaria and special gardens within cemeteries where the dead can be remembered. Even those in the death professions admit that cremation is a practical alternative, as Gene Raymond, a mortician, has stated: "When my time comes, I want to go up in flames. None of this waiting around. Four hours and you're done. They take you out, break up the big pieces, and put you in a jar. Otherwise, it'll take the worms twenty years to turn you into a puddle of ooze."[83] Today 700,000 Americans are cremated annually. Through individual preference or government pressures, cremation statistics continue to climb worldwide.

III
THE CORPSE AND
THE CAUSES OF DEATH

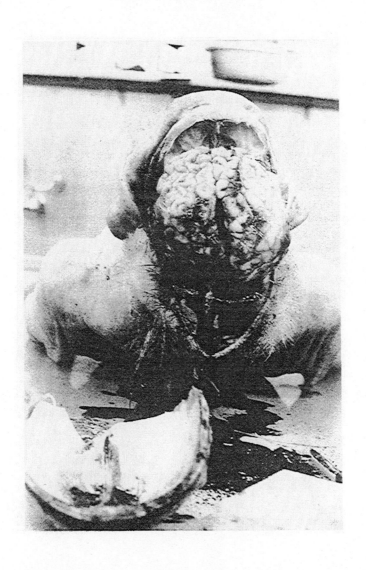

The Investigation

At the crime scenes, the victims are most certainly
dead, but at the point of autopsy, they become for the
detectives something more—or less. It is one thing, after
all, for a homicide detective to detach himself emotionally
from the corpse that forms the center of his mystery. But
it's another thing altogether to see that corpse emptied
of itself, to see the shell reduced to bones and sinew
and juices.... Even a homicide detective—a jaded
character indeed—has to witness his share of post-
mortems before death truly becomes a casual acquain-
tance.
　　　—David Simon, *Homicide: A Year on the
　　　　　Killing Streets*[1]

The Discovery

　　Corpses have been found accidentally and purposefully. They have been
reeled out of the water by fishermen, stumbled over by hunters, and spotted
by children in search of other treasures. They have also been located by psychics, police dogs, and infrared film. Murder victims that have remained hidden for years surface in crawl spaces and closets. The corpses of stranded
adventurers are found frozen in their last moments, having penned a final letter home. Abandoned bodies have been accompanied by posthumous apologies and have been fought over by competing legal jurisdictions. A civilian
may be more easily traumatized by his or her discovery of a body, but even a
hardened police officer will sooner or later meet with a corpse that strikes a
nerve and leaves an indelible impression.
　　Surprise at finding the body of the Reverend John Pinkerton in 1784 is

Part III title page: Autopsy. Photo by Jeffrey Silverthorne. Reprinted with permission of Book Beat Gallery.

107

preserved for posterity. The epitaph from his gravestone in Markinch, Scotland, immortalizes the discovery:

> After having spent a very chearfull evening at
> Balfour house with Mr. Bethune and his
> Family he was found in the morning in his
> Bedroom sitting in a chair by the fireplace with
> One stocking in his hand quite dead.[2]

Human remains are met with overwhelming sorrow when they are recognized as those of a loved one, rather than those of another victim in a string of killings. Police allowed serial killer Henry Lee Lucas to bring them to the place in Denton, Texas, where he had killed his girlfriend Becky Powell, and they reported dispassionately that a skull, lying in a pile of tangled brown hair, was found on the ground. In contrast, when police drove Mary Scaggs to the scene of a murder by California's Trailside Killer, the woman collapsed in tears when she saw strands of her daughter's long, blonde hair hanging from the trees.[3] In *Suicide of a Child*, the authors counsel parents that they may be especially troubled if the death occurred in the house: "You may have found your child or had to clean up the death scene or both. You will never fully lose the mental image of what you experienced: what you saw ... heard ... touched ... smelled and felt right then. The strength of the image and the dread of the place will gradually become less strong and any horror you may have felt will disappear in time."[4] On the other hand, those who did not see the child after death may imagine a scene much worse than the real one.

Many bodies have been discovered by strangers engaged in their daily activities. A British fisherman reeled in a brown paper parcel containing the decomposed body of an infant in 1896. It was traced to "baby-farmer" Amelia Dyer, who was sent to the gallows. In New York in 1897, a headless torso was discovered by two teenagers swimming in the East River, the pelvis was found in the woods near 176th Street, and the legs were found by two more boys swimming off the Brooklyn shore. Investigators identified the man as masseur William Guldensuppe, killed in a love triangle. (The scene of the murder was revealed when the blood that had drained from the cottage into a pond turned the ducks bathing in it pink.) In 1953, Beresford Brown examined the kitchen of his apartment with the aim of redecorating it. He peeled the wallpaper off a hollow spot, revealing a cupboard door. When he opened the door, the compartment contained three naked victims of the previous tenant, John Reginald Halliday Christie. Mrs. Sarah Jane Harvey spent 15 months in prison for the murder of her tenant Mrs. Francis Alice Knight. When Mrs. Harvey's son decided to clean and paint her house for her, he found the mummified body of Mrs. Knight on the floor of a closet on the stair landing, where it had secretly been stored for 20 years.

While it may be unsettling to discover a lifeless body, the position or location of the corpse has sometimes provided an additional shock. A photograph exists to document the extraordinary sight of a 45-year-old woman found dead in Germany standing upright in the corner of a timber yard. In *Blue Truth*, veteran Ft. Lauderdale police sergeant Cherokee Paul McDonald recounts the night he responded to an "unknown trouble" call and found a small dog hovering around the feet of a lifeless man who had remained standing at his kitchen sink.[5] A body discovered by workmen in the chimney of an office building was identified by his teeth as a known local burglar. A woman was found in her Bronx apartment in 1981 encased in a block of ice that had formed when a water pipe had burst. As the operator of a garbage truck was emptying his load at a landfill in 1986, a severed human leg tumbled out. Police searched the vehicle and wedged against a rear wall was a headless, armless torso with the second leg attached. The rest of the body was never located, and the victim remains unidentified. Worse than discovering a body at the dump, however, is finding one in the water supply. After receiving complaints of foul-tasting and smelly water from residents, workers found a decomposed body in the Princeton, West Virginia, municipal water tank.

Corpses do not always remain where they fall. An Ohio detective reports that it is not uncommon for his department to recover bodies in rivers or on beaches as far away as West Virginia or Pennsylvania. In New York in 1985, 85 corpses surfaced during the year in the Hudson, Harlem, and East Rivers. As a body decays, the head often becomes separated and is sometimes the only portion of the body which is found. When a body is dismembered, the head is sometimes the most difficult piece to find. Alfred Hitchcock is said to have remarked, "In all cases involving mutilation ... the biggest problem for the police is to locate the head."[6] The head of Hannah Brown, murdered and dismembered by James Greenacre in 1836, was discovered when it obstructed the gate on a lock in Regent's Canal in Stepney, England. In 1989, a woman's head with a gunshot wound washed up in the surf 13 miles north of Santa Cruz, California, and the head of a woman with the AIDS virus was found on a golf course near Trenton, New Jersey. In the same year, a woman's headless body was found on a New York City rooftop.[7] In cases where the body does stay put, it almost always suffers the damage of exposure. In the western United States, the body of a man was spotted hanging in the top of a tall pine tree. Exposed to the wind and sun for some time, the skin had become hard and dry and the weight of the body had stretched it to a length of eight feet.[8]

Through deliberate action, natural processes, or mistaken identity, a corpse may also be disguised or misrepresented. When a World War II air raid exposed a human skeleton that had been sealed in a steel pipe in Liverpool, the contents of the Victorian garments it was clothed in were examined. They contained materials dated in 1885, but the circumstantial evidence was refuted by Dr. Charles Harrison, senior pathologist of Liverpool University, who judged the man to have been dead less than ten years. In 1951, 16-year-old Ann Makinson of London found what appeared to be a large yellow doll in a sack above a cupboard in her family's home. The object was identified by pathologist Francis Camps as the ten-year-old corpse of a child who had died at age two-and-a-half or three. The story unraveled as Mrs. Makinson confessed to having slapped her daughter Muriel who then accidentally struck her head on the stove and died shortly thereafter. Her parents put her body away in a drawer rather than alerting the authorities. A child in Kensington, England, dug up the bones of what he thought to be a monkey from his garden and sent them to the local Natural History Museum. They were found to be the remains of a human newborn, but because the sex could not be determined and the bones were several years old, the matter was not investigated further. Hikers in the Rocky Mountains reported to authorities their discovery of some bone fragments; it was found that they were human remains, but that they had been cremated and deliberately scattered.

Some people, in anticipation of impending death, have prepared for the discovery of their bodies. Caught in a blizzard after reaching the South Pole in 1912, a month after Norwegian Roald Amundsen had become the first to do so, Robert Falcon Scott and his companions pitched their tent and resigned themselves to their fate. Captain Scott spent his last hours writing letters to the men's wives and his personal friends and making a final entry in his diary. Despite their urge to continue walking until they dropped, the party reasoned that their papers, records, and geological specimens would be lost if they did so. The bodies of the men were found in a state of perfect preservation by a relief party seven months later. The frozen bodies of Swedish explorer Salomon August Andrée and his two companions waited much longer to be discovered. Their balloon expedition to the North Pole in 1897 ended in tragedy when they missed their target, but their story was told by the photographic record left on the film found with their remains 33 years after their deaths. People who kill themselves are often mindful of the spectacle their bodies will present after death. Before hanging himself inside an abandoned house, a workman in England wrote a note in chalk on the wall outside: "Sorry about this. There's a corpse in here. Inform police."[9] According to Derek Humphry, proponent of active euthanasia, many who commit suicide in hotels have been thoughtful enough to leave notes to the staff expressing regret for the trauma and inconvenience caused.[10] Other suicides, however, intend the shocking discovery of the body as an act of revenge.

Scientists and psychologists can only speculate about the long-term effects of the surprise discovery of a corpse. When Lynn Thomas of Dubois, Idaho, was digging for relics in a cavern with his family, his eleven-year-old granddaughter Anna spotted a human hand sticking up from the ground, the limb of the victim of a still-unsolved murder. Forensic anthropologist

Douglas Ubelaker speculates: "I don't know what effect the discovery had on young Anna. It's hard not to believe the reaction was extreme and long-lasting, either in the direction of traumatizing her against caves and handshakes for the rest of her life, or of so desensitizing her that she will laugh her way through every horror film she ever sees. It's far more likely she'll look back on the event as a great adventure. I hope so."[11]

Those who stumble across a corpse are often so disturbed by the event that their memory of it becomes distorted. They will be most impressed by any blood on or around the body and will assume even a natural death was a murder if objects in the room are displaced. They will be so preoccupied with the bulging eyes and protruding tongue of a hanging victim that they won't remember what was around the neck. Although they will first notice the odor of a body that has been dead for several days, they may mistake a body for fresh that has spent time in cold flowing water. Even good observers may not be able to distinguish the color of anything but the corpse's hair because of decomposition. Following the discovery of a body, a person may experience post-traumatic stress disorder, which may cause their memories to become vague, disorganized, and unreliable.[12] In a few instances, the sanity of those who discover a body is in question because they fail to report the find. Edna Buchanan maintains that a nude body lay ignored on the front lawn of a well-kept Miami home for two weeks.[13] After arsonist Calvin Jackson killed a woman, he threw her body into the air shaft of an apartment building. The body fell four floors headfirst and pierced the ceiling of a second-floor room. The occupant of the room later complained to the front desk about the head which had been dripping into his sink for three days.[14]

Police officers become accustomed to seeing dead bodies, but are often taken aback by the smell. Homicide detectives joke that they know they have a really unpleasant death scene on their hands when everyone, including the morgue attendants, is standing *outside* the location. In *Homicide: A Year on the Killing Streets*, David Simon inventories the sights that become routine but never mundane to veteran police officers:

> And there is much to see, beginning with the bodies battered by two-by-fours and baseball bats, or bludgeoned with tire irons and cinder blocks. Bodies with gaping wounds from carving knives or from shotguns fired so close that the shell wadding is lodged deep in the wounds. Bodies in public housing project stairwells, with the hypodermic still in their forearm and that pathetic look of calm on their faces; bodies pulled out of the harbor with reluctant blue crabs clinging to hands and feet. Bodies and pieces of bodies that fell from balconies, bodies in beds, bodies in the trunk of a Chrysler with out-of-state tags, bodies on gurneys behind a blue curtain in the University Hospital emergency room, with tubes and catheters still poking out of the carcasses to mock medicine's best arguments. Bodies crushed by heavy machinery, suffocated by carbon monoxide or suspended by a pair of sweatsocks from the top of a Central District holding cell. Bodies on crib

mattresses surrounded by stuffed animals, tiny bodies in the arms of grieving mothers who can't understand that there is no reason, that the baby just
stopped breathing air.[15]

Police greet the saddening and sickening sights with gallows humor and other
defenses. The context in which a corpse is found often has its ironies, which
they are quick to note. A man who played Russian roulette and lost was found
by police with a bumper sticker above his head that read, "I'll give up my gun
when they pry my cold dead finger off the trigger."[16]

Death professionals seem most perturbed by the corpses of suicides. People who commit suicide often do so by taking poison and climbing into closets or other small, dark places. Paramedic Paul Shapiro believes that hanging bodies are the worst, with distorted faces and eyes that seem to follow
you around the room, staring as the body slowly swings around.[17] But police
and ambulance personnel are frequently bombarded with the results of violence not to the self, but to innocent victims. Tulsa detective Charles W.
Sasser writes autobiographically about the haunting effect that tracking down
a serial killer had on him: "The nightmares were so real that I could smell
death, even with my eyes open. I thought if I closed my eyes I might not
open them again. I didn't want someone ... coming out and throwing the sheet
off my stiff corpse and tossing me around to see if I had a .22 bullet hole in
the hairline at the base of the skull or a needle mark in my jugular. I didn't
want a homicide cop handling me like I handled so many others, and then
going and washing his hands because he'd handled me."[18]

Henry Bryant, deputy sheriff of Denver, has to distance himself from
the disturbing deaths he sees, despite his unique perspective: "My dad, you
know, was a mortician, and working with him, I've seen burnt bodies, drowned
bodies, bodies from accidents—I thought I'd seen it all. But each day of this
job you learn a lot more. You see things, still, you can't take this personally....
I've got a theory that dead's dead. A carcass. Just forget it, let it go."[19] Those
professionals who regularly converge on the death scene must work hard to
keep the dead in perspective, to avoid focusing on similarities between the
victim and members of their own families or themselves.

When bodies are known to exist, but have not been located, police have
several methods at their disposal for finding them. When the robbery-mur-
ders committed by the Bender family were uncovered in Kansas in 1871, investigators searched their property for evidence. When one man shoved a ram-
rod into a depression in the soft ground and pulled it back out, there was a
clump of hair sticking to the end of it.[20] Today dogs are trained to sniff out
corpses in response to the command, "Find dead." Photo reconnaissance is
sometimes carried out using infrared film to pick up the heat given off by a
decaying body. And heat-seeking equipment can also be used on the ground
to locate buried bodies. In extreme cases, psychics are employed to lead police

to the body of a missing person. And some dowsers claim to be able to locate bodies, as well as water, underground. Still, law enforcement agencies rely on the accidental discovery of bodies by citizens who spend time in places often used by murderers to dispose of their victims. "Hunters occupy a special place in police investigations," writes author Terry Landau. "Hunters occasionally call in the police when they stumble across the remains of people who breathed their last in the woods."[21] Once a body has been found—accidentally or after a deliberate search—the investigation of the death can begin. The corpse can be examined *in situ*, autopsied, and released to the family. The grieving by family members and the tracking of the killer by the police can proceed.

The Death Scene

The atmosphere changes when a dead body is present. The emergency medical technicians no longer hurry when a life is obviously past saving. The scene may draw a crowd, but the members tend to lower their voices. Civilians speak in hushed voices in the presence of death and in answer to police officers hoping for an eyewitness to the event. Rather than relying on the public for information, the officers gather evidence from the corpse itself and from its surroundings. The area is roped off, combed visually, and recorded manually and photographically. The corpse is the center of attention, but police examine it in context to deduce the nature of the crime—if in fact one has been committed—and preserve its details for further evaluation. In killings without eyewitnesses, without a confession, and without a relationship between the murderer and the victim, the crime scene must be scoured to provide a solution.

After police are notified of the discovery of a body, uniformed officers arrive at the scene and define its perimeter by roping it off with the familiar yellow tape. They note in their initial report the time, date, weather conditions, other officers present, a description of the location, the victim's clothing, and the position of the body. Additional patrol officers may be summoned if the crowd is unruly. Witnesses are isolated from one another to avoid tainting each other's testimony, and nonessential personnel are cleared from the scene. A corpse indoors is a more welcome scenario than a body in the street because the house allows police officers to keep details from gathering crowds and prying reporters and also provides clues to how the killer gained entry.[22] Detectives arrive and obtain a search warrant if the person who controls the location is unable or unwilling to sign a consent form. The detectives interview any witnesses and conduct the follow-up investigation. The coroner or medical examiner comes to the scene to pronounce death and make a preliminary examination of the body. His or her assistant coordinates with police and carries out any follow-up investigations. The hands and feet of the victim are often enclosed in plastic or paper bags to preserve any evidence. Morgue attendants may be allowed to remove the body, but an officer is usually assigned to accompany the corpse to the hospital or morgue to take additional photos and to take possession of the clothing. In addition, an officer often attends the autopsy to collect the slug when it is removed from the body. An identification section or major (or mobile) crime scene unit is generally requested to collect physical evidence.

Blood is an obvious clue and can reveal many things by physical and chemical analysis. Blood drops shaped like bowling pins indicate that a struggle occurred and point in the direction of travel. Drops in a sunburst pattern point to the fact that the victim was already bleeding when he or she was struck or fell.[23] The amount of blood may indicate whether the body was alive or dead before falling from a height. Blood splatter can reveal the relative positions of people and objects at the time of the crime and their movement afterward. It will indicate the number of impacts, whether the blow was made by a blunt or sharp object, and the distance and speed that the blood flew. The bloodstains may contain imprints of fingers, shoes, or fabric which could lead to the killer. If it has been washed away, its traces can be revealed chemically: orthotolidine will turn bloodstains bright green and phenolphthalein will turn them pink. Laboratory analysis will uncover the elapsed time since the spilling of the blood and in some cases the organ which it came from and the time and fat content of the last meal eaten by the deceased. Further analysis will reveal the stress level of the victim and any prescription medications or illegal drugs used by him or her.

Before the crime scene unit arrives, all officers are careful to avoid removing or adding anything to the scene. In addition to practical precautions, police must also take emotional ones, as David Simon points out in *Homicide*: "A good investigator, leaning over a fresh obscenity, doesn't waste time and effort battering himself with theological questions about the nature of evil and man's inhumanity to man. He wonders instead whether the jagged wound pattern is the result of a serrated blade, or whether the discoloration on the underside of the leg is indeed an indication of lividity."[24] The crime scene officers conduct a thorough and methodical walk-through and take photographs, noting the film, camera, lens, flash apparatus, and aperture used for each exposure. Officers prefer color film and photos that overlap each other, and they are careful to photograph the outside of the house and areas adjacent to the scene. The crime scene officers sketch the scene, "exploding" the walls in the drawing if they contain anything important, and they measure the body from two fixed points. Other officers may be assigned to assist in the evidence collection. Damp items are placed in paper envelopes and later spread out and dried. Liquid blood samples and rape kits are refrigerated. Dry items are collected in plastic bags, plastic or glass vials, or cardboard boxes.

Molds are made when necessary, using dental- or plaster-casting equipment, and fine particles are collected with a small vacuum. Chemicals may be sprayed to cause blood to fluoresce. Surfaces at the scene, on objects removed from the scene, and sometimes on the corpse itself are dusted or sprayed for finger and palm prints. Each item of evidence is packaged separately and labeled with an evidence tag. Processing the crime scene may take several days; during this period the location remains sealed.

Many details of the scene are kept secret from the news media to retain a means of verifying a possible later confession. Onlookers are barred from the area to avoid contaminating the evidence. And the body is soon covered with a sheet or carted away, leaving not even the fictional chalk outline. To the police, however, the dead body becomes an open book:

> A corpse has no privacy. Until you are dead, you are usually a total stranger to homicide detectives. Then, with a single-mindedness matched only by that of a jealous lover, they must know all about you—everything—even details your sweetheart or your spouse does not know. Secrets you would not tell your best friend. Particulars you didn't understand about yourself. Nothing is sacred. They want to know what you ate, what you wore, what you read. Your drinking habits and your sex habits. They will read your diary and your mail and scrutinize the contents of your safety-deposit box and your stomach. They are there, examining all that you held private, including every nook and cranny of your corpse, once they begin to disassemble it at the morgue.[25]

Once the evidence has been collected at the scene and submitted for evaluation, a technician in the laboratory conducts radiological, chemical, and microscopic examinations, maintaining the chain of custody carefully and issuing a detailed report. He or she shares the duties of analyzing the evidence on, around, and within the body with the coroner, medical examiner, pathologist, and forensic anthropologist so that the pieces of the puzzle can be assembled by prosecutors and a murderer can be brought to justice.

Medical Autopsy

When a person dies in a hospital, the family is often approached to obtain their consent for an autopsy. Techniques of persuasion include the truths that there are few religious objections to autopsy, that the procedure does not preclude later embalming and viewing of the body, and that the results may further medical knowledge in addition to yielding a specific cause of death. Like the medical-legal autopsy, the hospital autopsy begins with a Y-incision. Organs and their contents are then inventoried and specimens are sometimes retained for further study. The conductors of both types of autopsy steel themselves by repetition against facing the corpse as a symbol of death or a reminder of their own mortality. It is instead a door to unlock, a mystery to solve, or at the very least a careful job to perform. The body is dismantled, reassembled, and released in an atmosphere usually characterized by respect for the sometimes distasteful physical remnants that personify a life lived and a disease process understood.

As the pathologist begins the autopsy, the thing before him or her is both human and subhuman. It is shrouded in the odor of death and the smells of urine, feces, and blood, yet still retains a dignity in being so recently a member of the living. Pathologist F. Gonzalez-Crussi explains:

> Not long ago this was a child; now it is a corpse, overspread by the coldness and clamminess of corpses, yet still retaining something of the living human presence. The livid hue, the icy chilliness, and the sunken outline cannot undo the ineffable residuum of humanity that clings to the newly dead: this is why dissectors often place a surgical towel over the cadaver's face before beginning their task. The recently departed are already unsentient husks, but their corpses may still be honored or outraged, exalted or vilified, reverenced or debased.[26]

The autopsy is a humane but mutilating procedure which would devastate loved ones if they were allowed to witness it. The association of the physical form with the personality and consciousness of the deceased by those who knew him or her make the autopsy in most cases an operation necessarily conducted by strangers behind closed doors, although it was once conducted in the home by the family doctor. When the body is personalized, the pathologist has a difficult time carrying out the required duties. In *Hospital*, Michael Medved interviewed a morgue room supervisor who told him about a physician who watched the autopsy on his wife, interjecting comments about their life together: "When we were taking out the stomach he was saying how lobster always used to be her favorite food! It made everybody stiffen up. I don't think I'd ever allow it again."[27] For the pathologist, the patient has a name, a date of birth and death, and a medical history; knowing more than that is often counterproductive.

The autopsy begins with an examination of the body's exterior, including any wounds, scars, or tumors. A surgical incision is then made from each shoulder to the middle of the chest and then down to the pubic bone. The skin is parted, the ribs are cut or sawed, and the breastbone is removed. The pericardial sac around the heart is opened, and blood is drawn for cultures. Organs are removed altogether, individually, or in blocks after observing their relationship to each other in the body. The chest organs—heart, lungs, trachea, and bronchi—are lifted out as a unit, followed by the spleen and intestines, and then the liver, pancreas, stomach, and esophagus. The kidneys, ureters, bladder, and abdominal aorta are then removed, followed by the testes. After the body cavity is emptied and its organs are being opened to observe their internal structure, the brain is exposed by sawing off a large portion of the skull. The arteries, optic nerves, and cervical cord are severed to allow the brain to be lifted free and weighed, after which it may be fixed in formalin for later examination. During the procedure, muscle, nerve, and fibrous tissue samples may be taken for toxicological or microscopic analysis. If bone is removed, it is usually replaced with a prosthesis. The autopsy may take less than an hour or several hours, depending on the speed and technique of the pathologist, the number of assistants, and the findings. By removing organs en bloc for later examination, the pathologist can release an autopsied body in about 30 minutes. The results may take much longer to obtain and evaluate. In the lab, pathologists may culture specimens for bacteria and viruses, test body fluids for alcohol and drugs, and search for abnormal tissue patterns with an electron microscope.

By opening and examining the body, pathologists are able to confirm, deny, or expand upon the diagnosis made by the patient's physician or surgeon. They are often taken aback by the devastation they find when they enter the body: "At the dissecting table, even members of the AIDS care team are often surprised by unexpected areas of involvement and the degree to which the tissues of their patient have been laid waste."[28] Autopsy improves the accuracy of vital statistics, aids in the evaluation of diagnostic and therapeutic methods, and detects communicable or hereditary diseases. Gonzalez-Crussi points out that the medical autopsy is central to institutional efforts to upgrade the quality of medical care and teaching because it discloses, in about eight percent of cases, major diagnoses that were unsuspected during life.[29] Although corpses remind doctors first of their own mortality and second of the limits of their profession, autopsies are necessary to improve the quality of their care of the sick. In The Doctor, Edward Rosenbaum points out "Modern autopsy studies show that, in the best hospitals, good physicians miss the diagnosis in one patient out of four, and in one case out of ten the patient would have survived if the right diagnosis had been made."[30] A morgue room supervisor discloses that most of medicine is just a guessing game until they perform an autopsy and "find out what really happened."[31]

Hospitals often exert pressure on the staff to obtain consent for autopsies. Sometimes the medical students who get the most permissions from next of kin receive an award. When David Hellerstein was in training at Harvard Medical School, prizes were awarded for the greatest number of autopsies obtained, the most complete autopsies, and the highest percentage of patients receiving autopsies.[32] Families sometimes restrict autopsies to exclude the brain or limit them to include only the heart. Consent must be documented carefully, since surgeon William Nolen points out that pathologists live in constant dread that they'll perform an autopsy on someone whose next of kin has denied permission.[33] In some states, including California, a person can authorize his or her own autopsy prior to death by including instructions in a will.

In other states, next of kin must often be convinced before allowing the autopsy on a family member, even though a 1971 study of 30,000 people by Edwin Shneidman showed that 83 percent of those surveyed approved of an autopsy on their own body.[34] In *Battles of Life and Death*, David Hellerstein shares his persuasive techniques. Instead of trying to reason with the family, he agrees that the patient has suffered enough and assures them that he will be there to see that he or she doesn't suffer any more during what Hellerstein characterizes as a "small surgical procedure." In response to religious objections, he declares that there aren't any, and he offers to send a priest to talk to the family or to call in a rabbi to witness the autopsy. In the face of outright refusal, some naive family members are reputedly plied with what medical personnel know as the "gold ball story." They are persuaded to believe that the patient swallowed a gold ball for a test and that the body must be opened to retrieve it or its cost of $5,000 will be added to the hospital bill.[35]

In spite of the efforts of medical students, the autopsy rate in hospitals in the United States has declined over the years. By World War II, hospital autopsy rates had reached approximately 50 percent. The rate declined after the war for several reasons, notably the difficulty in obtaining consent, the fear of malpractice, and the fact that in 1971 the Joint Commission on Accreditation of Hospitals eliminated the compulsory 20 percent autopsy rate. Because autopsies are time-consuming and expensive (approximately $1,000) and are not reimbursed by insurance or Medicare, they are not done as frequently as was formerly the case. The national autopsy rate in U.S. hospitals is now about 20 percent,[36] much lower than the rate in other countries, including Switzerland (80 percent) and the previous USSR (up to 100 percent).[37] In America, autopsies are usually performed when the cause of death is unknown, when a genetic disorder is suspected, when research is being done on the process causing death, when organs are to be donated for transplantation, or when the medical inquiries of professionals and family members would be unanswerable without one.[38] Permission for autopsy may be withheld by Hindus, who find them distasteful, and autopsies are not permitted by the Muslim, Shinto, or Greek Orthodox churches, except when required by law.

The history of autopsy is intertwined with that of medical dissection. There is some question among scholars how early in time autopsies were performed in ancient Greece. Hippocrates (d. 377 B.C.) is said to have considered the autopsy an unpleasant task. Mummification familiarized the ancient Egyptians with human anatomy, and dissection was done in Alexandria to further knowledge of normal anatomy and disease process until about 200 A.D. Evidence of autopsies being carried out in ancient Rome and in the Middle Ages is scant and is based on paintings and manuscript illustrations, with actual references dating to the thirteenth century. The Catholic clergy discouraged autopsies, but Pope Clement VI allowed his physician to dissect the bodies of plague victims to determine the cause of the disease. The church also permitted an autopsy to establish the cause of death of Pope Alexander, who died unexpectedly in 1410. Pope Sixtus IV (d. 1484) permitted medical students at Bologna and Padua to open bodies in the continuing search for the cause of plague. By the sixteenth century, the Catholic church had accepted the practice. The Jewish religion forbade autopsy until the eighteenth century, when it was permitted in specific circumstances, and broadened the criteria in the early twentieth century. During the Renaissance, Italian physicians Bernard Tornius and Antonio Benivieni detailed and recorded autopsies, and by the eighteenth century, Theophilus Bonetus was able to publish a compendium of over 3,000 autopsies performed by 450 physicians, including Galen and Vesalius. Soon after, doctors began to correlate clinical observations with autopsy findings and to advance theories based on pathological findings. Pathologists such as Karl Rokitansky (d. 1878), who completed 30,000 autopsies in his career, had become proficient and prodigious.[39]

It was some time before the dangers of the autopsy became apparent. Ignaz Semmelweiss, a doctor practicing in the mid-nineteenth century realized that high death rates in the maternity ward of his Vienna hospital were the result of blood poisoning caused by the doctors' unsanitary practice of not washing their hands after autoposies or other procedures. Pathologists must safeguard themselves and those they come into contact with against contracting disease from the body they are examining. Medical threats in the morgue—as in the mortuary—include tuberculosis, hepatitis, HIV, and other communicable diseases. In addition to the illnesses which may be caught through contact with a corpse, its smell is also contagious, as a medical student discovered after observing an autopsy: "At home, I put all my clothes through the wash and take several showers, but the volatile formaldehyde vapours seem to have penetrated my flesh and I smell like a corpse myself for days."[40] Not only the smell, but the entire process is found distasteful by medical students and the uninitiated. The opening of the body has been taboo in many cultures in spite of the benefits and the fact that the body is returned to the family quickly and relatively intact.

After an autopsy, the skull cap is replaced, incisions are sutured, and the body is released to the mortuary. The carotid artery is often tied off by the pathologist to facilitate embalming the face and head. The restorative art of the embalmers will ensure that bodies will appear untouched by the scalpel: "Once they get hold of it and get it ready for the funeral, nobody knows the difference. All the incisions are covered by clothes. Sometimes they'll use a wig up on the skull, and even with the brain out, they can still embalm the face. Nobody would ever know. There's no mutilation with what we do. We really pay attention to that."[41] So says the morgue room supervisor in the same interview with Medved. Mutilation, however, is in the mind of the beholder. The body that appears intact may in fact be missing entire organs. While some hospitals replace organs that are not kept as specimens, others incinerate all autopsy tissue. Next of kin may find peace of mind in the fact that the results of the autopsy of a loved one, whether or not it pinpointed the cause of death, will advance science in many ways and for many years.

Medical-Legal Autopsy

There are times outside the walls of the hospital when the body does not yield up its secrets without some prying. The answers are sought by law enforcement officers who hope to solve a murder or rule out homicide, to clarify a natural death or identify the victim of an unnatural one. During a "triage" over which the medical examiner presides, he or she decides whether to certify the death and release the body, as in the case of an obvious natural death unattended by a physician, or to further investigate a violent or suspicious death. Further investigation warrants a ride to the morgue and the inevitable Y-incision. The same cut may be made by the hospital pathologist, but while medical autopsy is at the discretion of the family, medical-legal autopsy needs no consent of next-of-kin. The autopsy is carried out by coroners, pathologists, and medical examiners, who may in turn consult with toxicologists, radiologists, and forensic anthropologists (discussed in the next chapter). Performers of the medical-legal autopsy have haggled over corpses, testified in court about them, and set up makeshift morgues when their facilities were not adequate or accessible. They have been called upon to examine the bodies of the famous and the infamous and have the legal right to insist on an autopsy in cases of suspicious deaths, unattended deaths, bodies that are dead on arrival at the hospital, and even hospital deaths which occur during surgery. In their hands, the corpse is a wealth of evidence—the literal and figurative "body of the crime" referred to in the Latin phrase *corpus delecti*. Through them, corpses can convict their own killers, testify to their own self-destruction, or serve as evidence of a blameless death by natural or accidental causes.

In the United States, a jurisdiction may have an elected or appointed coroner of varying medical qualification. In many small towns, the local funeral director functions as the coroner. In addition to—or instead of—a coroner, the jurisdiction may have a medical examiner, a medically qualified official (often a board-certified pathologist) appointed to the post. Approximately 12 states have a coroner system, 22 have medical examiners, and 16 have both.[42] The duties of the coroner or medical examiner include investigation of deaths which occur through violence or suicide, those which occur suddenly or without the attendance of a physician within the previous 14 days, and any deaths which appear suspicious or which occur in prison. Many states recommend autopsy for all deaths that are violent, sudden and unexpected, suspicious, or employment-related or those that occur in prison or to psychiatric inmates, constitute a threat to the public health, or will be followed by cremation or burial at sea.[43] The autopsy of active duty military personnel is done at the discretion of U.S. military authorities. Pathologists estimate that one of every five deaths in the U.S. occurs under circumstances which warrant an inquiry.[44]

When a death is discovered, the medical examiner's office is notified and the M.E. or a deputy or assistant goes to the scene and later files a written report. The coroner or medical examiner may conduct an inquest, or judicial inquiry by a coroner's jury, to gain further knowledge of the circumstances surrounding a death. An autopsy is performed when the exact cause of death cannot be established with reasonable certainty and in all cases of homicide. Approximately 15 percent of investigated deaths are autopsied. The goals of the investigation are to deduce the specific cause of death and its manner: homicide, suicide, accident, or natural. Under the supervision of the M.E. or staff, the body is positively identified by next of kin. The findings of the medical examiner, including an estimated time of death, are used in legal proceedings concerning the death.

The office of coroner dates back to Norman times and, as set forth in the Magna Charta of 1215, required keeping written records of deaths, including a short explanation of the cause. There were forensic examinations before there were coroners, one of the first being performed by Antistius on Julius Caesar in 44 B.C. Ambrose Paré performed official autopsies in the fourteenth century. In eighteenth-century England, coroners were paid for the inquests they conducted and later for their expert medical testimony, autopsy, and analysis. Coroners in the U.S. and England have traditionally received a fee for each examination and have gone to great lengths to acquire it. In Brooklyn, New York, coroners used to employ people to push the drowned bodies in Newtown Creek over to the Brooklyn side, since each inquest was worth 12 to 15 dollars. In *Unnatural Death: Confessions of a Medical Examiner*, Michael M. Baden recounts that at the turn of the century, two rival coroners raced in boats to a body floating in the East River. They struck each other with their oars until one fell in. The winner hauled the body to shore as hundreds cheered.[45] A break between Douglas Cowburn, coroner at Southwark, England, and Bernard Spilsbury occurred when Spilsbury paid Cowburn a single fee for the examination of conjoined twins. Choosing the most important of the organs of the body for the pathologists' purposes mirrors their importance in defining death itself. For some it is the heart and for others the brain. If a body has been dismembered, the jurisdiction in which the heart is found generally takes control of the investigation. But when a man hanged himself from a roof in London and his body fell in one jurisdiction and the head in another, the district in which the head fell relinquished its claim to the other.[46] Upon examination, the brain and the liver are said to be the undisputed stars of the postmortem.[47]

The morgue, where the body is pried apart, is a place of superstitious dread to outsiders. To those who must frequent it, it is an austere place equipped with the necessary implements and fixtures to probe a human body for legal evidence. Among police officers, the place loses its mystique very quickly and only the constant traffic makes an impression:

> What still has emotional force for even veteran detectives is the autopsy room as a panoramic vision, a sort of Grand Central Station of lifelessness in which human bodies are at varying stops along the disassembly line. On a busy Sunday morning, the hallway outside the cutting room might be filled with eight or nine metal tables and the freezer may hold a half dozen more. To stand amid the overnight accumulation of homicides and auto accidents, drownings and burnings, electrocutions and suicides, overdoses and seizures—that is always a little overwhelming. White and black, male and female, old and young.... More than any other visual image, the weekend display in the tiled room reminds a homicide detective that he deals in a wholesale market.[48]

French author Jean-Luc Henning refers to modern morgues as underground parking lots. Depending on volume, they do serve as storage areas for the dead, who are parked in the drawers familiar to aficionados of the horror movie until the autopsy can be scheduled. Under normal circumstances the dead can wait four or more days in temperatures between 35 and 46 degrees, but the morgue can be particularly vulnerable during a power outage. When a blackout in New York City left 9 million people without electricity in July of 1977, Mayor Abraham Beane authorized the city hall generator to be used to cool the city morgue, where the bodies were decomposing in the heat. The typical examining room contains stainless steel tables with a water hose and drainage system, a sink, and a scale. A device is installed to record observations as the autopsy proceeds or after it is completed. Most morgues include a sealed and specially ventilated room for the examination of infectious corpses or those in an advanced state of decomposition.

A full autopsy may take several hours, but some cases, such as those involving trauma to the head, may require only a limited autopsy to make a ruling on the cause of death. The corpse is first identified and issued a toe tag, and any personal effects are inventoried. The body is scheduled for autopsy, if merited, and may be embalmed if it is likely to remain unidentified. It is photographed as it arrived and subsequently, as each layer of clothing is removed. The surface of the body is minutely examined for any marks or signs of trauma, for which reason hospital emergency teams are instructed to leave catheters, shunts, and other medical devices intact so the pathologist can differentiate between efforts to save the victim and those that caused death.[49] Eye and hair color, scars and tattoos, dental work, age, and general condition of the body are noted. Hands and fingernails are examined for blood, skin, or clothing fibers that may have come from an assailant. The position of any bullet holes is measured, and the angle of entry and the gun's distance from the body are calculated. If the victim was known to have been standing when shot, this information can be used to estimate the height of the killer. Clothing is examined for bullet holes or powder traces. The body is fingerprinted, measured, weighed, and x-rayed, and blood is drawn to determine drug and alcohol levels.

The internal examination of the body also follows a standard procedure. The chest is opened with a thoracic-abdominal incision from shoulder to shoulder and a midline incision down the abdomen to the pubis. Ribs and cartilage are severed, and the heart, lungs, esophagus, and trachea are removed as a unit. Each organ is then weighed, examined externally, and dissected. Blood is drawn from the heart, fluid samples are aspirated from the pleural and abdominal cavities, and microscopic slides are made from organ tissue. The organs of the abdomen—liver, spleen, adrenals and kidneys, stomach, pancreas, and intestines—are examined in situ and removed, weighed, and sectioned. The contents of the stomach are measured and samples taken. The genitalia are examined and vaginal and anal swabs are obtained for evidence of sexual attack. Blood, semen, and hair are collected for DNA typing. The uterus is opened to reveal possible pregnancy, and the bladder is removed and urine sent for analysis. Lastly, the head is examined, beginning with the eyes (for signs of hemorrhage) and the skull (for signs of injury). An incision is made through the scalp from ear to ear across the back of the head. The skin is peeled forward to expose the skull, the front portion of which is sawed through and removed to expose the brain. The brain, like the other organs, is examined, removed, weighed, and sectioned. After the autopsy, the death certificate is completed and filed, the report (concluding with the opinion on the official cause of death) is finished, and the case file and accompanying materials are turned over to the authorities. The body can then be released to the family. If the death was unattended or followed chronic illness, the family is required to wait 48 hours before cremating the corpse, in the event of further investigation into the cause of death. Any organs or tissues may be kept by the medical examiner if needed for evidence in a criminal or civil case. National standards require that wet tissue be held for six months, tissue in paraffin blocks for five years, and slides for twenty years.[50]

A murder victim's last expression will not be fixed on his or her face at death, nor will the last image be fixed on the eyes. But the body does contain a wealth of clues if properly and methodically examined: "Death marks the end of the physical body, but the body tells the story of its works and days at autopsy; sometimes a whole biography is there in the cast and color of blood and bone, the wounds and scars gathered in a lifetime. We can't see the last image on the retina, but we can see what was eaten, breathed, injected."[51]

condition of the body are noted. Hands and fingernails are examined for blood, skin, or clothing fibers that may have come from an assailant. The position of any bullet holes is measured, and the angle of entry and the gun's distance from the body are calculated. If the victim was known to have been standing when shot, this information can be used to estimate the height of the killer. Clothing is examined for bullet holes or powder traces. The body is fingerprinted, measured, weighed, and x-rayed, and blood is drawn to determine drug and alcohol levels.

The internal examination of the body also follows a standard procedure. The chest is opened with a thoracic-abdominal incision from shoulder to shoulder and a midline incision down the abdomen to the pubis. Ribs and cartilage are severed, and the heart, lungs, esophagus, and trachea are removed as a unit. Each organ is then weighed, examined externally, and dissected. Blood is drawn from the heart, fluid samples are aspirated from the pleural and abdominal cavities, and microscopic slides are made from organ tissue. The organs of the abdomen—liver, spleen, adrenals and kidneys, stomach, pancreas, and intestines—are examined in situ and removed, weighed, and sectioned. The contents of the stomach are measured and samples taken. The genitalia are examined and vaginal and anal swabs are obtained for evidence of sexual attack. Blood, semen, and hair are collected for DNA typing. The uterus is opened to reveal possible pregnancy, and the bladder is removed and urine sent for analysis. Lastly, the head is examined, beginning with the eyes (for signs of hemorrhage) and the skull (for signs of injury). An incision is made through the scalp from ear to ear across the back of the head. The skin is peeled forward to expose the skull, the front portion of which is sawed through and removed to expose the brain. The brain, like the other organs, is examined, removed, weighed, and sectioned. After the autopsy, the death certificate is completed and filed, the report (concluding with the opinion on the official cause of death) is finished, and the case file and accompanying materials are turned over to the authorities. The body can then be released to the family. If the death was unattended or followed chronic illness, the family is required to wait 48 hours before cremating the corpse, in the event of further investigation into the cause of death. Any organs or tissues may be kept by the medical examiner if needed for evidence in a criminal or civil case. National standards require that wet tissue be held for six months, tissue in paraffin blocks for five years, and slides for twenty years.[50]

A murder victim's last expression will not be fixed on his or her face at death, nor will the last image be fixed on the eyes. But the body does contain a wealth of clues if properly and methodically examined: "Death marks the end of the physical body, but the body tells the story of its works and days at autopsy; sometimes a whole biography is there in the cast and color of blood and bone, the wounds and scars gathered in a lifetime. We can't see the last image on the retina, but we can see what was eaten, breathed, injected."[51]

Medical examiners find that the bodies of those who die of gunshot wounds often contain bullets from previous shootings. The wrists of suicides will very often have "hesitation marks," small scratches on the skin made tentatively before the fatal cut. Many suicides also have scars on their wrists from past attempts. Bruising of the body, although sometimes confused with post-mortem lividity, can continue for a short time after death. If a body is exposed to flame, the heat will cause shrinkage of tendons and connective tissues, causing the hands to clench into fists and the arms and legs to draw up into the pugilistic or more acute fetal position. Muscles which were clenched at the time of death remain clenched, and a hand may contain a gun or the hair or clothing of an attacker. Jean Alexandre Eugene Lacassagne, professor of forensic medicine at the University of Lyon, experimented to find that the hands of a corpse could be closed around an object and produce the impression—after rigor mortis set in—that it was tightly gripped. In addition, Lacassagne determined that when people die naturally, their eyes are usually closed, but those who die suddenly have open eyes, which may be staring in cases of violence.

There are several formulas to determine time since death based on body temperature, but there are also many variables. Body temperature falls about one degree an hour after death. The rectal temperature subtracted from 98.6 degrees Fahrenheit and divided by 1.5 will reveal the approximate number of hours since death. The abdomen may also be punctured to insert a thermometer, but this may confuse the investigation. In any case, temperature is not a reliable indicator. The amount of clothing on the corpse, the ambient temperature and humidity, the victim's temperature during life, and the position of the body after death may all affect the cooling process. When a death is painful and violent, the body temperature may continue to rise for up to an hour after death, and a severe head injury will slow the temperature drop. The size of the body may also be a factor. Pathologists most often examine several of the changes in the body and make an estimate based on the comparison. The concentration of electrolytes that have seeped into the vitreous humor of the eyeball from the surrounding cells can be used to assess time of death, as can the rate at which various enzymes decay and the response of muscle tissue to electrical stimulation. The rate of digestion can also be used to narrow the time frame. If the food in the stomach shows no evidence of digestion, death occurred soon after eating. If the stomach is empty, death took place four to six hours after eating. And if the small intestine is also completely empty, at least 20 hours have elapsed since food was ingested.[52]

In addition to estimating the time of death, the autopsy seeks to answer the cause of death (the physical agent that brought it about), the mechanism of death (the pathological condition within the body that resulted in death), and the manner of death (natural, suicide, homicide, or accident). In many cases, cause of death will reveal or suggest manner of death. A person who has been found strangled is usually a victim of homicide because suicide by strangulation or suffocation is rare.[53] Death from a single gunshot points to suicide, while multiple shots indicate homicide. A suicide will rarely shoot through his or her clothing, so the shirt will be unbuttoned. On the other hand, a bathtub suicide will be found clothed because of to the victim's modesty.[54] Furthermore, the traits of murderers are inferred from the nature of their crime based on past investigative experience. The killing of a victim with little ritual may indicate a young killer. A particularly savage murder of a woman may suggest a killer with feminine physical traits.[55] Brutality, though, does not necessarily correspond to insanity, as the authors point out in *Alone with the Devil: Famous Cases of a Courtroom Psychiatrist*: "In deciding whether someone is psychotic or not, the method of killing is immaterial. The more bizarre process doesn't necessarily correspond to the more bizarre behavior or the degree of impairment."[56] But certain inferences from the killer's method may point in his or her direction. If the victim has wounds on the face, he or she was probably known by the killer. Wounds from behind indicate the killer was a stranger. If a male victim has bites on the chest, arms, or abdomen, his attacker was most likely a heterosexual male; if he has been bitten on the upper back, back of the shoulder, buttocks, or genitals, his killer was probably homosexual.[57]

The sights and smells of the body during examination lead easily to certain conclusions later verified in the laboratory. Poisoning does not always require chemical analysis to be initially detected. The skin of person who has ingested cyanide is cherry red, and an almond odor will often be noticeable. Immediate rigor mortis, eyes that are wide open, and a face frozen in a grimace are signs of strychnine poisoning. Inside the body, botulism will be evidenced by congestion and hemorrhages in all the internal organs, and poisoning with alkaline corrosives will result in gelatinous, dead areas of tissue. To back up their immediate convictions, pathologists send samples to the lab, which can routinely test for some 2,000 poisons. Carbon monoxide poisoning will slow the process of coagulation, so the blood will remain liquid for some time. The accumulation of carbon dioxide in the body, as in death by pneumonia, leaves the blood very dark and jellylike. The entrance site of an electrical injury, including a lightning strike, will show a central pale area with a bright red perimeter where the blood has been pushed by the heat. The entry wound of a bullet will present as a small, bruised hole, sometimes with a ring of grease around it. If the bullet has struck at an angle, the wound will be oval in shape and if the gun was fired within an inch of the body, the skin will contain a burn. If the victim was shot at close range (two to four inches), the soot on the skin can be easily wiped away, but if the distance was twelve to sixteen inches, the stippling of gunpowder residue will be embedded in the surrounding skin. Shots of longer range will neither burn nor stipple. A cyanotic victim with protruding tongue, frothing or bloodstained mouth, and petechiae on the face and whites of the eyes has almost certainly been strangled. Manual strangulation is deduced from a break in the hyoid bone in the throat, while ligature strangulation will leave a groove around the neck. If a ligature was used to commit suicide by hanging, the cord will not leave a straight line. In cases of homicide, the relevant portions of the body are often preserved as evidence.

Some factors contributing to death may be obvious on opening the body—lungs may be black, livers cirrhosed—but other causes require sophisticated analysis. In drowning deaths, microscopic diatoms will indicate by the extent of their travel through the circulatory system whether the victim's heart was beating when submersed and may narrow down the place of death by their variety. The chloride concentration of the blood is tested to determine whether the drowning occurred in fresh or salt water. If sand or weeds are found inside the lungs, drowning was the probable cause of the death (although drowning is a diagnosis of exclusion), but sand or weeds in the mouth and nose may indicate that the body was killed before being dumped in the water. In drowning deaths, the lungs are not necessarily filled with water. "Dry drowning" occurs when water enters the throat and causes a sudden laryngospasm, or constriction and closure of the airway. Bodies recovered from a fire will have soot in their windpipes if they were alive when the fire started; without this evidence of smoke inhalation, it may be assumed that the fire occurred or was set after the person was dead.

Coroners, medical examiners, and pathologists insulate themselves from the possible emotional and psychological consequences of their work in many ways. They may refrain from thinking of the corpse in human terms, or cover the face, or they may make light of the duties they are obliged to perform. Even the internationally famous London pathologist Bernard Spilsbury indulged in a little gallows humor, leaving a human leg in the kitchen for his cook to find and tying a ribbon around a human thigh bone to give to his dog at Christmas.[58] Thomas Noguchi, former chief medical examiner of Los Angeles County, calls humor a survival kit for those in his line of work. In *Homicide*, David Simon speaks of humor as a buffer between the living and the dead. It can be a weapon against the sight of body after body without their accompanying personalities or uniqueness: "For observers, the detectives included, this last stage of the autopsy is perhaps the hardest. The sound of the saw, the cranial pop from the lever, the image of the facial skin being covered by scalp—nothing makes the dead seem quite so anonymous as when the visage of every individual is folded in upon itself in a rubbery contortion, as if we've all been wandering this earth wearing dimestore Halloween masks, so easily and indifferently removed."[59]

Most pathologists also protect themselves physically from the occupational hazards of a contagious corpse, but the hazards only occasionally materialize. Spilsbury acquired an infection in his arm after performing a postmortem on a badly diseased body and got a similar disease the same way 20 years later. During the busiest part of his career, however, he was completing nearly 1,000 autopsies per year, a career total of over 25,000. Francis Camps and Professor Donald Teare each claimed to have conducted, with assistance, more than 80,000 over their lifetimes, Camps often dictating his report on one corpse while examining the next.[60]

Despite the rapidity and sheer numbers of examinations, however, each should be a solemn affair. Milton Helpern (d. 1977), retired chief medical examiner of New York City, advises: "The treatment of a dead body should not be personalized. It should be conducted with dignity and respect, remembering that any person, in any walk of life, through circumstance may require post-mortem examination. The autopsy room is the great democratizer."[61] Pathologists know well that the body on the slab could easily be their own. Francis Camps, professor of forensic medicine at the London Hospital Medical College in Whitechapel, confessed that his greatest fear in later life was having a postmortem examination performed on his body by his rival Keith Simpson, professor of forensic medicine at London University. Camps died a natural death outside the area in which Simpson normally worked, so the feared autopsy did not occur. Not only do autopsy technicians face their own mortality abstractly on a daily basis, they occasionally confront the deaths of those they know and care for. When Tony Olds, Jr., unwrapped the body of an 18-year-old shooting victim to photograph it at the District of Columbia morgue, he was shocked to discover that the young man was his cousin. Another technician, Louis Rogers, recalls the morning he chatted with a D.C. police officer and was called an hour later to pick up the officer's body after he had been gunned down by a stopped motorist.[62]

Similar but distinct circumstances have been imposed on coroners and medical examiners with the responsibility of examining the deaths of the famous and the infamous. With the spotlight on such cases, the autopsy findings often become an issue. When John Dillinger was brought down by federal agents in 1934, the Cook County chief pathologist Dr. J. J. Kearns recorded in his notes that the corpse had brown eyes and evidence of a childhood rheumatic heart condition. Dillinger's eyes were blue and he had no chronic medical conditions, leading to speculation that the body killed and examined was not his. Details that emerge from the autopsy can stun or merely startle. When English murderer John Reginald Halliday Christie was autopsied by Francis Camps after his execution by hanging, his stomach was found to contain the remains of a hearty breakfast.[63] The status of the deceased often dictates unusual protocols with regard to autopsy. The body of presidential assassin John Wilkes Booth was autopsied on board the ship *John S. Ide* by Dr. J. Janvier Woodward, who had autopsied Abraham Lincoln 12 days before. Afterward, attendants pretended to throw the body overboard so that it could be buried secretly in the Arsenal Grounds of the Navy Yard. Dr. Earl Rose, medical examiner in Dallas, asserted his authority over the body of President John F. Kennedy after the assassination, but was rebuffed at gunpoint by the Secret Service, who removed the body to the National Naval Medical Center in Bethesda, Maryland, for autopsy.[64]

Gonzalez-Crussi characterized the task of Dr. Milton Helpern, chief medical examiner of New York City, as "stamping the passport of those who unexpectedly embark for the beyond."[65] Another medical examiner says of his profession: "We know everything about everyone. But a day late."[66] The distasteful necessity that medical-legal autopsy represents before many of the departed can truly depart carries a long tradition and still retains lasting value. Only in this way can coroners and medical examiners learn the specific causes of death, particularly by violence, and teach by example how they can be avoided. With the assistance of specialists in the examination of hairs, fibers, bullets, toxins, and bloodstains, the pathologist can pinpoint human mortality. Through the information contained on the death certificate, patterns become evident, crimes and health hazards become apparent, and society can take steps to protect itself. Murder will out, but not always of its own accord.

Forensic Anthropology

The minute examinations carried out on the components of the corpse by forensic anthropologists raise suppositions which allow the dead to be identified and their deaths to be legally certified and avenged. The raw materials of the scientists are the bones, teeth, blood, and hair of the corpse. The fruits of their labors are detailed descriptions of the deceased while alive and a precise sequence of events preceding, causing, and following death. "The big difference between the pathologists and us forensic anthropologists, says scientist Clyde Collins Snow, "is that pathologists usually work on fresh bodies, while we usually have only bones to study. Bones can be puzzles ... but they never lie, and they don't smell bad."[67] A bone, for instance, may reveal by its muscle attachments the strength of the deceased and by its size an approximate height. Certain latent characteristics may be brought to light with chemical testing. Comparisons may be made by photographic superimposition and identifications by reconstruction. While the techniques of forensic anthropology do not guarantee that a murder will be solved or that a disaster victim will be identified, they do increase the chances.

Forensic anthropology is often a science of putting the pieces of a puzzle together:

> The severed head found in a plastic bag in a field in Indiana turns out to be an exact match with the headless torso recovered from a bog in Florida. The

mummified remains of a human female forearm and hand retrieved from a cellar crawl space in Poultney, Vermont, precisely fit the distal ends of an incomplete radius and ulna from a woman's body found the year before in an abandoned washing machine in Texas. The skeletal remains of another arm, this time a man's recovered in 1986 between the chimney and wall during the demolition of a house in Pennsylvania, belong on an incomplete body recovered at the crash site of a drug plane in Mississippi.[68]

When a murder is recent, the job of assembling the pieces is often a messy one. Bernard Spilsbury reconstructed the body of Emily Kaye, murdered by her lover Patrick Mahon in 1924, from four large segments, 37 smaller pieces of flesh, and various inner organs found at her bungalow. Even so, he could not disprove that the woman might have died accidentally, so the case rested on the fact that a knife was purchased before the death by Mahon, who was convicted and hanged. In 1935, Professor John Glaister of the University of Glasgow sorted out the two human heads and four bundles of body parts— including three female breasts—found on the bank of the Linn in 1935. Although the skin had been removed from the heads and fingertips, Glaister estimated the ages of what he reasoned were the remains of two women and determined cause of death to be strangulation and stabbing of one victim and battering with a blunt instrument of the other. Police charged Buck Ruxton with the murder of his common-law wife Isabella Ruxton and a woman who had come to her aid during the assault. Although the defense claimed that the remains were misidentified, a photograph of the larger skull superimposed exactly on a photograph of Mrs. Ruxton. The verdict of guilty was unanimous, and Ruxton was hanged. Sometimes the evidence remains in limbo for years. William Sheward cut his wife's throat and dismembered her body in 1851. Over the next few weeks, the pieces that were found in ditches around Norwich were preserved by order of the magistrate. Sheward confessed to the murder seven years later, and the remains were reexamined and found to possibly belong to his wife. Although he retracted his confession, the jury sentenced him to death.

Bones contain clues about accidental, homicidal, or natural death. The skeletons of children are less reliable than those of adults regarding gender, since the shape of the pelvic opening doesn't fully develop until puberty, but skeletons in general are highly informative about the individual and the circumstances of his or her death. The femur alone suffices to extract the height, sex, age at death, ethnic origin, and body weight, in addition to inferences about the dead person's walking patterns, livelihood, medical history, and cause of death. Other details may suggest foul play. Bending of the bone is forensic proof that the crushing trauma occurred at about the time of death and appeared to be the cause. Bones that have been burned while flesh-covered frequently have curved transverse fractures, irregular longitudinal splitting, and marked warping. The burning of dry bones causes cracking on the surface as well as longitudinal splitting. Shrinkage of bone in a fire depends on the fire's temperature and duration and the bone's density, but may be as much as 25 percent. Changes in bone color may also indicate the fire's intensity. Forensic anthropologists familiarize themselves with postmortem changes in the skeleton so as not to mistake mildewing for charring or the penetration of a plant root for trauma. The skull contains clues to age and sex, characteristics common to a race or ethnic group, and a singular key to identity, the teeth. In addition to matching dental records, the skull can be reconstructed to create a likeness of the deceased for possible identification, a method first attempted by German anatomist Wilhelm His in 1895. The technique was greatly improved upon by Mikhail Gerasimov (d. 1970) of Russia's Ethnographical Institute, but is still not legally considered positive identification. Photographic superimposition of the skull against an image from life is not legally admissible as final proof in American courts, either, but has gained limited acceptance in Europe.[69]

Hair also contains a wealth of information which is then used to link a murderer to a crime or to identify the dead. Hair found in the trunk of John Wayne Gacy's Oldsmobile matched that of Robert Piest, one of his victims. Hair caught in Mrs. Lucas's ring was found compatible with that of her matricidal son, Henry Lee Lucas, also responsible for dozens of other murders. And human hair found on the claws of a 400-pound grizzly bear killed in Yellowstone Park verified that it was the bear who had killed a woman the day before. A strand or two of hair may reveal sex, age, and race, but will most certainly indicate the part of the body from which it came, whether any bleaching or dying had been carried out on it, and if it fell out, was torn off, or was cut. Technicians can glean further information in the laboratory. When Royal Canadian Mounted Police found a few hairs in the hand of a dead woman in the mid–1960s, neuron activation revealed chemicals that were an exact match for the hair of one of the suspects, leading to his conviction for her murder. Chemists compared hairs from the corpse that had been found to locks of hair kept by the grandmother to identify the Lindbergh baby. Today DNA testing surpasses all other analyses in reliability. Even centuries later, a small hair sample may provide a window on a life and death. Scientists examined a lock of hair of John of Lancaster, duke of Bedford (d. 1435), and found it to contain mercurial embalming preservative. Hair clipped from the head of Napoleon (d. 1821) by his valet was analyzed by scientists 140 years later and found to contain evidence that the exiled emperor had been given steady and fairly massive doses of arsenic for about four months before he died.[70] Hair samples taken from victims of the ill-fated Franklin Expedition (1845–48) were subject to trace element analysis which proved that lead poisoning caused their deaths while they were stranded in the Arctic and surviving on canned food.

Identification of the dead can be a difficult task, and after disasters the process is assisted by dentists, pathologists, anthropologists, FBI fingerprint specialists, radiologists, photographers, and laboratory technicians. Identity has been verified by clothing, jewelry, fingerprints, dental work, tattoos, and scars, but is not foolproof. Military dog tags are considered only a presumptive form of identification of a body because they can become detached from it. Dental records are also becoming harder to match because of more widespread water fluoridation and better dental hygiene.[71] A team of scientists at Harvard has come up with a protocol for the identification of remains. The first question is whether they are human and next whether they represent a single individual or many. Investigators should try to determine when death occurred, the age of the decedent, and his or her sex, race, and physique. Significant anatomic anomalies should be noted, including signs of old disease or injury. Lastly, investigators should determine cause and manner of death. Even the first step is not as easy as it sounds, considering the fact that between 10 and 15 percent of presumed human skeletal remains sent to the FBI for analysis are proven to be something other than human.[72]

Often, identity needs only to be confirmed rather than determined. When Dr. Joseph Warren's son was killed at the battle of Bunker Hill and buried in a mass grave, Paul Revere identified the body by the dental work he had performed. The body of John Wilkes Booth was identified by several people. Dr. May identified a permanent scar on the back of Booth's neck, having originally sutured it, and the tattoo of his initials on his hand. Dr. Merrill, Booth's dentist, identified his fillings. And the family accepted the body as Booth's. Later assassin Lee Harvey Oswald was identified after death by fingerprints taken upon his enlistment in the marines and again during his arraignment after the shootings of President Kennedy and Officer Tippit.[73] Identification is often made by family members, but not as popularly depicted: "These days, pulling the metal slab out of the morgue wall so the body can be identified by next of kin is strictly movie hokum. Now there is a photograph, or for families that insist on something more, a video camera set up in the morgue, and a secluded viewing room with a discreet guard."[74]

Today's methods contrast markedly with those used in the Catherine Hayes case of 1726. When the head of her husband, whom she had bludgeoned and dismembered with the help of her two lodgers, was found intact on the shore of the Thames, the magistrate ordered that it be washed and the hair combed and that it be set upon a pole outside St. Margaret's Church, Westminster. Parish officers were ordered to take into custody anyone who showed signs of guilt at the sight of it, but it began to decay and was consigned to a jar. Friends of the victim recognized his head and lead authorities to Hayes, who was burned alive for petty treason.

Fingerprints have been a reliable means of identifying the dead, despite the difficulty in taking the prints. Alphonse Bertillon's method of identification by taking measurements from the body worked equally well on the dead as on the living, a fact he demonstrated by identifying a two-month-old body pulled out of a river, but it was eclipsed by the more efficient technique of fingerprinting. The fingerprints of corpses were first taken in England in 1905 to rule out the victims in a case where the killer left a bloody thumbprint on the lid of a cash box. Since then, several methods have been perfected to obtain prints from even the messiest of corpses, including injections to inflate wrinkled fingertips, hardening of pulpy epidermis with formaldehyde before printing, taking prints from the sloughed epidermis of the fingertips, and utilizing the identical but fainter patterns in the underlying dermis.[75] Officials in Wagga Wagga, Australia, fingerprinted a "glove" of human skin found in a river in 1933, establishing the identify of the victim and leading to the killer's conviction. Even partial or fragmentary prints may find a match. Clyde Snow verified the death of a victim of the Augusto Pinochet regime in Chile in the 1970s by fingerprinting the mummified tissue of a thumb found in a mine shaft with the fragmentary remains of 15 other victims. If fingerprinting the body proves unsuccessful, criminologists may, with the approval of local authorities, sever the hands of the victim and send them in a 70 percent alcohol solution in an unbreakable, airtight container to the FBI Laboratory for direct analysis.[76]

Another gruesome task of the forensic anthropologist is the identification not only of the victim, but of the species of maggot which is feeding on the body. If the larvae are removed and cultivated until they hatch, the timing data from their life cycle can be applied to the death. Pupae can be removed from under a decaying body and their cases analyzed to determine the number of generations of flies. That number can be multiplied by the length of the cycle to determine the period since the laying of the first egg. In addition, the species may indicate whether the victim was killed in or out of doors.[77] By this means and by experience, forensic anthropologists become adept at estimating time since death: "They know what happens to a skeleton after the passage of a month, a decade, a century, two thousand years. They know what happens when a skeleton is left on the prairie after an Indian massacre and buried years later by a passer-by. They can distinguish between evidence of murder and the results of a dog passing by and helping himself to lunch. Those experiences supply the context in which suspected or known murder cases can be interpreted far more precisely than before."[78] To interpret the data, scientists must first expose it. Trauma to bones is revealed by the removal of soft tissue, which is teased away with instruments, simmered away, or removed with chemicals or bleach.

Sometimes the forensic anthropologist bears an awesome responsibility, for instance, proving that a homicide took place based on evidence which does not include a body. Under constitutional protection against double jeopardy, a murderer once acquitted cannot be retried if the corpse is later found. Chicagoan Adolph Louis Luetgart and Englishman John George Haigh were both overly confident that no body was the equivalent of no conviction. Luet-gart disposed of his wife's body by dissolving it in a vat of boiling caustic potash in his sausage factory. Police found part of a tooth from her dentures and two rings, one of them bearing her initials, in a filter. The first jury was divided, but the second jury found Luetgart guilty and he was sentenced to life in prison in 1897. John Haigh destroyed the body of his victim with acid in a storehouse he owned. Detectives shoveled the resulting 28 pounds of greasy sludge into boxes and examined it at Scotland Yard, where it was found to contain a partially dissolved left foot, an upper and lower denture, three gallstones, and 18 fragments of human bone. The bones showed evidence of osteo-arthritis, which the victim was known to suffer from, a plaster cast of the foot fit her left shoe, and the false teeth were identified by her dental sur-geon. Haigh was found guilty and executed in 1949.[79]

In the ordeal of the bier, known in England until the seventeenth cen-tury, a person suspected of murder was obliged to approach or touch the body of the victim. Wounds bleeding at the touch, foam appearing at the mouth, or the body altering its position indicated guilt."[79] Today the evidence has little to do with superstition, and the proof is legally documented and repro-ducible. The forensic anthropologist works in tandem with the pathologist using the raw materials of human mortality:

> To the forensic pathologist, the outward structure of death is usually the horrid effect of violence on the frailty of the human body. The field of study is men, women, and children cut into small bits, bludgeoned into amor-phous, bloody tatters, carbonized by high temperatures, immersed in tanks of corrosive acids, bloated by prolonged immersion in water, half eaten by rats, tunneled by maggots, skinned by abrasives, blue from asphyxia, cherry red from carbon monoxide, inconspicuously pierced with ice picks, or blown into irrecoverable shreds by industrial explosions.[80]

To look beyond the gore and the dry clatter of bones, the benefits of such analysis are obvious. Persuasive and reliable evidence obtained in the field and the laboratory works to assure a conviction in cases of homicide. Techniques of positive identification allow families the dignity of memorializing the remains of loved ones killed in accidents, disasters, or wars. Study of the particular effects of a cause of death enable investigators to recognize diseases or other condi-tions more readily, saving steps and possibly saving lives in the future.

Exhumation

After being carefully laid to rest, the body is sometimes rudely roused from its grave. Adverse weather has been known to uncover buried corpses. Sometimes exhumations are a cultural prerogative. Other times bodies are

moved to a more appropriate tomb or so that cemetery space can be rede-
veloped. And occasionally graves are disturbed for less momentous and more
selfish reasons. Exhumations are often planned for the early hours of the
morning to avoid drawing the attention of cemetery visitors. If the event
doesn't provoke an audience, the results—a positive identification or a medical history of a famous historical personage—often do. Opening a grave may
reveal the ravages of decay, but may also uncover evidence of murder. For practical more often than whimsical reasons, exhumation has been an accepted
practice over the years.

The practical aspects of exhumation often necessitate retaining a low
profile. Disinterments are often scheduled early not only for economic reasons (the grave can be opened and closed the same day), but to avoid notice.
Douglas Ubelaker describes the bipolar reactions of mourners in Puerto Rico
taken unawares:

> The first visitors of the day were arriving at the cemetery, and I noticed sev-
> eral people watching us from a respectful distance, some with flowers des-
> tined for nearby graves still in their hands, as the leaky coffin was hoisted
> up from its watery resting place. It was clear from the expressions on their
> faces that this was not the kind of thing they expected to see, and when the
> lid came off, a couple of them dropped their flowers and moved quickly
> away. At the same time, those with different impulses or stronger curiosity
> came closer, craning for a look at whatever horrible thing was within.[81]

An even lower profile must have been sought by a New Jersey police chief
accused of ordering the opening of a grave to retrieve a hat he had loaned to
the grieving family for the viewing.[82] On the other hand, exhumations lead
to repeat business, and so are encouraged at Forest Lawn Memorial Park in
California in order to sell more caskets.

Many notable and notorious Americans have been shifted to a new resting place. After they received permission, the family of John Wilkes Booth
had his body removed from the Arsenal Grounds in Washington, D.C., to
an unmarked grave in the family plot in Baltimore. Other famous person-
ages have been moved to specially marked graves set aside or newly built for
those with a place in history. James Monroe was buried in New York in 1831,
but was transferred to Richmond, Virginia, on the centennial of his death.
Zachary Taylor was buried in 1850 in Washington's Congressional Cemetery,
taken later that year to his family plot in Springfield, Kentucky, and moved
a second time with his wife in 1926 to a mausoleum built by the U.S. government in Louisville, Kentucky. Abraham Lincoln was buried in Oak Ridge
Cemetery in Springfield, Illinois, in 1865, but was entombed beneath a tall
obelisk in the same cemetery in 1901. Jefferson Davis, buried in Metarie
Cemetery in Biloxi, Mississippi, in 1889, was reburied in Richmond's Hollywood Cemetery in 1893. George Patton was moved to a more accessible

location in the American military cemetery in Luxembourg three years after his death in 1945. Martin Luther King, Jr., was buried in South View Cemetery in Atlanta in 1968, but was later moved to Atlanta's Martin Luther King Memorial Center.

Bodies have been unearthed after burial for reasons both personal and political. The body of Napoleon was exhumed from his grave on St. Helena by order of King Louis Philippe, who hoped that restoring it to Paris would ingratiate him with the masses. Thomas G. Wheeler, author of *Who Lies Here?* chronicles that all reports agree that the emperor's body was in a state of almost perfect preservation despite 19 years underground: "There had been no attempt made to embalm the body, and yet there it lay, mocking by its youthfulness and beauty of countenance the aging men gathered about it."[83] Elizabeth Siddal (d. 1861), the wife of Dante Gabriel Rossetti, had retained her beauty in the grave, but was revisited for a quite different reason. Rossetti obtained permission from the Home Office to disinter her coffin, with the help of three other men, to retrieve a sheaf of poems he had buried with her seven years earlier. The manuscript had lain between her cheek and hair (which some say had grown to fill the coffin) and required disinfecting before being published in 1870. The bodies of Héloïse (d. 1164) and Abélard (d. 1142) were disinterred and reburied separately in 1630 by an abbess who disapproved of a monk and nun lying in the same grave; they were disinterred a second time and eventually reburied together in Père Lachaise.

Suspicion of murder is perhaps the most important reason a body is exhumed, and Lizzie Borden's killing of her father and stepmother is arguably the most well-known murder. Professor James E. Starrs of George Washington University proposes to exhume the bodies of Andrew and Abbie Borden from their Fall River, Massachusetts, graves and match the evidence on their bones with the cutting edge of the alleged ax, which is still available, thus solving part of the puzzle. Exhumation is sometimes necessary to confirm things that were overlooked at autopsy. The body of a woman found outside the District of Columbia in the 1980s was hurriedly autopsied and buried because she had maggots in her eyes, around her nose and mouth, in the chest area, and on the palms of her hands. The cause of death was recorded as unknown, but when forensic anthropologist Bill Rodriguez reviewed the photographs several years later the swarming pattern of the maggots suggested that they obscured deadly and defensive stab wounds. Upon receiving court approval, officials carried out the exhumation by lantern light in the middle of a snowstorm, thoroughly examined the remains, and reclassified the death as a homicide.[84]

Obtaining a court order for the exhumation of a possible murder victim can be a difficult step because it requires probable cause rather than mere suspicion. In addition, the family of the victim may protest the order, although the public often finds news of such posthumous prying fascinating. In his autobiography, Keith Simpson describes an exhumation in Barbados presided over by English officials: "Hundreds of gaily dressed men and women jostled outside the graveyard walls, and there were ice-cream stalls and hordes of children with great white eyes eager for an entertainment that had never come their way before. Policemen digging up dead bodies! Murder! English scientists! Scotland Yard!"[85] In fact, many statutes now permit exhumations if they are in the public interest. They are carried out to investigate the cause or manner of a death, to collect evidence of a crime, to determine the cause of an accident or the presence of disease, to gather evidence to assess malpractice, to compare the body with another person thought to be the deceased, to identify war and accident victims hastily buried without identification, to settle accidental death or liability claims, and to search for lost objects. In addition, they have been used to reconstruct historical events, such as Custer's last stand at Little Bighorn.[86]

When a body is to be exhumed, the next-of-kin are commonly invited to attend. While the autopsy of the remains used to be conducted at the graveside, the body is now removed to a laboratory for examination. Decomposed remains may be frozen to reduce odor. They are photographed, weighed, measured, and sometimes x-rayed. Hair samples and fingerprints are taken. Mold is cleaned off to reveal marks or scars. Dental structures are recorded, a standard autopsy is completed as fully as possible, tissue is tested for toxins, and the body is reburied.[87] The embalming process may remove evidence of a crime, the condition of the body will almost certainly have deteriorated, and the soil conditions may change the chemical composition of the body. In modern exhumations of possible poison victims, soil samples are routinely taken from above, beside, and below the casket to test against poison entering the decomposing tissue from the earth. It was believed in earlier centuries that a corpse exhumed as a possible murder victim would incriminate the guilty by showing signs of life. Today that responsibility is left to the forensic detectives.

Far from a legal need to exhume a body is the culturally entrenched idea of digging up the dead to clean, rebury, or distribute the bones. Trobriand Islanders disinter the dead and give away the bones as relics. The people of Malagasy exhume and rebury the dead in ceremonies so popular that during the cool seasons the roads are full of people traveling to reburials and the taxis advertise negotiable rates for trips to exhumations.[88] Huron Indians of North America held a celebration in which the bones of relatives were exhumed, cleaned, and carried in procession. In rural Greece, bones are retrieved from the grave after five years by the women of the family, who wash them with wine, pray over them, and pass them from person to person. During the handling of the bones and skull, the women comment on the frailty and futility of human existence before placing the remains in the village ossuary. Few Americans or Europeans would wish such familial duties, but some have been known to watch the exhumations of their spouses. When the body of French composer Hector Berlioz's first wife Harriet was moved, he described how he "With his two hands picked up the head, already parted from the body ... [and then] gathered in his arms the headless trunk and limbs, a blackish mass which the shroud still clung to."[89] Families may wish to attend the disinterment, but are rarely eager to witness the examination. In fact, when a funeral director was obliged to move a grave for road expansion one year after burial, he was proud to find that the corpse had remained perfectly preserved. But when he invited the family to inspect it, they emphatically refused.[90]

Land development often has dire consequences for the dead. In recognition, the Batesville Casket Company now equips some caskets with a memorial record tube to provide identification if the casket is moved. Today bodies are moved out of the way rather than to a place of more prestige like Père Lachaise. Cemeteries in Akron, Detroit, Houston, El Paso, New Orleans, New York, and the District of Columbia were moved to accommodate highway construction, and a cemetery in Baltimore gave way to a new airport.[91] In the 1920s, the burgeoning growth of San Francisco caused officials to have all graves removed from city limits and reinterred in the nearby town of Colma. But such large-scale manipulations of the dead do not belong only to the twentieth century or to the United States. From December of 1785 to October of 1787, 1,000 cartfuls of bones (the remains of an estimated 20,000 people) were removed from the cemetery of les Innocents in order to provide Paris with a park. The remains—consisting of a layer of earth over 10 feet thick, 80 vaults, and more than 50 large common graves—were deposited with some design in quarries which soon became known as the Parisian catacombs.[92] When cemeteries are relocated, some families refuse to have their loved ones moved. Lincoln Park in Chicago contains such a tomb, discreetly hidden with shrubbery. Reburial can be an expensive undertaking. In 1989, a Virginia resident found an affordable way to advance science *and* protect her ancestors from encroaching development and increasing vandalism. In exchange for having 23 members of the Weir family moved closer to the Liberia Plantation House in Manassas, descendant Jean Beach allowed scientists from the Manassas Museum, the Smithsonian Institution, the Armed Forces Institute of Pathology, and the University of Maryland to study the remains, which consisted mainly of hair, teeth, and crumbling bone fragments.

When graves are disinterred, there has often been curiosity about the condition of the occupants. The display of exhumed bodies was common in Mexican churches and has a long tradition in the cathedrals of Europe. The removal of thousands of occupants of les Innocents cemetery (discussed above) attracted the interest of several doctors, who increased their knowledge of both bodily decomposition and natural mummification. Their modern counterpart, Danish bone expert Vilhelm Moller-Christensen, exhumed a leper cemetery dating from 1250 to 1550 to second-guess early diagnostic techniques, which proved to be 70 percent effective. Cast-iron caskets used during the Civil War yielded—100 years later—corpses wearing intact uniforms and having recognizable features and internal organs. Concerned about her father's body rotting underground, one woman had his body exhumed two days after burial so she could visit him face to face rather than simply leaving flowers on his grave. The prospect of seeing the disinterred dead has a mesmerizing quality, not always equated with anthropological interest. When builders in Miami Beach unearthed a mass grave in 1923, which containing the bones of as many as 200 unidentified people, they built a road to allow the curious to visit. Today several have wondered what future diggers will think when they unearth today's dead, equipped with breast implants and damaged by attempts to save their lives: "Later I thought about how some time in the future they're going to be excavating graves from this time period and they're going to think that when a person reached a certain stage of debilitation that there was some sort of ritualistic sacrificing of them where we all jumped on their chests and broke their ribs."[93] So mused a critical care nurse who had participated in the vigorous but failed cardio-pulmonary resuscitation of an 80-year-old man.

The morbid fascination the living sometimes have for the dead is given added impetus when the dead are celebrities. When St. Giles Church in London was renovated in 1790, the grave of John Milton, who had died 116 years earlier, was exposed. A gravedigger exhibited the body in the church for two busy days, during which the shroud was ripped open, the ribs caved in, and the hair and several teeth removed as souvenirs. The vicar was said to have been outraged. Canon Thomas Gerrard Barber was more mincing upon taking a peek into Lord Byron's vault in 1938: "Reverently, very reverently, I raised the lid, and before my very eyes lay the embalmed body of Byron in as perfect a condition as when it was placed in the coffin 114 years ago. His features and hair easily recognisable from the portraits with which I was so familiar. The serene, almost happy expression on his face made a profound impression on me ... . I gently lowered the lid of the coffin—and as I did so, breathed a prayer for the peace of his soul."[94] In his book of medical anecdotes, Robert Mould points out the marked contrast between that account and the identification of the body shortly after death by friend John Hobhouse: "The decaying face that glimmered in the light of the candles was not the face of Byron: Hobhouse was able to identify the body by raising the red velvet pall and glancing at the foot."[95]

The French received an unprecedented opportunity in 1804 to observe the caskets, if not the bodies of the dead. The corpses of several notables were moved from their original location to Paris's newly opened Père Lachaise at the behest of the cemetery's founder Nicolas Frochot. Frochot acquired the bodies of Molière (d. 1673) and Jean de La Fontaine (d. 1695) to improve the

cemetery's standing among important Parisians. He also arranged the transfer of the remains of Louise de Lorraine, queen of Henry III, but later traded
Queen Louise for the bodies of celebrated lovers Héloïse and Abélard.[96] The
body of Oscar Wilde was also moved to the fashionable Père Lachaise, courtesy of a generous English woman who funded the operation. Upon the
exhumation of his grave at Bagneaux Cemetery, it is said his corpse was well-
preserved despite the quicklime that had been used at burial in an attempt
to reduce it to bones. English funeral director Harold Nicholson recalled the
common urge to catch a glimpse of the famous face:

> I never saw Oscar Wilde during his lifetime, but I very nearly saw him ten
> years after he was dead. … The soil had been placed on each side of the
> grave and, since it had been raining during the night, the sextons thought
> it wise to put three tombstones on the top of the earth so as to hold it down.
> There were many official representatives and journalists present at Bagneaux
> cemetery, and as they pressed forward to gaze into the grave one of the heavy
> stones became dislodged and fell upon the coffin, splitting the lid open. For
> a few seconds the face of Wilde could be seen, peaceful and white. Then
> the earth followed and in a few seconds his face was obliterated by mud.[97]

The status of the deceased seems to be directly proportional to a lack of
loathing on viewing the exhumed remains.

The examination of the bodily remnants of famous historic figures is said
to be justified by adding a chapter—usually on medical history—to his or her
biography. When the Soviet Ministry of Culture opened the sarcophagus of
Ivan IV (d. 1584 and better known as "Ivan the Terrible") in 1953, they found
what may be two reasons for his temper. The skeleton showed that he had
suffered from painful polyarthritis for much of his life, and his teeth indicated that the secondary incisors, canines, and premolars had come through
when he was in his fifties, which would also have been very painful.[98] The
tomb of King Edward I of England (d. 1307) was reopened in 1774 to document the burial clothes and goods. The skull of Alexander Pope (d. 1744)
was exhumed for examination by a phrenologist. The results are unrecorded,
but Pope's ghost is said to haunt the church at Twickenham as a result. Exhumations of the famous and infamous have been conducted to test several theories. President Zachary Taylor (d. 1850) was disinterred to determine whether
he was poisoned (the tests were negative). Marina Oswald Porter led the successful 1981 campaign to have the body of her husband Lee Harvey Oswald
exhumed to prove it was his after British writer Michael Eddowes suggested
that the grave contained the body of a Russian agent. The body was exhumed
from Rose Hill Cemetery in Fort Worth and examined at Baylor University
Medical Center at a cost of several thousand dollars. The remains were
identified as Oswald's from dental records and the scar from a mastoid operation. Permission to exhume and reautopsy the remains of John F. Kennedy

has been repeatedly denied. The body of Dr. Carl Weiss, alleged assassin of Senator Huey Long of Louisiana, was exhumed to search for bullets, which were not found. Members of a convention of Elvis-still-lives researchers want to exhume Elvis Presley's body to prove that it is not his and that he disappeared into the Federal Witness Protection Program.[99]

Occasionally, scientists have attempted to isolate the remains of the renowned from those of other occupants of common or confusing graves. A French team of anthropologists led by Pierre-François Puech of the University of Provence examined a partial skull exhumed ten years after Mozart's death in 1791 from a grave in a cemetery east of Vienna. Their study finds several correspondences with likenesses of the composer, and a reconstruction of the head bears a striking resemblance to existing portraits. A similar technique had been employed to identify the skull of Johann Sebastian Bach (d. 1750) in a collection of bones recovered from a cemetery in Leipzig.[100] American naval hero John Paul Jones (d. 1792) was brought from an obscure cemetery in Paris to a national shrine in Annapolis, Maryland. His leaden coffin was disinterred with four others and identified through a process of elimination. Before being transported and reinterred, the remains were examined, and lesions on the kidneys indicating nephritis suggested a cause of death.

In addition to identifying the famous, exhumation has uncovered whether a person in fact existed at all. In the eighteenth century, an ancient grave in Hathersage, Derbyshire, belonging to a John Little was opened. A thigh bone contained in the grave indicated the occupant's height to be seven feet tall, the conclusion being that the remains were those of "Little John" of Robin Hood fame. In a remarkable case in England in the nineteenth century, the body of shopkeeper Thomas Charles Druce (d. 1864) was exhumed at Highgate Cemetery and identified from photographs 19 years after death to quell claims by Druce's family that their patriarch was in fact not Druce at all, but the fifth duke of Portland (d. 1879) who had, according to them, led a double life and buried a casket of lead when he tired of the ruse. "Proof" of a person's existence has been obtained as a direct result of exhumation and as a byproduct. When it was realized that no likeness of Franciscan missionary St. Francis Solanus (d. 1610) had been made during his life, the viceroy of Lima ordered the body disinterred for a portrait. Artists took the opportunity to cast the skull of Robert Burns when his grave was opened for the burial of his wife.

In some cases, the dead are reexamined periodically. Abraham Lincoln was said to have had the body of his son Willy disinterred twice so that he could gaze upon the face of his favorite child. The body of James Smithson, founder of the Smithsonian Institution, was removed from the British Cemetery in Genoa in 1903, after which his skull was displayed to the press by the American consul in Italy. His skeleton was extensively examined by

Alexander Graham Bell and was photographed by Bell's wife. The following year, the remains were enshrined at the Smithsonian with full state honors, but in 1973 the sarcophagus was reopened and the bones given another once-over. In other cases, the dead are foisted on the living, whether they care to examine them or not. An extended storm resulted in a mudslide in the Verdugo Hills section of Los Angeles that caused a cemetery to spill its 100 occupants into the streets, stores, and even the living rooms of the community. Bureaucrats argued over who should take the responsibility—financially and otherwise—of sorting out the corpses, but the task of identification and reburial was taken up by the L.A. County Coroner's Office.

Graves are rarely perfect and not always permanent. The dead are settled, moved, and resettled. Christopher Columbus made two trans–Atlantic voyages after death, first from Seville to Santo Domingo on the island of Hispaniola in 1536 and then, after a brief respite in Havana, back to Seville more than a century later. The body of King John of Bohemia (d. 1346) was moved 11 times in 600 years, reaching a final resting place in the Cathedral of Luxembourg. The dead may be exhumed out of legal necessity or medical curiosity. Cemeteries may be moved by land developers, bones may be reclaimed from the earth for secondary burial, and bodies may be dug up by bad weather or disturbed individuals. Arthur Armbruster of Escondido, California, for instance, single-handedly exhumed the body of his 87-year-old mother twice in 1985 and drove her around in his van for weeks in search of an ideal burial site.[101] The idea of exhumation is often opposed on principle as distasteful, but with the enforced use of burial vaults or liners, modern caskets hold up quite well; they remain sealed for transport to a new location or yield remains that can be reexamined for historic or legal evidence.

The Deliberate Death

I left her there in the bedroom. After that, I believe I had
a cup of tea and went to bed.
    —John Reginald Halliday Christie commenting
    on killing his first victim, recounted by Robert
    Jackson, *Francis Camps: Famous Case Histories of
    the Celebrated Pathologist*[1]

Execution

Execution has been a varied punishment ranging from crushing the body
to pulling it apart. The often bloody destruction of a living criminal was long
intended to discourage others from pursuing the same career and was, as far
as possible, carried out near the scene of the crime. Public hangings drew a
crowd, but not of repentant thieves. They became a social event peopled by
all classes in which the scaffold was a stage. After the hanging, the body was
sometimes ignored and other times fought over. Capital punishment has been
argued against as cruel and unusual, unfairly applied, and lacking in its deterrent effect, but in practice it still thrills many. Where it is still legal, though
no longer a public spectacle, waiting lists to witness legal killings accumulate faster than the executions can be carried out.

Although American executions are no longer a spectator sport, there are
over 200 people eagerly awaiting the chance to observe one in Florida, where
the electric chair is the prevailing method. In "A Comment on Capital Punishment," Clarence Darrow writes that even though horror and cruelty is
necessary to capital punishment, familiarity lessens its impact on witnesses,
cheapening life and making killing more commonplace,[2] an opinion borne out
by recent statistics. Even though the face of the condemned was often cloaked,
after public executions were abolished in England in 1868, the public flocked
to the Chamber of Horrors at Madame Tussaud's wax museum to appease their
curiosity. In 1881, 250 people paid as much as $300 to see President Garfield's

assassin Charles Guiteau hanged. In only a very few instances, it seems, does a witness actually identify with the condemned. John Brady, convicted of felony murder and awaiting his own execution, watched the death of fellow inmate Nathan Lipscomb in 1961 and described his own reaction to the sight:

> When he walked into that gas chamber, it was me walking through that door into that gas chamber. When they strapped him into that chair, it was me they were strapping into that chair. When they sealed those doors, it was me they were sealing in there. When they dropped those capsules into that bucket, it was me that was going to breathe those fumes. When they hosed down that chamber ... it was my body they were hosing. When they took him out of that chamber, it was me they were taking out of that chamber. When they laid his body on that stainless steel hospital cart, it was me they were laying on that cart. When they wheeled him by my cell, so that I could see his body turned nearly purple from the bursting blood vessels, it was my body they were wheeling out, dead.[3]

In *Executions: The Legal Ways of Death*, George V. Bishop offers small consolation: "People who are executed by the inhalation of lethal gas do not offend the official witnesses with the facial contortions and eerie body color characteristic of an electrocution; there is no torn and burned flesh, or odors of bodily excretions that are typical of hanging; the messy bleeding and the final coup de grace of the firing squad is eliminated and, of course, there is always the unsightly head to be retrieved following a decapitation."[4]

The methods used to exact retribution for crime have been varied and vulgar. Stoning, prescribed by the ancient law of Moses, involved pelting the guilty party with rocks, which led to unconsciousness, death, and burial under the growing pile of stones. Crucifixion originated with the Phoenicians and was reserved for the lowest class of criminals. The condemned was scourged, forced to carry the transverse beam of the cross to the execution site, and nailed or tied to the assembled cross, which was then fixed upright. Death by crucifixion often took several days, prolonged by allaying thirst and hastened by breaking bones. Pressing was also a slow death, often intended to extract a confession; it consisted of piling increasing numbers of weights on the body until the condemned was crushed. The garotte, popular in Spain, was a method of strangulation aided by a mechanical device as simple as a stick with which to twist the cord or as complicated as a screw device operated by a series of levers. The mazzatello was a brutal and bloody method of execution used in Italy: the condemned was knocked in the head with a mallet and had his or her throat cut immediately thereafter. From 1241 to 1817, the English punishment of hanging, drawing, and quartering was practiced. The condemned was tied to the tail of a horse, dragged along the surface of the ground to the gallows, and hanged by the neck until half-dead. Then the body was cut down and disemboweled and the entrails were burnt. Finally, the body was beheaded, cut into quarters, and exposed for public viewing. In other cultures, animals have been put to direct use in the destruction of life. The Romans, Assyrians, and Babylonians all made public spectacles of pitting prisoners against lions. In the East, criminals were killed by allowing elephants to crush their heads or pull them apart using their foot and trunk. In *Man Is the Prey*, James Clarke recounts second-hand a story of civil strife in Brazil in which the locals nicked the skin of their prisoners and tied them in the waist-deep water of a river filled with piranhas.[5]

The lore of execution is filled with the savage sights of bloody deaths wrought by the state and by various brutal rulers. Fifteenth-century Romanian prince Vlad Dracul—to whom the legend of Dracula has been traced— was responsible for multiple atrocities on the citizenry. Better known as Vlad Tepes (Vlad the Impaler), he spiked his victims on stakes arranged in geometric patterns and accorded each a high or low spear, according to his or her rank. From 1450 to 1750, a person was broken on the wheel on the average of once a day in the squares of Europe. This method involved strapping a person to a wheel and shattering the limbs so that they could be braided into the spokes, after which the person was left exposed. In some instances, the cries of the condemned evoked so much sympathy that their tongues were pulled out to silence them or drums were beaten constantly to drown them out. Henry Norman describes a Chinese execution ground, at which 20 or 30 men were beheaded on the same occasion: "The place is ankle-deep in blood, the spectators are yelling with delight and frenzy, the heads are like bowling balls on the green, the horrible, headless bodies lie around in grotesque attitudes, the executioner is scarlet to the knees and his hands are dripping."[6] In eighteenth-century Germany and Hungary, a perquisite of the official executioner was to sell blood from the criminal executed on the block as it streamed from the headless trunk.

Blood was also the backdrop for France's Reign of Terror, during which more than 18,000 men and women were beheaded. During the French Revolution, Madame Roland (executed in 1793) said, "The time has come which was foretold, when the people would ask for bread and be given corpses."[7] And they were given corpses in abundance: noblemen, noblewomen, soldiers, workers, the wives of laborers and artisans, nuns, priests, commoners, and servants. The number of distinguished victims kept Madame Tussaud and her uncle, John Christopher Curtius, busy modeling their severed heads in wax. The volume of the executions was so high (as many as 90 in three days) that three new cemeteries were established. The guillotine in Paris had to be moved several times when shopkeepers and residents complained of the foul odors. And the executioner's assistant, positioned at the front of the machine, was provided with a shield or mask to protect him from the spurt of blood as the head was severed. Even so, executioners appealed for an allowance for new clothing: "Our clothes are ruined in a very short time, in spite of the precautions we take to prevent, in some degree at all events, the terrible effect that executions have upon them."[8] Sometimes the guillotine was erected over a sewer, other times bran was used to soak up the large amounts of blood.

Like the guillotine, the electric chair used in America has a sordid history. Since its development in the nineteenth century, the amount of electricity required to kill has been determined by trial and error. Too much and the meat will cook on the body, too little and death will be less than immediate. In New York in 1889, William Kemmler became the first person to be executed by electrocution, but he continued to move when he was pronounced dead. Warden and witnesses screamed, and the current was turned on for another 70 seconds, which burned the body terribly. Opposed to the use of electricity for killing, George Westinghouse commented that prison officials "could have done better with an axe."[9] Death in the electric chair is supposed to be instantaneous (and therefore painless), through paralysis and destruction of the brain. The process is supposed to be complete within two minutes, during which the body temperature rises to 140 degrees Fahrenheit. According to Amos O. Squire, M.D., chief physician at Sing Sing prison, a signal is given for the switch to be thrown. The buzz of the machine and the lurching of the figure in the chair against the straps is accompanied by the smell of burning. The face turns crimson, and a wisp of smoke rises from the top of the head. After a few seconds, the current is cut off and the doctor listens for a heartbeat. The switch is thrown again.[10]

Hangmen used to pride themselves on getting it right the first time. They devised formulas to determine the length of the drop based on the weight of the condemned. Hands and feet were tied so that the body would drop like a plummet. The executioners also experimented with the thickness of the rope and the placement of the knot, all in an effort to cause instant unconsciousness by dislocating the vertebral column and rupturing the spinal cord. Hangings in which the subject strangles while struggling on the end of the rope or in which the head has been pulled from the body are considered botched, but taken in stride: "If they [hangmen] occasionally make mistakes, strangle instead of asphyxiate or neck-break or vice versa, or pull off an occasional head, such incidents are mere accidents. Do we not *all* sometimes get out of the wrong side of the bed of a morning?"[11]

Ropes are stretched in advance using weights to simulate a body, but even despite precautions they have been known to fail. When Captain Kidd was executed in 1701, the rope broke and he fell to the ground, but he was raised again and successfully hanged. The bodies of those who were hanged were left in place for the period of time indicated in the execution order. At Execution Dock in eighteenth-century England, the bodies of pirates remained hanging until washed by several tides. While Lord Ferrers, hanged for shooting his steward, swung from the noose for an hour, the sheriff and hangmen passed the time by having a picnic lunch beneath the gallows.[12] The Lincoln conspirators were allowed to hang for half an hour before being cut down and buried. Like those who are hanged, those who die in the gas chamber (first used in 1924) are left in place for an hour after execution. This both ensures death and allows time for fans to draw the gas out of the chamber and the tray beneath the chair to be flushed with fresh water. After the door is opened, the body is sprayed with liquid ammonia to neutralize any gas that collected in the clothing or bodily orifices.

The people on death row, as do those in other death contexts, fend off fear with what is literally gallows humor. They have been known to joke about being fattened for the kill when they put on weight under sentence of death. Some condemned men have found humor in puns. George Appel, electrocuted in 1952, quipped before his execution, "Well, folks, you'll soon see a baked Appel." James Donald French, put to death in the electric chair in 1966, said to a newspaper reporter, "I have a terrific headline for you in the morning, 'French Fries.'" An hour before he was to die in the gas chamber for strangling two women, Richard Cooper told the chaplain that he was going to college—he had donated his body to science. "'Tomorrow morning,' he said with an air of triumph, 'I may be staring up at the college students from a table in some classroom.'"[13]

Many who have been executed have made a valiant attempt to continue living. In past centuries, well-meaning hangmen would tug on the legs of a condemned man as he hung from the gallows to ensure, if the neck was not broken, that strangulation would be quick. After being reprieved and cut down from the gallows in 1705, John "Half-Hanged" Smith described his 15 minutes of agony: "He, for some time, was sensible of a very great pain, occasioned by the weight of his body, and felt his spirits in a strange commotion, violently pressing upwards: that having forced their way to his head, he, as it were, saw a great blaze or glaring light, which seemed to go out at his eyes with a flash, and then he lost all sense of pain."[14]

A 1951 study by Jessie Dobson published in *The Lancet* indicated that the hearts of 10 of 36 criminals dissected after hanging continued to beat, three of them for five or more hours.[15] Today death in Florida's electric chair is followed by an immediate autopsy in an adjoining room to guarantee that the procedure has resulted in death. When the still-warm body of William Kemmler was dissected, his brain was said to be baked hard and the blood in the head had turned to charcoal. More recently, the electrocution of Ted Bundy caused a ring of skin on his head to be cooked away and a large burn to form on his right leg from the electrode. Warden Lewis Lawes of Sing Sing, an opponent of capital punishment, suggested that the legally mandated autopsy adds insult to injury and noted that the other prisoners on death row could hear the noise of the drills and saws as it progressed.[16]

Although it didn't last long, momentary consciousness after execution was of great concern to the French. The guillotine did its work so quickly that the detached head was thought to have time to ponder its fate as it fell into the basket or was held aloft by the executioner. Doctors and medical students tested such theories of lingering consciousness with pinpricks to the lips, ammonia under the nostrils, and stinging solutions to the eyes. One executioner arranged for a condemned friend to signal him after being guillotined and received a wink after the blade fell. A German anatomist, S. T. Soemmering, collected anecdotes of severed heads that ground their teeth, grimaced, and bit each other as they lay side by side in the basket. "If the air still circulated through their vocal organs," Soemmering insisted, "these heads would speak."[17] According to a legendary story, the head of Sir Everard Digby did just that. After being beheaded for complicity in the Gunpowder Plot in 1606, his executioner removed his heart and exhibited it to the people, exclaiming, "Here is the heart of a traitor." "Thou liest," articulated the head quite distinctly. The lips of Mary, Queen of Scots, continued to move for a quarter of an hour after her beheading in 1587. The head of Charlotte Corday, guillotined in 1793, was seen to blush after being slapped by the executioner. A witness of an execution by guillotine wrote that the humaneness of the machine may be overestimated:

> It appears to be the best of all modes of inflicting the punishment of death, combining the greatest impression on the spectator with the least possible suffering to the victim. It is so rapid that I should doubt whether there was any suffering; but from the expression of the countenance, when the executioner held up the head, I am inclined to believe that sense and consciousness may remain for a few seconds after the head is off. The eyes seemed to retain speculation for a moment or two, and there was a look in the ghastly stare with which they stared upon the crowd, which implied that the head was aware of its ignominious situation.[18]

Charles Dickens wrote of a Roman execution by guillotine which he witnessed in 1845, noting that the eyes were turned upward immediately afterward as if to gaze at the crucifix instead of the bag into which the head fell. Nineteenth-century physician Dassy de Lignieres suggested that severed heads hear the voices of the crowd and see the guillotine while dying, contradicting the *British Medical Journal* of the previous year (1879), in which three doctors discerned no sense of feeling or sight in the severed head of murderer Théotime Prunier.

The scientific investigation continued into the twentieth century. In 1905, Paris physician Dr. Beaurieux conducted an experiment during the execution of Henri Languille by calling out the man's name after he was guillotined. At the first and second call, the eyelids lifted up naturally and the eyes fixed and focused on the doctor, but a third call provoked no further movement.[19] He concluded that the disembodied head may remain conscious for 30 seconds. Following decapitation, facial muscles will contract in response to inflicted stimuli and much can be made of the fact that brain cells do not die instantaneously. Stories are recounted of men who still clenched a pipe or cigarette in their mouths after decapitation and St. Denis was said to have walked to his burial place carrying his head in his hands after being beheaded. And even prior to the French Revolution, doctors speculated about the postmortem awareness of the bisected corpse.[20] But as late as 1956, two French doctors wrote that "death is *not* immediate. Every vital element survives decapitation. It is a savage vivisection followed by a premature burial."[21]

Although the ethics of capital punishment do not fall within the scope of this book, it is worth mentioning that there are some instances in which the execution of one body results in the death of two. In some of the United States, pregnant women can be legally executed, although in the late stages they are granted reprieve. In Villarcia, Paraguay, a judge sentenced José Lopez to death by firing squad in 1984 for a shotgun killing, even though it meant that his Siamese twin Alfredo—who had tried to stop him from pulling the trigger—would also be killed.[22] The bottom line of capital punishment is making at least one living, breathing individual into a dead body, as George Orwell so eloquently described in 1931:

> It is curious, but till that moment I had never realized what it means to destroy a healthy, conscious man. When I saw the prisoner step aside to avoid the puddle I saw the mystery, the unspeakable wrongness, of cutting a life short when it is in full tide. This man was not dying, he was alive just as we are alive. All the organs of his body were working—bowels digesting food, skin renewing itself, nails growing, tissues forming—all toiling away in solemn foolery. His nails would still be growing when he stood on the drop, when he was falling through the air with a tenth of a second to live. His eyes saw the yellow gravel and the grey walls, and his brain still remembered, foresaw, reasoned, even about puddles. He and we were a party of men walking together, seeing, hearing, feeling, understanding, the same world; and in two minutes, with a sudden snap, one of us would be gone— one mind less, one world less.[23]

Whether it is just or even humane, execution—like murder and suicide— is a deliberate killing, the production of a corpse by starving the body of oxygen, applying fire or electricity, poisoning with gas or lethal injection, removing the head, or several other more creative methods used over the centuries.

Murder

The body, without which murder is difficult to prove and grief difficult to resolve, is only so much refuse to most killers once they are finished with it. Although some may use it to convey a message to police or the public, most murderers hope that it will not be found and go to great lengths to prevent discovery. Bodies have been disposed of in whole or in part: pushed out portholes, dumped from planes, hidden under floorboards, burned in the furnace, or buried in the garden. Some killers get satisfaction from the continued proximity of their victims and others have been undone by their urge to revisit corpses for which they are responsible. The body that results from a murder can be a burden, an object of fetish, a means to taunt police, or a legal weapon against the guilty. The death may be denied even in the presence of the corpse, or it may be relived using the body as a mnemonic device.

One way murderers have disposed of their victims is by reducing them to smaller pieces. In his history of forensic detection, Colin Wilson maintains that it is almost impossible to dismember a human body with a knife without detailed knowledge of the joints.[24] But a surprising number of amateurs have succeeded at the task without too much physical or emotional effort. British serial killer Dennis Nilsen characterized his murders of young men as unpardonable and disgusting, but the disposal of the bodies as merely the inevitable consequence that flowed from them. From his cell at Hornsey Police Station, Nilsen wrote, "The victim is the dirty platter after the feast and the washing-up is a clinically ordinary task."[25] The technique of Ivan Poderjay was anything but ordinary. After swindling his new wife Agnes Tufverson out of several thousand dollars in 1933, he bought a large trunk, 800 razor blades, and a large quantity of vanishing cream. He drugged Tufverson, put her in the trunk, and smuggled her aboard a ship leaving for England. Once in his cabin, which at his insistence was just above the waterline, Poderjay opened the trunk and spent what would have been his honeymoon voyage slicing Tufverson's flesh from her bones and feeding it to the fish. Afterward he greased the skeleton with cold cream and pushed it, too, through the porthole. Richard Crafts of Newtown, Connecticut was less meticulous when disposing of the body of his wife. He carved her up with a chainsaw and sent the pieces through a woodchipper, leaving only three ounces of evidence including hair, bone fragments, a tooth, and a fingertip from which police were able to identify the victim. John George Haigh reduced the corpses of his victims with sulphuric acid that he poured into the London sewer system through a hole in his basement. And in the early 1980s, Rory Thompson dismembered and flushed his wife down the toilet.

Serial murderer Ted Bundy implies that he and his peers are underestimated when it comes to hiding the evidence. He calls killers very rational people: "The more people they kill, the better they get at disposing of the bodies....You only find the bodies that a serial killer wants you to find. There's plenty more you'll never find."[26] Larry Eyler of Chicago discarded the dismembered bodies of 23 male victims in the garbage bin behind his apartment house before he was caught in 1984. People who commit crimes of passion are less apt to cover their tracks. In *What Cops Know*, Connie Fletcher states that murder has one of the highest clearance rates of any crime because the obvious suspects make no attempt to camouflage the fact that the killing was committed. Some murderers, if they have the time, simply procrastinate until they are forced by circumstances to dispose of their victims. In the late 1850s, Mrs. Sarah Meteyard opened her home to unwanted girls, but forced them to work in her shop. When one of the girls attempted to run away, she was tortured in an attic for three days and died. Mrs. Meteyard continued to bring food up to her to convince the other children she was still alive. The woman then hid the body and told her wards that the girl had run away again. When the smell of the decomposing body threatened to contradict her story, she enlisted her daughter's help in dismembering the body and dropping the pieces—after unsuccessfully trying to burn them—into a sewer that ran into the Thames. After she and her mother argued, Sarah Meteyard confessed and the two were hanged.

More savvy killers, even when a homicide was not premeditated, find seemingly ingenious ways to dispose of the evidence, but their plans sometimes backfire. Brian Donald Hume rented a private plane in which to fly over the English Channel and drop parcels containing the body of Stanley Setty, whom he had killed for a small sum. The first two bundles containing the head, legs, and murder weapon were disposed of successfully. But when he went into a dive to drop the third parcel, which contained the torso, coal dust clinging to it from its temporary storage in a scullery blew around the cabin. The package was dropped, but floated on the surface. Seventeen days later, the torso was found and identified, and Hume was sent to prison in 1950. Other killers delay in getting rid of the body out of a bizarre comfort or delight in its retained presence. Cecil Maltby killed his lodger Mrs. Alice Middleton in 1922, after which he put her body in the bathtub, boarded it over, and used it for months as a dining table. John Wayne Gacy, convicted in 1978 and executed in 1994, inhumed 28 of his teenage victims in a crawlspace in his house, resorting to dumping an additional five in a nearby river only when the crawlspace became crowded. John Reginald Halliday Christie buried his first two victims in the garden, sealed three dead prostitutes in an alcove off the kitchen, and entombed his wife under the sitting-room floor after allowing it to lay in bed for two days. When a skull surfaced in the garden, Christie threw it into a bombed house, where it was assumed to belong to a Blitz victim. The thighbone of one of the victims, Ruth Fuerst, was used to prop up a weak spot in the fence. "I think he got some feeling of satisfaction in continuing to live in Rillington Place with the dead bodies nearby," said Dr. J. A. Hobson, consultant physician in psychological medicine.[27]

There is another breed of killer who finds immense satisfaction in using the body or parts of it to tease investigators, as a means of self-congratulation for deceiving them or perhaps as a subconscious attempt to get caught. In 1888, Jack the Ripper sent part of a human kidney in a letter to George Lusk, head of the Whitechapel Vigilance Committee, and threatened in a letter to the Central News Agency to clip off the woman's ears on his next "job" and mail them to police.

On January 4, 1964, police officers found a greeting card wishing them "Happy New Year" on the foot of the last victim of the Boston Strangler. Italy's unidentified "Monster of Florence," responsible for the deaths of 18 people since 1968, sometimes mailed the severed genitals of his female victims to police. Other killers have scrawled messages with their victims' blood or carved them in their flesh. Nineteen-year-old William Edward Hickman showed his contempt for the father of eleven-year-old Marion Parker, whom he kidnapped in Los Angeles in 1927. After receiving $1,500 in ransom, Hickman tossed part of his daughter's body at Parker's feet as he drove away. When convicted, Hickman received the death sentence. Still others joke nonchalantly about their crimes, as if indifferent to any consequences. After poisoning her first two husbands with phosphorus in 1957, Mary Elizabeth Wilson suggested to the undertaker that she had given him so much work that he should quote her a wholesale price. Mrs. Wilson was convicted the following year and died in prison.

Once a victim has been killed, perpetrators have several options. They can flee the scene and hope that no evidence culled from the body or surroundings will be traced to them directly or indirectly. They can flee with the body and dump it at their leisure in a remote site, such as a river or wooded area. Or they can dispose of the body hurriedly or meticulously by burning it, dissolving it, dismembering it, burying it, or simply hiding it. Francis Camps' biographer points out the difficulties the killer faces in the aftermath of a murder: "Murder, it has been said many times, is a comparatively easy exercise to carry out, but if the disposal of the body becomes an urgent necessity problems arise. Even when there is plenty of space for burial, such as fields, open spaces, moors and woodland, the task is seldom easy; but when the murderer is surrounded by bricks and mortar, as well as nosey parkers, it must be daunting."[28]

Whether to circumvent the necessity of carting the body away in sight of potential police informants or to retain the company of the corpse, there are those who provide a resting place for their victims in or around their own home. Several serial killers, including Dennis Nilsen, Harrison Graham, and Fritz Honka, let rotting corpses accumulate in their apartments. But some killers retain trophies or continue to consult the corpse for their own pleasure (two tendencies discussed in later chapters). Many killers view the corpses as nothing but refuse. Its sight may invoke pleasurable memories of the killing, but its eventual smell will demand more practical action than reliving the crime.

Suicide

Unlike the murdered or the executed, the bodies of those who take their own lives are the objects of special attention in the form of dread or disapproval. Suicides have traditionally been denied a Christian burial and have been subject to superstitious practices designed to prevent vampirism or haunting. The methods they use as a means to self-destruction are often frowned upon. By jumping from a height, they jeopardize those below. By throwing themselves in front of a train, they force the conductor to do their dirty work. And by shooting or hanging, they traumatize those who discover their bodies and clean up after them. Although suicide has been carried out with discretion, discrimination against its practice has led to the deliberate misrecording of this manner of death, leading to statistical underrepresentation.

Suicide has sometimes occurred in clusters, in which an initial suicide sparks others of the same kind in a community. For example, one after another youth may be found dead of carbon monoxide poisoning in the family car. One of the earliest documented suicide clusters took place in the Greek city of Miletus in the fourth century B.C. Maidens of the city hung themselves in a wave of suicide that could not be stopped by family or friends. The suicides came to an abrupt end when a law was passed prescribing that women who hanged themselves were to be carried to burial naked through the marketplace. Posthumous indignity (discussed more fully in a later chapter) brought to a halt what heartfelt persuasion could not. Ancient and modern history also have their stories of mass suicide, in which hundreds of bodies are left for the enemy to discover. In 73 A.D. at Masada, an entire community of Jews killed their families and themselves rather than become slaves to the Romans who besieged them. When faced with the 960 bodies, the would-be captors could only wonder at their courage. In 1978, Guyanese and American officials were left to wonder at the more inexplicable deaths of members of the People's Temple and to sort out their bloating remains. The bodies of Jim Jones and more than 900 of his followers littered the camp that he had created in the jungle and had ended with his order of ritual suicide, compelled by loyalty and threat.

Suicide on a large scale may provoke marvel, but on a small scale it often raises more fears than questions. Superstition and suicide go hand in hand. And the hand that had turned against itself was buried separately from the body in Athens, with both parts banished outside the city limits. An old European belief held that suicides did not sink. In the Middle Ages, those who had killed themselves were buried at a crossroads for two reasons: the heavy traffic would prevent their spirits from rising and the number of roads would confuse the ghost and hinder its return home. Sometimes additional means were used to keep the ghost down, including placing a stone over the face or the more drastic measure of driving a stake through the heart. It was not until 1823 that England outlawed this practice. From the sixth century, suicides were denied burial in sacred ground and if they were allowed in the churchyard, they were relegated to the north side along with strangers and illegitimate or unbaptized children. In the early nineteenth century, the family of a suicide was required to bury him or her privately late at night without religious ceremony. It was further believed that the bodies of suicides were exempt from dissolution until the church granted release from this curse.[29] Today some nurses refuse to touch the body of a suicide.

While the general public is no longer as superstitious about suicide, they find fault with almost every means by which suicide is completed. Jumping is thought to be especially inconsiderate: "They almost always splash down on a public street, traumatizing all sorts of innocent passersby. And there's always the chance of one of them landing on someone. Kids stand by and wonder what the body looks like under the sheet. If a Jumper goes from very high, his brain matter may fly down the block. Why subject people to that type of abuse?"[30]

Jumpers have in fact landed on others. The Officers' Mess at the Presidio in San Francisco was moved to a new location after too many disturbances caused by leapers from the Golden Gate Bridge. In what Greg Palmer insists is a true story, a husband who told his wife he had fallen in love with another woman was killed by the disconsolate wife when she leapt from their fifth-floor balcony—and survived. When a person jumps from a ship, as did author Hart Crane, the body is rarely recovered. When a suicidal individual throws him- or herself in the path of an oncoming subway train, the body is recovered—but only in pieces, causing trauma to the rescue workers, the commuters, and the driver who has been forced to take a life. Suffering can be both psychological and physical. A police officer recalled with bitterness cutting down the body of a hanged man and falling when the rung of the ladder broke: "He almost killed me. Killed by a guy who killed himself."[31]

Suicide to end physical suffering has not been looked upon so harshly. In a letter dated February 23, 1756, Benjamin Franklin gave his opinion: "That bodies should be lent us, while they can afford us pleasure, assist us in acquiring knowledge, or in doing good to our fellow creatures, is a kind and benevolent act of God. When they become unfit for these purposes, and afford us pain instead of pleasure, instead of an aid become an encumbrance, and answer none of the intentions for which they were given, it is equally kind and benevolent that a way is provided by which we may get rid of them."[32]

Euthanasia is encouraged by many when a body is no longer able to function. Passive euthanasia, carried out by withholding "extraordinary" treatment, can be directed by a person in a living will prior to incapacitation. Active euthanasia, on the other hand, often has legal consequences. Depending on state law, a person who carries out another's request to be killed—even to escape certain and impending death by disease—may be found guilty of assisted suicide. One who puts an unconscious terminal patient out of his or her misery may be found guilty of homicide. Euthanasia, like suicide, is a deliberate death, but often by proxy. Participatory forms of it are in general discouraged in favor of letting nature take its course.

In history and today, the acknowledgment of suicide has been withheld in order that the body may be treated with respect. For centuries, suicide precluded a churchyard burial. Today the act is condemned less on religious grounds and more for social reasons. Derek Humphry, a well-known advocate of active euthanasia, blames the media: "In the past forty years the news media has felt free to be much more explicit in reporting the seamier side of life and one of the results of this openness is that suicides of a particular gruesome nature have been reported (or are those remembered). Thus suicide often has a connotation of a sinister, degrading act when even its strongest opponents would have to agree that, however rare, it is not always so."[33]

Suicide may not be bloody or violent, but it almost always leaves survivors to blame themselves and to ask why with only a corpse for an answer. In some cases, the body is used to convey a posthumous message, usually of contempt or anger. In advocating his more distinguished forms of self-deliverance, Humphry continues: "People who have hanged themselves have often done so as an act of revenge against someone else, for the shock of finding a garrotted person is one of the worst experiences that could be inflicted by one human being upon another."[34] His argument is that practitioners of suicide or voluntary euthanasia should be provided with a method that is both practical and aesthetic. As psychologists and social workers examine the reasons for suicide in an effort to reduce it, family members and strangers continue to clean up after the handiwork of those who have chosen to leave their bodies behind.

The Proliferation

Buried with my own hands five of my children in a single
grave. Many corpses were buried so superficially that the
dogs dug them up and devoured them. No bells. No tears.
This is the end of the world.
  —Agnioli di Tura, an Italian during the Black
  Plague, recounted by Daniel Cohen, *The Black
  Death*[1]

Accident

Accidents often occur when a man or woman is using a machine, usually a machine intended to make life more efficient or more comfortable.
Since the invention of trains, people have been killed in them or in their
paths. Automobiles and motorcycles have taken more than their share of victims. Airplanes have taken fewer lives, but more at one time. Even the unsink-
able ship sank. Human creations explode, collapse, or catch fire, killing their
inventors, operators, or occupants. But people have also been known to explode
or burn spontaneously, they have drowned in puddles, and they have accidentally fallen, smothered, choked, or hanged. People have been killed at
work in mines or at play by wild animals. Accidental deaths in their many
varieties point out the limitations of the human body as well as the limitations of technology to safeguard life and, after an accident, to save it.

Viewing the body of an accident or disaster victim is often a necessary
evil. Family members called upon to identify the body are pained first by the
sudden death and second by the devastation done to their loved one. Identity may rest on a birthmark, a scar, or a piece of jewelry evident among the
remains. In past decades, as after the fire at Our Lady of the Angels School
in Chicago in 1958, viewing was restricted to fathers or male relatives of the
victims. Today those of both genders are given the opportunity. Despite any
mutilation, the chance to see the body—to say goodbye—is beneficial to most

155

people, some of whom find comfort in spending time with the body. In *When Disaster Strikes*, Beverley Raphael cites several studies which confirm this:

> There is ... a tendency to expect that the deaths of a disaster are more terrible, mutilating, and violent than other deaths, as indeed they may be, and thus to expect that seeing the dead will somehow in itself be inherently damaging. There is very little to indicate that this is the case, however, and much to suggest that *not* being able to see the body may in itself contribute to the difficulties the bereaved experiences afterward (Singh and Raphael 1981). Indeed, in those disasters where this aspect has been investigated, none who have seen the body have regretted doing so (Lindy et al. 1983; Lundin 1984; Singh and Raphael 1981).[2]

Denial comes naturally to relatives in cases of sudden death, but is quickly overcome by witnessing the victims before they are put to rest.

For workers, the luxury of denial is not an option. Images of bodies torn apart by the world's most destructive forces burn themselves into their memories as they literally pick up the pieces. Even medical men find accident and disaster scenes traumatizing. Dr. Shacknove, one of the first medical men to arrive after the explosion of two ships in Halifax Harbor in 1917, was so affected by the horrible sights that he hanged himself in his office as identifications of bodies and detached limbs continued. Raphael points out that many rescue and relief workers dehumanize the remains in order to carry on their tasks, postponing distress and grief until later.[3] A North Carolina paramedic commented that seeing people die every day tends to "chip a little off your soul." A trauma doctor notes that violent death is something one never gets used to:

> It's always the same. There is the initial wave of shock, of course, but with repetition this tends to pass quickly. Then comes the numbness. The wave of nausea. But these things don't stick, either. What stays glued to your memory, oddly enough, is the smell. The smell of fresh warm blood spilled from ripped body parts. It's so faint and distinct an aroma that, at first, you don't even realize it's there. You may not be aware of it for a few hours or a few days even. But it always catches up with you. Usually later when things are quiet and your mind drifts. It's a brain smell. A smell that goes straight to some deep primitive center of your cortex. It's a profoundly disquieting moment when the reality of that smell finally hits. It's a feeling you can never quite shake.[4]

Like so many others in close contact with death, emergency and disaster relief workers turn to humor to mask the horror, ease the stress, and make light of their own fears.

Accidents occasionally provide an outlet for a very grim sort of humor. The following inscription on a 1798 gravestone in Burlington, New Jersey, is quoted in numerous collections of epitaphs:

Here lies the body of Susan Lowder
Who burst while drinking a Seidlitz powder.
Called from this world to her Heavenly Rest
She should have waited till it effervesced.[5]

A man killed in a gunpowder explosion was immortalized with the words "He rests in pieces," another favorite of epitaph-hunters. The industrial revolution can be blamed for extreme cases in which the pieces are difficult, if not impossible, to salvage. In *Sudden Endings*, Vin Packer reports the fate of men who fell into steaming vats and were sometimes not missed for several days: "All but the bones of them had gone out to the world as Durham's Pure Leaf Lard."[6] In the early 1980s, John Ramsey's body was unfortunately sliced and diced when he slipped into a coleslaw maker at a Baltimore plant. In California, Arturo Crisostomo was crushed in a giant mixing bowl when a co-worker turned on the beater. A 34-year-old worker was minced to death in Alabama in 1993 when a giant meat grinder he was cleaning started up unexpectedly. An Irish garbageman was killed in 1993 when he was sucked into his truck and compressed with the refuse. Edna Buchanan reports an unbelievable case she came across at the morgue: "His job at a Hialeah textile factory had been to keep the knitting machines running no matter what. Working alone, overnight, he had to make sure that no threads caught, that nothing snarled the works. The next morning they found him tangled in the machinery—knitted to death."[7] Worse yet, when a worker accidentally fell unnoticed into a brickmaking machine in Boulder, Colorado, in 1981, his body was mixed into a batch of bricks that were being processed. The bricks from that batch were later buried at a local cemetery.[8] In all of these violent endings, the means are so ludicrous as to obscure the real tragedy of the death.

The tragedy of accidental death is perhaps most apparent on the highways. As public health campaigns stress the importance of wearing helmets and buckling seat belts, tens of thousands die of motor vehicle accidents each year. Emergency workers spend a good portion of their time freeing bodies from automobiles, both of which may be crushed beyond recognition, or ministering to those who have been flung out the window or through the windshield. In *Last American Heroes*, Charles Sasser paints a bloody picture of a driver who ran off the road and hit some parked cars:

> Pieces of human flesh as well as teeth, hair, and bone fragments smeared the Toyota's compacted interior. Blood from the male driver and his three passengers ... drenched the interior like someone had splashed the seats and occupants with a bucketful of it. What was left of the driver occupied the four inches of space that remained between the steering wheel and the back of his bucket seat. He sat folded into it with his neck twisted at an angle, like the possessed Linda Blair in *The Exorcist*, who could ratchet her head around on her shoulders. His passenger in the front seat next to him had

merged with the metal on impact. The dead man had knees where his ears once were, while a part of his skull rested on the dash and the rest of his head went into the glove compartment. He wasn't merely dead; he was deconstructed.[9]

As every pedestrian is aware, a person does not need to be an occupant of a vehicle to become its victim. Race car drivers know the risks they take at high speeds, but members of the crowd in Le Mans, France, in 1955 got more than they bargained for. When a Mercedes driven by Pierre Levegh of Germany jumped the barrier, 87 spectators were killed, many by being beheaded.

Some people have had to pay a high price for adventure, a price that includes not only their lives, but their bodies. While exploring a cave in France in the early 1950s, Marcel Loubens fell to his death when a clamp broke. His companions covered his body with stones and it remained in the cave until it was brought up at the insistence of his mother two years later and buried in his home village. When a swimmer is attacked by a shark, the body is even less likely to be recovered. Studies show that in 12 percent of frenzied attacks, bodies were not recovered.[10] Human remains have been found in the stomachs of many hammerhead sharks, according to another source, and the whitetip oceanic shark is known for attacks upon the survivors of air and sea disasters.[11] In *Beasts Beyond the Fire*, Michael Jenkinson recounts the discovery of an arm found in the belly of a shark: "The fingertips were too shriveled from immersion to yield easy prints. Yet by peeling the skin, inverting it, and chemically treating it to remove the wrinkles, the victim was identified."[12] Those who swim in certain rivers may become the prey of crocodiles, who are said to have particularly fetid breath after eating a human. There was no comment about the breath of a 45 foot python killed by a bulldozer in Sumatra and found to contain two whole human bodies.

Of all deaths by misadventure, drowning is the most fraught with superstition. Native Americans believed that if a loaf of bread weighted with quicksilver were dropped into a river, it would stop over the place where a corpse was lying. Another belief attributed to Native Americans is that a rooster in a boat will crow when it passes over a body. According to popular belief, bodies can be located underwater by floating a lighted candle on the surface or by firing a gun across the surface (said to cause the gallbladder to break and the body to rise). In truth, bodies tend to float because of gases produced during decomposition. American police have found that drowned men float face down, while women who have drowned float on their backs. In a survey of boating accidents on the Chesapeake Bay, researchers found that most recovered male corpses were found with their pants unzipped, indicating that they had fallen overboard while urinating. Monica Myers, on the other hand, was performing her duty as mayor of Betterton, Maryland, when she fell off a catwalk during an inspection of sewage tanks and drowned. Others drown when their ships sink, as did the mighty *Titanic*. The bodies of John Jacob Astor and 327 other victims were still being plucked out of the ocean by four recovery vessels a month after the April 1912 disaster.

Even when a body is recovered after an accident, it may provide little in the way of explanation. While the victims of structure fires are blackened and charred, the remains of victims of spontaneous human combustion are obviously burned, but leave few clues by which to deduce the cause of such intense heat and fire. In St. Petersburg, Florida, 77-year-old Mary Reeser combusted overnight in 1951 while sitting in an armchair. All that remained of the chair were a few springs and a blackened circle on the carpet. All that remained of Mrs. Reeser were a human skull charred to the size of a baseball, a backbone with a fragment of fiber attached, and a foot encased in a satin slipper. Reports of similar deaths stretch back hundreds of years. In the eighteenth century, Countess Cornelia de Bandi of Cesena, aged 62, was reduced to ashes. Her stockinged legs and her half-burnt head were found on the floor of her bedroom, and it was remarked that the air was full of soot. Several theories have been advanced to explain spontaneous human combustion, but all have been found wanting. As an "unexplained phenomenon," it carries a stigma which rubs off on fire investigators who challenge the official determinations that a stray spark or errant flame could completely ignite a human body and leave the feet intact in their shoes.

The victims of air disasters are often found in pieces, but even the pieces are in shreds. Rescuers who searched for bodies following the crash of a DC-10 in Antarctica in 1979 described horrific scenes of "heads with smashed faces, opened skulls empty of brains, bodies without feet, and corpses that were charred."[13] Smaller remnants were collected in plastic bags which were sometimes punctured by bits of bone, spilling their fleshy contents thick with aviation fuel and hydraulic oil. When Flight 427 crashed in Pennsylvania in 1994, the site was declared a biological hazard due to the amount of blood from the 132 victims. The remains which must be collected, identified, and disposed of are the stuff of nightmares. After Eastern Airlines Flight 401 went down in the Florida Everglades in 1972, the driver of a panel truck was gagged and sickened by his cargo—a load of severed arms and legs. Later, as an undertaker prepared the body of a pregnant victim of the same crash, he realized the woman's fetus had been pushed far up into her chest cavity.[14] After the Antarctic victims were transferred to Auckland, New Zealand, disaster victim identification teams were confronted with "charred, carbonized torso fragments with the majority of flesh singed, arms and legs badly gashed (usually), ankles broken, and feet either dangling or missing, the stumps badly lacerated, with varying degrees of skull damage.[15] When an identification team consisting of pathologists, radiologists, dentists, anthropologists, photographers, FBI fingerprint specialists, and administrative personnel was faced with the task of sorting out the 248 victims of a downed U.S. DC-8 in Newfoundland in 1985, they were able to identify 231 victims with standard methods and the remaining 17 with comparisons of personal effects, anthropological features, and the process of elimination.[16] In the 1988 explosion of Pan American Flight 301 over Lockerbie, Scotland, all but six of the 259 passengers, whose remains were scattered over an 845-square-mile area, were successfully identified. In addition to identifying the dead, forensic teams determine the cause and mechanism of death, test for the presence of intoxicants in the victims, search for evidence of explosives or other intentional trauma, look for preexisting disease, estimate time of death, and determine the last survivor in the deaths of spouses.[17]

Ironically, some survive airplane accidents only to die of conditions on the ground while awaiting rescue. When a small plane with three occupants crashed in the Sierra Nevada mountains in 1976, one passenger died shortly after impact. When Lauren Elder watched the other survivor die of hypothermia in her arms, she considered her own fate ("Jay had been talking to me and then he was dead.... It would be so very, very nice to be out of the cold. And it would be so easy"), but instead walked to safety. In 1962 a flight from New Jersey to Frankfurt carrying military personnel and their dependents ditched in the North Atlantic after losing power in three engines. Because of high waves, it took a Swiss ship over an hour to retrieve the 48 survivors from their life raft. When a colonel was finally able to reach his wife, who had been only six feet away in the overcrowded raft, it was too late. She was one of three who had died unnoticed during the five-hour ordeal.

People can withstand tremendous shocks, including plane crashes and car accidents, but they are usually no match for a train. In *Paramedic*, Paul D. Shapiro notes that despite its toughness and resilience, the human body is opened with no resistance by a subway train. "People can die, and no one on the subway would even be aware of it."[18] An Iowa medical examiner gathering parts from a pedestrian killed by a train had to search more than a mile of track. In a book about the search for a missing person, William Dear vividly describes the damage a train is easily capable of: "Two things can happen when a person argues with a train, each of them hideous. He or she can be smashed off the tracks and propelled through the air, a broken, mangled, shattered mass of flying debris, or he or she can be hooked by the train and be dragged along, here the head squishing like a watermelon, there the back torn open to the spine, then a leg or an arm sailing through the air."[19]

The blood-drenched scene of a 1977 rail disaster in Granville, Australia, which resulted in 83 mashed bodies, prompted a doctor to comment that although he thought he was used to death, the quiet deaths at home or in the hospital had not equipped him for the sight. Even the accidental deaths he had experienced had been cleaned up by the nurses before he saw them.[20]

Similar devastation has occurred in coal mines, known for their danger and for taking their victims hundreds at a time. When a mine in Monongagh, West Virginia, exploded in 1907, one body was mashed flat, another was blown into 20 pieces, and a third was untouched and sitting in place. These were only a few of the 5 to 600 men who died in the tunnels that day and had to be hoisted to the surface. A workroom on the grounds of the mine became a temporary morgue where three undertakers and 30 embalmers worked in shifts as burial boxes arrived from Pittsburgh and Zanesville, Ohio. Many of the victims were not identified. Thirteen days later, another mine exploded in Jacob's Creek, Pennsylvania, killing 2 to 300 workers. Men who had been standing had had the tops of their heads blown away. Authorities were able to identify many of the victims, but their methods were slow and the mine began to smell so bad that the horses employed to haul the bodies out balked at entering the mine. To add insult to injury, when mine workers reentered the Monongagh mine a year later, they found a human heart left in a crevice by the explosion.

Accidents cause destruction to the body, often leaving it less than intact. Sudden death, coupled with disfiguring mutilation, can cause devastation to the victim's family, which may be called upon to identify the dead or may choose to reinforce the finality of the death by a last look at the remains. Co-workers, too, may be affected, having perhaps found the body, or in some unfortunate cases having flipped the switch that set the macabre accident in motion. Rescue workers, hoping to find victims with the potential for survival may instead be required to scour the ground for body parts. Like natural disasters, accidents result in horrible images of the dead, scattered or entwined, singly or in groups. Unlike catastrophic storms or lightning bolts, accidents involving machinery can only be blamed on our own ingenuity and sometimes our misuse of it. Falls, drownings, and killings by animals may be foolhardiness or sheer bad luck. In any case, when death takes us unawares, it is likely to pull us apart or at least force some bloodshed.

Disaster

A disaster is defined as an occurrence of widespread destruction. Occurrences which qualify by causing mass loss of life include earthquakes, volcanoes, and the tsunamis ("tidal waves") which they often provoke; lightning, flooding, tornadoes, and other weather phenomena; and epidemics of deadly disease. Disasters prescribe their own set of circumstances, some particular and some shared. Lava and water may overwhelm those who try to flee. Earthquakes and avalanches may preclude or prolong the recovery of bodies. As with accidents, identification by scientists and viewing by the family may not be possible due to mutilation. The sheer quantity of corpses—sometimes numbering in the millions—may affect their salvage and those who carry it out. Survivors may in fact be so few, as in times of plague, that the dead must be buried en masse. The forces of disaster create a new landscape, one that is initially littered with human bodies, along with other debris.

Earthquakes have caused thousands of deaths, mostly due to collapsing structures. When a building falls, it takes extended resources and time to recover the victims and occasional survivors from the wreckage. By the time they are rescued, survivors have sometimes spent several days confined in a tight space in close proximity with the dead. Occasionally, workers have had to cut through a dead body to reach a living victim. After prolonged relief operations, workers don masks against the smell of decaying corpses they have not yet reached. In many earthquakes, a percentage of the dead are never recovered. A massive earthquake in Alaska in 1964 killed 115 people, 82 of whom were presumed dead because their bodies were not found. Two of the missing victims were twelve-year-old Perry Mead III and his two-year-old brother Merrell, who plunged from sight when a crevasse opened under them after they fled their house with two other siblings. In addition to stealing its victims away, earthquakes have brought forth corpses for which they were not responsible. During the San Francisco earthquake and fire of 1906, rumors spread that buried bodies had been churned up by the disaster, which was scattering putrid corpses among those seeking safety in cemeteries.[21] In the mid-twentieth century, an earthquake in Ecuador did unearth the dead, demolishing mass tombs and strewing human bones and skulls. In the town of Pelileo, however, there was no one taking refuge in the cemeteries, no one to repair the graves, no one to dig new ones—no survivors at all among the 565 inhabitants.

Tsunamis, like other disasters, are quite capable of both exhuming the dead and causing additional deaths. When a seismic sea wave hit the coast of Peru in 1868, the force of the water opened the tombs of the Andean Indians to eyewitnesses like Lieutenant L. G. Billings of the *Wateree*, which was anchored in Inique Bay: "We saw to our horror that the tombs in which the former inhabitants had buried their dead, in the slope of the mountain, had opened, and in concentric ranks, as in an amphitheater, the mummies of natives dead and forgotten for centuries appeared on the surface. They had been buried sitting up, facing the sea. The nitre-impregnated soil had preserved them astonishingly, and the violent shocks that had crumbled the desert-dry earth now uncovered a horrifying city of the dead, buried long ago."[22] In addition to revealing the already dead, the wave piled up new corpses 20 or 30 feet deep in some areas. Thousands of people who were killed by tsunamis that struck Lisbon, Portugal, in 1755 were given mass burials at sea, which grieved the clergy but prevented an outbreak of typhus. Tsunamis, given impetus by volcanoes or underwater earthquakes, cause tremendous human devastation, chronicled by survivors. After a seismic sea wave struck a lighthouse in the Aleutians in 1946, the Coast Guard searched in vain for survivors and recorded in their log, "Went to light station; debris strewn all over place. Piece of human intestine found on hill." The remains of the men were found a few days later, far from the lighthouse. Ironically, a tsunami is rarely evident to those at sea, since the wave crests and forms its wall of water close to shore. When an undersea earthquake occurred off the coast of Japan in 1896, the resulting wave wiped out the city of Kamaishi, but fisherman returning home the following morning were made aware of the disaster only after encountering miles of strewn wreckage and floating corpses.

Like earthquakes, floods sometimes swallow their victims, who may or may not turn up later. The flood in Johnstown, Pennsylvania, in 1889 pounded some of its victims deep into the mud. One reporter documenting the countless corpses in disarray noted that the hands of almost all the dead stretched above their heads in a last effort to grasp at a straw.[23] The fate of the dead caused those still threatened by the flood to ponder whether their own corpses would be found and if so, whether they would be recognizable. In his history of the flood, Willis Fletcher Johnson documents the disfigurement of the dead, not only by the ravages of the water, but by scavengers who cut off fingers to salvage rings and sliced off earlobes to obtain the diamond earrings.[24] After the Johnstown flood, bodies were brought to two emergency morgues opened at a schoolhouse and a saloon. Within a day six other buildings, including a factory and two churches, were also converted into temporary morgues. Supplies including quicklime and embalming fluid were brought by rail to Johnstown. A Pittsburgh train eleven cars long carried nothing but coffins.[25] Although hundreds of bodies will never be found, it is estimated that the flood claimed 2,209 lives and entirely wiped out 99 families. The official death toll does not include the 40 people who died of typhoid and others who survived the flood only to die of their injuries or of exposure. Soon after the disaster, bodies were recovered at the rate of 10 to 15 a day, which later slowed to about one a day. For years corpses were found in and near the city—two of them as late as 1906. The flooding of the Missouri River in 1993 caused few fatalities, but washed away several hundred graves from a Hardin, Missouri, cemetery. Many of the bodies recovered could not be identified and were buried in a mass grave.

The victims of the eruption of Mount Vesuvius in 79 A.D. were brought to light centuries later. Of the approximately 18,000 killed by the volcano, some 2,000 skeletons have been excavated in Pompeii. Archaeologist Giuseppe Fiorelli (d. 1896) was the first to inject plaster into the cavities left by the bodies of fleeing inhabitants when the six to twelve feet of lava overwhelmed them. The castings reveal people in their last moments, covering their own faces and trying to save their children, both universal themes in the face of death. Volcanoes kill in a variety of ways, since they can spew molten lava, hot ash or pumice, or poisonous gases. When Mount Pelée erupted in 1902, wiping out all but a few of the 28,000 inhabitants of St. Pierre, Martinique, the bodies of the victims had reddened and boiled from the steam and intensely heated air.[26] A. L. Koster, one of the first to photograph the results of the eruption, reported that the bodies of many of the victims were greatly reduced in size, as if the moisture had been suddenly extracted from them. The swiftness with which death overtook the island was evident by the attitudes in which the dead remained: a clerk bent over a ledger with pen in hand, a man leaning over a washbasin from which the water had evaporated, and a family seated at their table, some clutching at their scalded mouths and throats.[27] The eruption of Mount Saint Helens in Washington in 1980 had limited casualties because the danger zone had been closed by authorities on the advice of scientists. In Columbia in 1985, however, volcanologists were unable to convince authorities of the imminent danger of Nevado del Ruiz. Explosions melted its summit glacier, causing mud flows that engulfed the 22,000 inhabitants of the nearby town of Armero.

People have been overwhelmed by lava, ash, water, mud, rocks, sand, and snow. A few of the residents of a town in Switzerland were killed by flying rocks during an 1881 avalanche, but the remaining 150 were buried under ten million cubic yards of rock. During the blizzard in the eastern United States in 1888, a man trying to make it back home after attempting to get to work on foot tripped over a pair of booted feet sticking out of a snowdrift. He pulled out the body after much effort only to find that he was too late—the man was frozen solid. Harold Osterman said about his experience, "Maybe it was wrong, but I just left him there. I knew he'd be found eventually, and there wasn't a thing I could do except get myself killed trying to do something about a dead body. ... It took me about two hours to go back over the three blocks I'd traveled from my apartment."[28] The cold at least prevents decomposition until the bodies can be recovered. During the 1954 Hurricane Carol, Audrey Burkett recalled seeing two people staggering toward her in the blinding rain as she cowered in the ruins of her house. A board flew toward the couple as she watched and decapitated the woman. The victim's husband located the bloated body after the flood waters receded, but her head was never found.

The victims of tornadoes are found soon after the disaster, but often far from home and out of context. In 1953 two men were lifted in their car by a tornado in Waco, Texas. When the tornado set the car down gently, the body of a dead woman lay across its hood.[29] The tornado that cut across Missouri, Illinois, and Indiana in 1925 blew babies from their mothers' arms and caused a journalist to remark that the scene of devastation resembled a battlefield, except that the victims were mostly women and children. Most of the men were at work in the mines when the tornado hit, but farmer William Rainey of Parrish, Illinois, was blown more than a mile from his home and found dead with both legs broken, a broken neck, a hole in his head, and a severed right arm. The body of Mrs. Lem Lounis, also of Parrish, was found in a field a quarter of a mile from her home. Her body was crushed, so her relatives identified her by her red hair.[30] As victims were found, dead and alive, structures that remained standing were pressed into service as makeshift hospitals and morgues. Opal Boren, a child living in Caldwell, Illinois, when the tornado struck, reached home after being dismissed from school to find that her house had survived, but many of her neighbors hadn't: "And then there was people coming and going all the time, come and see if they'd found their loved ones, and they came and went till morning. Some of the dead had been laid out on what we called the front porch out there, where Mother had to identify some of them. But, well, they had nowhere else to take them."[31] Victims of tornadoes are most often killed by flying debris. Olive Deffendall of Baldwin Heights, Illinois, remembered that the woman who lived across the street had been knitting in a chair in front of the window and was decapitated by the glass when it shattered.

While seeing the pitiful and plentiful bodies of victims may punctuate the untimeliness of deaths caused by disasters, witnessing the victims of lightning strikes can be particularly disturbing. Some people killed by lightning have had their clothes torn from their bodies and bear signs of great violence. Others appear unscathed and in many documented cases remain in the position in which they died:

> Horsemen have been killed while their horses remained untouched and the dead riders have remained rigid in the saddle. A girl struck dead while picking flowers was found standing upright still holding a daisy in her hand, and a man who was killed while feeding his dog was found turned to stone, as it were, caressing a petrified pet with one hand and feeding it with the other. A strange story from France tells of eight reapers who were all killed instantly while eating a meal under an oak tree. People passing later were startled to see eight statues, motionless, but in the act of feeding. One had his hand in a dish, another was carrying food to his mouth, and a third still held his glass in his hand. Not even their expressions had changed. Their eyes and mouths were still open, and it was only the change in their pallor that made them look unnatural.[32]

Being killed by lightning is an eerie end and may cause a corpse to decay quickly or to remain rigid. Lightning victims were believed by the Greeks to be incorruptible, having been smitten by Zeus. They were sometimes left where they were struck and an enclosure built around them.

In times of plague, the dead were sometimes of necessity left where they fell, which only spread the disease. The Black Death is estimated to have claimed nearly 43 million lives—between one fifth and one quarter of the world population. Entire ship crews died at sea, their vessels drifting aimlessly in the Mediterranean and the North Sea carrying only corpses. The plague entered Europe in 1347 when the Turkish army besieged the Crimean port of Kaffa and hurled the infected corpses of their comrades into the town with giant catapults. In England the levels of the churchyards were raised several feet to accommodate the dead, and communal pits were used when the churchyards reached capacity. Reusable coffins, in which a hinged end allows the body to be slid out, made burial more efficient. In Athens in 430 B.C., the number of dead resulting from plague caused some to resort to stealing other people's pyres or adding bodies surreptitiously to those already kindled. An epidemic of bubonic plague in Europe and Asia in the sixth century reached a mortality rate of 10,000 a day in Byzantium. Justinian ordered the roofs removed from fort towers, which were then filled with bodies, drenched with lye, and roofed over. When all the towers were filled, the dead were loaded on ships that were rowed out to sea and abandoned or burned. During the Black Death, the pope blessed the river Rhone in France so that throwing bodies into it would be considered a form of Christian burial.[33] In nineteenth-century England, cholera victims were sometimes buried within ten minutes of expiring.[34] During the influenza epidemic of 1918, the volume of deaths required the mayor of New York City to recruit street cleaners to serve as gravediggers.

Such "acts of God" as earthquakes and epidemics do not inspire confidence in a benevolent creator. Bodies that pile up, threaten additional deaths, or resurface years after the event that killed them are sorry sights to behold and yet they occur time after time. Like accidental deaths, deaths due to disasters are untimely, without reason, and usually without warning. Unlike suicide or execution, we do not have society or the victim to blame. We cannot vent our rage on an existing killer because the killer—a wave or a lightning bolt—is often momentary, whereas the death is permanent. Natural forces take their toll hundreds, thousands, and even millions at a time. Repeated droughts in India and Africa have caused several million deaths. A single monsoon in China in 1877 killed an estimated 10 to 13 million people. Natural disasters leave a glut of victims in unnatural positions and their survivors questioning their faith, cursing the elements, or both as they try to pick up the pieces of their lives and bury those whose lives have been taken so ruthlessly.

Human Sacrifice

In the many varieties of human sacrifice, the body is an offering made in honor of something or someone. Children and adults have been sacrificed by force and voluntarily, their lives and lifeblood offered to gods and idols. Sacrificial victims were interred in the ground to ensure a good crop and entombed in the foundations of new buildings as a protective measure. Servants followed their master into the tomb to serve them in the afterlife. Lives have been offered to gain success in war or to stave off epidemics. More recently, Japanese kamikaze pilots pledged their lives to their country. And protesters have immolated themselves to draw attention to the injustices of war. The corpse of a sacrifice victim, symbolic of the sacrifice itself, is the object of respect and ritual.

Foundation sacrifice was practiced in Europe, Africa, and Asia to protect new buildings. When the body was interred during construction, the soul was believed to appease the local spirits. In Japan, before effigies were substituted for flesh and blood, victims were known as "human pillars." In the nineteenth century, an Ashanti king in Africa sacrificed 200 girls and mixed their blood in the mortar of the walls to make his palace impregnable. Like buildings, ships were also christened with blood. Both Vikings and Polynesians rolled new ships into the sea over the bound bodies of sacrificial victims to redden the keels. Human sacrifice has also been undertaken to ensure the fertility of the fields. An ancient tribe in India offered victims to their earth goddess by shedding blood and planting flesh in the fields to ensure good crops of tumeric. In some cultures, the fertility rite extends to humans: additional sons were ensured to a woman if her firstborn male child were killed. In India, the children of humble parents were killed so that the wife of an exalted person would thereby conceive.

In another variation on the theme, retainer sacrifice, followers willingly or unwillingly suffered death to serve their ruler in the afterlife. A Scythian king was buried with all the members of his royal household, including cooks, grooms, and butlers. Sixteen graves in the royal cemetery of Ur, dating from 2800 B.C., contained anywhere from 6 to 70 victims. In prehistoric Central America, kings were often buried with jesters and dwarfs to amuse them, women to console them, and priests to act as spiritual guides. In ancient Japan, as many as 30 servants of dead noblemen performed hara-kiri to serve their master in the afterlife, a custom which persisted into the seventeenth century.[35] During the funeral of Attila the Hun in 453 A.D., 500 mounted warriors cut their throats so that they could accompany him to the next world. The tombs of two Chinese kings were opened to reveal more than 100 bodies in each and such sacrifices continued into the thirteenth century. Five hundred men and women threw themselves on the pyre of the Indian king of Narsynga when he died in 1516. Until the late nineteenth century, the attendants of Ashanti kings were sacrificed during the preparation of the body for burial. The kings of Dahomey were buried with their soldiers, eunuchs, singers, and drummers. Like faithful servants, wives have also followed their husbands to the grave by practicing suttee and other customs both ancient and universal. While Indian women roasted themselves in the fire, their Chinese counterparts hanged themselves, cut their own throats, took poison, or leaped into chasms. In many countries and times, people have vowed to die to show their devotion. In ancient Rome, noblemen practiced "devotio," a ritual suicide, to show their loyalty to the emperor. Japanese

Kamikaze pilots in World War II flew their mission for their emperor and in the process gave up their lives by flying their planes into bombs enemy ships.

Another earlier form of ritualized suicide, seppuku, was popular until after World War II. Known in the West as hara-kiri, seppuku consisted of cutting one's own stomach with a sharp knife, followed by decapitation carried out by a companion.

Human sacrifice was an accepted and frequent ritual in many cultures. The Old Testament describes the burnt offerings of children to Baal. The ancient Greeks held potential victims, the Pharmakoi, in readiness for an annual festival or for special sacrifices to avert plagues, famines, or other disasters. Early Christians were ready and willing to die for their savior. Members of the Donatist sect that arose in the fourth century were so desirous for martyrdom, since it was the quickest and surest way to heaven, that the church declared them heretics to prevent great numbers of Christians from committing suicide.

The heretics of the Spanish Inquisition were put to death dozens at a time by order of Ferdinand and Isabella. At the autos-da-fé of the seventeenth century, victims were burnt at the stake or sometimes strangled and burnt. But perhaps the most prolific sacrificers, and definitely the most well-known, were the Aztecs, who killed thousands in 18 annual ceremonies. While arms and legs were held by priests, the heart was cut out and the body was rolled down the steps of the pyramid. Afterward, the flesh was cut into pieces and cannibalized. Skulls accumulated in racks, and remains were sometimes kept as relics. In a four-day ceremony in 1487, some 80,000 people were sacrificed.

While it is said that those chosen must be willing to die to make a successful sacrifice, victims have included the less than willing. In Egypt, redheads were burnt alive to guard against drought or pestilence. Conquered enemies were killed to honor gods credited with the victory. People have been sacrificed to serve as messengers to the gods: infanticide was carried out by Polynesians when great men died, so that the babies could serve as intermediaries. And the builders of tombs have been murdered upon their completion to prevent graverobbing. The king of Dahomey sacrificed hundreds each year in honor of his predecessor. In India, members of the Thuggee cult strangled victims to dedicate to Kali into the nineteenth century. The Human Leopard Societies of Sierra Leone, practicing from the seventeenth into the twentieth century, were comprised of killers who obtained ingredients for medicines from the bodies of their victims. Rather than compliance, the chief ingredient of human sacrifice seems to be availability. An abundance of prisoners of war, a glut of heretics, a ready supply of young pilots—any of these, killed with ritual and tradition, will produce bodies that signify that the soul or spirit has been given up for a cause.

War

In waging war, the goal is victory—the conquest of a people or a nation. The means is the large-scale and hand-to-hand killing of the enemy on both sides. The result is combat casualties—corpses—in abundance. The dead were counted in the past by an inventory of ears cut from their heads; later, ears became souvenirs of a tour in Vietnam. The soldiers strewn on the battlefield were cremated on the spot in classical times; in the modern world they are returned to their families. "It is necessary that our civilization build its temple on mountains of corpses, on an ocean of tears and on the death cries of men without number," said Count Gottlieb Von Haeseler. And civilization has. World Wars I and II produced the representative unknown soldier, but they also produced millions of known and unknown victims, both military and civilian. Although war has been classified as a natural disaster, it forces death into unnatural poses, overwhelming in their numbers and brutality. War, too, is a sacrifice, usually to a cause which can't be measured in individual terms except by the bereaved.

Enemy shells and bullets kill in an instant, sometimes discreetly and other times luridly. Colin Wilson mentions a French soldier who continued to hold his rifle after death and another, whose head had been blown off, sitting with a cup half raised to his lips.[36] The men in the trenches in World War I expressed their preference for death by a bullet rather than artillery fire, which would rip apart their bodies. The air raid on Dresden, Germany, in World War II blew people into treetops, and the firestorm generated a heat so intense that it shrank the victims to half their size. Civilians met their deaths from fire, asphyxiation, bombing, and flying debris. In combat, bodies are torn apart, in which case identification becomes a problem, or torn open, causing fellow soldiers post-traumatic stress disorder or a grisly curiosity: "Watching guys die is a drag, but there's a weird educational side to war, too. Like the first time I seen a guy's guts laying on top of him, as disgusting as it was, I said to myself, 'Oh, wow. So that's what they look like.' If you want, you can go in there and help yourself to a handful, you can wash them off and keep them. You can perform major surgery, right there."[37] The opportunity is not a new one. An eyewitness of the sacking of Antwerp by the Spanish army in 1576 related that the Germans had been burned in their armor in such a way that "you might look down into the bulk and breast, and there take an anatomy of the secrets of Nature."[38]

As soldiers become more familiar with death, newly initiated civilians remain horror-stricken. Survivors of the bombing of Hiroshima and Nagasaki reported that their strongest emotional reactions came from witnessing the dead and injured.[39] Margaret Freyer witnessed the bombing of Dresden in 1945 and spoke of the dead, dead, dead everywhere: "All the people lying so close together that it looked as if someone had put them down there street by street, deliberately."[40] For Frances Faviell, who helped to sort the piece-meal victims of the Blitz in Chelsea in 1941, it was like completing a grisly puzzle. Making one body almost whole left another with large gaps. Many pieces didn't seem to belong to anyone, and there were too many legs.[41] After prolonged exposure to the dead, even civilians can become inured. In his diary in 1941, Emanual Ringelblum, who lived in the Warsaw ghetto during the Nazi occupation, chronicled: "Death lies in every street... . The children are no longer afraid of death. In one courtyard, the children played a game of tickling a corpse."[42] War makes an unwelcome neighbor of the dead.

To some, though, the dead are a proverbial gold mine. War dead have traditionally been stripped of their valuables, including their clothes and boots, by their opponents or by scavengers. In addition, many cultures in the past made a practice of robbing the dead of their appendages for the purpose of making an accurate count of them. An Egyptian mural indicates that phalluses were collected after at least one battle. In the thirteenth century, Ghengis Khan's army killed all the inhabitants of the city of Nishapur in one hour. Their ears were cut off and proved that 1,748,000 had been slaughtered. At the end of the Ming Dynasty in China, Chang Hsien-chung ordered a massacre in Szechuan Province, after which he instructed soldiers to bring the ears and the feet of the dead to him to be counted. In feudal Japan, the Imperial Army employed soldiers whose only duty was to count the number of severed enemy heads after each battle.[43] Soldiers invading Korea in 1597 under Japanese warlord Hiyedoshi Toyotomi severed more than 20,000 noses to prove their kills. In the Balkan War of 1912–1913, the Montenegrins replaced the practice of taking the head as a trophy with cutting off the nose and upper lip, including the mustache. In Vietnam, cutting off the body parts of the enemy was less a counting aid than a status symbol: "We had a thing in the Nam. We used to cut their ears off. We had a trophy. If a guy would have a necklace of ears, he was a good killer, a good trooper. It was encouraged to cut ears off, to cut the nose off, to cut the guy's penis off. A female, you cut her breast off. It was encouraged to do these things. The officers expected you to do it or something was wrong with you."[44] The carnage of war seems to provoke the suspension of normal mores, including both the fear and mutilation of the dead. As the saying goes, familiarity breeds contempt.

While Charles IX of France (d. 1574) remarked that "The body of a dead enemy always smells good," Washington Irving wondered that anyone could look down on the grave of an enemy and "not feel a compunctious throb, that he should ever have warred with the poor handful of earth that lies mouldering before him."[45] As pitiful as the enemy dead may be, the victors are content to leave them where they fall unless they are in the way. During the sacking of Carthage in 146 B.C., auxiliary troops were sent in to clear the streets of debris and civilian bodies for the Roman infantry. Care, however, is taken with the bodies of one's fellow fighters. After battle, the task of both the victorious and the defeated is to dispose of the corpses of their respective comrades that litter the battlefield. The Chinese removed the dead and wounded from the battlefield in wheelbarrows. The ancient Greeks cremated dead soldiers on the battlefield and shipped the ashes home. According to Aeschylus, the bodies were incinerated individually and the ashes labeled and stored in separate urns.[46] Germans of the early nineteenth century also turned to cremation as a hygienic method to dispose of battle casualties. Prior to the 1800s, the threat of plague or cholera induced armies to bury the fallen on the spot in common graves, the officers being consigned to the nearest church.[47]

During the Civil War, American families began to demand the return of their dead sons, giving rise to the trade of embalming. In addition, the haphazard burial of bodies near Gettysburg, which were exposed with each rainfall, led to the establishment of the Graves Registration Unit to identify soldiers and reinter their bodies in national cemeteries. Half a world away from home, combat casualties have been buried in American cemeteries overseas by the military, which erects for each a wooden marker bearing name, rank, and serial number. Still, there is pressure to return the bodies to their homeland: after the Second World War, 225,000 bodies were exhumed and taken back to America. The first shipload arrived in San Francisco in 1947 carrying 3,028 caskets. In addition, unidentified bodies were removed from cemeteries in Europe, Africa, Hawaii, and the Philippines as candidates to lie in the Tomb of the Unknown Soldier. The Tomb, which contains an unidentified soldier from every war in American history except the American Revolution, had been approved by Congress in 1921 to represent the hundreds of Americans who did not return home from World War I because their identities could not be determined. Today the U.S. military has begun to store a small amount of genetic material from each service person so that a body—no matter how damaged—can be identified by genetic fingerprinting.[48] Although war has not been abolished, the unknown soldier has.

The Nazis cared little for their victims individually or as a whole. The dead men, women, and children of the German concentration camps were picked clean of their belongings (including their hair) and disposed of by their fellow prisoners in ways their captors determined to be most efficient. Their identities were extinguished in ovens and open pyres. The camps of Belzec, Sobibor, and Treblinka together produced more than 25,000 deaths per day. In assembly-line fashion, victims were stripped of their clothes, herded into gas chambers, and hauled away for burial or burning, typically within three hours of arrival.[49] Prisoners were forced to become part of the diabolically efficient machinery of the camps. Bela Katz, a prisoner at Birkenau, had to put the body of his own father in a crematory oven. The resulting ashes of the dead were raked through for gold fillings or jewelry and were used to surface roads in the camp or sold as fertilizer.

In a memoir of his forced work on the death brigade at Janowska Camp in Poland, Leon W. Wells writes of the smell of death, which he and the other men couldn't wash off their hands, permeated as they were from the daily task of manipulating the bodies of their neighbors and fellow prisoners. The men were forced to retrieve the already decaying corpses from shallow mass graves and stack as many as 2,000 into a pyramid for burning. Out of necessity they learned the properties of dead flesh: naked bodies burn more quickly than clothed ones, and fresh bodies more quickly than decomposed ones. The SS men also learned by trial and error that women burn more rapidly than men because their bodies contain more subcutaneous fat. Sergeant Major Otto Moll, the overseer of the crematoriums, devised drainage channels in the cremation pits so that the fat from burning bodies would collect in pans and could be poured back on the fire to speed burning. Experiments conducted at Auschwitz in 1943 to save fuel concluded that the best oven load consisted of one well-nourished adult, one child, and one emaciated adult. Once it caught fire, this combination would continue to burn without requiring more coke.[50]

The men at Janowska Camp also learned to discern cause of death: open mouths with projecting tongues and bodies without bullet holes indicated that the victims were buried alive. Wells reports that a recognized face in the pile gave rise to stories about the life of the deceased. On the other hand, the members of the death brigade were able to distance themselves—mentally, if not physically. They sometimes sat on the corpses they would later burn as if they were benches, and their breakfast arrived on the same truck with the new corpses from the camp. Of the brigade members Wells recalls, "Their hands are caked with the fluids from the corpses so that one cannot differentiate between the flesh of their hands and the flesh of the corpses."[51] The prisoners and the dead were referred to by the Germans as "figures" and were for the most part indistinguishable from one another, the living being one step away from the dead they disposed of. "The fire is burning," writes Wells, "the smoke stings our eyes and the smell chokes us. Some of the bodies in the fire have their hands extended. It looks as if they are pleading to be taken out."[52] The world for the Jews and others persecuted by the Nazis was turned upside down as the living dead did away with the dead who appeared to live.

Like other causes of death deliberate and incidental, war has been described as hell. The history of war is the history of making corpses, face to face or from a distance, tens, hundreds, thousands, and tens of thousands at a time as weapons grew more advanced. "I spend 30,000 men a month," boasted Napoleon. The images of war are unsightly numbers of bodies, heaped in disgrace and robbed of clothes and often identity; victims innocent except by religion or nationality, bombed in their homes or driven out of their communities and shot; deaths of the young, armed with rifles, bayonets, and gas masks to kill their peers. In reality, making the "ultimate sacrifice" is much less romantic than it is depicted in poetry or movies. The words of war are equally unappealing: soldiers may be used as "cannon fodder" and the resulting scene described as a "slaughterhouse." Two words, "megacorpses" and "megadeath," have been necessitated by the development of atomic weapons, in which casualties are referred to by the millions. A government agency, the Civil Defense Mortuary Service, was even set up to handle the abundance of corpses in case of a nuclear attack. It is one thing to talk abstractly about— and even to plan for—human casualties and another to aim the rifle, throw the grenade, thrust the bayonet, or drop the bomb. Even so, Robert Payne envisions that "As long as there are military elites there will be massacres, and we cannot hope that they will be shocked into sanity by the sight of the dead."[53] The dead are merely the means to an end.

THE RECYCLING
OF THE CORPSE

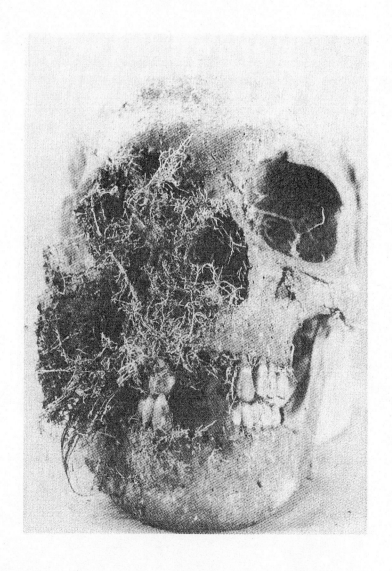

The Resuscitation

The freshly dead will, on occasion, move. Although such movement is usually limited to reflex twitches, perhaps the bending of a finger, or even the flexing of an elbow, it is not unheard of for a body to make a significant movement, like sitting up.
—Joseph Sacco, *Morphine, Ice Cream, Tears: Tales of a City Hospital*[1]

Denial of Death

Resistance to death is found among the bereaved in both anomalous and cultural situations. Kings have remained enthroned long after their hearts have stopped beating. Families have retained corpses in their homes while convincing themselves that their loved one is just sick. Corpses have been propped up to give the appearance of life and spoken to as if they had never died. To govern their posthumous existence, the dead are awarded legal rights which rival those of the living or extend to next of kin. In addition, bodies have been "rescued" from the fires that killed them, they have been the object of love letters, and they have in fact been married—to the living and to other corpses. Concurrently with the refusal of the living to accept death, corpses stage their own denial. The heart continues to beat after the brain has died, and the cells continue to live for a time after even the beating stops. The dead retain reflexes which may cause them to move or even sit up. And in the most extreme cases, female corpses have given birth.

When a death is acknowledged, grief often requires an interim period during which the life is mourned in the presence of the body. In many cases, the wake and funeral serve this purpose and sometimes include the spectacle

Part IV title page: **Roots growing in the facial area of a cranium found at the side of a road in Massachusetts. Photo courtesy of the Smithsonian Institution.**

of a widow throwing herself upon the casket in a last embrace. Some families take the opportunity before the viewing to help dress the body. In other instances, the hospital is the setting for a last goodbye: "One recent study of behavior regarding the dead in hospitals notes the common tendency for family members to continue to speak to and caress the recently deceased as a manifestation of their refusal to readily accept the death of one so close."[2] Affection shown to the body immediately after death may be less a denial than a postponement of the inevitable separation of the living and the dead. Spending a few minutes alone with the body allows the family to absorb the fact of the death gradually and together before facing the public with the news.

At other times, there is an outright refusal of the mind to admit the fact that the death of a parent, a child, or even a stranger has occurred, even when it is obvious. Being under extreme stress induces some people to prolong efforts to save a life that is far beyond saving. In many cases, parents intent on saving their own lives and those of their child reach safety only to find that they have been carrying a dead body. When Anne Wahle fled the burned-out city of Dresden by train with her children, she sat across from a woman holding a large suitcase on her lap. When the conductor attempted to take the bag and place it in an overhead rack, the woman became hysterical, the bag came open, and the charred body of a baby rolled out onto the floor.[3] In his book on arson, Peter Micheels notes that members of the fire department rescue even the bodies of people whose heads have been split open in the vain hope that they can be saved. Paramedics arriving at a home where a baby has died of sudden infant death syndrome must make a choice: they can leave the body there and let the family face the death immediately or they can rush it to the hospital, giving the parents false hope and delaying the process of acceptance.[4]

In spite of the ministrations of doctors, some people—yesterday and today—cling to the hope that retaining the body is the equivalent of retaining the life. Sir John Price (d. 1761) had the body of his first wife embalmed and allowed it to share the bed with him and his second wife. His third wife objected to sharing the bed with her two predecessors and insisted they be buried. Henrietta, duchess of Marlborough, became deranged at the death of her lover, English playwright William Congreve, in 1792. She had his death mask attached to a life-sized mannequin, which she dressed, conversed with, lay in bed with, and was buried with. Rather than resorting to an effigy, Pedro I of Portugal exhumed the body of his mistress, Inez de Castro, a few years after her murder in 1355 so that she could receive the honor of queen. The body was propped up on a lavish throne, securely tied, and garbed in regal robes. More recently, people have chosen to postpone disposal of the corpse to await possible revival. A Belgian family was found in 1989 to have kept the body of a 30-year-old diabetic daughter in the bedroom for 10 months awaiting a miracle cure for the disease. A Knoxville, Illinois, family kept the body of their father in the house for eight years, believing he was just sick. Sheriff Mark Shearer commented, "Let's just say they have abnormal beliefs in the power of healing."[5] Others, for whatever reason, have neglected to bury their dead, preferring their continued company: a 53-year-old woman of Gainesville, Florida, whose mother's body had lain for ten years under a blanket on the couch, a 65-year-old man who kept the corpse of his 89-year-old mother for a year and was found shot next to her body, and a 74-year-old Oklahoma man who retained his mother's corpse for four years after her death.

While some people do not want to admit a loved one's death personally, rumors feed the fires of the many who choose to disbelieve the death of a public figure. Adolf Hitler was believed to have escaped his fate at the end of World War II by flying to Spain or South America. James Dean was rumored to have survived his car accident in 1955 and to have been maintained in a coma in an Indiana hospital. John F. Kennedy was said to have survived his bullet wound to the head and been transferred to a top-secret wing of a Houston hospital (or to Alaska or the Swiss Alps or the Onassis mansion in Greece). And sightings of Elvis Presley, who died in 1977, continue to this day.[6] In contrast, many notables have "died" prematurely. Mark Twain's published obituary shocked him, and he quipped, "Reports of my death have been greatly exaggerated." And astrologer and almanac compiler John Partridge was put in the position of proving himself alive after his contemporary Jonathan Swift announced his death and published his epitaph in 1708.

Aside from misprints and wishful thinking, the body itself may feign death (as discussed in the next section) or to some extent ignore it. The human body can survive without the stomach, spleen, most of the liver and intestines, one kidney, one lung, and almost every organ from the pelvic and groin area.[7] Even when pieces are removed traumatically rather than surgically, the body struggles on. Former police officer Anne Wingate reported seeing a man whose lungs continued to work for half an hour after his brain had been blasted from his skull by a shotgun.[8] Once the body has been overcome by death, small parts of it live on for a time. Many cells continue to grow and replicate. Physiologists discovered that the sperm of guillotined men lived on for 24 or more hours. And some reflexes continue to function, resulting in almost unbelievable stories about corpses sitting up. When Jean-Antoine Chaptal assisted in the private dissection of a cadaver in 1893, the subject lifted his right hand to his heart and moved his head at the first thrust of the scalpel.[9] A report from Cincinnati, Ohio, in the late nineteenth century details the posthumous actions of a man who died of a gunshot, which included sitting up, raising his arms, shaking his fists, lifting his legs, clapping his hands, winking, and standing up. In her book on vampires, Manuela Dunn Mascetti writes:

> Within the throat and trachea regions of the body there are certain chem-
> icals and fluids that continue to function after death. The body has its own
> post-death system which continues to work, preparing the corpse for its
> deterioration and decomposition. Among these fluids there are some that,
> after the rest of the fluids have dried up, contract at a later point, drawing
> the other organs into this "dance" of contraction. In effect, the muscles and
> tissues within the stomach and lower digestive tracts are reduced and in this
> process the body arches forwards into the sitting position.[10]

Exaggeration, in addition to chemical processes, may account for some of the
perceived motion, although the moving of fresh bodies is a documented phenomenon.

Even when removed from the body, human tissue can continue to live.
Scientists have found that amputated cadaver fingers show growth of the
fingernails, and an injection of pilocarpine into the arteries of the fingers
results in the excretion of sweat.[11] There is considerable controversy in the
medical literature and folklore, however, about the continued growth of hair
in the grave. It is agreed that hair is one of the most indestructible of human
tissues, remaining intact long after the skin has vanished. It is not destroyed
by changes of climate or water and is resistant to many chemicals. But scientists find reports of hair-filled tombs to be fanciful, despite their numbers.
In one story, Colonel Morland of Napoleon's army was noted for his lush,
drooping mustache. After he was killed in action, his body was returned to
Paris in a barrel of rum. When the barrel broke some time later, the mustache was said to have grown to waist length. In his treatise on beards, Reginald Reynolds includes a report by Wolferus of a Nuremberg woman whose
grave was opened after 43 years, at which time hair was found growing
through all clefts in the coffin.[12] Plato and Democritus held that the growth
of the hair, beard, and fingernails in the tomb is caused by the soul, which
lives for a certain time close to the body. Forensic anthropologists and others claim that the hair only *appears* to grow as the skin shrinks around the
follicles. And yet a voice from the American Medical Association proclaims:
"Long after I have been pronounced physiologically dead and the mortician
has set me in the ground, I remind you that cellularly I am still alive. My
fingernails grow, my hair grows for three to six weeks, and it is a long time
before I return to dust." (Reverend Paul McCleane, Presbyterian minister,
director, Department of Medicine and Religion, American Medical Association).[13] If they do not agree that hair grows after death, scientists will at least
accede that it is one of the last parts of the body to disintegrate.

The uterus is also said to be resistant to decay, and the death of a pregnant woman does not always preclude the birth of her child. The *Guinness
Book of World Records* reports the longest recorded interval in postmortem
birth to be 80 minutes. Fanella Anderson was found dead at 11:40 P.M. on
October 15, 1966, and her son was delivered by Caesarian section at 1:00 A.M.

the following morning. In earlier times, opening the bodies of dead pregnant women was compulsory because of the possibility of delivering a living child. According to myth, Asklepios, the Greek god of medicine, had been cut out of his mother's body after she was killed on Mount Olympos. St. Peter Nolasco was believed to have been taken from his mother's womb after her death in labor in the thirteenth century. The posthumous Caesarean section was supported by the Catholic church, and priests were threatened with excommunication if they buried pregnant women before this operation. Delivery has also occurred spontaneously, both before and after burial. Gorgias of Epirus was born during his mother's funeral. In the Derbyshire parish register, it is recorded, "April ye 20, 1650, was buried Emme, the wife of Thomas Toplace, who was found delivered of a child after she had lain 2 hours in the grave."[14] In 1890, Lavrinia Merli was discovered two days after death to have given birth to a baby of seven months gestation. After dying of yellow fever in 1901, Madame Bobin was exhumed and found to have given birth in the coffin. In most of these cases, the delivery is discovered too late, and the child has died. According to one account, which includes neither date or place, a man who had been away when his wife died ordered her body exhumed and discovered an infant in the coffin which lived long afterward under the name of "Fils de la terre."[15] Perhaps the most extraordinary story of posthumous birth is that of a woman hanged during the Spanish Inquisition in 1551. Four hours after her execution a child (or according to another source, two babies) dropped from her womb as she hung from the gallows.

Men, too, have fathered children posthumously by donating their sperm. In addition to giving birth after death, women and men have been married posthumously. In China, from ancient times to the present, families have joined the unmarried dead in matrimony, placing single men and women in the same grave. The Romans were said to have provided a dead woman for every ten dead soldiers to serve as a camp-follower in the underworld. The living have also been wed to the dead in ancient and modern times. The Chinese allowed a man to marry a deceased woman, after which he would be considered a widower and would customarily take the dead woman's sister as his wife. When a young Masai warrior dies unmarried and without children, the family sometimes finds a bride for the dead man so that a child she bears by any man she wishes will inherit the property and name of the deceased.[16] In 1984, after months of legal struggle, a French woman was allowed to marry her fiancé, a police officer who had been shot to death in the line of duty. She held his picture as the ceremony was performed. With or without the formal rite, love affairs have been carried on beyond the grave. A year after the death of James Dean, the studio was still receiving 8,000 letters per week addressed to him from his fans.

While they are beyond any ability to act, the dead are accorded legal rights or specifically excluded from performing certain functions in many jurisdictions. A dead person may not serve on a jury, according to Oregon law. To arrest a dead man is unlawful in Maine, and to arrest him for a debt is a misdemeanor in New York. Although the decision has been challenged in at least two states, corpses cannot be counted as passengers to fulfill HOV-lane requirements. Lithuanian anarchist and social reformer Emma Goldman fared better as a corpse: she was allowed to return to the U.S. for burial after having been deported in 1919 as an illegal alien. The dead have been held accountable posthumously for centuries. Ninth-century Italian pope Formusus was put on trial after death, as was St. Thomas à Becket, archbishop of Canterbury, in the twelfth century; John Wycliffe, fourteenth-century English religious reformer; Joan of Arc in the fifteenth century; and Nazi official Martin Bormann in the twentieth.[17] In France, where laws apparently differ from those of Oregon, sixteenth-century outlaw Raymond Gui was placed on trial before a jury comprised of the shrouded bodies of three of his victims. He was convicted and executed.[18]

In a few cases, people have willed (or willed to) their own bodies. In 1890, a man signed a contract with the Caroline Institute in Stockholm to donate his body for dissection after death. When he tried to buy it back in 1910, they refused so he sued. He lost and had to pay damages to the doctors for having two teeth pulled without permission.[19] In the early twentieth century, a Frenchman bequeathed his entire estate to his corpse, to be expended for preservation of the mortal remains and the adornment of his mausoleum. In his case, the will was declared null and void by the court after being contested by his heirs. In most lawsuits, the next of kin or heirs are necessary to uphold the rights of the dead, such as the right of a child who dies in the womb as a result of an accident and sues for damages. Misidentification is often grounds for a lawsuit by family members. Four children were each awarded $500 by a Brooklyn hospital after it mixed up the bodies of two elderly widows. Beatrice Daigle of Rhode Island filed a $250,000 suit against her church after it was discovered that her husband's grave, at which she had been praying for 17 years, contained the body of a woman. Her husband's body was located, and the case was dismissed in 1979.

The effect a botched funeral or burial has on the deceased and the survivors often spurs litigation. A woman in New York City sued a funeral home for $10 million for the shock and emotional distress she experienced upon viewing the body of her six-foot, two-inch husband crammed into an under-sized casket and looking "as if his neck had been broken."[20] A Brownsville, Texas, family sued a funeral home after employees dropped the casket of their stillborn child, causing the baby to roll across the floor to the feet of the grieving family. The family of David Patterson was awarded a $1,500 discount on his funeral when the driver of the hearse was two hours late getting from Houston, Texas, to Bertainville, Louisiana. The funeral home is often the setting in which mistakes are discovered. When two women were involved in a car crash in Decatur, Indiana, the family of the dead victim granted permission to end life support efforts for the surviving victim they had been told was their daughter. The switch was discovered by a friend who viewed the body at the funeral home.[21] At Sisk Brothers Funeral Home in Connecticut, a family discovered the body of a stranger in the casket at the viewing. Their loved one had been mistakenly cremated. The funeral home filed a complaint against Yale–New Haven Hospital, claiming that the bodies of two men who had died on the same day had been tagged incorrectly.

The morgue is another location where misses and near-misses have occurred. The supervisor of a hospital morgue explains:

> You'd be surprised how many people forget to look at the name on the body. We had a case like that where we were doing a newborn baby. The resident was in the middle of cutting it open when I came over and checked the authorization. The baby we were supposed to be doing had died in open-heart surgery, but this baby had no surgical incision. It was also the wrong sex.... Fortunately we had a disposal permit. We do disposals for families — we cremate the infants. So we cremated the baby we did by mistake and then went ahead and did the autopsy on the right one. So nobody knew and nobody got upset.[22]

The family of a dead man victimized by a confessed necrophiliac were highly upset. They sued the 23-year-old woman and the Sacramento mortuary she worked for in the 1970s and were awarded $142,500. Legally, bodies have been fought over as well as fought for. When French Sergeant Aimé Druon was killed in 1952, his body was claimed by his natural parents and by the family that had taken him in at age 15, but hadn't legally adopted him. A 1959 decision ruled against the foster parents, but a 1963 decision by the supreme court of appeals reversed the earlier decision.

Life persists after death in numerous ways, above and beyond the metaphysical. The living try to will the dead back into existence by keeping their physical forms on hand. Bodies may be the subject of lawsuits long after they are buried. Burial may depend on who the corpse has been engaged to by next of kin, and exhumation may be called for if one's widow or widower has been crowned. Furthermore, the body itself does not relinquish life easily. Cells reproduce and a woman who has already reproduced may deliver her baby in the grave. A corpse that twitches or even sits up before autopsy or burial is grounds for a horror story, but the true horror begins not when the dead mimic the actions of the living, but when the living are mistaken for dead.

Premature Burial

In contrast to denying that a body is dead, some assume so incorrectly. People in a coma or trance were often mistaken for dead before the advent of the electrocardiograph (ECG) and electroencephalograph (EEG). Exhumations revealed that premature burial was a frequent occurrence. Even with the technology of the modern day, surprised people have awakened in the morgue. To prevent the usually irremediable error of burying the living, the people of the nineteenth century connected signaling devices to the grave, ordered the mutilation of their bodies in their wills, and placed the dead in "waiting mortuaries" to guarantee that life was extinct. Corpsehood is often anticipated, as when hospital personnel prepare a moribund but still-living body for removal or plague victims lay down in their graves to circumvent remaining unburied. But in earlier times and today, it is sometimes anticipated too eagerly.

Bodies showing no signs of life are assumed to be dead, but this is not always the case. In *Death Is a Noun*, John Langone catalogs several conditions that can cause a deathlike trance: asphyxiation, catalepsy, epilepsy, cerebral anemia, apoplexy, smallpox, cholera, shock, influenza, freezing, and being struck by lightning.[23] The 1896 book *The Encyclopedia of Death and Life in the Spirit-World* chronicles (through his unquiet ghost) the predicament of a man wrongly declared dead in Europe and placed in a casket for transport back to his American homeland:

> Picture to yourself, if you can, the horror of his position. The mind—the man—fully alive to all that was being done about him, but unable to make known his condition through the avenue of any of the senses. He knew when they first pronounced him dead. He understood their conversation when the question of the disposition of the body was being discussed; and he realized what was taking place when his body was being laid in the casket, and when the lid of the casket was being fastened. Imagine the terrible mental suffering of that man as he lived through those awful hours.[24]

The body of a man who became paralyzed after eating puffer fish in the 1880s was put in storage for a week pending burial. He awoke before the interment and reported that his mental faculties had remained intact throughout his ordeal and that he had greatly feared being buried alive.[25] Two days after an explosion in Halifax Harbor in 1917, William King regained consciousness in the mortuary, but was unable to alert the attendants until he was finally able to signal with his arm.

When a person has mistakenly been determined by a doctor or layperson to be dead, he or she faces the unfortunate and frightening prospect of waking up in a facility, vessel, or position reserved for the dead. Examples are both ancient and modern. Pliny the Elder reported that Acilius awoke on his funeral pyre. Fourteenth-century Italian poet Petrarch was almost buried after being in a trance for 20 hours. French General Baptiste de Montmorin (d. 1779) was pronounced dead on the battlefield five times and revived each time as he was about to be interred. In this century, Helen Francoeur, aged

82, of Massachusetts was hospitalized for dehydration and revived in a funeral home. A hypoglycemic Charles Herrell, aged 56, of West Virginia awoke in a body bag in a funeral home in 1980. Eighty-seven-year-old Carrie Stringfellow of Ohio and 37-year-old Frederick Kerr of New Zealand woke up just prior to being embalmed in 1989 and 1986 respectively.[26] A few patients have come close to having their organs harvested before they are ready to be divested of them. Thirteen-year-old Julia Braden of North Carolina revived as Dr. Thomas Rusk was about to remove her eyes and kidneys, which had been donated on her behalf by her father.

Some unfortunates betray signs of life on the slab, but their breath is cut short by procedures which—intended for a corpse—are fatal. A Parisian actress awoke from a trance in 1858 after embalming had begun only to die ten hours later as a result of the chemicals that had been injected into her veins.[27] The supervisor of a hospital morgue confessed in *Hospital: The Hidden Lives of a Medical Center Staff* that an old woman was discovered to be alive after the autopsy on her had begun. The Y-incision resulted in heavy bleeding and the patient breathed for several minutes before expiring.[28] When the cold, stiff body of a man was found in the woods in 1763 and brought to a surgeon, the autopsy incision both revived and killed him. An earlier precedent was set when Vesalius autopsied a man whose heart was still beating. In Virginia in 1889, the father of a young girl stabbed her in the chest with a knife to prevent her premature burial. She had only been in a trance, but the stab wound killed her.[29] Occasionally, attempts to ensure death have had the opposite effect. After Ann Green was hanged at Oxford in 1650, it was noticed that she was still breathing. A man stamped with all his force on her breast and stomach to put her out of her misery, but this served to revive her and she is reputed to have lived for many more years.[30] Margaret Dickson was hanged in Scotland in 1728, and her body was transported to her hometown. When the drivers stopped for a meal, they noticed the coffin shaking and found the woman alive inside. She was not hanged a second time.

But if a person has not awakened before burial, interment—like autopsy and embalming—is often fatal. The available air in a sealed coffin has been estimated at no more than three or four cubic feet, enough for only about 20 minutes.[31] Researchers estimate that many who were buried before embalming was common were buried alive, giving credence to horror stories of claw marks found inside caskets.[32] In 1742, John Bruhier documented 52 examples of premature burial and 72 mistaken diagnoses of death, and proposed that an "inspector of the dead" be appointed. In 1895, Franz Hartmann included in his book *Premature Burial* more than 700 cases and narrow escapes. T. M. Montgomery surveyed the burials made in Fort Randall Cemetery when it was moved in 1896 and found that nearly 2 percent of those exhumed had been victims of suspended animation. In a similar book published in 1905, William Tebb and Edward Vollum collected accounts of 219 narrow escapes, 149 premature burials, 10 cases of dissected alive, 3 almost dissected alive, and 2 who revived while being embalmed.[33] In the early 1900s, a case of premature burial was discovered an average of once a week. Dr. Alexander Wilder wrote of a scarlet fever victim who was exhumed after two months. The man had shattered the glass front of the casket and kicked out the sides and was found face downwards with his arms bent and with handfuls of hair in his clenched fists.[34] Even the air in the larger space of a vault does not stay fresh for too long, and it is no easier to escape than the grave. Scottish theologian Johannes Duns Scotus, who died in Cologne in the early fourteenth century, was found outside his coffin with hands torn from his futile attempt to open the doors of the vault. When a vault was opened in Rudenberg, Austria, in 1858, the skeleton of a man who had been entombed 15 years earlier was found sitting in the corner.[35]

There are some who defy the odds and are resurrected from the grave— by scavengers or sentimentalists—to resume their natural lives. In the seventeeth century, the three-year-old daughter of a French governor was pronounced dead at sea and sewn into a sack to be dropped overboard. A meow revealed that her pet cat had crawled into the bag and further inspection indicated that the child was not dead at all. She recovered to become the wife of King Louis XIV and died in 1719 at age 84. Max Hoffman also lived to the ripe age of 85 when his mother dug his body up after dreaming that he had not died of cholera and was trying to climb out of his coffin.[36] The story of Victorine Lafourcade of France is recorded by Edgar Allan Poe and others. She died in 1810, having married against her will. Her earlier suitor Julius Bossuet opened the coffin to cut a lock of her hair, whereupon she revived and fled with him. Another story is told of a woman who was buried in the public cemetery in Orléans. A servant opened the coffin that night to steal a ring, but was unable to slip it off her finger. He resorted to cutting it off, the pain of which revived the woman and scared away the thief. She struggled out of her shroud, returned home, and outlived her husband.[37] Constance Whitney was buried in a trance state in London and revived when the sexton opened the coffin to steal her ring. In 1919, a German nurse named Minna Braun overdosed on sleeping pills and was buried in an open grave. When the coffin lid was opened the next day to permit identification of the body, she was found to be alive and soon returned to her nursing duties.[38] Roberto Rodriguez of Pecaya, Venezuela, was lucky in reviving from his heart attack just prior to his burial in 1971. Unfortunately, the shock of seeing the "dead" man burst from the coffin and scramble out of the grave caused his mother-in-law to collapse and die, so she was buried in his place.[39]

It can be assumed that more people died of premature burial than were rescued from the grave, and this gave many people pause in earlier centuries.

Washing the body, as performed by the Greeks, had the reputation of reviving the apparent dead. Romans waited eight days before burying the dead, and the conclamatio, or calling out to the dead, was more than a ceremonial farewell. A watch held over the body, practiced also by the ancient Celts and Thracians, survives in the custom of the wake. An eighteenth-century Englishwoman was so fearful of being buried alive that she left her estate to her doctor on the condition that he visit her each morning for a year, which he fulfilled by mummifying her body and keeping it in the attic. Germans chose to await the decay of the body as a certain sign of death. "Waiting mortuaries" or "shelters for doubtful life," as they were called, first appeared in Weimar, Germany, in 1791 and soon sprang up in Berlin, Mainz, and Munich. In these repositories, the corpses were washed, dressed, and placed in a sloping position over a tray of antiseptic. Families surrounded the dead with flowers, took photographs, and awaited the onset of decomposition. The fear of live burial reached a crescendo in the nineteenth century, resulting in the design and patent of numerous devices from which the dead could signal from the grave. In a coffin invented by Count Karnicé-Karnicki at the University of Louvain in 1897, the pull of a lever by a buried person would cause a flag to wave or a bell to ring and thereby affect his or her rescue. Other instruments were perfected to prove death conclusively before burial, including a large pair of clawed forceps designed to pinch the nipples. Some suggested burying the dead with a bottle of chloroform, a knife, or a gun with which to commit suicide if they awake.

Many people dictated in their wills the procedures they wished to be carried out to insure against live burial. These included an incision in the body, the application of hot metal or boiling liquid, or dissection. Some ordered that a finger be amputated before the coffin was sealed. According to Philippe Ariès, when a testator specifies that the body is to be opened without offering any other reason, it may be assumed that the decision is inspired by fear of being buried while still alive. Hans Christian Andersen carried a letter at all times detailing the elaborate means by which his relatives were to guard against premature burial. George Washington died after requesting, "Have me decently buried, but do not let my body be put into a vault in less than two days after I am dead."[40] Frédéric Chopin's last words were: "The earth is suffocating.... Swear to make them cut me open, so that I won't be buried alive."[41] The wills of Washington and Chopin stipulate that the blood be drained or the head or heart be removed before casketing.[42] The widespread fear that dictates such actions may have originated during times of plague when the dead were buried hurriedly, but it has prompted scientists to seek more information concerning the determination of death.

In certain circumstances, people have assumed or been forced to assume the role of corpse while still alive. During the Black Death, there were not enough people to examine or bury the dead. Many victims, their families already killed by the disease, kept linen cloth ready, into which they sewed themselves in their last moments.

David E. Stannard notes similar circumstances in *The Puritan Way of Death*: "In one little hamlet in Cheshire in 1625, for example, literally everyone was killed off by an epidemic; and when the last adult came down with it he dug his own grave in his yard and buried himself, apparently because he knew that the only remaining survivors were children, who would have been incapable of removing his body from the house."[43]

Today hospital patients are sometimes treated like corpses, purposefully or accidentally. Elisabeth Kübler-Ross spoke of a patient who begged the nurse never to put the siderails of his bed up because it reminded him of being in a casket.[44] David Sudnow writes of a county hospital on the West Coast in which the nurses tied the feet and closed the eyes of moribund patients while they were still alive. John Donne, on the other hand, composed his own body for burial before expiring, closing his eyes and assuming a posture with his hands and body which required no alteration for shrouding or burial.[45] An unnamed man in Taunton, England, imagined himself to be a corpse and refused to move until a coffin was made. The insults of the people who attended his subsequent "funeral" in 1827 caused him to leap from the coffin, deciding he was alive after all.[46] King Charles V of Germany and Spain rehearsed his part as a corpse at his own funeral every day for the last three weeks of his life.

As Tom Stoppard muses in *Rosencrantz and Guildenstern Are Dead*, to be awake in the casket is a living hell. The truly dead, at least, are not aware of their confinement, or are they?

> Do you ever think of yourself as actually *dead*, lying in a box with a lid on it? ... It's silly to be depressed by it. I mean one thinks of it like being *alive* in a box, one keeps forgetting to take into account the fact that one is *dead* ... which should make a difference ... shouldn't it? I mean, you'd never *know* you were in a box, would you? It would be just like being *asleep* in a box. Not that I'd like to sleep in a box, mind you, not without any air—you'd wake up dead, for a start, and then where would you be? Apart from inside a box ... because then you'd be helpless, wouldn't you? Stuffed in a box like that, I mean you'd be in there for ever. Even taking into account the fact that you're dead, really... . I wouldn't think about it, if I were you. You'd only get depressed. (Pause.) Eternity is a terrible thought. I mean, where's it going to end?[47]

The dead may be aware of their surroundings, but many spiritual beliefs claim that they are not confined by them. In fact, it is said that the premature burial of Thomas à Kempis (d. 1471), which was evidenced by splinters of wood from the coffin lid embedded beneath his fingernails, worked against his canonization. It was assumed that no aspiring saint would have made such frantic attempts to postpone meeting his maker.

The Undead

Beyond mere spasm or partial latent life, some corpses have been revived by medical and supernatural means. In reincarnation, the soul leaves one body to inhabit another, but in resuscitation the soul is cajoled into staying with the body as it is repaired. Reanimation, a largely mythical idea, raises the question of whether the revived being even has a soul. Ghosts appear to be unembodied spirits, but zombies seem to be spiritless bodies. Unlike zombies, vampires have a will of their own, but according to popular belief they have traded their souls for their immortality. To have survived death bodily requires a second death to extinguish life. The resuscitated have postponed death, which will come again naturally, accidentally, or homicidally. The reanimated have tried to outwit it and must be deprived of life deliberately lest they succeed.

Many people are given a second lease on life after being brought back from clinical death with cardiopulmonary resuscitation or other methods of revival. In a letter written in 1773, Benjamin Franklin foreshadowed modern techniques in which children have been brought back to life after more than an hour underwater: "I wish it were possible from this instance to invent a method of embalming drowned persons, in such a manner that they may be recalled to life, however distant."[48] Franklin expressed a wish to be immersed in Madeira wine and later revived "as flies drowned in wine are sometimes later revived."[49] Methods of resuscitation were crude in 1895, when the *Chicago Herald* published that of Dr. Laborde of the Paris Medical Academy. To bring a person back to life, Dr. Laborde grasped the tongue, pressing down on its base and pulling it out full length with a steady motion at the rate of 15 or 20 pulls per hour until recovery.[50] Today's more sophisticated attempts focus on rescue breathing and heart massage, and the means to detect life have become sensitive enough to monitor even the most subtle signs. Some of the clinically dead have reported witnessing attempts to restore life to their inert bodies and other near-death experiences. But in cases of medical resuscitation, the patient has not truly been dead, according to some, because death is an irreversible condition. The question remains for the superstitious whether the irreversibly dead may then take on a posthumous life of their own.

Many doctors and scientists have attempted to prove that the body weighs less immediately after death because it has relinquished the soul, an entity determined to weigh as much as an ounce and a half. Ghosts are thought to be a visible form of this immortal soul which has left the body behind. Other legends have it that the body, too, can be made immortal. Just as people were afraid of being buried alive, they were also afraid of the "living dead" escaping from the grave. Headstones were originally intended to keep the dead in their place—underground. Tibetans used to believe in reanimated corpses and thought their touch was fatal. In Haiti, many still believe in the reanimated dead. Zombies are people killed and brought back to life by magicians who have extracted their souls and therefore control their bodies. A zombie is without will but can participate in ordinary activities. If it is fed salt, the zombie will realize its condition, kill its master, seek out its grave, and die. Otherwise, the creature is able to return to the grave only after reaching the age at which he or she would naturally have died. To prevent such a fate, corpses have been buried face down holding a dagger with which to stab the sorcerer who disturbs them. Another preventive method is to sew the mouth of the corpse shut so that it is unable to answer to its name.[51]

Another creature immune to physical death is the vampire, a body reanimated by its own damned soul or by an evil spirit. The vampire is especially feared because of its need to sustain itself with the blood of the living, which it obtains by biting the neck or chest of its victims. The supposed causes of vampirism range from the idiosyncratic to the momentous: being a seventh child, being born on or near Christmas, being buried too shallowly, dying with something on one's conscience, dying unbaptized, dying a violent death, or being attacked by an existing vampire. In Sicily and Greece, anyone who refused to avenge the murder of a family member was doomed to vampirism.[52] Vampirism was forecast years in advance by several signs, including being born with a caul or with teeth. Once dead, vampires were diagnosed by the condition of the remains some time after burial. Corpses whose hair and nails had grown or fallen off, whose eyes were open, or who lay in a different position than that in which they were buried were considered to have become vampires. A body intact long after decay should have progressed indicated vampirism. To prevent a corpse from becoming a vampire, the Finns nailed the body to the coffin or tied the knees together. The Chinese left the body unburied until the onset of decomposition. In other cultures, the corpse was kept in the house or in a shallow grave until it putrefied or even skeletonized before being buried deeply. Another sure solution was to cremate the body. Christians splashed the body with holy water or buried it with a communion wafer. Some people stuffed the mouth of the dead with garlic. To secure the death of a vampire, any of several violent methods were employed. The body could be transfixed through the heart with a wooden stake, but this had to be done in one blow. The body could be burned, or the heart boiled, or the head cut off. One remedy involved cutting the body in several parts, which were then boiled in wine. In the Balkans, suspected vampires were killed by driving nails into their skulls.

As science has devised the means to rescue the clinically dead, it has also put to rest legends involving the undead. Canadian ethnobotanist Wade Davis concluded from his research and his travels that Haitian zombies *do* exist, but have not returned from the dead. Instead, they have been intentionally drugged, buried—still conscious but completely paralyzed—and resurrected, during which they may undergo a near-death or out-of-body experience. They often suffer continued symptoms and become social outcasts.

While sorcery may have much to do with the events that precede and follow the poisoning of an intended zombie, the turning point or pseudo-death has been reduced to a chemical formula. Vampires have been unmasked by Paul Barber, who separates fiction and folklore from reality in *Vampires, Burial, and Death*. The eastern European vampires of centuries past were not the pale specters of the horror matinee, but ruddy creatures bloated with the blood obtained from their victims. A suspected vampire was exhumed as the cause of an epidemic when in fact, he or she was simply the first to die from it. Proof of vampirism, such as apparent lack of decay, is shown by Barber to be a natural consequence of burial, which may retard external decomposition and darken the skin color. Other symptoms are also of natural origin: blood may reliquify in the grave, rigor mortis will have worn off by the time an exhumation is performed, and the gases that have built up in the body may cause it to emit a "groan" when pierced by a stake. The stench traditionally associated with the vampire is evidence of the body's putrefaction, which—when complete—precludes the reanimation of the corpse. Although the legends are revived around the campfire and in the movies, modern science insists that there is no need to kill the dead.

Resurrection

Life after death often assumes bodily resurrection. At the Last Judgment, the dead will be called forth from their graves and those judged worthy will enter heaven. To prove that such things are possible, God and his followers have brought the dead back to life one or several at a time. Through prayerful intercession, Christian saints have not only been able to reverse death, but to repair mangled corpses. As Ezekiel witnessed in the valley of dry bones, the flesh and the breath can be restored to even long-dead bodies. Raising people from the dead has won the church converts and has been attributed to Christ, his disciples, and saints from Agnes to Vincent. Sometimes only the relic of a beatified person is needed to renew a tragically lost life. Many of the miracles performed directly or indirectly by the saints concerned children or adults whose deaths were premature. These miracles allowed them to resume their lives secure in the knowledge that a corpse is not necessarily a corpse.

Perhaps the most famous biblical resurrection, apart from his own, was that which Jesus performed upon Lazarus, who had been laid in his tomb four days earlier. When Jesus ordered Lazarus to come forth, the dead man obeyed, still bound hand and foot with graveclothes. The miracle made believers of many Jews who saw it occur. The actions of Christ were emulated by the saints to prove the power of their Lord and thereby win converts to Christianity. A squire who blasphemed St. Bernard of Clairvaux (d. 1153) fell lifeless after witnessing the saint cure a crippled woman. When St. Bernard brought the squire back to life, the man became a crusader. St. Francis of Paola (d. 1507) revived his nephew under the condition that the boy's mother allow her son to become a monk as he wished. St. Patrick (d. 493) resurrected the son and daughter of a king who promised that the whole city would be baptized in the new faith if they were restored. St. Vincent Ferrer (d. 1419) restored the life of a rich Jew who had left his sermon in anger and was crushed by part of the porch structure. When the man revived, he had been converted. Others performed their miracles before crowds. The pagan crowd that witnessed St. Martin of Tours revive a woman's only son in the fourth century converted to Christianity.

Those who had chosen to lead an especially holy life were often rewarded with resurrection by their peers in times of need. When a young monk was crushed by a wall, his life was restored and his bones healed by the prayers of St. Benedict (d. ca. 547). St. Bernard of Abbeville (d. 1117) brought back to life a novice nun who had been knocked down and crushed by a cart drawn by ten bullocks. In the fourteenth century, St. Colette restored a nun in her coffin who had died without absolution. St. Dominic de Guzman (d. 1221) revived a friar who lay in agony after receiving the Last Sacraments and the son of a Roman noblewoman who had left the ill boy at home so that she could hear the saint preach. Another boy who drowned after being sent to invite St. Hyacinth (d. 1257) to preach was restored by him. In an interesting reversal of roles, St. Winifride was restored by the prayers of her congregation after she was beheaded (ca. 650) by a prince to whom she had denied her body.

Miracles were practiced on religious colleagues, relatives, neighbors, and even complete strangers. Blessed Agnes of Prague (d. 1282) brought her niece back to life, and St. Teresa of Avila (d. 1582) revived her six-year-old nephew. St. Ambrose restored to life the son of an illustrious man of Florence. St. Dominic de Guzman (d. 1221) resurrected the nephew of a bishop who had fallen from his horse while riding recklessly. Some are chosen for resurrection because they died before making a sacrament. St. Catherine of Siena (d. 1380) revived her mother because she had not yet received the sacraments of the church. Joan of Arc (d. 1431) revived a stillborn baby so that it could be baptized. The child came to life, yawned three times, was baptized, and died again. When St. John Bosco (d. 1888) revived a 15-year-old boy, the young man made his confession but was allowed to die again at his own request. St. Malachy the Irishman (d. 1148) postponed anointing a woman who then died, so he cried and prayed over her body all night until "the woman opened her eyes and rubbed her forehead and temples with her hands, as people do who rise from a deep sleep."[53]

Victims of premature death were frequent subjects of resurrection miracles. St. Agnes of Montepulciano of the thirteenth century revived a child found floating in a bath. St. Colette brought several stillborn babies back to life. St. Bernardine of Siena (d. 1444) restored to life a young man who had been killed by a bull. St. Paul of the Cross (d. 1775) restored the life of a child who had fallen out a window. St. Francis of Paola (D. 1507) is credited with raising the same man back to life twice: Thomas d'Yvre of Paterna was restored after being killed by a falling tree and later after plummeting from a steeple. St. Francis Xavier (d. 1552) renewed the life of a boy who had drowned in a well and another who had been bitten by a cobra. Complete restoration of life can be achieved even when the corpse is not intact. St. Catherine of Sweden (d. 1381) restored to life a workman who had been mutilated in a fall from a roof who was then able to return to work the same day. St. Francis Solanus (d. 1610) revived and healed a five-year-old girl who had fallen from a height; her skull was split and her eye destroyed by the impact. A woodsman killed by bears hours earlier and horribly disfigured was raised from the dead by Blessed Margaret of Castello (d. 1320). St. Philip Benizi (d. 1285) restored a child killed and partially eaten by a wolf. When a man returned home from one of St. Vincent Ferrer's sermons, he found his wife had gone mad, cut the throat of their son, chopped up his body, and roasted a portion of it to serve to her husband. St. Vincent prayed over the pieces, which then reassembled and came back to life.

Not only have some saints been able to bring the newly dead back to life and to repair their mangled bodies, they have revived bodies that had already begun to decompose. St. Elizabeth of Hungary (d. 1231) is credited with the revival of a three-year-old boy dead since the previous day, another small boy who had been inanimate and rigid for some time, and a four-year-old pulled from a well with black skin and a swollen belly. St. Francis of Paola brought back to life a criminal who had been hanging from the gallows for three days; the man became a monk after his resurrection. A man entombed the day before and beginning to putrefy and a girl buried for three days were revived by St. Francis Xavier. But even more remarkable than saints who revive others are those who have willed their own resurrection after death. When St. Catherine of Siena was about to stoop to kiss the foot of St. Agnes in her coffin, Agnes raised her foot so that Catherine did not need to bend over. After the local prior would not allow the body of Blessed Margaret of Castello (d. 1320) to be buried in the church, the parents of a crippled and mute girl brought the child to the bier. Margaret's left arm rose and touched the girl, curing her and ensuring her own burial in the church. When Blessed Peter Armengol (d. 1304) was executed by the Moors and left hanging for six days, a friend arrived and cut him down, alive and well. Peter attributed his resurrection to the Virgin Mary.

Other saints used their power to affect justice. When his father was wrongly implicated in a murder, St. Anthony of Padua (d. 1231) ordered the grave of the murdered man to be opened and commanded the victim to declare in the name of God whether he was killed by Don Martino. The corpse sat up, raised his hand as if to swear an oath, and declared St. Anthony's father innocent, after which he requested and received absolution and sank back into his coffin.[54] St. Ignatius Loyola (d. 1556) restored to life a man who had hanged himself in despair after losing a lawsuit against his brother. The resurrection allowed him to express sorrow over his action, make his confession, and receive the sacraments before expiring again. To prove to the court that some disputed property was owned by the church, St. Stanislaus (d. 1079) resurrected a man who had been dead for three years. After the grave of Peter Miles was opened, the saint touched the bones with his crozier and they filled out with flesh. The man rose and accompanied the saint to trial, where he was acquitted. When offered a few years of life, Miles declined, returned to his grave, composed himself, and fell to pieces exactly as he had been found. As St. Vincent Ferrer pleaded in vain for an innocent man who had been condemned to death, he was passed by a funeral procession. He asked the corpse— who had nothing to gain—whether the condemned man was guilty and the corpse replied that he was not, but also declined an offer to remain alive.

Permanent or temporary resurrection sometimes occurred spontaneously, presumably the work of the Lord himself. After 48 Dominican friars were killed in Poland by Tartars, the mangled bodies chanted the hymn "Salve Regina." Others attribute miraculous resurrections to the intercession rather than the direct action of a particular saint. Through prayer, Blessed Sebastian of Apparizio (d. 1600) was said to have raised a boy killed by the kick of a horse, a child who had been pushed out a high window, an infant who drowned in a stream, a boy killed by a heavy beam, a girl who had frozen to death, and the fetus of a woman who then gave birth to a healthy baby. The intercession of Our Lady of Czestochowa at Jasna Gora, Poland, is credited with many resurrection miracles: a peasant woman condemned to drown for giving birth to a child out of wedlock, a judge who had died after a long illness but wished to live so that he could do penance for his sins, and a teenager who had accidentally died after being hanged in a mock trial. Most incredibly, Our Lady of Czestochowa restored life to three bloodied corpses brought to Jasna Gora and prayed for by the entire congregation after a remarkable series of events. A four-year-old boy slashed the throat of his younger brother in imitation of his father (the operator of a slaughterhouse), then hid in the oven which his mother unknowingly lit when she got home. The father returned home just after she had noticed the deaths of both boys. Thinking she had killed them, he crushed her skull with an axe before realizing the truth. He loaded the three bodies on a wagon, and at the church they came to life. Fame of this sixteenth-century miracle spread worldwide.

Resurrection has also attested to the veracity of holy relics. When St. Helen (d. ca. 330) uncovered three crosses from Calvary, she touched each

to the body of a dead man. The cross that returned him to life was designated the True Cross on which Jesus had been crucified. The body of a young
man laid out on the tomb of St. Cyril (d. ca. 1235) while his grave was being
dug came back to life, joined the Carmelites and lived another 12 years. The
dead could be restored simply by touching the corpse to the tomb of St.
Hyacinth. The application of the relics of St. Pacific of San Severino (d. 1721)
caused two people to return to life. The relics of St. Philip Neri (d. 1595)
gave life to a two-year-old boy when placed on his neck, and the hair of the
saint was used to restore a premature baby, who was baptized and died 20
days later. A piece of a garment worn by St. Rose of Lima (d. 1617) brought
the daughter of a laborer back to life, and a picture of St. Rose restored a
faithful servant when placed on his corpse. A young woman was revived when
her robe, which had been touched to a relic of St. Stephen, was placed on her
body. Similarly, a Spanish priest was brought back to life after being covered
with a tunic touched to a relic of St. Stephen. Oil from St. Stephen's shrine
restored a young boy to life. And the Bible tells of a man whose lifeless body
revived when it touched the bones of Elisha in the tomb.

Stories of resurrection are often difficult to believe but are documented
by the Roman Catholic church as part of a saint's beatification. That resus-
citations occurred naturally, but were taken to be miracles by a medically
naive populace belies common sense, according to Father Albert J. Hebert,
S.M., author of *Raised from the Dead*:

> Included in the cases detailed herein were men (or women or children) who
> had been dead for as long as twenty-four hours or even several days, per-
> sons who had drowned hours or days before the bodies were recovered, and
> others who had been hanged by the neck for days or even a week. There
> were others who had suffered violent deaths, having been thrown from
> horses, crushed under wheels, fallen from great heights or buried by falling
> walls, debris, or landslides; some had dropped into a mine shaft or plunged
> into a well. Finally, there were those who had been sealed in a coffin, wrapped
> in shrouds and actually buried under earth or stone, some for long periods
> of time…. Granted, there *may* have been a *few* cases in which a person was
> mistakenly judged to be dead. But to assume that people in other ages did
> not generally know how to determine the state of death is simply prepos-
> terous.[55]

If one accepts that a person truly dead can be returned to life, the idea of
the collective dead rising from their graves on Judgment Day is less far-
fetched.

To resurrect all the dead is as effortless to an omnipotent being as bringing one person back to life. Christians argue that if a saint can mend and give
life to a dismembered corpse, God should be believed capable of resurrect-
ing bodies that are decayed and corrupt. Thomas Lovell Beddoes put the
image of the body regathering itself into verse in the nineteenth century:

Thread the nerves through the right holes,
Get out of my bones, you wormy souls.
Shut up my stomach, the ribs are full:
Muscles be steady and ready to pull.
Heart and artery merrily shake
And eyelid go up, for we're ready to wake.[56]

Not only will the dead be whole again, they will—according to prophecy—
rise at the perfect age of 33 at which Christ was crucified. The dead will be
gathered from cemeteries and from the sea. It will not matter that corpses
have been cannibalized or cremated. At the Last Judgment, the risen will
become immune to physical evil, weakness, and pain. They will have command of their bodies, but will not be bound by them, having assumed sub-
tility (the qualities of spirit while remaining a body), agility (instantaneous
movement), and clarity (radiance and beauty). Believers are convinced that
physical death is spiritual—and to some extent physical—rebirth. Others feel
that resurrection miracles may be collective hallucinations and that the Last
Judgment is perhaps nothing more than historical and contemporary wishful thinking.

The 10 Donation

> We take cadaver organs and transplant them; we use
> human bodies for medical instruction; we perform
> autopsies to learn more about disease processes. In doing
> these things, we have lost no repect for human life or for
> persons. On the contrary, it is because of our fundamental
> regard for life and for the well-being of humankind that
> we do such otherwise distasteful things. We do not do
> them capriciously, arbitrarily, or without appropriate
> consent.
> —Samuel Gorowitz, *Drawing the Line: Life, Death,*
> *and Ethical Choices in an American Hospital*[1]

Anatomical Gifts

Dead bodies are donated in whole or in part to sustain the living, directly or indirectly. An anatomical gift of a kidney or heart may add years to a life that would otherwise have been lost. Whole body donation allows medical students to practice their skills on cadavers before applying textbook knowledge to living patients. With organ and body donation comes heavy responsibility. Consent must be obtained from next of kin, leading to the legal question of whether family members may nullify an anatomical bequest made in advance by the deceased. Respect must be maintained by medical personnel who, while in training, may be prone to playing pranks with the corpse as a distancing device. And questions of supply and demand must be faced as the need for more organs leads to ruthless harvesting and illicit markets for body parts.

Organ donation lends an earthly immortality to the dead whose parts, like their works or their children, survive them. Transplant of kidneys, livers, lungs, hearts, corneas, pancreases, and some glands has been carried out successfully. And in times of war, the blood of the dead has been used for transfusions. Organs are in constant demand in today's hospitals. In 1990, an estimated 2,206 people died waiting for an organ transplant. By the end of 1991, over 23,000 Americans were on the waiting list, with a new name being added every 30 minutes.[2] Bodies are also in demand in many medical and dental schools, where available bodies may be refused if they are obese, emaciated, autopsied, burned, or mutilated. One evaluation of a good medical school is the ratio of anatomy students to cadavers. While the number of people who die in hospitals is large, only a minute percentage of patients die under conditions that permit organ donation and only a portion of their families are approached for consent.[3] Of those who would be willing to donate their organs, only a small percentage have made arrangements to do so. Today such arrangements consist of carrying a signed and witnessed organ donor card or merely signing the release printed on the back of some state driver's licenses. While a third of Americans state that they are "very likely" to become organ donors, more than twice that number admit that they are "very likely" to donate the organs of a family member.[4] Still, some of those on the waiting list die of their illnesses before an organ can be found.

Much guilt is often spent awaiting an appropriate organ match. The wait causes depression and sometimes psychosis and leads to an increased suicide rate. Rapidly failing health as time slips by is a factor, but also contributory is the fact that the best organ donor is a young person who has suffered brain death: "Prospective heart transplant recipients, drowning in the fluids of their own hearts' failure, wait in motel rooms and apartments up and down the strip for motorcyclists to smash their brains out on California highways and provide new hearts for them."[5]

Competition for organs is fierce and is only mediated by tissue matching and a national waiting list maintained by the United Network for Organ Sharing (UNOS). "Thousands of people," says Dr. Donald Kayhoe, who oversees tissue-typing research for the National Institutes of Health, "look forward to claiming the heart, liver or kidneys from the latest seventeen-year-old boy who is killed on a motorcycle."[6] The families of the young victims are often prevented from meeting the recipients of the organs for fear that their death or rejection of the organ would cause them additional grief. Even after a successful transplant, the recipients of donated organs themselves experience varying emotions. Some report being haunted by the feeling that they are somebody else. Others feel excessively grateful to the donor's family or guilty that they benefited from the donor's premature death. In addition to organs, many tissues and substances from the human body can be donated. Before human growth hormone was synthesized, it was regularly extracted from the glands of the dead by coroners. Blood is collected for use in the laboratory in the United States, but in Moscow, cadaver blood obtained within six hours of death has been successfully transfused since 1930. Heart valves and veins may be used in heart surgery. Skin can be used to cover burn patients, and cartilage may be used in restorative facial surgery. Cartilage may also be implanted as a foundation for new bone to grow or be used to replace damaged joint tissue. Discs between the vertebrae may be transplanted to replace or reconstruct damaged discs, and the vertebrae themselves may be used as a source of bone marrow. Temporal bones may restore hearing in a recipient, and corneas may restore sight.

The family members of a person whose body is donated to science are not surprisingly out of contact with the anatomy class from the time of the donation to the reclamation of the ashes or body after many months in the hands of medical students. As may be expected, gallows humor is often part of the curriculum (although Jeffrey Iserson discounts such stories as "urban legends"): "Pranks have been going on in medical schools as long as there have been medical students. Putting skeletons on subways or sticking a cadaver's arm out of a car window at a toll booth I'm sure have been done many times."[7] During the final session of an anatomy lab at Harvard, one of the students hid brightly colored jelly beans in the nooks of a cadaver. Many explain the horseplay as a means of protecting themselves from the sobering realities of cutting open another human being. Dissection is often described as something other than a "normal" human act, made somewhat easier by the fact that the skin of cadavers is leathery: "They look as if they've been dead forever, as if they were *born* dead."[8] Students walk a thin line between personalizing and depersonalizing the dead: "It is hard for me to think of it (her?) as a living person, but when I do, I think of her with gratitude,"[9] said one. Another had to inform her instructor at the University of Alabama School of Medicine that one of the cadavers in the class was her great aunt. Unlike the subject of an autopsy, a cadaver is usually anonymous. Even so, some students cover the face, and others try to imagine the cadaver during life: "That body had once been round and plump and young, stubbed its toe and wept, fallen in love and been elated and made conversation, felt the slow, creaky onset of age, now was inert upon a metal table, gradually to be dismembered layer by layer, organ by organ, limb by limb."[10] An embalming school in Farmingdale, New York, requires its students to visit the sources of their cadavers—nearby institutions for the indigent—so that they will be able to look upon them as people.[11] Unwrapping the dead body of a stranger in the laboratory, a doctor-to-be faces his or her own mortality in an undeniable way, becoming either more callous or more caring. "The objects which before had filled me with extreme horror had absolutely no effect on me now. I felt nothing but a cold distaste," wrote Hector Berlioz (d. 1869) about his medical training in the early 1820s.[12]

Physically, dissection is often unpleasant and requires a certain amount of callousness. In their autobiographies, almost all medical students complain about the tenacious smell of the formaldehyde or formalin, a smell which permeates their clothes and hair and has been described as "beef soup and oil-of-wintergreen"[13] and "spiced honey gone rancid."[14] The chemicals used to preserve the corpse are said to pickle the hands and may have to be sprayed on the body over the course of the semester to prevent mold. The sight of human muscle tissue drives many to vegetarianism, if only temporarily, and causes others to have nightmares. The sight of the interior of a human body can be both revolting and fascinating: "What economy of colors there, compared to a tropical fish or a sunrise or even a pigeon's neck—dull red, indistinct gray buff, some splotches of green. But what opulence of forms—serpents, goblets, tapestries, coils, pouches, conch shells, washboards, sheets, waves, curls, fountains of translucent tissue."[15] For the medical student, the wonders of the body are found within the corpse, not in a lifelike visage. Anatomical embalming, often by complete immersion, is concerned with the preservation of internal and external structures and does not include any adjustment of the features, such as eye or mouth closure.

Dissection usually begins with the muscles of the back. Head, hands, and feet are covered with formaldehyde-soaked cloths and plastic bags to preserve them for later dissection. The external chest is anatomized next, followed by the arms and shoulders, legs, internal chest, abdomen, pelvis, feet, hands, neck, face, and head. During the semester, the cadavers may become dry and stiff, a condition that may be improved by the application of fabric softener. Beyond an extensive and extended dissection, whole body donation may result in the preservation of tissue for research and education. The users of slides and specimens are generally mindful of their origin and careful with these parcels of human remains: "I held the slide up against the light again. There was the cross-section of the finger, red with translucent agate lines coursing through. Yes, that had once been someone's finger—it had felt coffee cups and pieces of paper and buttons, scalded itself, shook hands, gestured in excitement, caressed faces. Now it lived between pieces of glass in a box.... If this was human flesh, however sliced, diced, dried, or stained, I should at least show it the courtesy of adequate attention."[16] The carving up of the dead human body may be distasteful, but it is not necessarily disrespectful. And those in the medical field do show their appreciation. An anatomical technician called the cadaver "all the encyclopedia volumes in the world in one body."[17] Some schools—including Tulane University, West Virginia University, the University of Arizona, and the University of Massachusetts at Worcester—conduct a memorial service for the cadavers that is attended by all who have come into contact with them. Unclaimed bodies are cremated or buried. Donated bodies are returned with thanks to next of kin if requested.

Consent is a byword in the modern hospital. The Uniform Anatomical Gift Act, adopted in some form in all 50 U.S. states, has made it possible for individuals to bequeath their bodies or parts of them for use immediately after death. In the majority of cases, the family is not allowed to cancel the donation. In the absence of prior arrangement by the deceased, permission to remove organs must be granted by the next of kin. Obtaining permission for both autopsy and organ donation is often the responsibility of medical interns who must approach the bereaved family at an obviously stressful time. Family members that object to mutilation of their loved one's body are assured that it will be treated with respect, and they may be allowed to place restrictions on its use. The result of such persuasions is still refusal in many cases. Relatives may fear that body donation circumvents the traditional funeral rite.

Objections to harvesting organs are made on ethical grounds by those who view organ donation as exploitation of the newly dead. It is feared that those who carry donor cards will be declared dead prematurely and that doctors will make only half-hearted efforts to preserve their lives. Brain-dead bodies which remain attached to respirators in order to keep transplantable parts viable are said to be incubators for their own organs.[18] In his book about nurses, Michael Brown describes some of the tasks of a certified registered nurse anesthetist:

> Organ harvesting is one of Mavis's strangest duties, keeping bodies functioning until the kidney, heart, or some other part can be removed. Pulmonary edema, bronchial clogging, and decreased blood flow to organs must be avoided, electrolyte balance and maximum oxygen saturation maintained. Regular arterial-blood gas checks, suctioning, cadaver positional changes, and blood-product infusions are all employed. Mavis knows they are being kept alive artificially when they come to her. They have to be declared dead beforehand. Still, they have a good blood pressure that she maintains with the appropriate drugs; their hearts are beating, vital signs normal. Then the kidneys come out and the heart comes out, lung, bone or ear tissue, and corneas. Then Mavis turns everything off, and they die. It feels eerie. In the heart it feels eerie, while the head knows it's right.[19]

Ethicist David Lamb disagrees and calls a still-breathing corpse morally repugnant.

Some family members—and some ethicists—fear futuristic visions such as that of Willard Gaylin of the Institute of Society, Ethics, and the Life Sciences. Twenty years ago, Gaylin advocated the physical maintenance of the lives of the brain-dead in "bioemporiums" for use in harvesting organs, practicing surgeries, and experimenting with new techniques and medicines.[20] While such places are as yet science fiction, exploitation is not. In 1988, five people were caught selling human corneas to customers as far away as Saudi Arabia. The corneas were harvested from bodies by doctors who assumed they were given to a Florida tissue bank. Instead, they were sold for up to $650 each.[21] The head of a state-run mental hospital in Argentina was arrested in the early 1990s, along with eleven of his staff, for the murder of patients from whom the blood, corneas, and organs were extracted and sold. Offering a financial incentive to families who donate the organs of a loved one, as is sometimes suggested, would only legitimize the sale of organs for transplant, which is currently illegal in the U.S.

The National Transplant Act of 1984 prohibits the purchase or sale of human organs, though a processing fee is often charged. Recipients of anatomical gifts are limited to hospitals, surgeons and physicians, accredited medical or dental schools, and tissue or organ banks. The gifts may be used for education, research, advancement of science, or therapy including transplantation.[22] When organs are donated, the procurement organization covers all hospital and physician costs associated with maintaining the body and recovering organs and tissues. Organ donation is endorsed by most major religions, including Catholicism, Hinduism, Buddhism, Judaism, and most Protestant denominations. The donation of organs may be followed by customary funeral arrangements and in some cases may be allowed to precede medical-legal autopsy. In spite of the arguments for donation, at least 5,000 human organs that are medically suitable for transplantation are buried in the U.S. each year. To encourage organ and tissue donation, some advocate a system of "mandated choice" in which all competent adults would be required to declare (for instance, on their drivers' licenses) whether or not they wish to become organ donors. Others less charitable suggest that organs be given only to those who have made arrangements to donate their own in advance of their need.

The organs that are available are removed from the newly dead by surgical teams. The heart has priority, followed by the lungs, liver, and other organs. Tissues can be retrieved up to 24 hours after circulation of the blood has ceased. The removed organs are placed in a cooled preservative and packaged in a triple-layered sterile barrier in a rigid container housed in an insulated, double-strength container. The heart must be transplanted within six to eight hours, heart and lungs together within four to five hours. The liver and pancreas will keep for 12 to 24 hours and kidneys for up to 72 hours.

In past centuries, would-be doctors had to break the rules: the mere opening of a dead body was either against the law or taboo. Unlike today, when it is an accepted part of the training regimen in medical professions, dissection in other times was out of necessity carried out in secret. In many cultures, it was forbidden to cut a body because doing so was thought to hurt the soul or invite retribution from the dead. In ancient China, a doctrine which considered the dead body to be sacrosanct prevented doctors from opening it. Hindu doctors were restricted to the study of children's bodies, because anyone who died over two years of age was cremated. Dissection and possibly vivisection of criminals was practiced in ancient Greece, but dissection was forbidden in Rome. Galen (d. ca. 201) was forced to base his suppositions about the internal structure of the human body on dissections of animals until he found a corpse left by a bandit and scavenged by birds. The ban on cutting the cadaver extended through the Middle Ages, though it was still sometimes done. Frederick II (d. 1250) was the first to permit the dissection of the human body in the Holy Roman Empire. Charles VI of France (d. 1422) issued a decree allowing the medical faculty of Montpelier to dissect one executed criminal each year.

Several other European universities petitioned for and were granted the right to perform dissections, with restrictions on the annual number or the origin of the cadavers. Venice officially sanctioned dissection in 1429 and built a theater of anatomy in 1446. An institute of anatomy was founded by Jacob Sylvius (d. 1555). King Louis XI (d. 1483) received instruction from visiting doctors: "It was decreed that whenever an especially renowned surgeon was passing through the kingdom, Court would adjourn to a nearby cemetery and the throne be set up beside a freshly dug grave. A condemned prisoner (who would have had his head lopped off) was tied, nude, to a slab at graveside and the visiting physician proceeded to dissect him, fully conscious, and to explain the working bodily functions to the attentive monarch."[23] In England, on the other hand, private dissections were forbidden, as John Deane found out in 1573 when he was fined "for having an Anathomye in his howse."[24]

Condemned men were the only available subjects for anatomical dissection for centuries. In England from the mid-eighteenth century, anatomists were allowed to dissect the bodies of executed criminals publicly in Surgeon's Theatre. Parliament passed a law in 1832 which protected the bodies of criminals by authorizing their burial on prison grounds and instead allowed executors and keepers of workhouses the power to assign to anatomists the bodies over which they had legal right. Faced with difficulty in obtaining subjects and in carrying out their examinations, dissectors became adept at getting around the rules. Sir Astley Cooper (d. 1841) testified before a House of Commons committee about how he acquired bodies for dissection, bragging, "There is no person, let his situation in life be what it may, whom, if I were disposed to dissect, I could not obtain."[25] Some men resorted to dissecting the bodies of family members. William Harvey, for instance, dissected his own father and sister in the seventeenth century. Others made the most of a single body, crafting wax models of those they dissected. Clemente Susini (d. 1805) made over 1,000 models with the help of his assistant anatomists.

Despite the means they had to take, both artists and scientists believed in the need to study the human form inside and out. Michelangelo (d. 1564) requested the right to dissect bodies from the hospital chapel of a monastery in Florence as part of his fee for his work there. When he had other opportunities to study firsthand the skeletal structure and musculature, he was said by his biographers to have applied himself so diligently that the stench of the bodies made him unable to eat or drink.[26] Just before his death in 1519, Leonardo da Vinci confessed to having personally dissected more than 100 bodies. For some the desire for knowledge gained through the opening of a dead body was seemingly insatiable: Xavier Bichat (d. 1802) was said to have dissected 600 bodies in a single winter, and a doctor who later became physician to Louis XVI boasted of having dissected 1,200 cadavers. Doctors craved dissection not only of the average man, but the exceptional one. Anthony White, Chief Surgeon of Westminster Hospital, paid three-foot-tall George Trout ten pounds for the right to dissect his body after death, but was in fact survived by him.

Many people, including doctors, are more willing to donate organs than their entire body. Organ donation is an immediate surgical procedure and does not disrupt postdeath activities, whereas the use of a donated body may span years and may prevent or postpone a traditional funeral. If consent is obtained, the interval of delay between the pronouncement of death and organ removal may be as little as ten minutes. Soon after the removal, the body may be claimed by next of kin for burial or cremation. When a body is donated in its entirety, the school often assumes responsibility for final disposition. Many will, upon request, return the ashes of the cremated cadaver to the family. In some cases, the cadaver itself may be claimed for burial. As bodies are picked apart for transplantation of their useful organs and tissues and picked clean for educational and research purposes, there is bound to be some corrupt gain and some tasteless games. But potential organ and body donors must continue to subscribe to the idea that the benefits of allowing doctors access to living human tissues and students access to cadavers outweigh the disadvantages. The Latin inscription over the Theatrum Anatomicum in Paris reads, "Here is the place where death enjoys helping life."[27] The same motto can be seen in the faces of those who have lost a son or daughter but have gained some peace of mind by putting their earthly remains to good use.

Experimentation

Unlike organ donation, the use of corpses for scientific experimentation is not saddled with the need for consent. The bodies involved are usually unclaimed, and the experiments unpublicized. When the public is made aware of tests conducted on the dead, there may be an outcry about the lack of respect shown to human bodies, which are shot at, guillotined, or simply allowed to decay in the name of science. But like the medical student in the gross anatomy lab, the scientist uses the corpse to obtain information that could not be had using models. The dead are employed to serve the living: solving murders, replicating history, or making cars safer. With a few exceptions, the ends justify the means.

At the University of Tennessee's Anthropological Research Facility established in the late 1970s by Bill Bass, bodies are allowed to decay under monitored conditions. The corpses of the unidentified or unclaimed dead are donated by the medical examiner's office, and between 30 and 40 per year are placed on the ground or on concrete slabs within a fenced enclosure. Some bodies are buried shallowly, and the occasional corpse is wrapped in plastic to mimic the treatment of murder victims. The rare embalmed body provides useful comparative data. Exposed bodies are photographed at regular intervals and buried bodies are periodically exhumed for examination. Changes in vegetation and in the composition of the soil are noted, as is maggot activity, and seasonal variations in decay are recorded. While the ARF's findings may not apply in every situation because of different climates,they have helped anthropologists in their understanding of decay, disarticulation, and disintegration of the dead. This knowledge, when applied to discovered human remains, will indicate the length of time the body has been exposed and under what conditions, giving authorities a frame of reference regarding possible homicide. The revolting aspect of the research is validated by the need for such information, which has resulted in the development of additional facilities in California and Texas.[28]

From murder investigations have occasionally arisen equally gruesome experiments to test the methods of killing and disposing of the victim. To test whether hot potash solution would actually reduce a corpse to the lumpy residue found in Luetgert's sausage factory, authorities used the same technique on a cadaver and achieved the same results. To assess whether the body of a victim purportedly incinerated in the furnace of her apartment building in 1945 could actually be reduced to the unidentifiable fragments obtained from it, anthropologist Wilton Krogman of the University of Chicago was consulted by the prosecution. Dr. Krogman obtained an unclaimed body of a woman about the same age and weight of the victim and placed it in the furnace, raising the temperature to its maximum. The corpse was completely reduced in three and a half hours. When the evidence was presented to the grand jury, the janitor of the building was indicted and subsequently sentenced to life imprisonment. U.S. Army wound ballistics experts fired bullets through the wrist of a cadaver to test whether Texas Governor John Connolly was hit by the same bullet as President John F. Kennedy during their Dallas motorcade in 1963. Experiments were also conducted separately by Dr. Alfred J. Olivier at the Aberdeen Proving Grounds and by Dr. J. K. Lattimer of Columbia University to reproduce the assassinated president's wounds by firing identical bullets into human skulls. Investigators have also used corpses to mimic the clues left by killers. In an English investigation, examiners made trial bites on the breast of a female body in the morgue using dental impressions from the suspect.[29]

Cadavers have been used in many experiments to test military weapons and protective gear. In 1892, the U.S. Army tested the effect of bullets on various parts of the anatomy. Ballistics pioneer Dr. Louis LaGarde performed his experiments on corpses suspended from their necks or heads at Bellevue

Hospital.[30] Between the Korean and Vietnam wars, the U.S. Army conducted field tests using cadaver legs and heads obtained from the Baltimore medical examiner's office. The legs were dressed in routine-issue pants, socks, and boots to test the effect of land mines. The heads were put in newly designed helmets to test their effectiveness.[31] The use of corpses to improve the safety of equipment is complemented by their use to train doctors and nurses effectively. Since the turn of the nineteenth century, the French army has shot corpses to teach the effects of gunshot wounds to medical personnel. Today bodies unfit for organ donation are occasionally kept on a ventilator to test new medications. Newly dead bodies are also used to test medical devices and appliances, to refine techniques such as laser surgery, and to allow health professionals practice before using skills such as intubation on living patients.

Tests on bodies have also been carried out in the public interest for the purpose of refining execution methods. The inventor of the guillotine, Dr. Louis of the French Academy of Surgery, tested his device first on sheep and then on a number of male and female human corpses. The results of his testing caused him to give the blade a slanted edge and to increase the length of the drop.[32] While Dr. Louis was attempting to devise a humanitarian means of beheading a person, some would argue that contributing to the development of capital punishment was not humanitarian at all. Harder to fathom is the objection to automobile testing using human cadavers. Research on auto safety at the University of Virginia, the Medical College of Wisconsin, and Wayne State University involves strapping human bodies onto metal sleds that crash at speeds of 35 miles per hour. The bodies are then autopsied and x-rayed. For every test using a cadaver, hundreds of computer simulations and dummy tests are performed. Similar testing has been conducted by the U.S. Army and the Department of Transportation, and at Heidelberg University, where the research was protested by the Roman Catholic German Bishops' Conference and the question of consent was raised. The University of Virginia does inform families of the intended use of the donated body, but at Wisconsin and Wayne State, families are informed of the specific use only if they ask.

In addition to being used to make the future safer, human bodies and parts of bodies have been used by modern researchers to verify the past. Scientists at the University of Glasgow carried out experiments on amputated human limbs to determine that the natron with which ancient Egyptians mummified the dead was used in solid rather than liquid form. Dr. Pierre Barbet did a number of experiments in the 1930s to verify that the man originally wrapped in the Shroud of Turin had in fact been crucified. Using unclaimed bodies at St. Joseph's Hospital in Paris, Dr. Barbet attached them with square nails to a wooden cross in his laboratory, after which he analyzed and photographed them. His experiments revealed that those condemned to be crucified were nailed through the wrist rather than the palm as popularly depicted: "Raising the cross from the floor, Barbet knew that his theories would literally either stand or fall when he brought the cross to a totally upright position and slid the beam into a hole on the platform. When he did so, the body slumped down about ten inches. The chest area expanded in size as though the victim had taken a deep breath and were about to exhale. The head was pulled forward and down, the chin touching the collarbone. The knees jutted out. The body stayed on the cross."[33]

Barbet also explained the blood streaks on the shroud which showed the wrists to have been in two different positions by determining that suffocation would occur unless the crucified person periodically stood on the nails that held his feet. Barbet was by no means the only person to try to authenticate the image on the shroud, a task which is ongoing. Monsignor Giulio Ricci of the Vatican and Dr. Nicolo Miani of Rome's Sacred Heart Medical school spent months wrapping corpses in winding sheets to determine the height of the man wrapped in the shroud, whom they believe to have been Jesus Christ.

Experimenters have sometimes gone too far. Dr. Roger Kerris, medical examiner of Oahu, prepared to testify in a battered child case by dropping babies that had died of SIDS on their heads. Because he had not consulted the parents of the dead children, his testimony caused pandemonium and revulsion.[34] Other times, researchers have not gone far enough. Sentencing for a 1962 murder in England depended on whether a puncture wound in the chest and back of the victim had been made by a bullet wound (a capital offense) or a swordstick. Dr. H. J. Walls, director of the Police Laboratory at New Scotland Yard, happened to possess an ancient swordstick and tried it out on a corpse. "The experiment was inconclusive, for he confessed a certain revulsion at trying to impale the corpse and probably failed to apply the necessary enthusiasm," writes Colin Wilson.[35] The nine-day trial resulted in a sentence of life imprisonment for manslaughter, although later chemical tests proved that the wounds were caused by a bullet. Tests on portions of the body rather than the entire corpse meet with more approval. Members of the German army carried out experiments to determine whether a 1953 death was a suicide by hanging or murder by a karate blow to the throat followed by hanging. Lieutenant Colonel Frank Elliott and Detective-Superintendent Colin MacDougal gave human larynxes of different ages blows of varying strengths and found that a high proportion of those hit sustained discernible damage. Prosecutors commended them for doing their homework.[36]

Experimentation using human corpses is an accepted part of legal, military, medical, and historical research. The physical simulation of crimes and procedures of the past and present can prove or disprove our theories and beliefs. Ethical objections to such use of the dead are considered by many to be groundless. Despite ancient superstitions, the corpse cannot be "hurt," though it can sustain mutilation. If broad consent is obtained by the family at the time of the body donation or if research is conducted only on unclaimed bodies, there is little basis for objection. Bringing admittedly gruesome experiments to light in an atmosphere of condemnation only makes the research— which will surely go on—more difficult. As far as the public is concerned, what we don't know won't hurt us and may in fact help us.

The Ingestion 11

We are very far from caves containing blade-scarred
human bones—until our ship or plane goes down,
until we become lost in a frozen land, until our city is
besieged by enemy troops. Then, with our food supplies
dwindling or gone and famine wasting our bodies, we are
transported back to those caves, and we are faced with the
same bleak choices our ancestors had. Most often we
make the decision they did, and newly scored bones soon
litter the campsite or the deck or accumulate in the
bottom of the boat. The dead are not always wholly
interred when the burial party is starved.
—Edward E. Leslie, *Desperate Journeys, Abandoned
Souls: True Stories of Castaways and Other Survivors*[1]

Animal Scavengers

There are numbers of animals that have, when given the chance, par-
taken of human meat. Alligators, sharks, fish, and crabs have consumed bodies they found in rivers or oceans. The corpses of those who have died on
land have become food for vermin (insects and rats), domesticated animals
(cats, dogs, and even pigs), and wildlife (leopards, tigers, and bears). Hyenas,
jackals, and the other less notorious carrion-eaters have been attracted by the
number of bodies resulting from mass disasters. "Man's best friend" has made
a meal of his or her master when confined with the corpse for any length of
time. Pets have also been known to steal part of a body from the casket as
easily as a steak from the grill. The results of all of this ingestion and digestion are mutilated bodies and strewn skeletons, often difficult to identify. The
actions of animals may be a detriment to the work of the forensic anthropologist and a nightmare to the family of a devoured victim, but they oper-
ate as natural custodians in the cycle of decay.

Alligators have often swallowed a human meal, in whole or in part. A body abandoned in the ocean may become food for crabs, which will consume the soft parts within a few days. Bodies found in San Francisco Bay have shrimps at their orifices. Another sea creature fond of human flesh is the sheatfish or wels, weighing as much as 700 pounds and measuring up to 15 feet in length. Specimens caught over the centuries have contained a right hand and two rings (1558), the body of a seven-year-old child (1754), and the body of a full-grown woman in eighteenth-century Turkey.[2] The barracuda is a more notorious carnivore, that was in times past believed to prefer the bodies of blacks to Caucasians and to disdain the taste of Frenchmen.[3] The shark is perhaps the best-known oceanic predator and has often been cut open to reveal its human meals, which it takes as long as 20 days to digest. In 1932, fisherman caught a 12-foot brown shark whose stomach contained a human arm and right hand probably belonging to the victim of a recent aircraft accident between Key West and Havana. On land, bodies are more accessible to insects, which are said to respond to a "universal death scent," and to rats, who will eat the tissues of the face and hands, the flesh and small bones of the feet, and the abdominal organs. After receiving extreme unction, Italian poet and playwright Pietro Aretino (d. 1556) cautioned his survivors, "Keep the rats away now that I'm all greased up."[4] It is often more difficult to keep away the flies, an omission which results in the maggot activity discussed in the chapter on decay.

It is the smell of decay which leads dogs to the dead, a trait exploited by police to find missing bodies. Ubelaker and Scammell suggest that when dogs are not on a leash, they find many more bodies than they bring home, but do not speculate about whether they make a meal of them. The authors do note that dogs confined with their dead owners have no qualms about eating their flesh. When an unfortunate Tennessee woman died of natural causes in her home, her three dogs—two German shepherds and a collie—survived on her remains until they were found two weeks later. Neither of the woman's daughters were eager to adopt the dogs, nor were any of the locals who read the newspaper advertisement and had heard the story. When the feces of the dogs were x-rayed in an attempt to recover the victim's diamond ring, authorities found instead hairpins, three teeth, and a painted toenail still wrapped in a section of pantyhose.[5] Nearly 2,000 years earlier, an Italian suffered the same fate. Excavations in Pompeii revealed that a dog trapped in a room with a human corpse had eaten the body and gnawed the bones.[6] According to Kenneth Iserson, an appetite for the flesh of victims' burned bodies is the reason firetrucks no longer carry the traditional Dalmatian.[7]

When the plague enveloped Europe, hungry wolves ventured into Paris, where they fought with dogs, pigs, and cats over the unburied dead. The skies were blackened by ravens and vultures.[8] In remote African districts, the scavengers are more exotic. Unburied bodies satisfy the appetites of leopards, hyenas, and jackals. The lordly lion is said to have the least discriminating nose of all.[9] The tiger is reported to gorge itself on the bodies resulting en masse from natural disasters. In the arctic, polar bears are responsible for the exhumation of a number of Eskimo corpses, but rarely eat them. Hungry hyenas dig up recent graves for the purpose of consuming the occupants. It has been common in many places to cover new graves with stones to keep the animals from penetrating them. Without a companion to perform this service for him, Alexander Selkirk—marooned on the island of Más á Tierra in the early eighteenth century—professed that one of his greatest fears was having his body devoured after his death by his pet cats. Animals that may not otherwise have had the chance to taste human flesh, will take advantage of human mishap or misfortune. When a brawl erupted at a wake in Puerto Rico in 1912, the coffin overturned and fell through the floor of the house. The body spilled out into a pen of domestic pigs that ate most of it before they could be driven off.[10] According to a story some insist is apocryphal, the heart of Thomas Hardy was eaten by the family cat when it was being prepared for burial in 1928. When the body of the Duke of Orléans was eviscerated in 1723 so that his heart could be taken to Val-de-Grace, the prince's great dane was in attendance. Before he could be stopped, the dog had pounced on the heart and eaten a quarter of it.

While casket-raiding stories may be exaggerated, the victim's manner of death is at least already known. The work of animals and insects on the body or bones of the abandoned dead often misleads investigators: "Animal activity is one of the most frequent sources of skeletal alterations in murder cases, and it can be one of the most confusing, especially to the inexperienced examiner. I have seen numerous examples of carnivore damage mistakenly associated with cause of death, and I have also seen cases in which the real cause of death was hidden among the tooth marks of a rat or dog."[11]

In *Bones*, Ubelaker and Scammell discuss a case in which a body had been mummified by exposure to cold, dry conditions and yet could not be identified visually because rats had eaten away the lips, cheeks, most of the nose, and all soft tissue for a diameter of four inches around the empty orbits of each eye.[12] It is known that dogs, wolves, coyotes, and foxes eat human corpses in a definite order, beginning with the face, hands, and spongy parts of the arm and leg bones. In addition to altering evidence on bones and removing flesh from them, animals sometimes strew the bones over a wide area or destroy them entirely.

By dumping the bodies of their victims in remote areas, murder victims may consciously or unwittingly take advantage of animals' capacity to reduce the body to bones, which are then scattered, fractured, or disguised. But while animals may sometimes destroy a body, other times they call attention to a corpse that might otherwise never have been found. Birds circling a carcass may signal investigators searching for a missing person. If the body is found, however, it is often difficult to separate cause from effect. When the contents of a beast's stomach are revealed to be human, it may be only a guess whether the animal caused the death or merely disposed of the remains. It is the continuing effort of forensic anthropologists to reduce such guesswork to science. When the situation is known, such as the confinement of a pet with a deceased owner, the instincts of the animal may be acknowledged or the event may be viewed as a regrettable form of survival, akin to the human practice of cannibalism in times of duress.

Cannibalism

Like animals, some humans have a taste for human flesh. Men like Peter Stubb of the sixteenth century, Alferd Packer of the nineteenth, and Albert Fish of the twentieth combined the acts of murder and cannibalism. Others acquire the taste or pursue it when required by cultural ritual, drinking the blood or eating the flesh of deceased relatives. Still others turn to cannibalism or necrophagy when no other means of sustenance is available: during famines, after accidents, or adrift at sea. The consumption of human flesh is held to do more than provide protein. It has been variously believed to transfer strength and other properties of the victims, to allay grief, and to cause madness or death. The history of cannibalism—more than 400,000 years of it—is a history of contradictions. It has cured and killed, it has been a sacrament and a punishment, it has been abhorred and relished, and it has been condemned in some instances and tolerated in others. As Sweeney Todd said to Mrs. Lovett, "The history of the world, my sweet—is who gets eaten and who get to eat."[13]

For some, human flesh is a delicacy. The evidence of crushed skulls leads scientists to speculate that Peking Man relished human brains half a million years ago. In the third or fourth century, St. Jerome wrote that the North Britons had plenty of cattle and sheep, but considered the occasional human ham or slice of female breast a luxury.[14] The natives of Fiji determined that the best way to cook a man was to bake him whole, and one chief was credited with having eaten 900 people. Native New Zealanders were said to slaughter and bake over 1,000 prisoners at a time, and Melanesian Islanders considered human brains a gourmet dish. The Bafum-Bansaw of Africa pumped palm oil into the corpse to let it marinate.[15] Unlike cannibalism forced by circumstance, voluntary cannibalism makes no attempt to dissociate the meat from the human body. Shih Hu, fourth-century ruler of the Huns of northern China, occasionally had a woman from his harem beheaded, cooked, and served to his guests, while the uncooked head was passed around on a platter to prove he hadn't sacrificed the least beautiful.[16]

Others learn to tolerate the taste of human meat in cultures where cannibalism is a show of force over one's captives. Until the mid-nineteenth century, natives of Fiji used to rub pieces of flesh over the lips of infants to train them in the practice of the cannibalism of their enemies. Especially hated enemies were stripped of their ears, noses, tongues, fingers, toes, and limbs and made to watch as these were cooked and consumed. Women held as slaves in a South American tribe were impregnated so that their captors could eat their babies. The Batak tribe of Sumatra ate adulterers, traitors, spies, deserters, and members of attacking war parties. A native missionary in the Cook Islands in 1879 recorded one of the benefits of war for the participants:

> When people were killed, the men tossed the bodies back and the women fetched and carried them. They chopped the bodies up and divided them. ... When the battle was over, they all returned home together, the women in front and the men behind. The womenfolk carried the flesh on their backs; the coconut-leaf baskets were full up and the blood oozed over their backs and trickled down their legs. It was a horrible sight to behold. When they reached their homes the earth ovens were lit at each house and they ate the slain. Great was their delight, for they were eating well that day.[17]

As recently as 1975, Cambodian soldiers practiced cannibalism on captured prisoners or enemy corpses, whose lungs, livers, hearts, biceps, and calf muscles were eaten. Those in the company of cannibals have to consider the possibility of being consumed. In the seventeenth century, a Jesuit missionary was tortured and cannibalized by the Iroquois, who roasted and ate his heart and flesh stripped from his legs, thighs, and arms, in addition to drinking his blood. Dr. Albert Schweitzer bravely faced up to the possibility of such a fate, penning the unused epitaph, "We have eaten Dr. Schweitzer and he was good to the end ... and the end wasn't bad."[18] Many cannibals, however, disdain the taste of white flesh. Australian aborigines found the flesh of white men to be salty and to cause nausea.[19]

In some cultures, cannibalism is associated with bereavement rather than conquest. It is a sacred duty rather than a show of power or a practical necessity: "'Sarco-cannibalism' is done with extreme repugnance and dread and usually followed by a violent vomiting fit. At the same time it is felt to be a supreme act of reverence, love, and devotion."[20]

In Indonesia, the bodily liquids resulting from decomposition are allowed to drip over rice, which is then eaten by members of the dead person's family. In this way, the living share in the death and the deceased is thought to exist in the living.[21] According to Herodotus, the Issedones mixed the flesh of the dead with beef and conducted a funeral feast. For some tribes of Australia, the loss of a loved one was assuaged by carrying a piece of his or her body and eating a tiny bit of it when overcome by grief. The eating of dead family or community members follows prescribed ritual. Members of some Venezuelan tribes indicate during their lives those by whom they wish to be eaten after death. The body of a dead Australian Bushman was apportioned according to custom: mother and child could partake of one another, but father and child could not.[22] In Papua, New Guinea, cannibalism was practiced by the women of the Gimi tribe over a number of days. The corpse was believed to retain vestiges of awareness and was persuaded to dissolve inside the grieving women. The Irish were said to have drunk the blood of dead relatives until the sixteenth century. In this century, the Amahuaca of eastern Peru were still grinding up the teeth and bones of the dead to concoct a drink for the bereaved. Ritual cannibalism is thought to keep the soul within the tribe and shows pious desire to partake of the good qualities of one's forebears.[23]

The meat of men and women is said to contain strength and potency. George Rushby quoted a Tanzanian about its unique properties: "It tastes better and is much sweeter than elephant meat or any other meat, including gorilla and chimpanzee. Also, as you know, when you place a piece of elephant meat in the pot to boil, it just lies there at the bottom like a stone while it is being cooked—it is quite dead. But if you boil a peace of human meat it bumps and bounces around and jigs about in the pot; it has life."[24]

This life was believed transferable, thus eating the heart gives one courage, the reproductive organs give power and virility, and the liver adds strength to the soul. Believers have often exploited or abused these magical properties. A Fijian chief fortified himself with human flesh whenever he had his hair cut. Navajo witch doctors rely on corpse powder for their evil magic, and human remains are a necessary ingredient in Haitian voodoo potions. An Australian sorcerer reputedly digs up a corpse and eats the bones. And in the Banks Islands, a sorcerer eats a morsel of the corpse to ally himself with the ghost and is then able to direct its destructive powers against any target.[25] As late as 1949, a potion made of charred flesh and fat mixed with herbs was used by the natives of Basutoland to strengthen warriors before battle, protect the village, or ward off evil spells.[26] Some Venezuelan tribes would collect the fluid from a corpse as it decayed and make a potent drink reserved for medicine men. Members of the Human Leopard Society obtained human fat and blood in the late nineteenth century for use in a magical and protective potion.

The life-sustaining properties of human meat have been put to practical use by those in dire straits. The will to live drives some to eat the dead, some to murder the living, and some to go about the latter democratically. Perhaps the best-known example is that of the Donner party, a California-bound group of 87 people stranded in the Sierra Mountains in the winter of 1846. Less than half of the group survived, most of them resorting to cannibalism and one to murder. The widespread taboo against cannibalism accepts its practice only in a desperate situation when one is devoid of any other source of nourishment. In such cases, the public was not intolerant and objected to prosecution in cases of survival cannibalism provided certain proprieties were observed.[27] These may include preserving the anonymity of the dead, or in more intimate circumstances stripping the body of its individuality. Three crew members rescued from the rigging of the waterlogged *Thekla* in 1892 had survived by eating the body of a fourth, but first cut off the man's head and hands and threw them into the sea. A prelude to eating the flesh of the dead has sometimes been to drink their blood. This done, there is nothing left but to parcel out the body to those willing to partake of it. "Cannibalism seems to follow a pattern in instances of starvation: once the decision is made, the initial sections removed from the body are the meatier areas like the buttocks, thighs, lower legs, and arms. Recognizable human parts, such as hands and feet, are not eaten at first. As time passes and hunger continues to tear at the survivors, the options of where the flesh comes from are reduced, and bone marrow, organs, arteries, and skin are consumed."[28] When this has been carried out and rescue is still not forthcoming, survivors must face the necessity for a martyr from their own ranks. Sometimes the weakest among them becomes food for the rest, but more often a lottery is conducted.

Richard Parker, cabin boy on the *Mignonette*, had the misfortune to be the first to fall ill after their ship was lost in a storm in the South Atlantic in 1884. Parker, Captain Tom Dudley, mate Edwin Stephens, and able seaman Ned Brooks had drifted in an open boat for 24 days and considered drawing lots some time after their two tins of parsnips and the turtle they caught were consumed. When Parker became violently ill after drinking a considerable amount of seawater, they killed him, stripped his body of clothes, and cut out and ate his heart and liver. (Ironically, Richard Parker had the same name and met the same fate as the cabin boy in Edgar Allan Poe's *The Narrative of Arthur Gordon Pym*, which the captain was said to have been reading on the voyage.) The men had been living on Parker's flesh for four days when they were rescued by a passing vessel. They made no attempt to cover up their deed afterward, although Captain Dudley did try to explain it in a written statement:

> What must our poor brain and mind have been when that awful impulse came to put the poor lad out of his misry [sic] for he was dying at the time the salt water killed him and the terrible deed was done for the sake of something to eat and exist up that ghastly food it makes my blood run cold to think about it now and would to God I had died in the boat I should have saved the pain from those belonging to me whatever. I can assure you I shall never forget the sight of my two unfortunate companions over that gastly [sic] meal we all was like mad wolfs who should get the most and for men fathers of children to commit such a deed we could not have our right reason.[29]

After the rescue, the courts found the captain's actions as heinous as he did, despite the well-known "custom of the sea." Dudley and Stephens were sentenced to death after Brooks became a prosecution witness, but their sentence was later commuted to six months in prison.

As rescue becomes less hopeful, victims of misfortune become inured to their means of survival and remain determined to make their only food last. In a failed attempt to rescue the eight survivors from the *Earl Moira* in 1838, the captain of another ship noticed that a body from which pieces had been carved was suspended from the mast to keep it fresh. Survivors of a plane crash in the Andes Mountains in 1972, celebrated in the book and movie *Alive*, had natural refrigeration to preserve the human meat. Although they preserved certain proprieties, such as leaving the dead wife of a survivor untouched, some still refused to eat the bodies of their dead companions. Those who did not partake of the flesh died, and those who did—16 men among the original 45 passengers—gradually became more casual about it. Upon their rescue after 10 weeks in subfreezing temperatures, the area around the fuselage in which they camped was littered with the refuse of cannibalism, particularly feet, which contained too many bones to be worth eating.[30] Another source quotes one of the survivors as he tossed a skull to another during the identification procedures after their rescue: "You should know who this guy is; you ate his brains!"[31] Their shame at having broken one of society's taboos returned after their story made headlines, and the men became reluctant to talk about their ordeal.

The misfortune of men and women consigned to choose between cannibalism and death was popularized by Eugène Delacroix (d. 1863) in his painting *The Raft of the "Medusa,"* which now hangs in the Louvre. In preparation, the artist visited the sick and dying in hospitals and borrowed corpses and severed limbs to sketch in his studio. While Delacroix's efforts were painstaking and the painting a success, the event on which it is based was more lurid than the canvas could describe. The *Medusa* was wrecked in 1816 en route to Senegal carrying more than 400 passengers. A raft was hurriedly constructed to accommodate the 150 persons who did not fit in the lifeboats. The raft was towed by one of the boats, but was soon abandoned and drifted off the coast of West Africa. The 29 men and one woman remaining alive on the third day resorted to cannibalism. Human flesh was readily available, but the means to cook or cure it were not. The *Medusa*'s midshipman said afterward, "Among the unfortunate people spared by death, the most starved ones rushed onto the remnants of one of their brothers, tore flesh off the corpse and fed themselves with this horrible meal. At that moment a great number of us did not touch it. Only a short time later, we were forced to do so."[32] For almost two weeks, the living were surrounded by and subsisted on the dead. Only 15 people on the raft survived, and 5 of these died a short time after rescue.

Alferd Packer was a more dubious character, being the lone survivor of a group of six prospectors he led into the San Juan Mountains of Colorado in 1874. Packer was convicted of murdering one of the men, Israel Swan, but the conviction was overturned. He was retried for killing all five and spent 17 years in prison as the only person in U.S. history to be convicted of cannibalism. Packer claimed he had killed in self-defense, using his victims as food only as an afterthought when he ran out of supplies. He admitted, however, that he had grown quite fond of human flesh and was quoted in the *Saguache Chronicle* of March 23, 1883, as saying that he found the breasts of the men "the sweetest meat he had ever tasted."[33] Some of those who have eaten human flesh to survive have been pleasantly surprised by the taste. When the *Francis Mary* was shipwrecked in 1826, the bodies of those who had died were cleaned and cut up by Ann Saunders, who had been engaged to the ship's cook. When she served the brains of the ship's apprentice, the captain's wife declared the dish the most delicious thing she had ever tasted.[34] A sailor on the damaged schooner *Sallie M. Steelman* (or *Stedman*), adrift for 43 days in 1878, butchered a black member of the crew who had threatened to shoot the captain and cooked his flesh. He claimed the meat tasted "as good as any beefsteak he ever ate."[35] Ned Brooks, one of the crew members of the *Mignonette* who had survived by killing and eating Richard Parker, stated plainly, "I can say that we partook of it with quite as much relish as ordinary food."[36] Typical means of preparation in the absence of fuel is to cut the flesh into slices, wash it in salt water, and dry it in the sun.

It does not always require bad weather or the malfunction of machinery to reduce men and women to cannibalism. Herodutus reported that some troops ate their own fallen warriors to prevent their bodies from being desecrated by their enemies. During Napoleon's Russian campaign, starving soldiers ate the flesh of their fallen comrades to preserve their own lives. In late nineteenth-century China, conditions of famine resulted in children under age twelve being butchered to support the lives of others. The buttocks of either sex were reported to bring the highest price. Eight hundred years earlier, human-meat restaurants had sprung up out of necessity in Hangcho, China. Menus included the flesh of old men, women, girls, and children, each with a special name.[37] In eleventh-century France, the flesh of humans was sold openly in the marketplace. Famished Huron and Iroquois Indians turned to their only means of sustenance in the seventeenth century: mothers ate their dead children and children their fathers. John Smith reported that Jamestown colonists survived starvation by disinterring the body of a murdered Indian and eating his boiled and stewed corpse. Even in this century, conditions in Russia during World Wars I and II provoked cannibalism. It was also practiced after World War II by a group of Japanese soldiers hiding in the Philippines. In some extreme situations, people have offered themselves up to preserve the lives of their companions. After the shipwreck of the sloop *Betsy* in 1756, Commander Philip Aubin reported, "When pressed with hunger and despair, my mate, Williams, had the generosity to exhort us to cut off a piece of his thigh to refresh ourselves with the blood and to support life."[38] In China in the 1870s, a man cut a piece of flesh from his arm to make a soup for his ailing mother and a young woman placed a piece of her flesh in her dying father's medicine; both parents recovered.

The need to use ourselves or fellow humans for food seems remote in this day and age, but in the quote that opens this chapter, Edward E. Leslie points out that this is a mistaken assumption. Only an acute or prolonged hardship lies between us and our worse fears. Cannibalism was practiced during the famines of the Middle Ages, sometimes on the flesh of corpses snatched from the gallows or from fresh graves. During the siege of Paris in the sixteenth century, citizens consumed horses, asses, cats, dogs, and then rats. When the animals were exhausted, they turned to tallow, soap, and leather for nourishment. When this too was gone, they ate the bodies of those who had died of starvation and finally resorted to disinterring the dead, whose bones were ground into a dough that was made into bread. The use of the bodies of the dead seems less palatable, but also less objectionable, than butchering one's fellows for food.

Somewhere between legend and fact lies the cannibalism of the Sawney Beane family, who backed themselves into a corner in fifteenth-century Scotland. The corner was a cave on the coast of Galloway, from which Beane and his wife ambushed and killed passersby. When it became too risky to sell the victims' valuables for food, the victims themselves became dinner for the couple and their increasingly large family, which grew to 14 children. The human flesh was dried, salted, and pickled, and the bones were stacked in another part of the cave. When the proverbial larder became full, excess pieces of flesh were tossed into the ocean. After the Beanes had killed an estimated 1,000 people, a victim escaped to alert authorities. A massive search revealed the cave and its occupants, which by then included numerous third-generation Beanes raised on human flesh. The entire family of 27 men and 21 women were arrested and executed by authority of James VI. The Beanes were not the only people to kill their fellow humans and live off their flesh for long periods of time. Silesian landlord Karl Denke battered to death strangers who came to him for lodging. He was discovered in 1924, and a search of his residence uncovered the remains of 30 bodies, both male and female, pickled in tubs of brine, along with a ledger he kept of his victims. Denke had been subsisting on human flesh for at least three years and chose to hang himself before he could be tried.[39]

Many murderers have interspersed regular meals with feasts of human flesh. Albert Fish, arrested in New York in 1934, confessed to killing and eating 15 children. His last victim, a ten-year-old girl, was cooked as a stew with onions and carrots. In a letter he intended to send to the victim's mother, he described his treatment of Grace Budd in 1928: "Grace sat in my lap and kissed me. I made up my mind to eat her.... I choked her to death, then cut her in small pieces so I could take my meat to my rooms, cook and eat it. How sweet and tender her little ass was roasted in the oven. It took me nine days to eat her entire body."[40] Fish was tried, found guilty, and electrocuted. Later this century, the culinary arts of Gary Heidnik were uncovered in Philadelphia. Heidnik cut up the body of a victim, froze some of the flesh in bags, and ground the rest of it in a food processor. He mixed the ground meat with dog food and fed it to both his dogs and his female prisoners. Another twentieth-century cannibal is Ottis Toole, companion of notorious serial killer Henry Lee Lucas. After their joint killings, Toole would often roast and eat the victims. When asked why he never joined Toole in the feast, Lucas casually commented, "I don't like barbecue sauce."[41] Andrei Chikatilo of Russia was convicted in 1992 of killing and eating more than 50 children and young women. He ate their hearts, stomachs, fingers, noses, genitals, and the tips of their tongues.

Even more dastardly than closet cannibals are the misdeeds of those who butcher the dead and feed the flesh to unknowing public, or worse—to the victims' horrorstruck relatives. In Germany after World War I, Fritz Haarmann murdered between 28 and 50 people, aged 13 to 20, by biting them on the throat. The "Hanover Vampire," as he was dubbed, dismembered his victims' bodies and sold the meat as sausages until he was caught in 1924 and sentenced to death by decapitation. Another German, Georg Grossman butchered the bodies of his female victims and sold the cuts as beef or pork. On the island of Coloane in Macau in 1985, Wong Chi Hang poisoned the owner of the Black Sands Resort and eight of his family members, took over the business, and served the flesh of his victims to his guests as dim sum until he was arrested in 1986. In Hainan Province, China, it was discovered in 1990 that the spiced meat in the popular dumplings Wang Guang had been serving at his White Temple Restaurant had been obtained from the buttocks and thighs of bodies at the crematorium where his brother worked.[42] Neighbors of infamous killer Ed Gein, one of whose victims was discovered dressed out like a slaughtered deer, remembered after his arrest numerous packages of "venison" he had presented to them over the years.[43] Others have been more forceful than sly. Vlad the Impaler, fifteenth-century king of Wallachia and probably a cannibal himself, forced mothers to eat their children and husbands to eat their wives. Another of his pastimes was holding a feast in which he served families crabs that had feasted on the decapitated heads of their relatives. He enjoyed taking his own meals amidst impaled and groaning victims from among the tens of thousands of residents of Wallachia that he had killed. Vlad committed murder and forced cannibalism to sway opinion, feeding three of their number to a group of captured Tartars and threatening more of the same until they agreed to fight the Turks.

Madness and bitterness have been the cause and the result of many episodes of forced cannibalism. During the Black Death, a raging peasant was reported to roast noblemen in the presence of their wives and children, who were then forced to eat their flesh. In the *Decameron*, Boccaccio recounts the true story of Sieur Guillaume de Roussillon, who killed his wife's lover, had the cook make a ragout from his heart, and fed it to his wife—an act which caused her to throw herself from the window.[44] Out of fear or pride, others have disguised their feelings after such a meal. Harpagus, who was served a meal afterward revealed to be the flesh of his sons because he had offended a Persian king, was asked how he enjoyed the food and remarked, "At the king's table no dish can displease."[45] Chinese general Yue Yang was knowingly fed the flesh of his son, who had unsuccessfully tried to reconcile the two warring sides. The general chided the severed head for the boy's ineptness, filled a bowl with the meat, and ate until the bowl was empty.[46] While cannibalism that is compelled is a means of proving one's power, cannibalism that is unforced often seems to spring from a sense of daring or an attempt to flout the mores of civilized society. A medical student at Jerusalem's Hebrew University ate a human brain to win a 12-dollar bet, after which he was suspended from the school. The Very Reverend William Buckland, dean of Westminster, whose taste spanned mice, crocodiles, and puppies, claimed to have eaten the heart of King Louis XIV of France. In the eighteenth century, Charles Domery once supplemented his double ration in the army with the leg of a dead soldier. Another eighteenth-century man, Nichol Brown, won a bet by slicing, broiling, and eating the leg of a gibbeted man.[47]

In the abundant stories of cannibalism are found occasional tales of poetic justice or simple bad luck. Joachim Burghard, for instance, ate his sister but died after contracting the plague which she carried. The deaths of hundreds of New Guinea tribesmen in the 1950s were caused by contact with human brain tissue eaten during mourning, a revelation which secured a Nobel Prize for Dr. Carleton Gajdusek in 1976.[48] A crew member of the shipwrecked vessel *Peggy* escaped with his life—though not his sanity—in 1765. His impending doom after having lost a lottery conducted by the survivors caused him to go deaf and insane and ironically made the others afraid to eat him for fear they would go mad too. Captain David Harrison of the same vessel reported that another crewman, who was too eager to wait for his share of the first victim to be fried, died after eating the liver raw. The historical linking of cannibalism with insanity or death may have been an attempt to limit its practice, above and beyond the natural revulsion most people feel. While many of the modern serial killers who have practiced cannibalism are pronounced sane under the legal definition, in past centuries such behavior was equated with madness or possession. When Peter Stubb was captured near Cologne, Germany, in 1589 and confessed to having killed and eaten at least 16 people, he was executed as a werewolf. The Algonkian tribe of North America believed that once an individual had tasted human flesh, he or she developed an insatiable desire for it that manifested itself in the "Windigo (or Wiitiko) Psychosis."[49]

Cannibalism has held a fascination for many. While it is condoned in the Bible when absolutely necessary, it is generally looked upon with disgust. Circumstances powerful enough to force humans to overcome their strong taboos against it are awe-inspiring. The stories of the survivors of the raft of the *Medusa* and the Andes plane crash become almost mythical in their proportions. Curiosity about the people put in such positions was evidenced in the nineteenth century by the popular pastime of visiting the jail cell of "Colorado Man-Eater" Alferd Packer and the display of the dinghy in which Richard Parker had been consumed. Such interest was cultivated by the cannibals to raise money, sometimes for their legal defense. In this century, curiosity has been measured by sales of *Alive* in the bookstore and at the box office and the number of sightseers who flocked to cannibal killer Jeffrey Dahmer's Milwaukee apartment building, since razed. But today, fewer practitioners of cannibalism are eager to become the center of attention. The "custom of the sea" is no longer condoned and even biblically sanctioned survivor cannibals shun the public for fear of becoming social outcasts.

The Dissolution

The metamorphosis from flesh to bone is not one
especially designed to be regarded affectionately by the
average observer.
—Thorne Smith, *Skin and Bones*[1]

Deliberate Exposure

As an alternative to the burial or entombment practiced in most cultures, exposure of the dead to the elements accomplishes skeletonization in a fraction of the time. Occasionally, it is intended as punishment, usually for the infamous or executed. Sometimes it is the disposal method used by murderers, who abandon the dead in woods or desert. Other times, burial follows a period in which the corpse remains in the home or community until after it has begun to decompose. In certain cultures, however, exposure is a technique applied democratically, but often exploiting the feeding patterns of animals. As it decays, the body is a loathsome sight. Deliberate exposure functions as a deterrent to crime, a catalyst for grief, or a preventative of the contamination of the earth.

Animals make meals of corpses as readily when they are freely offered as when they come across them by accident. Several cultures have made use of the appetites of various beasts to dispose of their dead. Natives of the Solomon Islands lay bodies on a reef so they will be eaten by sharks. In the French penal colony on Devil's Island, dead prisoners were thrown to the waiting sharks each day at four o'clock. During the days of the African slave trade, slaves who died during transport in the holds of ships were thrown overboard to be eaten by sharks, which followed the vessels for this reason. Some African tribes threw corpses to the crocodiles. Ancient Ethiopians threw their dead into lakes to return to the fish the nutrients they had consumed during their lives. A Masai tribe relied on hyenas to dispose of the dead. The Djurs of the Sudan abandon their dead to termites. Mongolians abandoned their

222

dead to be eaten by wolves, eagles, and other carnivores. The nomadic tribes of Central Asia dismembered the dead and left the pieces to be devoured by wild animals.

Birds have been used to consume the dead in Tibet and Persia. Until the 1950s, the people of Tibet took their dead to a hill, where they cut the bodies into small pieces and fed them to the birds. The bones were ground and kneaded with barley so that they, too, would be eaten. The corpses were prepared by workers who lived in huts built of skulls and bones. The Parsees of Persia exposed dead bodies in treetops or on platforms in circular "towers of silence." The body was washed and dressed, but before exposure the clothes were removed by the corpse bearers. Within a couple of hours, vultures picked the bones clean. In two to four weeks, the sun-dried bones were swept into a central pit. Because scavenger animals were considered by these Zoroastrians to be as unclean as the corpse, they were the logical choice for disposal. Interment, sea burial, or cremation would pollute the pure elements of earth, water, and fire, although the bodies of the poor, lepers, beggars, and infants were weighted and thrown into rivers and streams. In India, remains are dumped into the Ganges after cremation. To keep the river free of human debris, the government has stocked it with specially developed snapping turtles that weigh 70 pounds and each consume a pound of flesh each day.

In some cultures, the dead are retained within the household or within the community for a specified time. A Malaysian tribe sometimes delayed burial for many years, while the Dyaks of Borneo buried the body after several months. The Möis of Indochina lodged their dead in open coffins in the branches of trees, burying the bones after two years. Although they have now abandoned the practice, Australian aborigines used to expose bodies in trees, then place the remains on ant hills, and later collect the bones. Some Philippine tribes still use tree burial. Native Americans of the plains wrapped their dead in buffalo hide or deer skin and placed them on platforms or in trees to either rot or be devoured. Balinesians and some tribes of northeastern India exposed corpses on platforms. The Kapauku Papuans of West New Guinea left the bodies of drowned persons to the elements after erecting a protective fence around them. The bodies of women, children, and the aged were only semi-interred, with their heads remaining above ground. Heads collected by headhunters of many tribes remained on display, hung in trees, fastened to poles, or set on piles of stones.

Others deliberately expose the dead, but in remote areas, relying on scavengers or the elements to erase evidence of a crime. Pathologist Sir Sydney Smith explains: "Because the desert is so lonely, a dead body can lie undiscovered for days or weeks, even when it is close to a village. Then identification is very difficult, for all the soft parts quickly disappear, and nothing is left but the skeleton; and even that may be partially destroyed by wild dogs. On the whole, the desert is a pretty good place for murder."[2]

In Uganda, Idi Amin relied on the appetite of crocodiles to dispose of the truckloads of corpses of those slaughtered under his rule as enemies of the state. Other killers retain animals for the purpose of keeping their crimes a secret or simply use human flesh as an easily replenishable source of food for them. Texas nightclub owner Joe Ball fed his wives and waitresses to his pet alligators. California rancher Joseph Briggen used human flesh to fatten his prize-winning hogs. In ancient Rome, the leopards used in the colosseum were fed human meat from the bodies of gladiators felled in the games. Ancient Bactrians of Afghanistan kept dogs to eat the dead. More recently, Lord Avebury, 58-year-old British peer of the realm, announced in 1987 that he was changing his will to have his body fed to the dogs at Battersea Dog's Home.[3]

When people die naturally, it can sometimes be difficult to dig a grave, especially for those close to death themselves. Lieutenant d'Anglas, a survivor of the *Medusa*, recounts the unfortunate fate of a fellow passenger on the third day of their trek through the Sahara: "The wife of a corporal, Elisabeth Delus, collapses onto the sand, dead. The sight of this corpse troubles our imagination; it predicts our own fate. But we have neither the courage nor the strength of will to dig a grave for her."[4]

"Let my carcass rot where it falls," said Lord Byron, and George MacDonald wrote in 1866 that "We should teach our children to think no more of their bodies when dead than they do of their hair when cut off, or of their old clothes when they have done with them."[5] But in many cultures, proper disposal of the dead has been mandated. It was a sacred duty for early Hebrews to bury an unburied body, but the Egyptians and the Greeks were forbidden to bury the dead in certain instances. The bodies of executed criminals were left exposed. In addition, the Greeks refused burial to the infamous, although they practiced the death penalty on generals who neglected to bury or burn the slain after battle. Native Alaskans left the bodies of "bad men" to rot.

Deliberate exposure of the dead is in some cases linked with superstition, as when the bodies of those who have drowned are left above ground. Other times it is linked with religion, for instance by the Zoroastrians of Persia, who chose a method of disposal which would not foul the sacred elements. Exposure is sometimes an efficient means of reducing the corpse, especially when it is fed to carnivores. Other times it is meant to take time, perhaps to parallel the grief of those who secure their dead in trees or in their midst. And sometimes the time is meant to punish, for instance by leaving executed persons to rot. Time is also at issue when murder victims are dumped: the killer rids him- or herself of the body as quickly as possible, without a care that the body may not vanish for some time. Exposure resulting in immediate consumption or decay out of sight of the living may be the equivalent of burial, while decay witnessed over time by the bereaved suggests an acceptance of mortality more profound than that experienced by those of us who pack the dead away or give them over to be burned.

Decay and Decomposition

Unless it is postponed or circumvented, decay quickly follows death. Without precautions, the body becomes a host to many organisms. The tissues and liquids within undergo changes in color and texture and eventually fall off the bone. Although it is a natural process, putrefaction causes smells repugnant to all and is often thought to be contagious. On the other hand, a body that has been buried is expected to return to the earth and provides the theme of many poems. In some cultures, death is not complete until the dissolution of the body. The time required varies depending on internal factors, such as weight and embalming, and external conditions, such as the amount of moisture and oxygen. In some cases, corpses undergo drying or chemical changes which result in partial, temporary, or complete preservation. In most cases, however, only deliberate mummification will save human remains from becoming the dust of metaphor.

The contagion of the dead is a fear as strong now as it was in ancient Greece. The vapors given off by the corpse as it decomposes are believed to contaminate the earth and the air. Ancient Romans and nineteenth-century cemetery reformers advocated burial outside city limits to distance people from the dangerous miasmas that rise from the graves. The planting of trees in cemeteries was intended to reduce the poisonous fumes in the air. Nonetheless, gravediggers often fell ill or died as a result of their contact with the dead. Hughes Maret reported the following incident in 1773: "On the fifteenth of January last, according to Pere Cotte, priest at the Oratoire, a gravedigger who was digging a grave in the cemetery of Montmorency struck a cadaver buried a year before with his shovel. There emerged a noisome vapor that made him shudder.... As he was leaning on the shovel to fill in the hole he had just made, he fell dead."[6]

On another occasion in 1773, a grave was being dug in the nave of the Saint-Saturnin church in Saulieu. An existing grave was opened during the excavation and emitted an odor so foul that everyone in the church was forced to leave. One hundred fourteen of the 120 children preparing for their first communion fell dangerously ill and 18 of those present—including the priest and the vicar—died.[7] Gravedigger Thomas Oakes died while digging a grave at Aldgate Church in 1838; Edward Luddett died instantly when he attempted to remove Oakes from the hole. As disease processes became better understood, deaths were attributed to cholera and plague contracted from the dead. Those who worked with corpses soon learned to take precautions, and embalming grew in popularity as a sanitizing process. When Tom Dudley, captain of the *Mignonette*, died of plague in Sydney, Australia, at the turn of the century, his body was wrapped in disinfectant-soaked sheets and placed in a coffin. The coffin was taken downriver, filled with sulphuric acid or perchloride of mercury, and buried in an exceptionally deep grave.[8] Embalmers still protect themselves and the public from contagious corpses, but the fumes of the dead continue to plague the living, as was seen in Riverside, California, in February 1994 when proximity to the body of Gloria Ramirez felled six emergency room workers.

In general, the odors issuing from the dead are disagreeable, but not noxious. But the stench of human rot is said to be unparalleled and unforgettable: "It is a smell from which human beings recoil instinctively, as if slapped. It is a thing that human beings find more repulsive than almost any other sensory experience. People who experience it for the first time always say that it takes weeks for the stench to leave their nostrils and that, even years later, simple memory can cause it to recur full-force."[9] Pathologist F. Gonzalez-Crussi remarks, "Bathe a decomposing cadaver in sweet perfumes, and it will smell of rotting carrion on a bed of roses,"[10] but some of his colleagues attempt to mask the smell with lit cigars, coffee, or a daub of menthol under their noses. Those in emergency medicine, like pathologists, are familiar with the smells of death and categorize DOAs as "fresh, ripe, or very ripe."[11] As medical students found out in their anatomy labs, the smell of death is difficult to get rid of, but out of context it has sometimes not been recognized. Nanetta Lowery, a 21-year-old woman who lived above serial murderer Jeffrey Dahmer, told reporters she had often complained to the management about the smell: "It got in my clothes and I couldn't get it out, even after washing. How were we supposed to know it was dead people?"[12]

The fate of several smelly corpses has been recorded in history. Samuel Pepys (d. ca. 1701) writes of the death of a relative whose corpse smelled so strongly that it was banished to the courtyard.[13] William the Conqueror (d. 1087) suffered a worse disgrace. The obese king had died of an internal abscess that festered and caused his corpse to explode at the funeral, driving worshipers from the church.[14] While the condition of his body may have hastened this result, the natural decomposition of bodies produces quantities of hydrogen sulfide, sulfur dioxide, methane, and ammonia that create enormous pressure inside the body and inside the casket. The gas that forms inside the body will eventually cause a submerged corpse to rise to the surface of the water, even if it is weighted. When the flesh decomposes and the gas has an outlet, a floating body may sink and will eventually become skeletonized. When bodies are consigned to the water, the skin of the palms and soles may become very wrinkled. Overall, the skin becomes white, soft, and foul-smelling. The body bloats, the eyes protrude, and the skin soon loosens and darkens, eventually sloughing off.

Numerous chemical changes take place inside the dead body, one of which may be the hydrolysis and hydrogenation of body fats, a process whereby muscles, viscera, and fatty tissues are replaced with a light, soapy, waxy substance called adipocere. The smell of this substance is said to be especially strong. The formation of adipocere in adult bodies takes a year or more and usually occurs when the body has been in contact with water. Other changes take place in days or weeks. Livor mortis, or change in color, takes place soon after death, and the face and vulva or scrotum begin to discolor and swell. A greenish coloration appears over the right lower abdomen within two or three days, rigor mortis (discussed in the Foreword) comes and goes, and the abdomen distends with gas that turns the skin from green to purple to black. Gas may also cause the tongue and eyes to protrude, the intestines to be pushed out through the vagina or rectum, and fluid to be purged from the nose, mouth, and other orifices. Surface veins appear brownish, and within a week the skin may develop blisters that burst. Soon the epidermis sheds in large irregular patches, and blood-stained fluid may run from the mouth and nostrils. The eyeballs and brain liquify, nails and hair loosen and fall off, and tissue is converted to a semiliquid state. Later the abdominal and thoracic cavities burst open and the body dissolves.[15]

Several factors affect the decay of the body, which occurs in four stages: fresh, bloating, decaying, and dry (skeletal). A rule of thumb holds that "one week in air equals two weeks in water equals eight weeks buried in the ground."[16] If the body is exposed to heat or the deceased had a fever, decomposition will progress more rapidly. Warm temperatures also hasten autolysis, the destruction of tissues by the body's natural enzymes. A body exposed in the winter will decay more quickly from within, and the skin is more likely to stain, mold, and discolor because it does not slough off as quickly. Clothing or shrouds speed up decay of the body. Thin people and those who died suddenly and in good health decompose more slowly than others. Deep burial also retards decomposition. Bodies that have been buried three to four feet deep may take many years to skeletonize. Corpses that have been embalmed may decay more slowly over the first six months, depending on the amount of body fat. Embalming may also retard larval activity and disintegration, as a group of researchers found:

> After about three weeks of warm weather exposure the hands had shriveled and started to lose pigmentation, there was pronounced tissue loss in both legs, the hair had begun to detach, and the body cavity aspiration points in the groin and under the arm had begun to decompose. But the body was still fully articulated and retained most of its flesh, even though a non-embalmed cadaver would have already disintegrated. After two more months, the tissues of the embalmed murderer's face had shrunk only slightly, and there was some attrition due to rodent activity around the ears, nose, and lips, but even the eyes were still intact... . It was still intact after another four months, and by then the process of deterioration had gone about as far as it ever would.[17]

Like embalming, quicklime (often thought to reduce a body more quickly) is a preservative. Lime combines with body fat to produce a hard soap that resists insects and bacteria and retards putrefaction.[18] Different parts of the body may also decay at different rates. In soil that is naturally acidic, bone is poorly preserved, but some organic remains may survive. In alkaline soils, organic remains decay quickly, but bone is preserved.[19] Body parts that are more resistant to decay than others include the bones, teeth, cartilage, hair, and nails. The female womb, a very hard and compact muscle mass, is said to be the organ most resistant to decay. A body in hot, dry air may mummify in some places and decompose in others, particularly where body parts are pressed together or where they are in a tight location from which fluids cannot easily evaporate.[20]

The dissolution of the body is often furthered by insects, if they have access to it. Folklore is rife with the image of worms gobbling up our earthly remains, as they do in two versions of a popular rhyme:

> Did you ever think when the hearse goes by,
> That some fine day you are going to die?
> They'll put you in a wooden shirt
> And cover you over with gravel and dirt.
> The worms crawl in, the worms crawl out,
> They're in your ears and out your snout.
> Boo hoo, boo hoo, boo hoo hoo hoo.

> Whenever you see a hearse go by
> You think of the day you're gonna die.
> They wrap you up in a bloody sheet
> And then they bury you six feet deep.
> The worms crawl in, the worms crawl out,
> Eating your guts and spitting them out.

In his dictionary, Ambrose Bierce (d. ca. 1914) defines "worm's-meat" as "The finished product of which we are the raw material. The contents of the Taj Mahal, the Tombeau Napoleon and the Grantarium."[21] The physical fate of the body after death is obviously grounds for humility because flies are not choosy about the bodies on which they lay their eggs. In open air, thousands of eggs may be laid in the corpse's nose, mouth, ears, and any injured area. In hot weather, maggots can strip a body to the bones in about two weeks. Even in cold weather, maggots can survive in the warm environment caused by decay inside the body.

William "Tender" Russ, a 61-year-old gravedigger, complained to his interviewer that the modern burial service omits the biblical verse from Job about the worms feeding sweetly on the body. "They say these things are morbid. Well they *are* morbid. It is what people need when they are staring down at the grave-dirt."[22] Maggots are a reminder of mortality, but are both a help and a hindrance to forensic anthropologists, who examine them to determine time of death and then must work around them to search for cause of death. Flies were a reminder to serial killer Dennis Nilson of the victims he had deposited beneath his floorboards. Twice a day he sprayed his apartment to kill the flies as they emerged from the decaying flesh of the dead. While the larvae of the blowfly are most commonly associated with the eating of flesh, the *Wall Street Journal* reports that the most predominant pest in the mausoleum is the phorid fly. The phorids lay their eggs on the corpse before entombment or inside the casket. If the adults can't squeeze through the casket seal, they lay their eggs along the crack so their offspring can squeeze through after hatching. It is claimed that a single pair of phorid flies in a crypt could produce 55 million adults in as little as two months.[23] Exposed bodies become prey to an even greater variety of insects, including several species of fly and beetles.

As disfavorable as it is, ingestion by insects is merely one of the ways by which dead bodies are recycled. The corpse as fertilizer is a theme that has pervaded poetry and resulted in the harvest of bodily remains for practical purposes. In England in the 1830s and 1840s, tons of human bones were crushed in mills and used as fertilizer. In China, bones have been salvaged for this use from necropolises. Nineteenth-century economists favored cremation over burial, knowing that ash is an excellent fertilizer. Others urged that cemeteries be converted to farmland. "The pretty flowers that blossom here / Are fertilized by Gertie Greer," reads a typical epitaph. Many people have requested burial in their flower gardens, but the idea of the body becoming part of the vegetables we eat has been characterized as cannibalism once removed: "After death, and through the process of decay, the human body is converted into other organic chemicals. These may be absorbed by plants, and people may eat these plants or their fruit. Thus the atomic elements making up the deceased person can eventually come to be in other people."[24] The reality of the "earth to earth" phenomenon is not as inviting as the poets would have us believe. "Dust to dust they say. It makes me laugh. Mud to mud, more like," says William "Tender" Russ.[25]

While Omar Khayyam writes of herbs springing from unknown but lovely lips,[26] poets also use the inevitable decay of the female form to remark on human vanity. "See, ladies, with false forms / You deceive men, but cannot deceive worms," writes Cyril Tourneur in "Thou Shell of Death."[27] Even the handsomest and wealthiest of men must also bloat and rot in the grave. The decay of the flesh removes all signs of individuality, except for variations in bone size and structure. Seventeenth-century English Puritans preached that the soulless corpse will be a horror to all who behold it. Epitaphs of the 1700s make reference to the decayed body to compare it to the resurrected dead and to existence in human memory. Corpses are put away because they are objectionable to the senses, but also because they are no longer useful. *Mummies* author Georgess McHargue writes that bodies which did not naturally decay would be as bothersome to have around as old tin cans.[28] Plastic surgeon Robert M. Goldwyn, on the other hand, mourns that "My human canvases will have desiccated into nothingness along with me."[29] This, too, is vanity and despite such sentiments, the flesh will melt.

For some, death has meant the complete dissolution of the body. The period of mourning was intended to correspond to the amount of time it took the corpse to decay. In ancient Greece, the rate of decay was believed to be in direct proportion to the social standing of the deceased. The Greek Orthodox church stated that only the bodies of excommunicants did not decompose. Thus Greek curses include "May the earth not receive you" and "May you remain undecomposed."[30] Roman Catholics believe that only saintly corpses are exempt from decay, although the devil rejoices in parodying the works of the Lord.[31] Scientifically speaking, mummification can occur naturally under the right conditions, but decay is the general rule. Whether casketed or merely shrouded, bodies do in fact become food for worms. Many people authorize the cremation of their bodies to avoid the usual fate, and many others merely avoid thinking about it, but the rotting of the body after death—as poets so eagerly point out—is a counterpoint to our earthly vanity.

THE KEEPING
OF THE CORPSE

The Preservation

Burial ... [is] often preceded by strenuous efforts to keep
the body just like life, and the usual method is to make a
mummy of it by drying or embalming or by a mixture of
the two. No satisfactory method has yet been found, and
except in America most people have stopped trying.
—Barbara Jones, *Design for Death*[1]

Cryonic Suspension

Cryonics, the freezing and storing of the dead, is an attempt to lengthen
human life. By keeping corpses intact indefinitely, practitioners hope—but
do not promise—that their condition will be reversed by future scientists.
The prospect raises several ethical questions, just as the preparation raises
many legal ones. Cryonic preservation is an expensive and risky undertaking.
It is something more than a fad and something less than a science. Schooled
skeptics claim that the methodologies of cryonicists are based on false suppositions. At that, believers continually reiterate that—as in the case of Pascal's Wager—there is everything to gain and nothing to lose by trying.

Cryonics is big business, requiring funds set aside in trust for the future
maintenance of one's frozen corpse. In 1988, the American Cryonics Society
boasted 81 members who had contracted to be cryonically suspended at death.
The cost of full-body preservation was $120,000 in 1993. Neuropreservation,
in which only the head is frozen, costs $50,000, but requires faith that future
scientists will have the know-how not only to restore life to the dead, but to
grow new bodies, perhaps through cloning. Nationwide, a total of between
12 and 35 people (or their heads) are currently in cold storage in Arizona,
California, Florida, and Michigan. Of the more than 1,000 members of the

Part V title page: The head of Tollund Man, an Iron-Age fertility sacrifice preserved in a Danish peat bog. Reprinted from P.V. Glob, *The Bog People*, with permission of the original pub-
lisher, Gyldendal.

233

various cryonics societies, at least 100 have made arrangements for suspension and the numbers are growing. Membership in the Alcor Life Extension Foundation was 29 ten years ago and 353 in 1993.

In addition to financial arrangements, cryonic suspension involves cooling and packaging the body. Those who have made plans for cryonic suspension wear ID jewelry or carry a card with an emergency number and cryonic stabilization information. When death occurs, immediate action is necessary. Cardiopulmonary resuscitation is carried out until the body can be attached to a heart-lung machine that cools the blood and the body more than 30 degrees in 15 minutes. Medications are administered, including blood thinners, calcium channel blockers, and free radical inhibitors. The brain may be observed through a hole made in the skull as the temperature is monitored. The body then spends nearly two days in a bath of silicone oil as it is cooled to -108° F. It is then wrapped in two sleeping bags, placed inside a protective aluminum pod, and lowered into a unit containing liquid nitrogen. Over the next 24 hours, the body cools to -321° and is transferred to a permanent upright storage container. If cryonics technicians are not immediately available when a death occurs, the mortician is instructed to replace the blood with solution used to preserve organs for transplant, pack the body in ice, and transfer it to a cryonics organization. There the body will be placed on a heart-lung machine and the preservative solution replaced with glycerol and sucrose before the freezing process begins. If the deceased has opted for neuropreservation, the chest is opened and preservative and cooling solutions are injected into the blood vessels supplying the head. The head is severed at shoulder level and placed in a silicone oil bath, a can of liquid nitrogen, and finally transferred to permanent cold storage (with several other heads). The headless body is then cremated.

Salesmen of frozen storage are hopeful about its outcome and the benefits they may reap from it: "To be a cryonicist, you must be able to take one look at a frozen body and envision a burgeoning industry of storage tanks, insurance sales, cryonics lawyers—you must be able to imagine the world on ice."[2] You must also imagine a future world in which countless damaged cells could be repaired or replaced. Opponents of cryonics argue that not a single major human organ has been successfully preserved by freezing and that organs and tissues simply crack at temperatures below -200°. They point to the damage caused by the formation of ice crystals and the resulting imbalance of electrolyte solutions.[3] "They're freezing meat not living cells," says Dr. David Pegg, a cryobiologist at Cambridge University.[4] (Many scientists believe that cryonics enthusiasts are demeaning the value of cryobiology, a legitimate field within the scientific community. They are denied membership in its official society.) In their defense, cryonicists do not claim to have any answers beyond preservation of the body without decay. Greg Palmer confirmed this during his tour of Alcor Life Extension Foundation while researching *Death: The*

Trip of a Lifetime: "Nobody I talked to at Alcor, from Carlos [Mondragon, Alcor's previous president] to the guy who tops off the nitrogen, claims anything other than a slim chance for success, no matter how much you pray *or* pay. What they do emphasize is that a slim chance is better than no chance."[5] In *No More Dying*, Joel Kurtzman and Phillip Gordon concede that "The procedure used probably amounts to little more than an ice pack on a dead body."[6]

Nevertheless, many have espoused the hope that cryonics offers. The average cryonaut is a nonreligious, apolitical, intelligent, unmarried white male in the lower to middle income bracket.[7] Dr. James H. Bedford, a 73-year-old California psychology professor, was the first to undergo cryonic preservation in 1967. Shortly thereafter, rumors surfaced that Walt Disney (d. 1966) had been frozen at death. Greg Palmer comments: "Walt was obviously a big resurrection fan, but he was far too romantic for the freezer. I suspect he's really in a glass coffin hidden in a cavern beneath Space Mountain. And there he waits, not for science, but for a kiss."[8] In reality, Disney was cremated and his ashes were deposited at Forest Lawn Memorial Park in Glendale, California. Although they are surely represented in the group contracting to be cryonically suspended, few celebrities have acknowledged their plans to the public. The notable exception is Dr. Timothy Leary (d. 1996), who announced in 1989 that he planned neuropreservation. Cryonics clients, celebrities or not, have a stab at physical immortality as either a reanimated individual or a curiosity for future scientists to study.

Practitioners of cryonics put their faith not only in the science of the future, but in the continued financial health of the organization. This faith is not always well-placed, despite prepayments and trust funds. One of the first organizations of its kind, the Cryonics Society of New York, went out of business in 1975 and the bodies in its care had to be dispersed. One of its clients, Andrew D. Mihok (d. 1968), had already been defrosted and given a military burial when his widow was unable to make payments for his long-term care. The Cryonics Society of California had worse luck. The families of nine cryonically preserved people investigated the facility in 1980 and found that the nitrogen supply had been depleted and the bodies were all badly decomposed.[9] Only the corpse of the first cryonaut, Dr. Bedford, was saved and transferred to the Alcor Life Extension Foundation then in Riverside. Alcor warns its clients that in the event of an emergency, patients in whole-body suspension may be converted to neuropreservation. Not only are cryonics societies burdened by financial difficulties, they also sometimes run afoul of the law. The staff of Alcor was charged with murder in the case of Dora Kent, a woman who had terminal cancer and had made arrangements for neural preservation. She died while at the Alcor facility and was pronounced dead by a volunteer physician who was present. Some time after she was decapitated, police officers arrested the staff and the coroner insisted that the head be decanted and autopsied. Alcor fought the arrests and the autopsy and won, but was told by the Health Department to maintain a medical doctor on staff. The diploma of their appointed "resident physician" Dr. Donovan hangs on the wall above the flask in which his body is cryonically preserved.

Cryonicists sidestep rules, but they also fight—perhaps in vain—to change them. Jack Zinn, president of the American Cryonics Society, advocates changes in the law that would allow him and his colleagues to freeze bodies that are still alive in order to leave future scientists more living cells to work with. Such ideas stretch the definition of death and provoke questions that future ethicists may face. Assuming limited resources, who will decide (and how will they decide) who gets resuscitated? Will the resuscitated suffer pain or brain damage? Will it be considered merciful to suspend a baby with disabilities in the hope of a future cure? Will resuscitated people be able to afford treatment for their medical condition? When cryonic suspension becomes the rule rather than the exception, will intentional death (suicide or homicide) necessitate obliteration of the body? Will failure to freeze one's next of kin become an error of omission punishable by law? How will the institution of marriage be affected? In what ways will life insurance provisions and estate distribution need to be revised? And perhaps most importantly, asks Isaac Asimov, how will our species evolve if it is not renewed? Some of these questions were considered by the "father" of cryonics, Robert Ettinger, some are currently being argued, and some remain rhetorical. One way or the other, time will tell.

Mummification

Mummies. The mere word conjures up images of exotically bandaged bodies once housed in elaborate tombs and now unclothed for our edification and curiosity. To stare into the face of a man, woman, or child who lived and breathed hundreds or thousands of years ago is unlike looking at a portrait or even a photograph. The mummy is a time traveler, minus consciousness. Through the deliberate actions of ancient cultures or the accidents of nature, scientists have meat on which to base their theories and the layperson has a window into other worlds. Mummies have not always been treated as anthropological treasures. They have been used as fuel, fertilizer, even medication. Out of greed, they and their treasures have been plundered. Under the guise of study, they have been unwrapped haphazardly. While they are rarely restored to their tombs, many mummies are now x-rayed rather than dismantled. They are in moisture- and temperature-controlled environments, but are still in a sense sideshow attractions.

The bodies discovered in the peat bogs of Denmark, Germany, Holland,

Sweden, Norway, and the British Isles drew crowds before and after it was revealed that they were fertility sacrifices from the Iron Age and not victims of modern violence. Nearly 700 bodies have been uncovered since the first documented case in 1781, many of them in a remarkable state of preservation because of the acidity of the water and the exclusion of air. Tollund Man was found eight or nine feet beneath the surface of a Danish bog by two men cutting peat in 1950. Observing the noose around his neck, the men contacted police, who then called in archaeologists from Aarhus University. The body was removed en bloc to the National Museum in Copenhagen, and an autopsy was conducted. It revealed that the man was more than 20 years old when he died, and he was hanged, rather than strangled. His skull was undamaged, but the brain had shrunk. The heart, lungs, and liver were well-preserved. The contents of the stomach and intestines proved to be a blend of plant remains and seeds, including barley, linseed, and knotweed, which were eaten 12 to 24 hours before death. It was decided to chemically treat only Tollund Man's head, which is the best-preserved head to have survived from antiquity in any part of the world. The treatment caused the head to shrink by 12 percent, but has allowed museum-goers the chance to see the face of a man who walked the earth 2,000 years ago: "The majestic head astonishes the beholder and rivets his attention. Standing in front of the glass case in which it is displayed, he finds himself face to face with an Iron Age man. Dark in hue, the head is still full of life and more beautiful than the best portraits by the world's greatest artists, since it is the man himself we see."[10] While Tollund Man and the other bog bodies have been darkened by the action of the peat and flattened by its weight, it is not difficult to see why they were mistaken for our contemporaries. Even the prints are still visible on their hands and feet.

Two years later and eleven miles east of Tollund, Grauballe Man was unearthed. Unlike Tollund Man, his throat had been cut, but his stomach also included a gruel made up of a variety of grains, including clover, ryegrass, buttercup, and camomile. Examination showed that Grauballe Man was at least 30 years old, had rather bad teeth, had not done any heavy work, and had died in winter or early spring. Despite a claim and several "identifications" that the body was that of a peat cutter who had disappeared in 1887, pollen analysis and carbon-14 dating proved that he lived between 210 and 410 A.D. A plaster cast was taken of Grauballe Man, and his body was preserved without shrinkage by a tanning process, followed by treatment with glycerine and oils. Smoking was used to preserve the body of a man found in 1871, the first bog body to be photographed. Other bog bodies have been returned to the peat or buried in churchyards when they began to decay upon exposure to the air. The bodies also include women: one exhumed in 1835, another in 1842, and a third in 1879. Although most of the sacrificial victims have been found naked, some fragments of cloth and some complete garments have also been unearthed. Several of the bodies were pinned down in the peat, probably for superstitious reasons, by tree limbs and forked sticks—no match against modern diggers. Bodies of Native Americans dating back 8,000 years have been similarly preserved in a bog in Florida.

Like peat, ice also carries ancient men and women through to the present day with little deterioration of their flesh. Frozen mummies, like other bodies, are often found by accident. In 1991, tourists climbing the Similaun glacier in the Swiss Alps came across the body of a 35- to 40-year-old man killed accidentally 5,300 years ago whose remains were so remarkably intact that even the color of his eyes was evident. Scythian tombs discovered in the Altai Mountains of Siberia in 1924 contained three skeletons and four human bodies dating to 430 B.C. and still bearing the body tattoos applied during life. The bodies that had not been skeletonized proved to have been embalmed, probably since burial could only be carried out at certain times of the year. The brain had been removed through a hole made in the skull, which was then filled with dirt, pine needles, or pine cones. The plate of bone was secured back in place with a twist of horsehair, also used to sew up the eye sockets and other orifices. Plaits of hair removed prior to trepanning the skulls were found near the heads. The entrails were removed and replaced with sedge grass. The legs, arms, and buttocks contained deep holes that may indicate introduction of a preservative, possibly salt. Decapitation of two of the bodies and the dismemberment of one point to tomb-robbing.[11]

Other frozen bodies have surfaced or been brought to light by scientists. Prehistoric Inuits have been found in the ice near Barrow, Alaska, and in Herjolfsnaes, Greenland, Inuit bodies were preserved wearing the everyday clothing of medieval times. Bodies do not have to be ancient to be of interest, however. A scientific mission to locate buried members of Sir John Franklin's ill-fated arctic expedition of 1845–48 succeeded in 1981 and solved a historical mystery. The bodies of 20-year-old Petty Officer John Torrington, 33-year-old Private William Braine, and 25-year-old Able Seaman John Hartnell were painstakingly exhumed from the permafrost of Beechey Island in the Arctic Circle. The bodies were examined and returned to their frozen graves. The cause of death of these three men in 1846 (and presumably the other 126 men in the expedition) was not starvation, but complications of lead poisoning from the lead solder used to tin the food they relied on for so many months.

Mummification will occur naturally in conditions of heat, cold, aridity, airlessness, salinity, or alkalinity. The bodies of newborn infants are easily mummified if they are concealed in a dry place because they are sterile and therefore contain no destructive bacteria. Adult bodies have been mummified when they were left in an environment of very low humidity and protected from insects or carnivores. The body of Count Christian Friedrich von Kahlbutz (d. 1702) was found to have been preserved naturally when his crypt in Germany was opened in 1783. The naturally mummified male corpse found beneath the altar of the Church of St. James Garlickhythe in London is estimated to be about 300 years old. Natural mummification leaves the skin leathery and like parchment, and the organs have decayed long before. Some cultures intentionally make use of preservative conditions, allowing their dry climate to desiccate the body, wrapping it with absorbent materials, or burying it in soil with favorable properties. Mummification is achieved deliberately by eviscerating the body, replacing soft tissues with plastic materials, drying by fire, smoke curing, use of resinous substances, or filling the body with antiseptic substances.[12] Tibetan lamas were disemboweled, packed with lacquer-saturated padding, and wrapped in silk. The body was placed in the lotus position and allowed to dry for several days in a room filled with salt and heated air. The body was covered with gold leaf, conveyed to the Hall of Incarnations, and seated on a throne in the company of lamas of past ages.[13] Artificial mummification was also practiced in Australia, China, South America, the United States, and of course Egypt.

The mummies of Egypt are the most famous, swathed in ritual and bandages since they were first prepared in 2600 B.C. The ancient Egyptians carefully prepared and anointed their dead to prepare them for life after death. The body was meant to remain intact and recognizable so that it could be reinhabited by the soul. Once popularized, mummification was not easily discouraged. Egyptian Christians continued to preserve their dead more than two and a half centuries after conversion. All told, the ancient Egyptians mummified more than 500 million human bodies. As the Egyptians perfected their techniques, only inferior embalming or external forces caused the body to deteriorate. Many of the mummies that survived did so in remarkable condition, with even their eyelashes in place. Mummification was thought to have arisen when the Egyptians noticed the preservation of bodies which resurfaced after burial in the desert sands. The drying of the body prevented decay, so they attempted it deliberately using natron, a salt collected from the shores of the Wadi Natsrun, a lake outside Cairo. The sodium carbonate in the natural salt dissolved fat. The unclothed body was placed on a slightly sloped table, and natron was heaped over it to leach out the liquids over a period of 40 days. The body emerged darker in color and 75 percent lighter in weight, with skin taut or shriveled in some places and loose and rubbery in others.

Before the dehydration of the corpse, it was eviscerated and washed. A diagonal incision was made in the lower abdomen through which the intestines, stomach, liver, spleen, and lungs were removed. The female reproductive organs were also taken out, but the heart—considered the seat of intelligence—was left in place. Until approximately 1500 B.C., the brain was also left untouched, but it then became customary to remove it piecemeal through the nostrils, eye sockets, or a hole in the skull. Temporary stuffing consisting of rags, straw, wood shavings, sand, dried grass, and bags of natron was inserted into the empty abdominal cavity to speed drying and prevent crushing during dehydration. The body was washed again after treatment with natron and dried to prevent mold. The skin was packed with linen, sawdust, or mud to restore its fullness, and the empty skull was filled with sawdust, resin, and linen. Broken limbs were splinted. Bags of resin-soaked linen were inserted in the abdominal cavity, which was then sewn up. The eyes (sometimes replaced with onions or small stones), nails, and external genitals were given special attention. Preparation was not complete without anointing the body with oils and resins. The skin was rubbed with oils, wax, and spices. Hot resin was applied—sometimes sparingly and other times in abundance—to waterproof and toughen the mummy. The blackened and brittle appearance of bodies coated with resin gave mummies their name, "mummiya" being the Arabic word for the bitumen or pitch they believed the bodies had been dipped in.

The careful bandaging often took upwards of two weeks. Wrappings were frequently made of used domestic articles, such as towels or clothing, and varied in width from one centimeter to five meters, depending on whether they were used to fill hollows, envelop the entire body, or create a pleasing design around the exterior. As much as 300 meters of cloth was used in the preparation of a single mummy. As each layer of bandages was added, so were jewelry, amulets, and a layer of molten resin. The jewelry was meant to protect the body and was, as evidenced by the lack of clasps and counterweights, intended solely for the use of the dead. Other ornaments were added for aesthetic reasons. The mummy of Queen Ahmose-Nefertari, who had died in old age, was decorated with 20 strings of human hair to replace her own which she had lost. Placement of the arms was dictated by custom or class. Nonroyal mummies had outstretched arms, with those of women placed along the inner or outer thigh and those of men placed over the genital organs. In the Eighteenth Dynasty (1567–1320 B.C.), the arms of the pharaoh were crossed over the chest, as were the arms of all male mummies in the Ptolemaic period (330–305 B.C.). Later mummies, particularly those which were transported for embalming or burial, were equipped with labels. Masks were made of cartonnage, a kind of cardboard made of layers of papyrus. Just before mummification went into decline in the Roman period, the external appearance became the most important aspect of the preparation. Bandages were cleverly patterned, and portraits painted on board covered the face.

Even the organs which had been removed from the body were given special treatment. After being washed and dried in natron like the corpse, they were sealed in four canopic jars that were placed in the tomb. Each jar was topped with the image of a protective deity: human-headed Imsety guarded the liver, baboon-headed Hapy the lungs, jackal-headed Duamutef the stomach, and falcon-headed Qebehsenuef the intestines. In addition, everything used during the embalming process was entombed in a special cache near the body:

> Nothing which had been in contact with the deceased's flesh could be thrown away. Every piece of linen stained with blood or soiled with fluids, all the natron wadding which had absorbed the fats, each scrap of material which had been used to clean the body, even the natron in which the body had been buried and which was impregnated with the liquid exuded, all had to be preserved. There were vessels filled with used sawdust and pots of damp natron, jars of greasy stuffing material and vases of rags soaked in the discharges from the body. The embalming chamber was swept out and the rubbish put in sacks, so as not to lose even the tiniest particle of the dead person.[14]

Understandably, those who prepared the dead for eternity—employment full of grisly sights and smells—were disdained except for their skill as mummifiers. The embalming establishments and the cemeteries were both located on the west bank of the Nile, because of the association of the setting sun and the underworld, but also because of the smell. The embalming profession was looked upon with awe and disgust: "The embalmer's fingers are evil-smelling, for their odour is that of corpses," reads a contemporary papyrus.[15] Embalmers often lived on the same side of the river where they worked and were provided with their own necropolis. They inherited their profession as either "cutters," who eviscerated the body, or "salters," who preserved it. Their assistants washed the body and organs and prepared the ointments and bandages. The embalming system was governed by an administration which collected dues and offered a contract for a specific geographical area to each embalmer.[16]

Mummification was first practiced only on royalty, who sometimes conferred the privilege of the "king's gift" on dignitaries. Embalming was later available to all, though at varying prices and degrees of quality. Greek historian Herodotus documented the three methods of embalming that were based on how much the family could afford to spend. The costliest preparation included incising the flank and removing the organs, rinsing and spicing the body cavity, drying in natron, washing, wrapping, and anointing. The lesser methods included purging the abdomen and drying in salt or simply emptying the liquified organs through the anus after an injection of oil. The methods are estimated to have ranged from the equivalent of $300 to $1,200. Legal, as well as economic factors, sometimes discouraged proper disposition of the mummy. Bodies were deprived of burial if a judge found truth to any accusations that the deceased had led a bad life or if money borrowed against the mummy by relatives had not been repaid. The bodies of some of those who were embalmed fared better than others. Carelessness on the part of the embalmers sometimes caused the corpse to partially decay. The large number of rectal and vaginal prolapses found in Egyptian mummies are thought to be due to expanding gases produced by decay. Occasionally, limbs have been lost or rearranged. This may in some cases be blamed on political unrest, which caused workers to mummify too hastily to effect proper preservation. Even royalty did not guarantee a person perfect preservation. The flesh of King Tutankhamen was badly burnt by the excessive use of resins. It may be because of its inadequate mummification that the body of this young king was replaced in his chamber in the Valley of the Kings, although he is without most of his treasures. The pharaoh Amenophis II was also robbed of his grave goods. French archaeologist Victor Loret opened the tomb in 1898 and found the body of Amenophis and the mummies of eight other New Kingdom pharaohs whom he removed to Cairo. When word leaked out that the tomb still contained treasure, looters stormed past the armed guards and tore the mummy of the king to pieces in their search for valuables.

Mummies were meant to remain undisturbed, but few have, for reasons both good and bad. "Do not inter me in order to disinter me," asks a funerary epigram from Egypt's Late New Kingdom. Georgess McHargue points out in *Mummies*, however, that contemporary tomb-robbing allowed ancient Egyptian embalmers the opportunity to assess how well their attempts were succeeding.[17] Plunder sometimes began in the embalming tent with the pocketing of amulets and talismans intended to be wrapped with the mummy. Often, mummies were evicted from their final resting places so that the chambers and sarcophagi could be reused by subsequent kings or the tombs as local family vaults. Other times, those who had sealed the royal tombs led graverobbers to the burial chambers for a share of the spoils. No mummy was found in the great pyramid of Cheops, which had been plundered despite its careful architecture. Robbers hacked mummified bodies apart with axes and daggers to obtain the hidden jewels. In less elaborate tombs, looters left the passages open to jackals that would devour the corpse. Despite the patrolling of tombs and the prosecution of looters under Rameses X, graverobbing was out of control. By the Eighteenth Dynasty, not one royal tomb remained unpillaged. Until recently, the entire city of Gurna was said to be inhabited by looters.[18] In addition to the ransacking of their tombs for valuables, mummies have been hoarded for purposes ranging from the practical to the absurd. In nineteenth-century Canada, rags for paper-making became so scarce that manufacturers imported thousands of mummies for their wrappings. During the Civil War, Augustus Stanwood, owner of a paper mill in Maine, ran short of rags and made pulp from the bandages of Egyptian mummies. Because he was unable to bleach the resulting brown paper, he sold it to butchers and grocers to wrap food. Unfortunately, this caused a cholera epidemic. Until the early twentieth century, mummies were imported for use in the manufacture of bituminous paint: "The ancient Egyptians, when they put away their dead, wrapped them in clothes saturated with asphaltum, and could never have realized the fact that ages after they had been laid in the tombs and pyramids along the Nile, their dust would be used in painting pictures in a country then undiscovered and by artists whose languages were unknown to them."[19] The mummies did not even make it out of a tomb in Thebes: they were ignited to illuminate the chamber while the robbers committed their plunder. Mummies have been used as a source of heat as well as light. Nineteenth-century natives of western Thebes broke up the resin-coated bodies with hatchets for use as fuel or filled their ovens with the wrappings.

Oddly enough, mummy in the form of a powder or ointment became a sought-after edible commodity between the twelfth and seventeenth centuries. It was available in most apothecary shops in the form of fragments or as a thick, oily, black paste. Mummy powder was the ground flesh of corpses buried in the sand and dried. Egyptian mummy powder contained bitumen, and Arabic mummy powder had been anointed with aloes, balsam, and myrrh. "Funeral balm," a concoction of pitch and herbs, did not contain flesh but was sold as such. During the Middle Ages, powdered mummy was recommended by Arab physician Avicenna for the treatment of abscesses, contusions, coughs, diseases of the throat, fractures, liver disorders, migraine, nausea, palpitations, paralysis, poisoning, rashes, stomach ailments, and ulcers. "Mummy balm" or "Egyptian salve" was sold by European druggists in the sixteenth century, although by then it was believed to cure only gastric pains (taken internally) and bruises (used externally). French surgeon Ambroise Paré objected to its use and asserted that it caused "many troublesome symptoms, as paine of the heart or stomake, vomitting, and stinke of the mouth."[20] Still, it was carried in pulverized form by France's King Francois I in case of sudden illness or accident.[21] In 1793, the hearts of the French kings themselves were said to have been sold to make mummy powder.

In 1586, London merchant John Sanderson returned from Cairo with 600 pounds of mummy parts for sale to the Turkie Companie, in addition to "divers heads, hands, armes, and feet, for shew."[22] In 1658, Sir Thomas Browne lamented the frivolous use of the bodies of the ancients: "The Egyptian mummies, which Cambyses or time hath spared, avarice now consumeth. Mummy is become merchandise, Mizraim cures wounds, and Pharaoh is sold for Balsams."[23] Criticism came from many quarters, and still the fad continued. The demand for mummy led to a ready supply, often made up from the bodies of contemporary Egyptians. One European dealer found in the mid-fifteenth century that Alexandrian merchants had been selling him the remains of derelicts who had died of disease.[24] Other traffickers dealt in the flesh of the aged, the poor, executed criminals, and those who had died in hospitals. The muscles from fresh corpses were pickled and resinated to fill European need. Although its origin and content are probably not documented, mummy powder is still preserved in European medical museums and reportedly can still be purchased in an occult pharmacy in New York.

Others sought mummies not for their curative powers but out of curiosity for the exotic. In the 1830s, mummies could be purchased at auction at Sotheby's for under £40. Public or private unwrapping of mummies was popularized by men like surgeon and anatomy professor T. J. Pettigrew. The unwrapping was generally carried out by hand as a spectacle for view by honored laymen.[25] Even the procurement of the mummies or their goods was not conducted with any scientific integrity, save a written record. Italian Egyptologist Giovanni Belzoni (d. 1823) recorded his entry into a Theban tomb for the purpose of searching for papyri:

> [I was] surrounded by bodies, by heaps of mummies in all directions; which, previous to my being accustomed to the sight, impressed me with horror.... After the exertion of entering into such a place ... nearly overcome, I sought a resting-place, found one, and contrived to sit; but when my weight bore on the body of an Egyptian, it crushed it like a band-box...I sunk altogether among the broken mummies, with a crash of bones, rags and wooden cases, which raised such a dust as kept me motionless for a quarter of an hour, waiting till it subsided again. I could not remove from the place, however, without increasing it, and every step I took I crushed a mummy in some part or other. Once I was conducted from such a place to another resembling it, through a passage of about twenty feet in length, and no wider than that a body could be forced through. It was choked with mummies, and I could not pass without putting my face in contact with that of some decayed Egyptian; but as the passage inclined downwards, my own weight helped me on: however, I could not avoid being covered with bones, legs, arms, and heads rolling from above.[26]

It was English Egyptologist Sir Flinders Petrie (d. 1942) who established guidelines for the exploration of tombs and the study of human remains.

The fascination with Egyptian mummification has led some to choose it as a method of disposal. The service is provided by a company in Salt Lake City founded in 1975 by a man who now calls himself Summum Bonum Amon "Corky" Ra. His secret recipe includes the use of phenol, formaldehyde, solvents, salts, and other undisclosed chemicals. The body is immersed for several months, wrapped in gauze, sealed with latex rubber, and covered with layers of fiberglas and resin. Hundreds of clients have contracted for the $40,000 service. For an additional charge, they may have their bodies encased in a gold-leaf veneer or placed inside a customized sarcophagus.[27] Others with similar ideas for preservation include the "father of embalming," Dr. Thomas Holmes, who patented a process of electroplating bodies to transform them into statues, and archaeologist W. F. Jones, who suggested encasing bodies within transparent blocks of methacrylate resin. Such bodies would (or will) provide a puzzle for future archaeologists.

Our attempts to view the faces of the past are in obvious conflict with the religious beliefs of the ancient Egyptians, but are nevertheless useful for their scientific value. The social value of gazing at the forms and features of

2,000-year-old bodies is more dubious. In *The Egyptian Way of Death*, Ange-Pierre Leca contends, "Only a poet could be fanciful enough to persuade us that mummies are beautiful."[28] While they may not be beautiful in the classical sense, the sight of a mummy is an emotional experience, as Christina El Mahdy counters in *Mummies, Myth and Magic in Ancient Egypt*: "No one can look dispassionately upon the face of an Egyptian mummy. Even the seasoned Egyptologist cannot remain unmoved."[29] Gazing at mummies out of curiosity's sake, however, has been considered a faux pas. In the early twentieth century, the mummy of the priestess Amenra was believed to put a curse on those who stared at her as she lay in the British Museum. And in 1980, Egyptian President Anwar al-Sadat ordered the mummy hall in the Egyptian Museum in Cairo to close because he did not think it fitting that idle visitors should stare at the dead.[30] Almost all royal mummies have been disrobed and displayed, with Rameses II touring the world under a passport listing his occupation as "king (deceased)."[31] To date, Amenhotep I remains the only pharaoh of the Cairo royal mummies to remain wrapped as found a century ago.[32]

In the laboratory, the unwrapping of mummies has revealed a number of curiosities. Flies, beetles, cockroaches, crickets, small lizards, and even a mouse have been found preserved in the resin applied to the body during its preparation.[33] Sir Max Armand Ruffer discovered parasite eggs on the mummies he examined. The unwrapping is rarely easy, but is now documented photographically. At the autopsy of the anonymous mummy dubbed "PUM II," it took nine men seven hours to penetrate the bandages with chisel, hammer, and electric saw. The operation was recorded on videotape and in more than 1,000 photographs.[34] In 1852, Johan Czermack was the first to examine mummy tissue successfully under a microscope. The advent of radiography allowed insight into the cocooned body without unwrapping it. In 1898, Sir Flinders Petrie became the first to x-ray a mummified body. Since then, many scientists have taken advantage of the technique, which became more useful when the machines became more portable. Because of this portability, James E. Harris and Kent R. Weeks were able to radiographically catalog all of the royal mummies in the Egyptian Museum in 1966, almost 100 years after Gaston Maspero and Elliot Smith became the first to study the same mummies from an anatomic viewpoint. Today, the techniques of endoscopy, histology, and chemical and physical microanalyses are in use. CT-scanning and magnetic resonance imaging are also employed.

Modern scientists have performed some curious manipulations of mummies in the laboratory and museum. They have rehydrated mummified eyeballs and allowed them to reexpand to their former size. They have taken what they have learned and applied it to the modern dead, mummifying upon request (and payment) and substituting polyurethane for the traditional resin. But they have also verified royal lineage. Samples of hair were taken from the mummy of an elderly woman found in the tomb of Amenhotep II. They matched hair found in an inscribed locket in the tomb of King Tutankhamen, proving that she was his grandmother, Queen Tiye. They determined the bodies of two premature infants found in Tutankhamen's tomb to be the offspring of the young king and his wife Ankhesenamun. While they have often made astounding discoveries, Egyptologists have occasionally paid the price for their curiosity, scientific or otherwise. While "King Tut's Curse" was a fabrication, some have died as they explored ancient tombs. The deaths are attributed not to superstition, but to the combined effects of lack of oxygen and an accumulation of gases from decomposed bodies.[35]

More often, it is the mummies that suffer. Some coffins were inscribed, "Do not die a second time," in the hope that the corpse would not be destroyed. Unfortunately, importation has often led to "second death," and the statues placed in the tomb as substitutes for annihilated bodies have all been carted away. Mummies housed in a San Francisco museum were said to have crumbled to dust during the earthquake of 1906. A mummy brought aboard the *Titanic* by an English lord was lost at sea when the ship went down in 1912. A mummy was blasted out of its glass case and demolished when a bomb fell on the Royal College of Surgeons in London in 1941. Even those that survive the journey and their stay in a new land are no better for it: "But the sarcophagus is now empty, and its lid is broken, and the king's new friends have put him in a cheap wooden house; and written on a piece of cardboard, and tacked on the glass case in which he now lies, is the name he was so fond of cutting in granite."[36] In addition to robbing them of much of their dignity, the price of even scholarly inquiry is the damage of the mummies themselves. Their wrappings are destroyed as the body is uncovered. Their hair, loosened by the natron drying process, may fall out when the body is disturbed. Samples of flesh and fabric may be removed for testing. And the transfer of the bodies to different atmospheric conditions causes them to decay, imperceptibly but inevitably. We have learned from the past, but may have robbed the ancient Egyptians of their future.

The Veneration

Men ... have made fools of themselves for the jawbone of
a saint, the toenail of an apostle, the handkerchief a king
blew his nose in, or the rope that hanged a criminal.
Desiring to rescue some slight token from the graves of
their predecessors, they have confounded the famous and
the infamous, the renowned and the notorious, great
saints, great sinners; great philosophers, great quacks;
great conquerors, great murderers; great ministers, great
thieves; each and all have had their admirers, ready to
ransack earth, from the equator to either pole, to find a
relic of them.
            —Charles Mackay, *Extraordinary Popular Delusions*
            and the Madness of Crowds[1]

Souvenirs

Sometimes parts of the dead body are sought and retained. When their
origin is the body of a holy person, these pieces are called relics and are held
up to the veneration of the faithful. When their origin is secular and they do
not belong to a famous person, they are better referred to as souvenirs and
are more likely hoarded in secret. Serial killers, for instance, tend to collect
in their homes various pieces of their victims, sometimes after a crude attempt
at preservation. Witnesses of historical executions have publicly grabbed at
or privately procured a remembrance of the event: a tuft of hair, an inch of
rope, a handkerchief dipped in blood. Warriors of various lands and ages have
also kept souvenirs to prove their prowess to themselves or others. For some,
these bits of flesh have magical properties; for others they are a physical focus
for the remembrance of a violent death. Unlike relics, which are usually kept
out of love, souvenirs are collected out of lust.

Headhunting is the procurement of a souvenir which proves one's physical

247

prowess and accords the victor the power of the vanquished, which resides most notably in the hair. The natives of North America scalped their victims because the hair was believed to contain the soul. Ancient Scythians scalped their dead enemies, cleaned and softened their prizes, and hung them from their bridles. The Montenegrins of the Balkan peninsula attached entire enemy heads to their belts. The Jivaro Indians of South America were careful to preserve the flowing hair on the heads they hunted and shrunk. The heads, or "tsantsas," were avidly collected and painstakingly and secretly prepared. After killing the victim, the head was cut off close to the body. The skin was slit from the nape of the neck to the forehead and peeled toward the face using wooden or metal knives. After the skull and jaw were removed and discarded, the eyelids were sewn shut and the mouth sewn or held closed with slivers of wood. Water was heated in an earthenware pot that had never before been used. The head was boiled for two hours, along with a special vine believed to prevent the hair from falling out, until the fat and flesh fell away and it was then dried and cooled in the shade. The pot was thrown away, and the slit up the back of the head was sewn together. Small pebbles were heated in the fire and poured inside the head. The features were reshaped using a hot stone wrapped in a leaf. Progressively smaller stones and finally heated sand was poured into the head as it shrank. Some of the eyelashes and brows were plucked to maintain proportion with the face, and the facial hair was singed off with a flaming stick. The hair of the head and beard retained its original length, often more than half a meter. The crown of the head was pierced and laced with a string so the tsantsa could be suspended on a rack about three feet above the fire. The head was smoked overnight and buffed with a cloth the following day. The hole in the neck was closed with needle and thread.[2] By the end of the nineteenth century, European museums were as greedy for shrunken heads as were the Jivaros. The Indians supplied the demand by stealing or exhuming the bodies of paupers and selling their preserved heads for 25 dollars apiece.[3] In 1976, a Jivaro tsantsa sold at Christie's for $9,350 and the Ripley's Believe It or Not Museum was said to have purchased two at auction for $22,000. Warriors of many cultures have kept souvenirs of their conquests. According to superstition, soldiers who carry the finger of a dead comrade with them will be protected from harm. In the wars of this century, it is a piece of the enemy that is collected. An American soldier who returned from Vietnam reported that he and his fellows were expected and encouraged to collect the ears, noses, penises, or breasts of those they killed. A soldier who had a necklace of ears was considered a good killer. Like shrunken heads, war souvenirs are hoarded not only by those who obtained them and often glut the market:

> After World War II, trophy skulls of the enemy dead appeared all over the country, not just on bookshelves and mantelpieces but at dumpsites, in trash

receptacles at roadside rest areas, in people's gardens, and in all sorts of other places where they had been disposed of by collectors who apparently developed second thoughts about the meaning of victory. Another wave of trophy skulls arrived on these shores after Vietnam, and in at least two instances wholesale quantities of immaculately clean, carefully packed crania were recovered by police still in their shipping crates, evidence that the spoils of war had become a profitable import industry.[4]

The modern warrior is more easily parted with his trophies than the native headhunter, who was buried with his. Soldiers still sell their souvenirs, but collecting has been slowed by official decree. Although collecting human body parts has been against army regulations since World War I, the commander in chief of the Pacific Fleet issued an order in 1942 that no part of an enemy's body be used as a souvenir. His order urged unit commanders to take stern disciplinary action. Any confiscated skulls were (and still are) to be sent to the Armed Forces Institute of Pathology. Nevertheless, U.S. Marines were known to make letter openers from Japanese bones, and when the remains of Japanese soldiers were repatriated from the Mariana Islands in 1984, 60 percent had missing skulls. In the late 1980s, a special diving team was sent by Japan to the Truk lagoon in the South Pacific, where amateur divers were still making sport with the remains of the war dead.

The serial killer, on the other hand, defies regulations but rarely shares his or her souvenirs. John Reginald Halliday Christie kept a box of pubic hair belonging to his wife and the other women he had killed. A British serial murderer removed the front teeth of his victims. Other killers have kept even more grisly remembrances and used them as household objects or for special purposes. Jerry Brudos of Oregon made paperweights from the severed breasts of his female victims and collected their shoes—still containing their feet. Another man killed his girlfriend and cut off her ear to use as a bookmark. New York's Alex Mengel scalped one of his victims and wore the relic as a disguise during his next crime. "Sunset Slayer" Douglas Clark of Los Angeles decapitated a prostitute and kept her head for purposes of oral sex; his girlfriend obligingly painted the lifeless face with makeup. Some killers collect in volume: a man arrested by Egyptian police in 1920 was found with the heads of 20 women in his home, and a killer caught in Hong Kong in 1982 had several bottles containing female sex organs under his bed. Others prefer variety: Ed Gein of Wisconsin decorated his house with human lips dangling on a string from the windowsill, skulls on the bedposts, a drum made from human skin stretched over a coffee can, a skull fashioned into a soup bowl, wastebaskets and lampshades made of human skin, a chair upholstered with human leather, and the skinned faces of nine women mounted on the walls. Gein added to his wardrobe by crafting bracelets out of human hair, belts and vests from human skin, and several pairs of leggings made from human legs. His spare parts included a cup containing four noses on the kitchen table, ten heads sawed off above the eyebrows, and a shoebox of vulvas.

The activities of killers like Ed Gein have fueled many horror movies, but before the vicarious thrills of movies and television, the public satisfied its curiosity directly by visiting places of death and carrying away a physical reminder of the horrific event. The bloody bedsheets in Petersen's Rooming House where President Abraham Lincoln died were torn up and dispensed as souvenirs. At the execution of England's Charles I in 1649, guards and spectators scrambled to dip handkerchiefs in the king's blood, scraped up bloodied earth from beneath the scaffold, or tore off pieces of the blood-soaked pall.[5] When Louis XVI was guillotined in 1793, the crowd rubbed handkerchiefs, shirts, and paper in the blood as mementos. When Elizabeth Broadingham was strangled to death and burned in 1776 for murder, witnesses of the execution scooped up her ashes afterwards as souvenirs. As she viewed a victim killed by the Bender family in Kansas in the 1870s, a woman surreptitiously snipped off two or three curls of hair with which to make herself a commemorative wreath. An estimated 2,000 people visited Coffeesville, Kansas, after members of the Dalton Gang were brought down and tore pieces from the clothing of the dead robbers. And when John Dillinger was killed by FBI agents in 1934, Chicagoans converged on the alley outside the Biograph Theater to dip their handkerchiefs in the puddles of blood.

Trade in the souvenirs of murder and execution has been brisk, profitable, and sometimes fraudulent. The unsentimental wife of Eugene Aram made a daily collection of his bones as they dropped from the gibbet in which his body was enclosed. She then enlisted her children in selling them to tourists as souvenirs. When Maria Marten was murdered in 1828, crowds flocked to the places of her death and burial: "A lock of her hair was sold for two guineas, and the purchaser thought himself fortunate in getting it so cheaply."[6] Following the nineteenth-century execution of African-American Sam Hose in Georgia, members of the crowd of 2,000 severed his ears, fingers, flesh, bones, liver, and heart. Those unable to get a piece paid extravagant sums to obtain one.[7] More recently, an unscrupulous man did a brisk business in clippings of his own hair sold at five dollars each with a written guarantee that they came from the Lindbergh baby. Sellers of souvenirs find a ready market, since headhunting of one sort or another has been a hobby for generations. A tidy profit probably could have been made from sales of Ed Gein's handicrafts, had they not been reburied in a cemetery plot paid for by the Madison (Wisconsin) Archdiocese.

Relics

The bodies of saints have been parceled out to cathedrals all over the world. Bits and pieces have been smuggled and bestowed, hoarded and exhibited, stolen and retrieved. The authenticated relics of Christian saints have been deemed worthy of worship and function as symbols of faith. Religious relics have been sworn on, prayed over, and carried in funeral processions. While secular relics are not subject to the same sort of veneration, they, too, are figuratively clutched to the breast out of love and respect. They are held up, in whole or in part, to public or private worship. The bodies of political leaders, the skulls of composers, and the hearts of poets provoke the same sort of awe and have caused the same kinds of avarice as the finger or toe of a Christian martyr.

In some cultures, a portion of the physical remains of a loved one is intended to comfort the bereaved. New Zealanders embalmed the heads of family members by removing the brains, stuffing the cavities with flowers, baking them in an oven, and drying them in the sun. The relics were kept in baskets, scented with oil, and brought out on special occasions during which their relatives would cry over them. In the Torres Strait in Melanesia, the widowed spouse was presented with the tongue, palms, and soles of the corpse. The Sangos of the Ivory Coast keep a large basket in the family home containing the vertebrae of their ancestors. In Western culture, the heart of the deceased has sometimes been kept in the family as a sentimental reminder of the love they shared. The wife of Lieutenant General Vaubrun, killed in battle in 1675, had his heart embalmed and encased in glass; she was said to have gazed at it seven hours a day for the remaining 29 years of her life. The widow of John Baliol had her husband's heart embalmed and placed in an ivory casket that she carried with her everywhere for 20 years. Mary Shelley was presented with the heart of her husband Percy Bysshe Shelley after it failed to burn at his cremation in 1822; she preserved it in a silken shroud and carried it wherever she went. Women are not the only ones to retain such relics so fervently. Marshal Bourmont (d. 1846) of France carried the heart of his son, killed in battle, for 16 years. While the heart is treasured by some, the widow of the French governor of Canada in the eighteenth century refused such a relic, explaining that she did not want a dead heart which, when beating, did not belong to her.[8] As an alternative to the heart, the head is sometimes the relic of choice for grief-stricken survivors. After Sir Walter Ralegh was executed in 1618, his widow had his head embalmed and kept it by her side in a red bag until her own death several years later. After the execution of Sir Thomas More in 1535, his head was exposed on London Bridge, drawing large crowds. When his daughter Margaret learned that the head was to be removed, she bribed a custodian to obtain it and preserved it as a relic. Even today, the bereaved continue to latch onto a piece of a lover or beloved friend. A woman who had been involved in a disaster kept in her possession the hand of a friend which she could not bear to relinquish.[9]

Over the centuries, people have sought means by which relics of family members can be easily kept and savored. At the turn of the nineteenth century, Pierre Giraud advocated a process in which the bones of the dead were vitrified and memorial portrait medallions were made from the glass. Today inventor Philip Bachman has patented a process which freeze-dries corpses and deposits them in urns, although he admits that "no one really understands what might happen if boiling water were inadvertently poured over the remains."[10] While flesh may be embalmed and bones may be cleaned or transformed, the easiest memento to preserve—and one of the most effective remembrances—has proven to be the hair of the dead: "Who would not treasure the lock of hair that once adorned the brow of the faithful wife now cold in death, or that hung down the neck of a beloved infant now sleeping under the sward? Not one! They are home-relics, whose sacred worth is intelligible to all: spoils rescued from the devouring grave, which to the affectionate are beyond all price."[11] Hair need not be hidden away as abhorrent to anyone outside the family. In addition, it can be worked into jewelry or wreaths, as the English rediscovered in the eighteenth century. By the mid-nineteenth century, hair jewelry could be commissioned or made at home by following instructions that included soaking in baking soda, drying, knotting, and hanging with weights. Mourning jewelry ran the gamut from rings and bracelets to brooches and pendants. Sometimes the hair of a loved one was folded into a locket, other times it was woven into a picture of a mourning figure or a willow tree. Later, it was occasionally accompanied by a photograph. In many cases, the hair of the dear departed was collected and added death by death to a family wreath, which hung in the parlor. Despite the fad, hair did not need to be reworked to be of value. Before George Washington was placed in his coffin, a lock of his hair was cut and presented to his wife Martha. Today bereavement counselors recommend that the parents of a stillborn or miscarried child retain a lock of hair as a keepsake.

The hair of the renowned has been particularly sought after. After Napoleon's death in exile in 1821, locks of his hair were distributed among his retinue. Bones, too, comprise secular relics. The thighbone of Charlemagne (d. 814) housed at Aix-la-Chapelle has traditionally been thought to cure lameness. But the fleshy parts of genius are equally valued. The hands of philosopher and mathematician René Descartes (d. 1650), and sculptor Antonio Canova (d. 1822) have all been preserved. The heart of explorer David Livingstone (d. 1873) was retained after his death. The heart of Frédéric Chopin (d. 1849) is secreted in Warsaw's Church of the Holy Cross. Astronomer and physicist Galileo (d. 1642) has the dubious honor of having his hand, finger, and fifth lumbar vertebra on display in various Italian cities. Emperor Franz Josef is similarly divided within Vienna—his heart in the Augustiner church, his body in the Capuchin church, and his viscera in St. Stephen's Cathedral.

The skulls of the famous are of particular interest to phrenologists and others and are often the objects of much skepticism and speculation. After Mozart was buried in 1791, the gravedigger at St. Mark's cemetery gave his skull to artist Jacob Hyrtl. The skull was bisected by the artist's brother, who was an anatomy professor, and the top half made its way to Salzburg in 1901. A paleontologist examined the cranium in 1990 and found that the structure resembled a portrait of Mozart and that a faint fracture with traces of bleeding may have caused the dizziness and headaches the composer complained of in 1790.[12] During a visit to Rome in 1788, Johann Wolfgang von Goethe (d. 1832) described his reaction at seeing the skull of Raphael: "It was wonderful to look at—a brain-pan of beautiful proportions and perfectly smooth, without any of those protrubances [sic] and bumps which have been observed on other skulls.... I could hardly tear myself away."[13]

Goethe obtained a cast of the relic to reflect upon, unaware that it did not in fact belong to Raphael at all. A substitution occurred in the case of Franz Josef Haydn (d. 1809). Amateur phrenologist Johan Peter bribed officials for the privilege of exhuming the head, which he skeletonized and studied. Some time later Peter bestowed the gift on Joseph Rosenbaum, the secretary of his patron Prince Esterhazy. Meanwhile, the prince decided to have Haydn's body reinterred on his estate. When this was carried out in 1820, it was discovered that the skull was missing. When Peter tipped off the authorities, Rosenbaum denied possession, but he later succumbed to pressure and offered up a skull he obtained for the purpose from a Vienna mortuary. The skull was rejected as that of a much younger man, but a second skull of the correct age group was accepted as genuine. On his deathbed, Rosenbaum returned the genuine skull to Johan Peter, who in turn bequeathed it to the Vienna Conservatory of Music. Instead of following his instructions, his wife gave it to their family doctor, who gave it to the Austrian Institute of Pathology and Anatomy, which gave it to the Society of the Friends of Music in Vienna. In the early twentieth century, Haydn's skull was claimed by the local government for reburial with the remains. After a tug of war between the Vienna Council, which wanted it displayed in the Historical Museum, and the Society, the skull was finally reunited with the rest of the body in 1954.[14]

Famous heads, mummified over time, are almost as popular as the skulls within. Like some skulls, they have had tortuous journeys. The head of Sir Thomas More, once a family relic, became the property of St. Dunstan's Church in Canterbury, where it was only recently removed from public view. The head of Sir Walter Ralegh was buried with the body of his son in Surrey, with or without the protective red bag in which his widow had stored it. Oliver Cromwell's head lay safely with his body when he was buried in Westminster Abbey in 1658. It was two years later that he was exhumed, hung on a gallows, and decapitated. His head was fixed on a spike on the roof of Westminster Hall, where it remained for nearly a quarter of a century. After it fell off in 1685, it was variously housed in a soldier's home, in a private museum in London, and with a London jeweler. By 1814 it had been added to the private collection of Josiah Henry Wilkinson. The head, bearing the marks of the ax and pierced with a spike shown to be of the same age as the head, was declared to be genuine. It was willed to Sidney Sussex College in Cambridge and was reinterred near the entrance to the college chapel in 1960.[15]

Other parts (some of them less savory) of famous persons have been detached and offered for sale or perusal. What was purported to be Napoleon's penis was auctioned at Christie's in 1971, but failed to reach the reserve price. It was offered by mail order and was finally sold to an American urologist in 1977 for $3,800. The sex organs of Grigori Rasputin (d. 1916) and John Dillinger (d. 1934) are said to have been preserved. Napoleon III tried to purchase the relics of Madame Tussaud. Bodies become dismembered through time or greed, as Tom Weil points out in *The Cemetery Book*: "The melancholy of anatomy is that it keeps disintegrating on us. Scattered around the earth lie all manner of mortal remains—bones, limbs, skulls, relics, skeletons, mummies, corpses, fleshy fragments—honored or coveted by families, the devout, collectors, antiquarians, curiosity seekers and other connoisseurs.[16]

In special circumstances, the entire body of a leader has been preserved for indefinite display to his followers. Joseph Stalin was on view in a glass-enclosed tomb in Moscow's Red Square from his death in 1953 until 1961, when his body was entombed behind the shrine of Vladimir Lenin (d. 1924), who is still on view. The body of Mao Tse Tung can be visited in Tiananmen Square in Beijing, where a mechanism lowers the corpse—presented under a trapezoidal crystal—into a freezer each night.

The bodies of many Christian saints are also on view throughout the world, but unlike carefully embalmed bodies such as that of Lenin, they have been preserved miraculously. The "incorruptibles" have not decayed despite years, decades, or even centuries in conditions unfavorable to natural mummification. The tomb of St. Catherine of Genoa (d. 1510), for instance, was opened to assess her condition 18 months after burial when it was discovered that a water conduit ran under an adjacent wall. Despite a damp shroud and rotted casket, the body was spotless and so was redressed and exposed to large crowds before reburial. The remains of St. Julie Billiart (d. 1816) had not decayed after being buried three months in the height of summer. The body of St. Francis Xavier (d. 1552) was found incorrupt ten weeks after death, despite the use of lime to hasten decomposition, and was still preserved after five further months in direct contact with the earth. The chief medical authority of Goa found no evidence of artificial embalming or preservatives. Examination 142 years after death showed the state of the body to be remarkable, as noted by Bishop Espinola, Pere Joseph Simon Bayard, and others in their official report: "The tongue is quite flexible, red and moist, and the chin is beautifully proportioned. In a word, the body has all the appearance of being that of a living man. The blood is fluid, the lips flexible, the flesh solid, the colour lively, the feet straight and the nails well formed."[17]

That bodies have remained intact is taken as an indication of sanctity, but not always accepted as proof of sainthood. Although skeptics chalk it up to covert embalming, miraculous preservation is defined as the retention of life-like flexibility, color, and freshness *without deliberate intervention* for many years following death.

The earliest incorruptible saint is St. Cecilia, martyred in 177 A.D. when she refused to sacrifice to pagan gods. When Pope Pascal I wanted to transfer her remains to a basilica dedicated in her honor, he could not locate her grave until she directed him in a vision. When exhumed in 1559, she still lay in the position in which she had died. Her body was placed on view for a month and was then interred beneath the main altar. The body of St. Mary Magdalen de' Pazzi (d. 1607) was found to be entire and fresh during a transfer of her remains a year after death. The body has yellowed over the years, but has remained incorrupt and still smiles. The body of Blessed Rose Philippine Duchesne (d. 1852) was found in such an unchanged condition a few years after death that a photograph was made to remember her by. The body of St. John of the Cross (d. 1591) was found to be supple, and when a finger was cut off as evidence of preservation, blood flowed from it. At the most recent exhumation in 1955, the body had become slightly discolored, but was still moist and flexible. Twenty-seven years after his martyrdom, blood also flowed from the mortal wound suffered by St. Josephat in 1623.

Other incorruptibles include Blessed Sebastian of Apparizio (d. 1600), enshrined in Puebla, Mexico, and Blessed Anthony Bonfadini (d. 1482), whose body was found intact in 1902 and was still well preserved in 1945, when it was last examined. St. Hubert (d. 728) was found in perfect condition in unstained robes 13 years after death. The body of Blessed Antonio Vici (d. 1461) was exhumed a year after his death when a flame burning on the covering slab drew attention to it. The body was found intact and perfumed and was still intact and flexible when the tomb was opened again in 1599, 1649, and 1809. The corpse of St. Catherine of Bologna (d. 1463) was exhumed and found incorrupt when miracles began to occur at her grave 19 days after her death. She was seated before a window so she could be seen by the public and can still be viewed in a larger chapel, although her skin has been darkened by the flames of candles. The body of St. Margaret of Cortona (d. 1297) is light in color, dry, and intact, with full eyes and fingernails and toenails in place. The corpses of Bernardine of Siena (d. 1444), Blessed Bertrand of Garrigua (d. 1230), St. Zita (d. 1278), St. Sperandia (d. 1276), St. Peregrine Laziosi (d. 1345), and the Venerable Maria Vela (d. 1617) were also found in a state of preservation years and again centuries after death. The body of St. Teresa Margaret of the Sacred Heart (d. 1770) was examined in 1805 and found to have a healthy color and to be "somewhat dry but nevertheless, surprisingly elastic and pliable."[18]

Many incorruptibles have stood up to contemporary and modern scientific inquiry. A well-examined body is that of St. Etheldreda (d. 679), who was brought to light 16 years after death "as free from corruption as if she had just died and been buried on that very day," as described by the Venerable Bede. An incision that had been made just before death was found by the surgeon who made it to have healed, and the linens in which she was shrouded were still entire and fresh. The washed and redressed body survived the destruction of the church by several centuries, only to be destroyed during the Reformation. A left hand, found in the early nineteenth century, has survived and was examined by a church delegate, a surgeon, and an expert from the Victoria and Albert Museum—all of whom were impressed to find a tendon under the shriveled flesh of the 1300-year-old relic.[19] The body of St. Ubald of Gubbio (d. 1160) has been subject to several official examinations which track the deterioration of the relic. During the most recent exam in 1960, doctors found the brown, dry skin to have become mummified. The nails were still in place, but the upper lip and tip of the nose had corroded.

Perhaps the most famous incorruptible is St. Bernadette Soubirous (d. 1879), discovered in a state of perfect preservation during her beatification 30 years after death. Coated with wax, the body has been on display since the early twentieth century in Nevers, France. When bodies have been found in an incorrupt state, artificial means have been taken to sustain their condition, but often cause more damage than they prevent, in addition to casting doubt on the original incorruptibility. Blessed Arcangela Girlani (d. 1495) was discovered incorrupt three years after death, but the skin of the face was stripped away during the faulty application of a chemical in 1932; a mask was made in 1960 to conceal the wounded face. A wax mask was also made to cover the face of the once incorrupt St. Jean Marie Baptiste Vianney (d. 1859). Part of the skull of St. Theophile was deliberately left exposed when his relics were encased in a wax figure. The incorrupt body of St. Vincent Pallotti (d. 1850) was cleaned with alcohol and formaldehyde in 1949; the following year, a silver mask and coverings were made to place over the face and hands. The body of nineteenth-century visionary Catherine Laboure was found incorrupt in 1933 and was maintained by artificial means. On display in Paris, her blue eyes are open, but her incorrupt hands were amputated for enshrinement in a special reliquary and replaced with models of wax. The body of St. Philip Neri (d. 1595) was found entire four years after death, although it was covered in cobwebs and clothed in rotten garments. The corpse was embalmed several times thereafter, lastly in 1622 when flakes of the saint's skin were distributed as relics, and the face was eventually covered with a silver mask. The face of St. Piux X was also concealed with a bronze mask. Exhumed in 1951 and found to be incorrupt, his body was injected with a preservative chemical which turned the skin brown. In a few cases, treatment at the time of death or repair afterward has resulted in successfully prolonging preservation. The body of St. Charles Borromeo was embalmed soon after he died in

1584 and is enshrined in an intact state in Milan. The incorrupt body of St. Rita of Cascia (d. 1457) has become slightly discolored, but is otherwise perfect. An eyebrow which had moved in position and the right cheekbone which had become dislodged were fixed with wax and string.

In the quest for relics, even the bodies of the incorruptibles have been dismantled, officially or unsanctioned. The Catholic church tried to curb the dismemberment of the bodies of the saints, but was unsuccessful. As the number of churches grew, so did the demand for the bodies of saints and martyrs to enshrine in them. The practice of venerating relics was popular in the fourth century, but their distribution began in earnest during the seventh century to protect them from plunder by the barbarians. Relic-hunting became widespread during the Middle Ages. Pieces were carried home by pilgrims who dedicated churches in their honor. When the incorrupt body of Venerable Catalina de Cristo (d. 1589) was translated to Pamplona, the arm and hand were detached and left in Barcelona and are incorrupt to this day. The body of St. Francis Xavier, housed in Goa, India, has lost several parts to remote enshrinement. A number of toes are missing, the left hand was removed and divided, the internal organs were removed and distributed, and the shoulder blade was given away. After the death of St. Teresa of Avila, her incorrupt body was parceled out by relic-hunters during her many exhumations: the right foot and part of her jaw went to Rome, the heart and left arm went to Alba de Tormes, a toe was smuggled away in the mouth of a cleric, and the left hand ended up in the possession of Generalissimo Franco.

One of the most famous relics is the heart of St. Clare of Montefalco (d. 1308), which was found to be imprinted with symbols of Christ's Passion:

> The crucifix ... is about the size of one's thumb. The head of the Crucified inclines toward the right arm. The clearly formed corpus is a pallid white, save for the tiny aperture in the right side which is a livid reddish color. White tissue covers the loins of the Crucified as a loin-cloth. The scourge is formed of a hard whitish nerve, the knobbed ends of which represent the tongues of that cruel instrument of torture... . The crown of thorns is of tiny sharp nerves resembling thorns. The three nails are formed of dark fibrous tissue and are exceedingly sharp. The largest of these was attached to the inner wall of the heart by a thread of flesh.[20]

The incorrupt heart is enshrined in two pieces, one in a bust of the saint and the other in a jeweled cross. The body of St. Clare is also intact, though her hands have darkened. Similarly, the heart of blind and deformed Blessed Margaret of Castello (d. 1320) was found to contain holy images on three pearl-like pellets, including a picture of Christ in the manger. Like St. Clare, Margaret's body is still incorrupt and is on display at the School for the Blind in Citta de Castello, Italy. Another famous heart is that of St. Veronic

Giuliana, which bore symbols of the Passion corresponding to drawings the saint had made before her death.

While some incorrupt holy bodies have remained whole and others have been broken up deliberately, some eventually disintegrate over time. St. John of God died in 1550 while kneeling in prayer, an attitude retained unsupported for some time by the corpse. His body remained fragrant and intact for 20 years, but eventually disintegrated. The incorrupt body of St. Agnes of Montepulciano (d. 1317) partially decayed after three centuries. The bones, brain, and incorrupt hands and feet were enshrined in an effigy which can be seen in Montepulciano, Italy. The body of St. Rose of Lima (d. 1617) was fresh and fragrant 18 months after death, but desiccated by 1630. The preserved body of St. Albert the Great (d. 1280) had been reduced to a skeleton by 1483, but the head was almost intact and the eyes were still in their sockets. The eyes and heart of St. Jane Frances de Chantal (d. 1641) were said to swell at times, although the rest of the incorrupt body had been skeletonized. The incorrupt body of St. Camillus de Lellis (d. 1614) was eventually reduced to bone by flood waters of the Tiber River, although his incorrupt heart and right foot are in possession of the Order of St. Camillus. The body of St. Francis de Sales (d. 1622) was still fresh ten years after death, but later turned to dust and bones. St. Frances of Rome (d. 1440) was found in a state of preservation several months after her death, but had been reduced to bones after nearly 200 years. When agents of King Henry VIII were sent to destroy the relics of St. Cuthbert in Lindisfarne in 1537, they expected to find bones. Instead the tomb revealed the body as pliable and fresh as it had been found 11 years after death and again 417 years after death. The monks were allowed to rebury the body, which by 1827 had been skeletonized. The remains of St. Edward the Confessor (d. 1066) were found incorrupt in Westminster Abbey thirty-six years after his death, but had been reduced to a skeleton by 1685.

In a few cases, only a portion of a saint's body has remained incorrupt. When the relics of St. Anthony of Padua were transferred to a basilica built in his honor 32 years after his death in 1231, his tongue was found to be intact and was placed on display in Padua as a tribute to his eloquence. His jaw and forearm were removed for enshrinement in reliquaries. On the 750th anniversary of his death in 1981, St. Anthony's sarcophagus was opened and found to contain, in addition to his bones and skull, his perfectly preserved vocal chords, now also on display. When the tomb of St. John Nepomucene was opened in 1719, his body had become dust and bones, except for the tongue, which was brown and slightly dry and is now enshrined in Prague. Bodies which have not remained incorrupt have been even more easily distributed. The body of St. Anne was shared among several churches. During his visit to Apt, where a large portion of St. Anne's relics had been deposited by her two cousins, Charlemagne left the greater portion of them with the bishop of Apt, distributed some to his friends, and brought others back to Aix-la-Chapelle. Another collection of her relics housed in Nazareth was brought to Constantinople in 710 and distributed to churches including St. Anne at Auray in Brittany and the Basilica of St. Anne de Beaupré in Canada. St. Catherine of Siena (d. 1380) is divided among numerous European churches. Her head is in the possession of the Church of St. Dominic in Siena, three fingers and her left foot reside in Venice, a hand and shoulder blade in Rome, and a rib in Florence.

Even the smallest holy relics have a physical presence which may provoke or reaffirm one's religious faith, hence their display in churches and cathedrals. Kissing the relics of saints is understood by Christians as a spiritual union. While many relics are on permanent display, some are only exposed on special occasions. The skull, arms, legs, and breasts of St. Agatha, martyred in 251 A.D., are enclosed in an effigy which is exposed three times a year in Catania, Sicily. The partially preserved body of Blessed Sibyllina Biscossi (d. 1367) is displayed three times each year. The body of St. Francis Xavier was exhibited in 1974 and 1975 to more than 200,000 visitors, and in 1949 his right forearm was taken on a worldwide pilgrimage in honor of the 400th anniversary of the saint's arrival in Japan. The incorrupt, but slightly darkened body of St. Isidore the Farmer (d. 1172) was exposed for ten days when it was transferred to Madrid in 1969. Relics have been carried in procession and are sometimes worn by a bishop in a pectoral cross suspended over the breast by a chain. In the eighteenth century, parish clergy carried a reliquary containing the remains of a saint in local funeral processions. A reliquary containing the incorrupt heart of St. Rose of Viterbo (d. 1252) is carried in procession each year. In Sri Lanka, a tooth which survived Buddha's cremation in 483 B.C. is carried in an annual procession.

Some relics are not publicly displayed at all. At the pope's Sancta Sanctorum, the heads of Saints Peter and Paul and Christ's umbilical cord were on view until the chapel was closed to the public at the end of the sixteenth century. The remains of St. Peter are entombed beneath the papal altar in Rome. The relics of St. Simon and St. Jude are entombed under the altar of crucifixion in St. Peter's Basilica. Those of St. Bartholomew are kept in a large sarcophagus in an altar of Rome's Franciscan monastery. And the body of St. Ignatius of Loyola lies in the altar of Il Gesu. The relics of St. James the Less and St. Philip were placed in a crypt of the Basilica of the Holy Apostles in Rome. Rome also conceals the remains of Saints Cosmas and Damian beneath the altar of the church dedicated to them. The crypt of the Carmelite church in Paris contains the bones of 117 ecclesiastics beaten to death in 1792.

The most valued relics are those coming from or associated with Jesus Christ and there are many in existence. In 700 A.D., a monk doubting the miracle of transsubstantiation that takes place during the Catholic mass was the catalyst for the communion wafer to turn into a circle of flesh and the wine to become blood. The flesh was recently found to be striated muscle tissue from the heart wall and the blood was human type AB. Of the relics of Christ's followers, the most eagerly sought was the heart. That of St. Francis de Sales is enshrined at the Monastery of the Visitation in Treviso, Italy. The incorrupt heart of St. Vincent de Paul (d. 1660) is housed with the Daughters of Charity in Paris. The hearts of St. Ignatius (d. 107) and St. George (d. 303) were also preserved as relics. Also highly venerated were heads, arms, and legs, with fingers and teeth of less importance. The head of St. Ladislas is enshrined in the Cathedral of Gyor in Hungary. The incorrupt arm of St. Francis Xavier, which baptized 100,000 people, is housed in a chapel in Il Gesu of Rome. The forearm of St. Jude Thaddeus is kept in a silver reliquary by the Dominican Fathers in Chicago, and the incorrupt right hand of St. Stephen of Hungary is enshrined in the Cathedral of St. Stephen in Budapest. Relics often consist of bones, which are sometimes bejeweled. The skeleton of St. Idesbald (d. 1167) is kept in the church of Notre Dame de la Poterie in Brige, Flanders. Even the least of body parts has been revered, including the toenails of St. Peter distributed as relics throughout Europe.

Some relics have been known to exude fragrances and oils—further proof of their sanctity. Drops of liquid known as manna have been collected from the bones or bodies of saints. When the relics to not produce manna, they have sometimes been anointed with oil or water, which is then collected in vases, cloths, or sponges. The remains of St. Albert the Great exhaled a delightful fragrance when his body was found incorrupt three years after death; the bones remaining 200 years later still had a perfume. As it lay in state, the body of St. Paschal Baylon (d. 1592) gave off a copious flow of sweat, which was collected by the faithful. The bones of St. Alphonsus filled a vessel with perfumed oil during the process of his beatification. When the bones were dried and placed in a casket in 1892, the casket was opened four hours later and found to contain a white, sweet-smelling oil. The relics of St. Andrew produce manna on the anniversary of their rediscovery beneath the floor of the basilica in Amalfi, Italy. The relics of St. Nicholas, including a tooth and a bone fragment, were said to form a clear liquid. The hands and feet of Blessed Matthia Nazzarie (d. 1319) gave off an oil intermittently until 1920, then continuously until the relic was encased in plastic. A liquid issued from the remains of St. Sharbel Makhlouf (d. 1898) in such abundance that his garments were changed twice a week. After his body was placed in a special chapel, the liquid dripped from and collected in the bottom of the casket until 1965, when the remains had become skeletonized. Oil still flows four months a year from the relics of St. Walburga in Eichstatt and is believed to have curative powers. In contrast to oils exuded by the body, the relics of other saints consist of their blood, which may reliquify several times a year, as in the case of St. Januarius. The blood of St. Pantaleon in Ravello, Italy, liquifies on his feast day in July. The blood of St. Patricia, which liquifies frequently, was collected when it flowed from the socket of a tooth removed as a relic. Fresh blood spilled and was collected from the arms of St. Nicholas of Tolentino 20 times.

The manipulation and transportation of the bodies of saints over the years has resulted in misplaced and mishandled relics. When the tomb of St. Wunibald (d. 761) was opened in the Church of Heidenheim in Bavaria in 1968, it was found to be empty. The relics of St. John Southworth (d. 1654) were rediscovered by workmen during an excavation; they had been hidden in 1793 to save them from destruction during the French Revolution. The relics of St. Mark were brought to light in 1808 during enlargements of the choir of St. Mark's Basilica and are now enshrined under the high altar. The bones of St. Nicholas of Tolentino disappeared in the late fifteenth century, but were found beneath pavement in 1926. When the remains of St. Agnes were examined in 1605, her head was missing. Three centuries later, it turned up in the treasury of the Vatican. Over time, the collection of relics has been competitive and contradictory. A half-dozen churches claimed to have thigh-bones of the Virgin Mary, and as many as 15 claimed to possess the foreskin of Jesus Christ. Relics were occasionally salvaged by contemporaries from the funeral pyre or burial pit. The wife of the martyred St. Adrian recovered his hand when rain put out the fire that killed him in the fourth century. Relics were conferred upon churches and individuals, but they were also purchased. King Canute of England, was said to have paid a fine sum in the early eleventh century for the arm of St. Augustine. The search for relics covered the globe, and the Roman catacombs, in particular, were scoured for particles of holy martyrs. The size of one's collection was a status symbol: "Public displays of human anatomy—especially religious relics—were once fairly common. Relics were to the Europe of half a millenium ago what baseball cards or antique beer cans are to America today. Impassioned collectors back then assembled exhibits of holy bones."[21] A ruler of Saxony possessed 17,000 holy relics. Frederick the Great acquired more than 19,000 holy bones in the fifteenth and early sixteenth centuries.

As they proliferated, it became important to authenticate holy relics. The skills of several holy people made this possible: stigmatic Therese Neumann and Venerable Ann Catherine Emmerick were both able to distinguish false from true relics. More scientific means were used to identify bones thought to belong to St. Mary Magdalene. Upon opening her tomb in 1279, part of the lower jaw was found to be missing. The missing piece, which had been sent as a relic to the Basilica of St. John Lateran in 710, was matched perfectly against the skeleton, prompting Pope Boniface VIII to issue a bull confirming the authenticity of the remains. The relics of St. Dominic were confirmed by documents found in the tomb during exhumation in 1383. Some investigation was required in the mid-fifteenth century when churches in both Padua and Venice claimed to have the body of St. Luke. The bones in Venice proved to be those of a young man, while the bones in Padua were those of an appropriately older man whose skull was missing. Since the saint's head was known to be in Rome, the Paduan relics were accepted as authentic and are still enshrined in the Basilica of Santa Guistina. The disappointed Venetians were threatened with excommunication for the continued promotion of their relics as valid. The bones of St. Peter were examined in our own time and confirmed to be those of a large man who lived during the first century. Today the transfer and authentification of relics for personal devotional use and for installment in the altars of new churches is the duty of the Vatican's vicar-general.[22]

The worthiness of relics for worship has sometimes been questioned. In revolutionary France of 1793, the opening of the tombs at Saint-Denis revealed a number of dubious relics, including the finger of St. Bartholomew, the arm of St. Eustache, the chin of St. Louis, a bone of the prophet Isaiah, and the bejeweled shoulder of John the Baptist. They were brandished before a crowd and dispersed as ridiculous objects of veneration that nourished superstition.[23] The incorrupt body of St. Benezet (d. 1184) was seized and destroyed during the French Revolution, although fragments remain in Avignon. A few bones belonging to St. Germaine Cousin (d. 1601) survived the destruction of her corpse in 1795. Revolutionaries found the hidden body of St. Jeanne de Lestonnac (d. 1640), profaned it, and buried it with the carcass of a horse in 1791. In 1562, the tombs of St. Bonaventure and St. Francis of Paola were plundered by the Huguenots and their bodies publicly burned. The remains of St. Guthlac (d. 714) were secured in an Anglo-Saxon abbey, but were completely destroyed during Danish invasions. The body of St. Louis Bertrand (d. 1581) remained incorrupt for over 350 years only to be destroyed during the Spanish Revolution in 1936. Several relics were destroyed during the reign of Henry VIII, including those of St. Hugh of Lincoln (d. 1200), St. Werburgh (d. 699), and St. Withburga (d. 743). The incorrupt body of St. Andrew Bobola, martyred in 1657, was disinterred and disrobed by the Red Army. When the body was released by the Bolshevik government after it had been concealed in a Moscow museum for a year, the ears, nose, lips, some fingers, an eye, and large pieces of skin had been torn from the body. The mutilated relics were buried beneath the altar of a church in Poland. Relics that survived or were saved from such treatment, rather than losing their cultlike following, were considered even more precious.

In addition to suffering desecration by authority of kings and governments, relics were so coveted by some people that they were occasionally stolen. In 1969, a portion of Pope Sylvester's skull and St. Teresa of Avila's foot were pilfered in Rome, but later recovered. The left foot of Blessed James de Blanconibus (d. 1301) was also stolen. The bones of St. Lucy were stolen at gunpoint in Venice in 1981, but recovered a month later. During his second exhumation, St. Paschal Baylon was robbed of a finger and a portion of his ear; exhumed a third time, he lost both feet, which were returned under threat of excommunication. The Blessed Bernard Scammacca (d. 1486) prevented the burglary of his own incorrupt corpse. A nobleman and his companions entered the monastery where the body was enshrined, hoping to remove it. As they tried to lift the relic, it suddenly became heavy, and they were caught in the act by the awakened friars. St. Nicholas of Tolentino also prevented the removal of part of his remains. When his incorrupt body was exposed 40 years after death, a German monk detached both arms to take home, but was thwarted when after walking all night, he was in the same place he started. The head of St. Hugh of Lincoln was stolen in 1364 and later discarded in a field, where it was guarded by a raven until it was recognized. Relics were taken surreptitiously from a saint's shrine or directly from his or her body. When St. Elizabeth of Hungary lay in state in 1231, mourners removed her hair, nails, and nipples. When St. Hugh of Lincoln made a pilgrimage to Normandy to pay respects to the remains of St. Mary Magdalene, he took the opportunity to bite off two pieces of bone from the saint's arm to bring back to England. Anonymous relic-hunters availed themselves of a toe and some fingers of the incorrupt martyr St. Josephat (d. 1623).

Part of the value of relics lies in inspiring faithful reflection, but they were further believed to impart their holiness to others by their proximity to the living or dead. In the Middle Ages, oaths were sworn while touching holy relics. Egyptian Christians (Copts) tied bags containing a small relic or dust from a saint's tomb to the neck of the corpse. Sacred relics have also been thought—up to the present day—to be able to avert evil or disaster and to cure illness. The relics of St. Vitus were looked to in cases of demonic possession. Those of St. Anthony in St. Didier, Dauphine, France, were visited by medieval plague victims in search of relief. The coffin containing the remains of St. Stephen was said to have trembled and exuded a heavenly odor which cured the various diseases of the 70 people present. Holy relics are thus imbued with heavenly powers. Just as imploring a living saint may have effected a miracle, praying to a dead saint in the presence of his or her bones may benefit the unwell. Just as bones and hair are considered in many cultures to be endowed with magical properties, the mere fragment of a saint is considered sacred and worthy of veneration and special care. As with mummified Egyptians or Iron Age Europeans, the incorrupt body of a martyr provides the viewer with a literal glimpse of the past, a name that will henceforth leap out of the pages of a history book or Bible because the face has been seen.

Catacombs

Catacombs are visible repositories of earthly remains. Unlike the bodies in modern mausoleums, which are separated from the living by marble and bronze, the mummified bodies in catacombs crowd the viewer. They are their own monuments. Holy men in some cases, the poor public in others, they are not subject to tests or spirited away to museums, although they draw crowds of both scientists and tourists. Spectators come to the catacombs of Paris not only to see the spectacular tombs of the cemeteries above, but to view the actual bones of those consigned to the ossuary below. The patterns created from the bones and skulls, and the sheer numbers of them—like dozens of mummified monks standing row upon row—fuel our morbid curiosity. But our presence also pays homage to the sacred and secular lives lived, however anonymous they may now be.

Touring catacombs has been a pastime of the living for generations. Sixteenth-century Peruvians lined up at San Andrés Hospital for a view of the mummies. After being reopened to the public in 1874, the Parisian catacombs—still a popular tourist attraction—were visited by Napoleon III, Bismarck, Emperor Francis I of Austria, and Crown Prince Oscar of Sweden. The Capuchin monastery at Palermo in Rome was considered appropriate for Sunday walks among the mummified bodies of holy men and laypersons, which now number over 8,000. John Lloyd Stephens, a nineteenth-century American traveler, recorded his impression of a young woman he saw in the catacomb: "Her face was bare, the skin dry, black and shriveled, like burnt paper; the cheeks sunken; the rosy lips a piece of discolored parchment; the teeth horribly projecting; the nose gone ... and a long tress of hair curling in each hollow eye."[24]

Since the turn of the seventeenth century, the Capuchins dehydrated bodies by sealing them in chambers for six months, bathing the bodies in aromatic herbs and vinegar, and then exposing them to the sun. A small number of bodies were dipped in arsenic or lime, but most were simply dried. The shriveled bodies were stuffed with straw, dressed, and installed in the catacomb. This treatment originally intended only for the monks was soon demanded by the public, and the increasing numbers of mummified dead were displayed in segregated corridors: one for men, one for women (with a special section for virgins), one for professional men, one for priests, and one for the Capuchin friars. Relatives who came to visit the dead would sometimes change their garments. Nathaniel Hawthorne expressed surprise at the resulting mummies' lack of disagreeable odor: "The same number of living monks would not smell half so unexceptionably!"[25]

In the early eighteenth century, the Franciscans in Toulouse, France, earned a large clientele with their method: bodies were buried in soil that consumed their flesh, then exposed to air, and finally lined up in rows vertically or horizontally in their charnel house. In some repositories, the dead bear placards with their identities or have their names and death dates penned on their craniums. In many, however, the dead are nameless, if not featureless. In addition to their famous locations in Rome and Paris, catacombs can also be found in Palermo, Syracuse, and Naples, Italy, and in Israel, Ireland, Greece, Syria, Iran, and Cyprus, but the dead have not been free of further misfortune. The 20 natural mummies housed in a chapel in the cathedral in Venzone, Italy, were destroyed by an earthquake. The bodies of adults and children that line the walls of an underground pantheon in Guanajuato, Mexico, have been evicted from their graves. When family members could not afford to pay for their perpetual care, buried bodies were exhumed after five years, undressed, disinfected, and stood up along the walls. They are somewhat decayed and somewhat desiccated, with what look like horrible grimaces on their faces. The caretaker, who calls them "fossilized," points out the hair and beards that still cling to their heads and the shape of the unborn baby in the womb of a woman who died while pregnant. The catacombs of Rome were appropriated for use by Christians who worshiped in them and deposited there the bodies of their saints and martyrs, over whose tombs they would say mass. The bodies were placed or sealed in niches carved in the walls of the galleries. By the fifth century, over 40 Roman catacombs were in use and comprised 750 miles of galleries extending to a depth of 80 feet. The catacomb of St. Callixtus once housed the bodies of nine popes from the third century. The catacomb of Priscilla contained the remains of seven popes and several saints. The catacomb of Saints Marcellinus and Peter boasted a number of saints and more than 30 martyrs killed during the persecution of Diocletian. The use of the catacombs was prohibited by Emperor Valerian in 253 A.D., so they were abandoned only to be rediscovered in 1578. Of the estimated 194,000 dead originally entombed, almost all were removed to churches as relics or have crumbled to dust.

Many catacombs also contain ossuaries, where the bones of those less well-preserved are stacked or stylized. Churches dedicated to San Francisco in Lima and Cuzco, Peru, contain skeletal decorations and memento mori phrases spelled out with bones. Philippe Ariès describes the galleries of the Capuchin church and the cemetery of the Confraternità della Orazione e Morte:

> Each bone is used according to its shape: Pelvic bones are arranged in rosettes, skulls are stacked in columns, tibias or limbs support the arches of niches, vertebrae form garlands or serve as candlesticks. The work is attributed to an eighteenth-century monk. Here the charnel is no longer merely a repository; it is a stage set in which the human bone lends itself to all the convulsions of baroque or rococo art. The skeleton is exhibited as a theatrical prop and itself becomes a spectacle. Of course, it does not have the vegetative life that seems to persist in the mummy; it has lost its individuality. It is a collective life that animates this decor through the grinning mouths of hundreds of heads, the gestures of thousands of limbs.[26]

Charnel houses, or ossuaries, became common in fourteenth-century England as the church and churchyard became overcrowded with human remains. Galleries piled high with bones were used to hold catechism classes and charity gatherings despite the smell.[27] An ossuary at St. Leonard's Church in Hythe, Kent, in England contains 8,000 thighbones and 2,000 skulls exhumed from local burial grounds in the late Middle Ages. Other ossuaries are located in Evora, Portugal, at São Francisco and in Cologne, Germany, at St. Ursula.

The Parisian catacombs were originally the Montrouge gypsum quarries, usurped for the disposal of the bones of as many as 6 million people who had overcrowded the city's cemeteries. The remains were disinterred from 30 graveyards and moved under cover of darkness, though with appropriate solemnity, beginning in 1786 when the quarry was consecrated for burial. The galleries and passages 60 feet underground include bones both artistically arranged and economically stacked. Plaques on the wall indicate which churchyards certain groups were removed from, but even the remains of famous Frenchpersons cannot be picked out from the multitude. Stunning in their numbers, the bones of ossuaries may appear sculptural and belie their status as memento mori. Bones with a little bit of flesh still adhering tell another story:

"Unlike mere bone piles or even a skeleton, which bear only sketchy resemblance to an actual human being, the mummies at Guanajuato—like the desiccated but well-preserved bodies at Palermo's Capuchin catacomb and those at St. Michan's in Dublin—combine the contradictory characteristics of temporality and eternity: in the figures one sees both the living and the departed, death with a human face and humanity with the skull beneath the skin."[28] The mummies once visited by loving family members are now looked at with wonder and dread by a variety of people related only by a common mortality.

The Exhibit

I was surprised to find that the great man's brain weighed
no more than that of an ordinary mortal.
　　　—Dr. Edward Curtis in a letter to his mother after
　　　he assisted at the autopsy of President Lincoln,
　　　recounted by John K. Lattimer, *Kennedy and*
　　　Lincoln: Medical and Ballistic Comparisons of Their
　　　Assassinations[1]

Medical Specimens

Unlike relics or souvenirs, medical specimens are collected for their supposed scientific value. The brains of the famous, for example, are enthusias-
tically weighed and compared. After examination, the parts are rarely restored
to their rightful owners. They may become part of a private collection, collect dust on a lab shelf, reside in a medical museum, or be sold on the auction block. Specimens of the illustrious or ignominious dead have been stolen
from autopsy; anonymous limbs have been sold by mail order. Pieces and
parts have been microscopically examined, photographed, cast, and sketched.
While the collection of medical specimens has bordered on souvenir-hunt-
ing, it has in fact furthered science in objectively measured ways.

The popularity of preserving and displaying anatomical specimens
reached its height during the Enlightenment. Vascular injection of red wax,
mutton fat, and turpentine was used to preserve body parts that were then
exhibited as remarkable creations of God. Other preservatives included salt-
peter, pitch, resin, beeswax, tallow, arsenious oxide, mercuric chloride, or a
mixture of tar, salt, camphor, and cinnamon.[2] Frederick Ruysch (d. 1731) used
fixatives of his own creation to preserve organs, limbs, and entire bodies of
infants and adults. The collection so impressed Peter the Great in 1698 that
the czar later purchased it and had it transported to St. Petersburg. The
founder of Bellevue, Dr. Granville Sharp Pattison, amassed a collection of

1,000 sugar-cured specimens, but they were destroyed in a fire. Today such anatomical collections are on display in medical museums, but appear most spectacular to nonmedical viewers. The Hunterian Museum at London's Royal College of Surgeons groups organs into categories including "locomotion" and "digestion" and also has a collection of skeletons. The Mütter Museum in Philadelphia contains among other things the skeletons of a dwarf and a giant, a large array of skulls, a corpse mummified by the formation of adipocere, a sectioned human head, the shared liver of the original Siamese twins, and a skeleton wearing a varnished circulatory system. These displays reveal the inner appliances and structures of the human form and the gross exaggerations of it—things that may become routine to surgeons, but are a novelty to the uninitiated. Because they focus on the extraordinary and allow the ogling of human remains, such museums are frowned on by some.

To maintain their specimens, collectors must battle nature—human and otherwise: "A curator's task is never easy: he must come to terms with prohibitions of religious dogmas, prejudices, his own inner fears, and the ceaseless inroads of organic decomposition. Nevertheless, and in spite of secular difficulties, anatomical dissection and preservation of organs have been assiduously performed."[3]

Specimens can be preserved indefinitely with the newest method, plastination or biopolymerization, and will remain both flexible and odorless. But purveyors of bodily merchandise have run afoul of shipping regulations, particularly when preservation has not been successful—or was never initiated. In the 1970s, George Dashnau opened the first mail-order supply house specializing in human skulls. A century and a half earlier, a surgical student at St. Bartholomew's Hospital was taken into custody after two boxes he had packaged to send to London burst open in the Lion Coach Office. One box contained a man's head and the other the body of an elderly woman. While noting that the specimens were intended for dissection, the local press chastised, "We trust the parties will think it necessary for the sake of decency, to pack their *treasures* a little more carefully."[4] Upon opening a leaky box in 1986, United Parcel Service employees were a little surprised to find that it contained 12 human heads. The find prompted an investigation of the Philadelphia specialist who had been mailing body parts to medical schools for 15 years.[5]

Medical specimens have not always reached their destination, and when they have, they are not necessarily put to any use. Jay Leno recounts the apocryphal story of a bottle containing a human brain that was found on a shelf in a vacated apartment and taken to Lutheran General Hospital to be pronounced dead. The head of Egyptologist Sir William Flinders Petrie (d. 1942) was send to England by his wife in hopes that researchers could uncover the biological basis of his genius. Because it was wartime, the head was misplaced in the basement of the British Museum. Preserved body parts easily lose their identity, although Richard Selzer comments that "It seems a soulless thing to cut out the best part of a man, and fail to label it: Liver of Henry Huckaby, b. 1914, d. 1977."[6] Only fame ensures properly identified specimens, although eccentricity will sometimes suffice. Hannah Beswick willed the use of her remains for looking, rather than dissecting. Her body was preserved and displayed at her request in the Natural History Museum of Manchester for 30 years.

Of individual organs, brains are the greatest prize, and the Brain Institute of the Soviet Academy of Sciences was founded in 1926 to study them. The most famous brains the institute has examined are those of Vladimir Lenin, Joseph Stalin, Maxim Gorky, and Andrei Sakharov. The Max Planck Institute for Brain Research hoards its specimens and only reluctantly agreed in 1989 to cremate the 10,000 glass slides containing sections of brains obtained from children killed by the Nazis at a euthanasia center.[7] The inventory of the Musée de l'Homme includes the brain of French anatomist and anthropologist Paul Broca and the skull of René Descartes. The brain of Albert Einstein was retained at his death in 1955 by Princeton pathologist Dr. Thomas S. Harvey. Dr. Harvey studied the brain and distributed microscopic sections to his colleagues, but could not find anything unusual about it. In fact, very little evidence supports the belief, widespread in the nineteenth century, that the size of the cranium is proportional to intellect.

Skeletons are popular specimens and are perhaps the most easily prepared (usually by boiling and sometimes with the assistance of scavenger beetles), preserved, and manipulated. Photographs of the students enrolled in the Women's Medical College of Pennsylvania in the 1890s show them posed familiarly with articulated skeletons. The Smithsonian Institution has found room for 33,000 human skeletons, including the 1,700 which comprise the Terry Collection from Missouri and are accompanied by a description of the living individual, photographs from life, and sometimes a death mask. The bones are put to good use by forensic anthropologists:

> Probably the last thought in the minds of the anthropologists who amassed this army was that it would ever play a major role in fighting crime. It was assembled as a standing resource for the solution of other kinds of mysteries: where we came from, how we lived, where we are headed. But once a body has lost its soft tissue and gone to bones, a single drawer in this collection of human skeletal remains contains far more data for analyzing, interpreting, and identifying the victims of crime or misadventure than all the millions of fingerprints ever recorded.[8]

As long-lasting as skeletons, but more cumbersome, are the castings made of anatomical models. In the eighteenth century, William Hunter cast the corpse of a man who had been flayed and hanged from Tyburn Tree. Since World War II, Medical Plastics Laboratory of Gatesville, Texas, has sold models made by full-time and freelance employees from cadavers, organs, and skeletons. Many famous painters and sculptors made use of corpses in their work or as practice for the portrayal of the living form. Leonardo da Vinci and Michelangelo both sketched the dead. In the sixteenth century, renowned artist Bartholomaus Torré of Arezzo made sketches of cadavers and body parts. The U.S. National Library of Medicine has prepared a digital record of the human body by recording the minutely sliced bodies of a man and a woman with a CT scan, an MRI, and standard photography.[9] But excised organs or bones are not always used for study. In 1813, royal surgeon Sir Henry Halford autopsied the body of Charles I, who had been executed in 1649. He stole the severed fourth cervical vertebra and used it as a salt holder at the dinner parties he hosted, until commanded by Queen Victoria to return the specimen to the coffin. Other specimens have been reunited at great length with the bulk of the remains. A bidder at Sotheby's paid approximately $3,000 in the 1970s for the skull of Swedish philosopher Emmanuel Swedenborg (d. 1772) with the intention of reuniting it with the skeleton.

Collections begun decades or centuries ago have been incorporated in the exhibits of modern medical museums. The head of Australian outlaw Ned Kelly was acquired by the Australian Institute of Anatomy in Canberra in 1921, when the old Melbourne gaol was demolished. After workers uncovered Kelly's coffin, local students availed themselves of souvenirs from the remains. Specimens still used to illustrate the formation of adipocere to students at the Forensic Museum at Edinburgh University were obtained by Sir Sydney Smith. The pathologist kept two heads, two legs, two arms, and numerous internal organs from a pair of murder victims he autopsied. Despite their dubious means, collectors have sometimes been thwarted. Physiological marvel Alexis St. Martin had been shot in 1822, leaving a hole in his stomach through which the process of digestion could be observed. At St. Martin's death in 1881, Sir William Osler tried to acquire the famous stomach for the Army Medical Museum in Washington, D.C. The family objected and allowed the body to partially decompose in their home before releasing it for burial. While the Army Medical Museum does not have St. Martin's stomach, it does have in its holdings thousands of gross and skeletal anatomical and pathological specimens, many of them from men who fought in the Civil War during which the museum was founded. While the soldiers are no longer remembered, their identities and the name of the battle in which they died are attached to their bones for posterity.

Curiosities

Curiosities are just that—preserved bodies or pieces thereof that turn up in unexpected places or are willed for specific purposes. Curiosities have no redeeming value medically or religiously, but may be of interest artistically, culturally, or historically. A pair of boots made with a human skin purchased from a widow and tanned by a nineteenth-century American were donated by the maker to the Smithsonian Institution. The reduction of human bones to trinkets and skin to upholstery is a puzzling phenomenon when intended by the deceased and a disturbing one when it is carried out against their wills and at the expense of their lives. Of less serious nature are anecdotes of misplaced mummies, mysterious skulls, and postmortem mannequins.

Several people have made provisions for specific uses of their bodies after death. The intention of André Tchaikovsky (d. 1982) to donate his skull after his death to London's Royal Shakespeare Company for use in the production of *Hamlet* was thwarted only by the fact that the company does not use real skulls because they are easily broken. The request of the mistress of nineteenth-century French novelist Eugène Sue was carried out after her death: a set of his books was bound in skin taken from her shoulders. A contributor to *The Lion* in 1829 revealed the instructions he had left in his will: his body was to anatomized and the skull given to the London Phrenological Society, the skin was to be tanned and used to upholster an armchair, his bones were to be crafted into knife handles and buttons, and his flesh was to be used to fertilize a rosebush. Surgeon Richard Selzer, overly familiar with medical specimens, muses about—but has probably not formalized his plans for—the treatment of his own remains after death: "So, I have decided. No gourd, nor royal drinking cup, nor forest strew for me. Upon the wall of some quiet library ensconce my skull. Place oil and a wick in my brainpan. And there let me light with endless affection the pages of books for men to read."[10] Czech revolutionary leader Jan Zizka (d. 1424) had a less sedentary plan. He requested that his skin be made into a military drum so he could continue to work for the Bohemian cause.

Skin was a commodity in the concentration camps of Nazi Germany. At Buchenwald, Ilse Koch ordered the execution of prisoners with interesting tattoos on their skin so she could have the tanned leather fashioned into lampshades and gloves. In Dachau, Dr. Franz Blaha was ordered to remove and prepare the skin of the dead: "It was chemically treated and placed in the sun to dry. After that it was cut into various sizes for use as saddles, riding breeches, gloves, house slippers and ladies' handbags.... . The skin had to be from healthy prisoners and free from defects. Sometimes we did not have enough bodies with good skin....The next day we would receive twenty or thirty bodies of young people. They would have been shot in the neck or struck on the head so that the skin would be uninjured."[11]

Although no one was allowed to cut the skin of a German, the Jews were sometimes forced to make penknife cases and other items from the flesh of their fellow prisoners. When found today, items such as these are often buried in simple ceremonies. The SS also favored shrunken heads and skulls obtained from the emaciated bodies of their captives. Because the Nazis prided themselves on quality, it was dangerous for their captives to have clear (or tattooed) skin or strong, straight teeth.

Some characters from history have had body parts preserved not as luxury items, but as warnings. When Seminole Chief Osceola died in prison, his doctor decapitated the corpse and used the head to frighten his children when they misbehaved.[12] Peter the Great (d. 1725) had the head of his unfaithful mistress placed in a jar of alcohol, which remained in his bedroom as a warning to other mistresses. He was also said to have done the same with the head of the lover of his wife, Catherine I. Others have used the dead as proof. While the mother of Paul-Marie Verlaine stored her miscarriages in alcohol in the cupboard, actress Jean Seberg exhibited her miscarriage in a glass coffin in her hometown to assure the public that she had not been impregnated by a leader of the Black Panthers, as was rumored. The hand of "Three-fingered Jack" and the head of his murder accomplice Joaquin Murieta were cut off and shown as proof that they were dead; the relics were later sold for $36. In cases where the news may have been disheartening, premature death has been concealed temporarily by allowing the body to be seen in a lifelike pose. At his request, El Cid was mounted on his horse posthumously during the next battle, which was won. When millionaire William Crockford died in 1844, his corpse was seated in a chair visible through the window of his gambling club. Word of his death would have destroyed confidence in one of his horses and caused it to be withdrawn from the race.

The body of Elmer J. McCurdy had quite a colorful existence after the death of its occupant. McCurdy, a train robber, was killed by a posse in Oklahoma in 1911. A local undertaker embalmed the body, put it on display, and charged a nickel a peek. The stationary show came to an end in 1916, when the corpse was claimed by two men posing as McCurdy's brothers. The men exhibited the body across the country as a sideshow attraction for decades; its integrity was maintained with lacquer and paint and its mouth became stuffed with carnival tickets. The mummy of McCurdy finally came to rest in a funhouse in Long Beach, California, until a crew showed up to film an episode of "The Six Million Dollar Man." When McCurdy's arm broke off after being hit with a stage light, it revealed bone. His identity was uncovered, and the body was returned to Oklahoma for burial. A French bandit, Louis Dominique Cartouche, was kept on public display by one of the executioner's assistants because of his infamy and his height, which was only four and a half feet. A skull that occupies a prominent place near the cash register of a Kansas beer hall had more interesting fictional histories conjured up after the bar owner had a hole drilled in it to suggest a bullet hole.

Bodies and body parts have turned up in surprising locations. In *A Journey to Paris in the Year 1698*, Englishman Dr. Martin Lister described how he had come across the well-preserved leg of a mummy while browsing among the books in St. Genevieve library. British artist Robert Lenkiewicz was found to have hidden the body of a 72-year-old friend in his home. He hoped to regain custody of the corpse after it had been taken from him and to keep it "for the rest of my life, something like a large paperweight in the library."[13] Canadian sculptor Rick Gibson and the owner of a London gallery showing his work were fined several hundred dollars in 1989 for outraging public decency with the piece *Human Earrings*: attached to the ears of a head modeled by the artist were matching freeze-dried aborted fetuses.[14] More commonly, libraries sometimes contain books bound in human leather. After William Cordes was executed in Bury St. Edmunds in 1828 for murdering Maria Marten, his skin was used to bind an account of his trial that was given to the town museum. Campi, another murderer executed later in the century, had his skin tanned and used to bind documents relating to the case, including his own postmortem examination. In 1891, a physician commissioned a human hidebound copy of Hans Holbein's *Dance of Death*, which had inspired a number of copies bound in human leather. Most recently, the widow of Donald Eugene Russell (d. 1994) of Eugene, Oregon, went to court to defend her husband's will that his body be skinned and tanned and the leather used to cover a book of his verse. The court sided with the State Mortuary and Cemetery Board that such use would violate state laws against the abuse of corpses.

It is arguable whether carrying out the stated wishes of an individual with regard to his or her own body after death is a violation of anything other than bad taste. And taste, like law, changes over time: "There are many examples in archeological literature of human bones being modified to serve as bowls, medallions, or trinkets... . These things rise and fall with the tides. In the time of Byron and the Romantics, it became fashionably scandalous for the cognoscenti to toast each other's health from ornately decorated drinking steins made of human skulls, sometimes even from the heads of their friends or intellectual celebrities of the day."[15]

For the Romantic poets, the skull of a contemporary was a personal memento mori. The owner of an anonymous skull may find that it serves as food for thought or merely a conversation piece. Putting a body to good use, physically or philosophically, would probably be condoned by the deceased. Those who will the use of their skin as leather may intend it to be a small piece of physical immortality. Those who appropriate the skin of executed murderers to bind accounts of their crimes have effected a form of poetic justice. But those who execute people to obtain their skin exemplify life without respect for life and death without legitimate purpose. It is one thing to acquire a preserved head, limb, or fetus and charge a fee at a carnival sideshow for the privilege of seeing it. It is quite another to value a tattoo more than the heart which beats beneath.

RESPECT FOR THE CORPSE

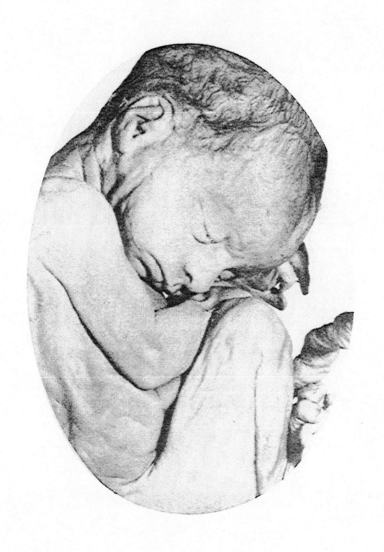

The 16 Shamed

Posthumous indignity is a fear that has remained wide-spread long after the passing of the body-snatchers. We still endow a lifeless corpse with the capacity for feeling hurt and the expectation of respect. All forms of defile-ment of the dead, especially the thefts or mutilation of corpses, are regarded by the majority as deeply distasteful.
—Robert Wilkins, *The Bedside Book of Death: Macabre Tales of Our Final Passage*[1]

Ransomed Corpses

The high price some people have had to pay for their celebrity is a mon-etary sum exacted from their survivors after death. The families of the famous sometimes receive offers for the right to display the bodies of the deceased. Some instead receive threats demanding money for the safe return of the stolen corpse. Others even less fortunate learn that the remains they entombed have been removed with no clues to their graverobbers or their whereabouts. To foil such plots, special measures have been taken by wary families. Still, locks are broken, tombs are penetrated, and casketed bodies are spirited away by the covetous, the curious, or the merely greedy.

Offers to purchase the rights to a corpse have been turned down or thwarted. The body of presidential assassin Leon Czolgosz was not released by prison authorities after his electrocution in 1901. Officials were leery of his brother's demands for the remains, with what turned out to be good reason. After they doused the body with sulfuric acid and buried it in an unmarked grave, they learned that a New York crime museum had offered the brother $5,000 for permission to display the body. The father of gangster John

Part VI title page: Twenty-five week fetus. Reprinted with permission from Keith L. Moore, *The Developing Human: Clinically Oriented Embryology*, Fifth Edition (W.B. Saunders, 1993), Fig. 6-10.

277

Dillinger reportedly refused an offer of $10,000 for the use of his son's body in a sideshow like the body of Billy the Kid, which was supposedly exhibited by several traveling showmen. "There isn't enough money in the world to get me to place my boy's body on exhibition," Mr. Dillinger said.[2]

Those who steal a body and then demand a sum leave little room for relatives to bargain, but have rarely been successful. In the late 1870s, the body of millionaire T. A. Stewart was stolen in New York. The $25,000 ransom was not paid, and the body was never recovered. In England in 1881, the body of Alexander William Lindsay, the fifth earl of Crawford and Balcarres, was stolen. The demand of £6,000 was never met, but the body was later recovered. In 1978, thieves stole the body of Charlie Chaplin (d. 1977) from his grave in a Swiss cemetery. The ransom was not paid, and the body was found 11 weeks later in a shallow grave in a distant cornfield. Remains have been held hostage not only for their supposed worth, but until the debts of the deceased have been paid by his or her family or friends. A king of Egypt forced his subjects to pay their taxes by withholding the urns containing the ashes of their ancestors. In 1700 the body of John Dryden was seized to collect a debt, and in 1784 the body of Sir Bernard Taylor suffered the same fate. In 1816 a man who passed as a mourner gained access to the room in which the body of Richard Brinsley Sheridan lay. He impounded the corpse on behalf of a creditor and refused to release it for burial until the sum had been paid. Although common law in the United States holds that the corpse may not be withheld as security for funeral costs, the body of James McDill (d. 1989) resided in the basement of a Flint, Michigan, funeral home until $3,600 was received from the family for his burial.

Attempts were made to steal and ransom the bodies of two of the most famous men in American history. Eleven years after Abraham Lincoln's death in 1865, a gang of thieves broke into his tomb in Springfield, Illinois. They succeeded in forcing the sarcophagus open and partially removing the casket, but were not successful in their plan to hide the body in the sand dunes of Indiana pending payment of $200,000 and the release of a counterfeiter from Joliet Prison. The men were arrested, charged with breaking a lock on a tomb, and sentenced to one year behind bars. Eleven days after Elvis Presley's death in 1977, four men were arrested for attempting to steal his body. They had plotted to break into the mausoleum, remove the corpse, and demand a ransom. The publicity such plots generate has caused the families of the famous and infamous to take special precautions when entombing their dead. After learning the hard way, Robert Todd Lincoln embedded his father's coffin in two tons of concrete in 1901 to discourage further attempts to snatch it. John Dillinger's grave was sealed with scrap iron and cement because his father feared the body might be exhumed by someone intent on verifying Dillinger's identity.

Families have gone to great lengths to protect the posthumous privacy of public figures. The body of John Wayne (d. 1979) was buried in an unmarked grave in Pacific View Memorial Park and Mortuary in Newport Beach, California. To confuse possible bodysnatchers regarding the exact location, several graves were dug simultaneously. Some bodies have been at risk of being stolen not for their celebrity or their infamy, but for their oddity. The bodies of the original conjoined twins, Chang and Eng Bunker, were cast in plaster for posterity, in addition to being autopsied. Just to be on the safe side, the joined bodies were guarded around the clock for a year after their interment. Bodies no longer of use to those who have vacated them continue to be of value to those willing to rob the grave, but usually only before decay has become too advanced. Bodysnatching is most likely to occur within days of death, when the corpse is still salvageable. Bodysnatchers are unconcerned with the name of the corpse they have resurrected. But it is the identity of the body which drives people to pay to see it in a sideshow or pay to have it returned to its rightful owners—the next of kin.

Public Exhibition

The bodies of notables are honored with the formal viewing ceremony known as lying in state. The notorious, on the other hand, are subject to an impromptu display at the morgue, funeral home, or place of execution. The public has historically clamored for a look at the corpses of criminals and pirates—the victims of legal execution, lynching, and justifiable homicide. The practice of gibbeting or hanging in chains left the killers and convicts on display until their bodies disintegrated. Intended as a deterrent, gibbeting fed the same morbid interest that caused people to line up for a look at the morgue.

When John Dillinger's body was put on display at the Chicago morgue, 100,000 curious people filed past. A crowd estimated at 15,000 turned up to view the body of Leo Frank after he was lynched in 1913 for the murder of schoolgirl Mary Phagan. Following the hanging of John Holloway in 1831 in Sussex, England, 23,000 filed past his body in the town hall. Those who have been executed by federal agents, by the enraged public, or by the legal system do not need name recognition to become popular attractions after death. Billy Cook was sentenced to 300 years in Alcatraz for random murders committed across the country after World War II. Tried for another murder in California, he was sentenced to the gas chamber and the sentence was carried out. Afterward, the undertaker laid out Cook's body in a blue suit and encouraged visitors with a welcoming "Step right up!" Thousands of men, women, and children took the opportunity to see the body of a man who had been gassed by the state. After a much more controversial conviction and execution in 1927, the bodies of Sacco and Vanzetti were kept on view for three days to accommodate the thousands eager to pay their respects or simply have a look.

Having a look at the dead was a popular sport in Paris until after the turn of the twentieth century. Sightseers were obliged by workers at the city morgue, who arranged the corpses for daily display. Also on daily display were bodies hung in chains in England and Europe. Once a method of execution by exposure and starvation, hanging in chains became a form of posthumous punishment in which the executed person was strung up after death to deter others from committing the same crime. In ancient Rome, the executed were exposed opposite the forum until their bodies rotted and were then dumped in the Tiber River. The French attached the body to a gibbet of stone and wood erected along the highway outside the city. A fourteenth-century writ commanded the bailiffs of Easthampstead to "cause chains to be made, and to hang the bodies in them upon the same gallowes, there to remain so long as one piece might stick to another, according to the judgement."[3] So that it wouldn't decay immediately, the body was painted with pine resin or boiled in pitch and was sometimes bound with leather straps. The prepared body was raised in chains or an iron frame on the gallows or from a post erected near the scene of the crime.

But the gibbeted bodies were not symbols of misguided lives, as intended, but curiosities. Before decay, spectators could catch a glimpse of a notorious highwayman. As decay progressed, they witnessed the mysteries of the body's interior. An Englishwoman related that the body of an executed wife-murderer, which she used to pass by as a girl in the early 1800s, became the nesting place of a pair of starlings until they were stolen from out of the rib cage. Spooky to some, exposed corpses were sought out by others. In the eighteenth and nineteenth centuries, the ferryman was kept busy transporting London's thrill seekers to the foot of Execution Dock, where pirates remained suspended from the nooses in which they had been hanged. Taverns with a view of gibbeted bodies offered telescopes or spyglasses to their eager patrons. When the corpses were removed by legislative enactment in 1834, newspapers of the day made a great outcry that holidaymakers were being deprived of their amusement.[4]

The last body to be hung in chains was that of a murderer named Cook in 1834 outside Leicester in England. General rioting led to the removal of the body and prompted William IV to abolish the practice by statute. But the exhibition of bodies continues, although sometimes cloaked with good intentions. The people of Atlanta, who had been so angered by the murder of Mary Phagan that they lynched her accused killer, were allowed to view her body. It was seen by 6,000 people, the largest crowd to view a murder victim's body in Atlanta. Other victims have been exposed to the public in hopes that someone will recognize them. In Cleveland, authorities allowed the exhibition of the body and head of a victim of the "torso murderer" at the morgue. Several thousand filed by over the next few days, but the victim was never identified. Public exhibition has traditionally been intended to shame the dead and succeeds in that regard. Exposure has made a novelty of the corpses of pirates, an example of local murderers, and a mockery of powerful and legendary lawbreakers. It has not, however, been a successful deterrent. The sight of John Dillinger on the slab did little to discourage those who followed in his footsteps and even in the early stages when the bodies on the gibbet were identifiable, few identified with them.

Posthumous Punishment

While the public exhibition of the bodies of the infamous after death may seem vulgar, several more extreme measures have been taken to "punish" the dead. The corpses of criminals have been denied burial, dissected, or dismembered as part of their lawful sentence. Political figures have been brought forth from their graves and executed for the first or second time as a symbol of the death of the previous regime. Religious enemies have been burned, captives have been skinned, and the graves of the disliked have been desecrated. Because they are undertaken posthumously, such punishments cannot be considered cruel and unusual, except to the memory of the deceased. The fear of such treatment—threatened before death by law or example—has been used to deter crimes against the state, against religion, and against oneself.

During its long history, the Catholic church has tried the dead for heresy and had those found guilty disinterred from sacred ground and burned or reburied elsewhere. Pope Stephen VII and later Pope Sergius III had the body of their predecessor, Pope Formosus (d. 896), dragged through the street and his fingers cut off. The Church of England convicted Thomas à Becket, archbishop of Canterbury, of high treason nearly 400 years after his death and had the remains exhumed and publicly burned. The dismemberment of the corpse was often explicitly directed in the legal death sentence. In English law under Edward III, those convicted of high treason were half-hanged, after which their entrails were removed and burnt before them, their heads severed, and their bodies quartered. Other times, mutilation of the body of an executed man or woman is carried out at the whim of the crowd. When Elizabeth Brownrigg—a murderer—was hanged in 1767, the executioner carried out his duties as quickly as he could while the assembled mob attempted to dismantle the scaffold and shred the corpse. A piece of the felon is sometimes displayed as a warning to others, much like the gibbeting discussed in the previous chapter. The skin of Richard de Podlicote, hanged in 1306 for stealing the Crown Jewels, was stretched across a chapel door to discourage would-be thieves.

Before executions were private affairs, they provided a forum for shaming the victims of the ax or gallows: "These executions [of Mary Ann James for forgery and Amelia Roberts and William Davis for robbery in 1818] and many others unfailingly drew crowds [that were] bent on making sport of death and saw nothing unseemly in mocking the dying. It was not unknown for rowdies to cut down victims not yet dead and haul them through the streets like figures at a carnival and roysterers considered it great fun to toss a stiffening corpse from one to another."[5]

Even when the condemned have cheated the executioner, their corpses have not escaped punishment. When a man named Valazé was arrested and sentenced to death with several fellow Girondins, he committed suicide rather than suffer execution. His corpse was guillotined with the rest of the prisoners, however. Michael Lancelin killed himself in his prison cell in Belgium in 1807 and was guillotined after death as a warning to others in similar situations. Suicide itself was grounds for posthumous punishment, forms of which were undertaken to stem waves of self-destruction. When suicide rates swelled during the plague, officials succeeded in lowering the numbers by threatening to display the corpses of all who killed themselves. In France, suicides were sometimes dragged head-down through the streets. The pregnant body of Marie Jaguelin was tried posthumously for suicide and infanticide, then dragged on her face through the town. After the fetus was cut from her stomach, her corpse was hanged by the feet and burned at the stake.

Restrictions imposed on the disposal of the body after death have been used as a punishment for one's deeds during life. The ancient Romans denied burial to criminals who died while being punished and simply hurled their bodies from a cliff. Felons were traditionally buried at crossroads for the superstitious reason of disorienting their souls if they chose to linger, but also to shame them by separating their bodies from the flock. An Act of Parliament in 1823 finally allowed the burial of murderers in churchyards, but only between nine o'clock and midnight. Churches often reserved the least desirable burial sites—those on the north side—for suicides, felons, and the unbaptized. Such discrimination resulted in the punishment of the unfortunate family of the deceased, as when families were prevented from recovering the bodies of executed relatives for burial, rather than direct retaliation for the wrong committed. Burial of some condemned people was circumvented by the award by law of the body to anatomists for public dissection. The far-reaching consequences of crimes, even those against oneself, were meant to be borne in mind *before* illegal acts were carried out.

But even a standard (or substandard) burial does not exempt a person from the wrath of a crowd bent on revenging a social, political, or religious crime. The body of the viscount of Narbonne, who had taken part in the murder of the Duke of Bourgogne, was exhumed from a mass grave in 1424. His corpse was cut into 21 pieces, each of which was hanged on a gallows. In

France, the Convention unearthed royal remains from St. Denis and threw them in a pit. A furious Russian mob dug up and burned the body of Grigori Rasputin after his assassination in 1916. In the thirteenth century, the body of French theologian Amalric of Bena was dug up and burned as punishment for his heresy. Servant Barbara Thutin of Koenigsburg was exhumed, hanged in her coffin, and burnt at the foot of the gallows as an example to her contemporaries because she had purposely infected her master and herself with plague.

The use to which some corpses are put adds insult to injury. Indians of Peru made the stomachs of their captives into drums. Nero used to light the arena and his garden at night with the oil-soaked bodies of crucified Christians. The corpses of kings and statesmen have been held up to ridicule by succeeding rulers. After conquering Egypt, Persian king Cambyses had the body of King Amasis exhumed, whipped, pricked with needles, plucked of hair, and burned. When the Stuarts were restored to the English throne in 1660, Charles II ordered the body of Oliver Cromwell and two compatriots to be dug up, hanged, and decapitated. The heads were impaled on spikes and carried through London as the crowd pelted the heads with rocks and garbage. The bodies were discarded under the gallows. As the Revolution got underway in France, the vault of the Bourbons was opened and the intact body of Henry IV (d. 1610) was leaned against a pillar in public for a period of two days. During this time many indignities were carried out against the corpse, including the removal of a lock of hair from the king's beard by a soldier who used it as a false mustache. The Bolsheviks were said to have desecrated the tombs of the czars in the Kremlin until losing their nerve after exposing the well-preserved face of Ivan the Terrible.[6]

While the destruction of burial sites has often been carried out as a show of force by conquerors, the mutilation of the bodies they contain is an even more personal insult. The purposeful mishandling of the corpse of a king or a family member is reacted to with outrage or, at the very least, distaste. The desecration of graves robs the dead of their dignity; if dignity were lacking to begin with, it robs them of the right to decay in peace. The executed and dethroned pay their price before death with their lives and possibly after death with their souls; extracting a price from their physical remains only shames their survivors—and their mutilators. In *Death: The Trip of a Lifetime*, Greg Palmer claims that "what really shows the human being's consideration for the dead is the care we take, not with the bodies of friends, but with the bodies of strangers."[7] Perhaps the toughest test is the care taken with the corpses of those who were hated during their lives.

The Anonymous

Rather than another demonstration of the human's ability
to emotionally complicate the simplest matters, I think
the way we get rid of the bodies of our fellow citizens is a
unique demonstration of our humanity. We take great
care with the bodies we know, and our grief at death is
often exaggerated when there is no body.
—Greg Palmer, *Death: The Trip of a Lifetime*[1]

The Aborted and Newborn Dead

The deaths of babies are especially disturbing. The parents are often
encouraged to interact briefly with the body to facilitate their grief in instances
of miscarriage, stillbirth, or neonatal death. In some cases, parents are accused
of abuse or neglect resulting in the death of a newborn child. The courts in
earlier centuries had difficulty discerning whether a baby had been stillborn
or abandoned after death. Infanticide was a common practice, treated leniently
by juries when prosecuted. It often went uncharged, but not unnoticed as
infants were discarded in dumps or rivers. Today fetuses are deliberately
removed from the body prior to birth, and their tissues are incinerated or used
for research. Abortion is sanctioned by law, but ethically objected to by some,
including many of those who see the results on a daily basis.

Nurses who work in hospitals that allow abortions are saddled with the
task of assisting in the procedure or parceling out the fetal remnants. Many
have expressed their revolt at disposing of perfectly formed fetuses, or worse,
ignoring those whose hearts are still beating. One doctor admits that none
of his colleagues wants to perform abortions after ten weeks because by then
the human features of hands and feet are visible. Suction abortion tears the
fetus out of the womb, while dilation and curettage cuts it out. Either way,
the procedure leaves a bloody byproduct that is obviously human in origin. A
morgue room supervisor provides his perspective on terminated pregnancies:

284

"We get a gauze sack, filled with what looks like foamy blood clot. There's some tissue in it, but most of it's placental and you really can't tell what it is.... But a lot of times we get fetuses that are large enough for you to see it's a person. You get like a hand, a foot, a head, an eye. You just can't imagine what it looks like. Like this body that's very developed, at an early age, has been blown apart and there's just fragments, like limbs and bloody pulp."[2] In the later stages of pregnancy, saline abortion (in which salt is introduced into the uterus and the dead fetus is subsequently delivered vaginally) and hysterotomy (in which the fetus is removed by Caesarean section and allowed to die) result in babies lacking nothing but life. Pictures of these potential human lives piled in garbage cans form the most potent right-to-life propaganda.

For those opposed to abortion, it is small consolation that the products of it are no longer considered waste. Fetal tissue is today a valuable commodity. Hospitals and abortion clinics contract with universities, commercial firms, and brokers to provide tissues to researchers. The volume of such exchanges, made through the payment of a service fee, is estimated to be 15,000 specimens annually. The tissue is used in research, which sometimes includes transplant. Transplantation of fetal pancreases and livers has been performed in more than 100 countries around the world, including the United States. Researchers hope such procedures will eventually cure people with Parkinson's disease, Alzheimer's disease, Huntington's disease, and diabetes. In 1993 it was revealed that ova could be retrieved from aborted female fetuses, nourished to mature quickly, fertilized by in vitro methods, and transferred to the body of a woman hoping to become pregnant—creating a child whose biological mother was never born.

The 30 million abortions performed annually worldwide leave a ready supply of raw material, but the enthusiastic use of fetal tissue has led some ethicists to become wary. Cases have been documented in which women have become pregnant with the intention of aborting the fetus and using its organs. More generally, the sale of fetal parts by women, clinics, and hospitals makes women manufacturers of a commodity, whereas the sale of human organs for transplant is prohibited. Modifications in abortion techniques for the purpose of obtaining fetal tissue may lengthen the procedure and jeopardize the woman's physical or mental health. In the U.S., some steps have been taken to regulate the fetal tissue industry. Congress banned research on living fetuses in 1974 after public outcry over an experiment to study the cerebral oxidation of glucose in which a team of American and Finnish scientists attempted to keep alive the heads of 12 fetuses aborted through hysterotomy. In early 1988, the Reagan administration declared a moratorium on federally funded research involving transplantation of tissue from elective abortions. The ban did not include the use of fetuses for nontransplantation research or any use of fetuses resulting from ectopic pregnancies or spontaneous abortions. Later that year an amendment was passed which made it illegal to sell fetal organs and organ subparts for transplant purposes. In 1993, President Clinton lifted the ban on the use of fetal tissue by executive order, but the restriction on the sale of transplant tissue remains in effect. In his book *The Human Body Shop*, Andrew Kimbrell points out the abuse of the female body and the unregulated use (or misuse) of aborted fetuses. In his view, the use of fetuses from induced abortions for transplant or research should be put on hold until the ethical and legal problems are fully resolved.[3]

Fetal tissue is big business, but was once merely a dirty business. Unwanted babies were killed *after* birth by smothering or exposure. The birth of children, especially illegitimate ones, was concealed, and the babies were tossed onto the rubbish heap: "In the eighteenth century it was not an uncommon spectacle to see the corpses of infants lying in the streets or on the dunghills of London and other large cities."[4] The coroners of earlier centuries had difficulty telling whether a baby was born dead or abandoned after birth, and juries were less likely to convict the killer of a baby than the killer of an adult. In the eighteenth century, the bodies of infants were hidden in trunks, haystacks, stairwells, and coalbins. During the winter of 1896, the bodies of 40 newborns were found floating in the Thames and traced to a woman and her son who disposed of unwanted infants. The infanticide rate began to fall, however, as the industrial revolution created a demand for child labor.

The subjects of today's abortions and yesterday's infanticides are nameless and, to all but a few, faceless. The aborted fetus is counted, but remains anonymous. The modern means of contraception after the fact is considered by many to be morally wrong, but socially necessary. Like capital punishment, abortion has been successfully defended in the Supreme Court but has strong dissenters among those who have seen it performed. Unlike capital punishment, abortion kills the innocent, although whether the victim is a "person" is still hotly debated. In contrast, parents whose newborn baby dies naturally or accidentally are encouraged to personalize their loss. They are urged by hospital staff and bereavement counselors to name the child, take photographs of it, and hold it before it is taken away. Despite the attentions of the medical staff, one grief-stricken mother commented, "The hospital is very lonely when your husband goes home and you know that your baby is in the morgue and not the nursery."[5] She does not belong with those who have deliberately ended their pregnancies, and she is pained to be near those who have had successful deliveries. She and her husband have been helped through their grief by giving their baby an identity.

The Unidentified Dead

In the United States, approximately 1,500 bodies that cannot be initially identified are found each year. Some are transients or teenage runaways, others are prostitutes or kidnap victims. The bodies of those who are unclaimed or unidentified undergo a different disposal procedure than those of the rest of us. After a mandated waiting period, during which identification may be attempted by publishing or televising photographs of the face of the corpse, it is cremated or buried in a common grave. The family of the deceased—unaware of the death—may presume several years later that death occurred, but they have no corpse to mourn or bury. In rare cases, the body released to the family by the morgue or to the funeral home by the hospital has been misidentified, an error which causes much anguish when eventually discovered. When next of kin have occasionally refused to identify a body or no next of kin have been found, the death will go almost unnoticed. Unidentified soldiers, on the other hand, have been glorified. The existence of tombs of unknown soldiers prove that the unidentified are not always unmourned.

Attempts to determine the identity of a person found dead of natural or deliberate causes meet with success when a person fitting the description is reported missing by family or friends or when the face of the deceased is recognized after a photograph is circulated. In the former case, the concerned individuals are called to the medical examiner's office to verify whether or not the body in question is that of their loved one. In the latter instance, police may receive a call from a relative, friend, neighbor, or fellow law enforcement officer who was acquainted with the deceased. In the hope of such calls, police may request the broadcast of a photograph by local television stations and its publication in regional newspapers. If this is unsuccessful, a photograph and information may be submitted to *Search*, a magazine that functions as a central registry of missing persons and contains a section of photographs of the unidentified remains of those found dead of natural causes, suicide, drug overdose, and murder.[6] Information may also be relayed to the FBI's National Crime Information Center, where features of the remains are compared with missing-person reports in their files. If the face is disfigured, the photograph submitted to the media may be retouched. If it has been skeletonized, police may—usually with the help of a computer or trained sculptor—model a face based on the characteristics of the skull.

When all attempts at identification have failed and a legally mandated waiting period has elapsed, the remains are disposed of. In the District of Columbia, unclaimed bodies are cremated after 30 days. The medical examiner's office operates its own crematorium and deposits the ashes of each body in a box marked "John (or Jane) Doe" that is later buried. The unclaimed dead of New York City have been boxed and transported to Potter's Field on Hart Island since 1870. The pine boxes containing adults are buried three deep and those of infants seven deep. From the 6,000 graves, which are recycled every 25 years, an occasional body is claimed and exhumed. Exhumation is also undertaken in cases of misidentification. When an unidentified woman died of a drug overdose in Washington, D.C., in 1989, she was taken to the medical examiner's office, fingerprinted, and held. A few days later, Wally Williams hesitantly identified the body as that of his wife Lynette, who had been missing for two weeks. It was after an open-casket wake and funeral and the burial of the body supposedly hers that the real Lynette Williams turned up alive and well. The fingerprint identification of the dead woman revealed her to be Andrea Bassil, whose mother was contacted. In compensation for the unfortunate mix-up, the medical examiner's office offered to exhume the body and pay for another funeral.

It is a small consolation, but at least Bassil's mother received a body to bury. When two men died on the same day at Yale-New Haven Hospital, their identities were transposed before their bodies were transported to their respective funeral homes. The mistake resulted in the wrong body being cremated, but the death was grieved for just the same. Bodies that remain unidentified may also remain unmourned. Accidental deaths and war casualties sometimes leave no traces. Airplanes and ships carrying dozens of passengers have crashed or sunk without bodies or wreckage being found. Hundreds and sometimes thousands of troops have disappeared during wartime: 4,000 in the Pyrenees during the Spanish War of Succession in the early eighteenth century, 650 French soldiers during a 15-mile march on Saigon in 1858, and nearly 3,000 Chinese soldiers during the sacking of Nanking by the Japanese in 1939. When soldiers are missing in action or civilians are missing for years on end, it is at some point assumed that they are dead, but families are denied the finality of a funeral or memorial service in the presence of the remains. They may have lingering doubts about the death and harbor a shred of hope that their loved one may still be alive. War may necessitate mass burial in which the dead—soldiers and civilians—are not individually memorialized. The Civil War prisoners at Andersonville died dozens at a time, totalling 13,000 altogether, and were buried in nearby trenches. When Allied troops liberated the German concentration camps, they were forced to inhume in mass graves the tens of thousands of corpses they found.

Ironically, the bodies of some unidentified soldiers are buried with honors and mourned by the nation as a whole. The unknown soldier becomes a symbol of all those who have given their lives for their country. The anonymity of the remains makes the martyrdom all the more poignant. The first unknown American soldier, killed in the Revolutionary War, was buried in Union Cemetery in Lackawaxen, Pennsylvania. Unknown soldiers form the majority (54 percent) in the 79 national Civil War cemeteries: more than 12,000 in Vicksburg, Mississippi, and at least that many at the site of a Confederate prison in Salisbury, North Carolina. It was by an act of Congress after World War I that unknowns were selected for enshrinement at Arlington National Cemetery. In 1921, four unidentified American soldiers were exhumed from each of the American cemeteries in France. One of the caskets was chosen by a U.S. Army sergeant and shipped to Washington aboard a cruiser. The remains arrived on November 9 and lay in state at the Capitol until Armistice Day, when a service was held at Arlington Cemetery, taps was sounded, a national salute was given, and the remains were thus formally committed to the now familiar sarcophagus. The rite was repeated with bodies from among the 3 percent of soldiers who remained unidentified after World War II and the Korean conflict. A fourth crypt in the tomb, intended to house the remains of a casualty of the Vietnam war, was finally filled in 1984 by one of the few unidentified bodies recovered.

While genetic and manual fingerprinting assure that unknown soldiers will be difficult to find in the future, unidentified civilians continue to turn up. Common graves were once an economical means of disposing of those without money, a method detailed in the report of a municipal committee in 1842:

> In accordance with [the plan] generally observed or adopted throughout London: this is, the opening, what is called a public grave, thirty feet deep, perhaps; the first corpse interred was succeeded by another, and up to sixteen or eighteen, and all the openings between the coffin boards were filled with smaller coffins of children. When this grave was crammed as full as it could be, so that the topmost coffin was within two feet of the surface that was ... considered as occupied ... A typical metropolitan church, St. Martin-in-the-Fields, had a burial ground 200 feet square, which was estimated to contain 60,000 to 90,000 bodies.[7]

Potter's fields are now filled with those without names.

The Plundered

Corpses were bought and sold, they were touted, priced,
haggled over, negotiated for, discussed in terms of supply
and demand, delivered, imported, exported, transported.
Human bodies were compressed into boxes, packed in
sawdust, packed in hay, trussed up in sacks, roped up like
hams, sewn in canvas, packed in cases, casks, barrels, crates
and hampers, salted, pickled or injected with preservative.
They were carried in carts and wagons, in barrows and
steam-boats; manhandled, damaged in transit, and hidden
under loads of vegetables. They were stored in cellars and
on quays. Human bodies were dismembered and sold in
pieces, or measured and sold by the inch.
—Ruth Richardson, *Death, Dissection and the
Destitute*[1]

Graverobbing

The dead are easy victims for the unscrupulous. With only external
defenses—the cemetery gate, the depth of the grave, or the lock on the mausoleum door, they have been robbed of their clothes, their jewelry, their teeth,
even their bones. The spoils are sold at a profit or kept for reasons ranging
from historic interest to use in magic ceremonies. Even their caskets have been
usurped for reuse or firewood. But graverobbing has not always awaited interment. Victims of disaster have been stripped of their valuables as they wash
ashore, soldiers have been robbed of their teeth or shoes as they lie on the
battlefield, and bodies have been divested of their organs en route to the crematory. The definition of graverobbing is called into question by Native
Americans, who accuse archaeologists of plundering the sacred burial sites
of their ancestors.

Teeth of the dead have been sought after in many places and times. In
Etruria in 800 B.C., good teeth were surgically removed after a person's death

and used to make dentures for the upper classes. The ancient Jews made false teeth from the teeth of dead people and animals. The teeth of the healthy young soldiers who died in the battle of Waterloo were prized, and dentures referred to as "Waterloo Teeth" were sold for years throughout Europe. Casualties of the American Civil War had their mouths ransacked for the same reason. In this century, the teeth of the dead have been plucked for their monetary value rather than for reuse. Gold fillings were harvested from the dead in the Nazi concentration camps before their corpses were buried or cremated. The same motive led David Sconce, the son of a funeral home owner and the manager of the Pasadena Crematorium in the mid–1980s, to extract gold teeth from incoming corpses with pliers, a task he referred to as "popping chops" or "going to the mine." Since the average gold crown weighs in at one tenth of an ounce, one author estimates that Sconce may have made as much as $280,000 by selling the precious metal.

Those who are not a part of the funeral industry have less of an opportunity to plunder the bodies of the dead. Scavengers must content themselves with stealing jewelry from the victims of occasional accidents or disasters. On Woolwich Quay in 1878, thieves stole watches, rings, bracelets, necklaces, and hair combs from the bloated bodies of victims of the wrecked *Princess Alice*, hacking off fingers and hands in their frenzy. Fingers were also cut to retrieve rings from the bodies that washed ashore in New Jersey after the ocean liner *Morro Castle* burned en route to New York in 1934. When two ships exploded in Halifax Harbor in 1917, prowlers removed rings and rifled the pockets of the dead. After the San Francisco earthquake in 1906, thieves caught cutting fingers and ears off corpses to obtain rings and earrings were lynched.

David Sconce's punishment was not nearly so harsh, despite the fact that he plundered not only gold, but the organs of the dead. After misleading his clients to obtain signatures on a release form allowing his staff to remove "tissues and pacemakers" before cremation of the body, he extracted eyes and organs to be used for transplant and research. Sales of the body parts were arranged through a company he initiated and named the Coastal International Eye and Tissue Bank. In addition to the sale of the gold from the teeth of those he cremated, Sconce hoped to add more than $1 million to his gross annual income through this enterprise. The CIE&TB was approved as a non-profit organization by the California Department of Health Services in 1986, but Sconce was brought up on charges including stealing body parts the following year. The charges were dropped in 1989, but he pled guilty to several other felonies and was sentenced to five years in prison.

The traditional graverobber often escapes punishment by operating under cover of darkness. In Victorian times, many graves were robbed by the men who dug them. The gravediggers sold the lead and wood from the coffins, the clothes from the bodies, and sometimes the bodies themselves (an enterprise discussed in the next chapter). Today graves are opened in search of valuables, such as military insignia or jewelry, or merely for the thrill: "Every state in the Union contains cemeteries that have been plundered for their bones by looters whose motives range from childish derring-do through morbid curiosity to Satanism and plain old-fashioned madness."[2] In Brazil, graves have been raided to search for gold teeth, to obtain coffins to sell to local undertakers, and to gather bones for use in magic ceremonies. In the U.S., the motivation is often wanton destructiveness. In the Washington, D.C., area, a crypt was desecrated in the early 1980s and the occupant decapitated with a knife. The family afterward chose to have the mutilated body cremated. In 1983, vandals who broke into Bayside Cemetery in Queens, New York, opened several crypts, broke into the caskets, strewed the remains about the mausoleum, and scrawled graffiti on walls and headstones. One case, *The People v. Robert Fennell*, set a precedent when the mausoleum was interpreted to be a building by the New York State Supreme Court, and Fennell was convicted of burglary in the third degree. In 1992 the mausoleum of automobile manufacturer Ransom Olds and family was burglarized of five urns and the casket of an infant. No payment was requested for their return, and the crypt of the family patriarch was not disturbed.

Another form of graverobbing—archaeology—has been criticized, but legislation concerning its practice has been enacted. More than 25,000 Chinese tombs were plundered between 1988 and 1990 to retrieve antiquities.[3] In the U.S., the remains of Native Americans have been disinterred, studied, and placed in museum display cases around the country to the objection of their descendants, who have formed an association—American Indians Against Desecration—in protest. In some regions, the looting of Native American burial sites is said to constitute a major part of the local economy.[4] The activism of the Indians has led to decisions at the Smithsonian Institution and elsewhere to remove Native American skeletal materials from public display. While the contemporary Indians do not have family ties to the dead, they do feel a spiritual bond, a symbolic identification, and a psychological relationship.[5] By passing a bill authorized by Senator Daniel K. Inouye of Hawaii, Congress authorized the Smithsonian Institution to return approximately 20,000 Indian remains to tribes that could identify them. Museums in New York, Boston, and Palo Alto followed Washington's lead, and more than 20 states have passed similar legislation on the issue, which broadens the traditional definition of graverobbery to include not only plunder and vandalism, but what was once thought of as legitimate scientific claim-staking.

Bodysnatching

Bodies have been stolen from the grave not only for their valuables, but for their flesh. Bodysnatching was a possibility to be guarded against in the eighteenth and nineteenth centuries. With law limiting the subjects of dissection to the executed or indigent, or to a certain number per year, anatomists turned to the black market for the centerpieces of their lectures. Bodies were dug up under cover of darkness from private plots and potter's fields. Demand led two famous "resurrectionists" to circumvent exhumation by killing their boarders and selling their bodies. As the means of obtaining corpses grew more devious, the attempts to prevent bodysnatching grew more clever. Guards were posted, bodies were allowed to decompose before they were left unchaperoned, and justice was served when the most famous resurrection man was himself publicly dissected.

In medieval Europe, the scientific study of anatomy was virtually abandoned when Pope Boniface VIII issued a bull excommunicating anyone who cut up a human body. Study of human anatomy resumed during the Renaissance, but the availability of cadavers was curtailed by law. The Council of Edinburgh authorized that the body of one executed criminal per year could be used by anatomists, while a 1694 decision also gave Edinburgh surgeons the right to dissect the bodies of a small number of prisoners, foundlings, and stillbirths. In England, public dissection was allowed on only a small number of executed criminals per year under an act of Henry VIII. The lawmakers of late eighteenth-century Massachusetts made available for dissection not only the bodies of the executed but also the bodies of slain duelists. To supplement these meager rations, anatomists purchased newly dead bodies that were offered to them with no questions asked. In the seventeenth century, medical students were sometimes expected to provide their own cadavers for anatomy lessons and often became so adept at procuring them that they sold their services to finance their schooling. "It is said that in Scotland anatomy students could pay for their tuition with corpses rather than coin, which suggests their tutors' complicity," writes Ruth Richardson in *Death, Dissection and the Destitute*.[6] The demand for bodies far outweighed the legal supply, with Edinburgh alone requiring 1,000 annually during the early 1800s. Several famous professors carved up the bodies of their own family members when others (even those procured illegally) were unavailable. Rondeler of the Montpellier Medical School dissected his own child before his students. William Harvey dissected the bodies of his father and sister. Medical schools relied almost exclusively on their students, unscrupulous undertakers, and local bodysnatchers to obtain cadavers for dissection until 1832, when Parliament passed the Anatomy Act. The act allowed unclaimed bodies to be turned over to medical establishments, effectively substituting the poor for the executed.

Exhuming freshly buried bodies was the most labor-intensive way to obtain subjects for dissection. But resurrectionists were purposeful and efficient: "It was part of his trade to despise and desecrate the scrolls and trumpets of old tombs, the paths worn by the feet of worshippers and mourners, and the offerings and the inscriptions of bereaved affection.... The coffin was forced, the cerements torn, and the melancholy relics, clad in sackcloth, after being rattled for hours on moonless byways, were at length exposed to uttermost indignities before a class of gaping boys."[7]

The most experienced of the bodysnatchers used short wooden spades to dig a hole at the head of the grave and piled the earth they removed on a piece of canvas. When they reached the coffin, they snapped the lid in half with a crowbar or iron hooks and hoisted the body out using ropes or a hook under the chin. They stripped and bagged the body, replaced the earth, and rearranged the flowers on the grave. Resurrectionists had many tricks of the trade. The clothes the corpse was wearing were left in the grave until the 1820s, before which time their removal (not the removal of the body) would have constituted a felony. The robbers dug in shifts, so the task could be completed more quickly. Graverobbers were also said to be fond of telling horrific ghost stories to discourage late-night visitors to the graveyards from which they stole bodies. The infamous bodysnatcher "Old Cunny" (discussed below) dressed the bodies he resurrected in old clothes, propped them up next to him in his buggy, and carried on a heated, one-sided conversation with them during transport.

Because anatomists were in need of *fresh* bodies, resurrectionists often—but by no means exclusively—frequented the cemeteries of the Jews, who buried their dead soon after death. Those who could afford to do so posted guards at the grave for the first few weeks, but even many of these could be bribed to look the other way. Others had no choice but to take their chances. Potter's fields and African-American cemeteries were easy targets. Laurence Sterne, author of *Tristram Shandy*, died penniless in 1768 and was buried at St. George's in Hanover Square. His body was dissected at Cambridge two days later. While the well-to-do had the means to guard against unauthorized dissection, the less fortunate could only dread it: "To the rich it was a monstrous obscenity to be guarded against with forethought and precaution, but to the poor it was the first horror of sickness and the last terror of death, that their bodies ... should be in danger of being unburied by ghouls, carted to the dissection table, and cut to pieces by the apprentice doctors."[8]

The only recourse was to allow the corpse of a loved one to putrefy under careful watch so that resurrection would be pointless. In some cemeteries, houses were erected in which the newly dead were allowed to decompose for up to three months before burial. Even those who tried to protect their own bodies after death were thwarted. Irishman Charles O'Brien (d. 1763) feared that his eight-foot-tall body would be a prime candidate for the anatomy museum and made arrangements to be buried at sea. Members of the funeral escort were persuaded financially by surgeon John Hunter to fill the coffin with stones and allow him to take possession of the corpse, which he then dissected and skeletonized.

In 1827 two Irishmen—William Burke and William Hare—discovered a means surer and more direct than exhumation or bribery to obtain bodies to sell for dissection. They produced corpses themselves by murdering tenants in Hare's Edinburgh lodging house and by so doing became the most infamous resurrection men in history. They lured 15 travelers one-by-one into the house, got them drunk, and suffocated them by holding their mouths closed and pressing on their chests. After the two men (who in fact had been assisted by Hare's wife and Burke's mistress) were brought to trial, "burking" became synonymous with smothering. The bodies were sold for eight to fourteen pounds each to anatomy instructor, Dr. Knox, who was immortalized with Hare and Burke in ballads of the day:

> Up the close and doun [*sic*] the stair,
> But and Ben with Burke and Hare,
> Burke's the butcher, Hare's the thief,
> Knox the boy that buys the beef.[9]

The punishment of William Burke fit the crime: he was executed before a crowd of 20,000 and publicly dissected in 1829. Tickets to the anatomy demonstration were distributed to important citizens and outstanding medical students, causing 2,000 members of the student body to riot until they were given permission to file past the corpse. The general public was allowed to view the partly dissected body the following day and as many as 40,000 took the opportunity to do so. Some sought souvenirs, and it is said that Burke's skin was tanned after dissection, sold for a shilling an inch, and used to make wallets and tobacco pouches. Burke's skeleton still hangs in the Anatomy Museum at Edinburgh University. William Hare, on the other hand, suffered a different fate. After turning king's evidence against his partner, he fled to England. He was recognized by some workmen and thrown into a pit of lime which blinded him. He spent the rest of his days begging in London.

Murder was not a prerogative only of Burke and Hare. Helen Torrence and Jean Waldie were hanged in Scotland in 1752 after they stole and killed an eight-year-old child and sold the body in exchange for drink and a small sum. In the early 1800s, an Irish woman offered the bodies of her living children—one thirteen years old and the other two months old—for dissection but was not satisfied with the offer and was reported to the authorities. But despite the example of Burke's punishment, bodysnatchers still resorted to murder. Thomas Williams, John Bishop, and John May killed three people in 1831 by drugging their rum and drowning them in a well. Two of the gang were hanged and the third exiled to Australia. The most recent example of homicidal bodysnatching is that of a security chief at the Free University of Barranquilla in Columbia, who was arrested for clubbing 50 people to death.

He sold the bodies to an institute of the university for $200 and was paid with checks drawn on the university's account.[10]

Little pity is lavished on resurrectionists, while their living victims—the families of the exhumed—receive considerable sympathy. The robbing of bodies leaves mourners doubly grief-stricken. Tom Hood characterized the emptiness of the coffin in his poem "Mary's Ghost":

> Don't go to weep upon my grave,
> And think that there I be;
> They haven't left an atom there
> Of my anatomie.[11]

There were many graves left empty by the resurrectionists of the eighteenth and nineteenth centuries. An Edinburgh resurrectionist even disinterred and sold the body of his own sister. It is estimated that by 1850, 600 or 700 bodies were snatched annually from the burial grounds of New York City. The epitaph on a gravestone in Hoosick Falls, New York, details the fate of Elizabeth Sprague's corpse for posterity:

> She was stolen from the grave
> by Roderick R. Clow & dissected
> at Dr. P. M. Armstrong's office
> in Hoosick, N.Y. from which place
> her mutilated remains were
> obtained and deposited here.
> Her body dissected by fiendish men
> Her bones anatomised,
> Her soul we trust has risen to God
> Where few physicians rise.[12]

Bodies were distributed within the U.S. and within the U.K., where they were shipped from rural areas to London and Edinburgh in casks, trunks, and packing crates.

Corpses were snatched not only from the cemetery, but also from the scaffold and the undertaking establishment. In the early nineteenth century, several American funeral directors were accused of stealing children and killing them to receive a fee given for the burial of indigent youths. As recently as 1975, funeral directors were said to have resorted to illicit means to obtain the state burial allowance for the poor. During the heyday of bodysnatching, corpses were not only manufactured by murder, they were sabotaged, commandeered, and resold. Hospitals purchased bodies they knew had been retrieved from the hospital graveyard, and competing gangs of resurrectionists broke into anatomy schools to mutilate corpses delivered by their rivals. At least one anatomist was swindled into buying the bagged body of a man who was not dead, but dead drunk. If a person dropped dead in the street, a resurrectionist would take the opportunity to claim the body as that of his "cousin" and sell it after being awarded custody. Bodysnatchers were also known to send their wives to the anatomy lab to demand the return of their "relative" so the corpse could be sold a second or third time. Bodies were sometimes purchased from the family of the deceased and occasionally from the living in advance of death. Joshua Jones of Ellisberg, Pennsylvania, sentenced to be hanged for killing his wife in 1838, sold his body to Dr. Amos French for ten dollars and spent the money on food. Early eighteenth-century surgeons employed agents to barter with Newgate prisoners for claim to their bodies after death—unless dissection was already part of the prisoner's sentence. When that was the case, payment was made by the Company of Barber-Surgeons, which was charged with anatomizing the condemned.

Several famous doctors were associated with bodysnatching, and several bodysnatchers became famous in their own right. Sir Astley Cooper, president of the Royal College of Surgeons, was nicknamed "King of the Resurrectionists" because of his boast that he could obtain for dissection any body he wanted. The services of resurrectionists were also commissioned by the founder of Bellevue Hospital, several of the presidents of the New York Academy of Medicine, and the founder of what later became the George Washington University School of Medicine. One bodysnatcher, George Christian, operated his business out of the Surgeon General's Office in Washington, D.C. Another, Ben Crouch, was known as the "Corpse King" and was hired by anatomists to give their students resurrection lessons.

While it was sometimes a messy business, bodysnatching could turn a tidy profit. Adult bodies were sold for four guineas, and the bodies of children were sold by length—six shillings for the first foot and ninepence for each additional inch. After expenses, resurrectionists took home more than 10 pounds per week, 20 times the average earnings of an unskilled worker.[13] In 1828 a gang of six or seven men testified that they had sold 312 bodies the previous winter at four pounds, four shillings per corpse for a grand total of 1,328 guineas (several thousand dollars). Corpses were a commodity in great demand. Most of the bodies were purchased for use as cadavers, but some were bought for their fat. Human fat, a remedy for wounds and disease and raw material for the manufacture of candles and soap, commanded a high price in the eighteenth century.

Graverobbing was lucrative, but also exacted a price—sometimes legal retribution and other times just desserts. An 1827 magazine relates the story of a sailor who assisted some students to rob a grave only to find that they had exhumed the body of his sweetheart, who had died a few days before he returned from sea. Many anatomists feared the fate of their own bodies after death, as expressed in the poem "Surgeon's Warning" by Robert Southey:

my 'prentices will surely come,
And carve me bone from bone,
And I, who have rifled the dead man's grave
Shall never rest in my own.[14]

A notorious Irish-American bodysnatcher of the 1800s named William Cunningham never made it to the grave. "Old Cunny" was often ridiculed by the medical students he supplied. In retaliation, he sent the body of a smallpox victim to the school and was pleased to hear that a number of students had contracted the disease. When "Old Cunny" died, his widow sold his body to the Medical College of Ohio for 15 pounds. Resurrectionists were also at risk while alive. Two medical students caught snatching a body near Edinburgh in 1832 were committed to gaol voluntarily, fearing the violence that the crowd threatened. When two surgeons began to dissect the body of a hanged man in the 1820s, they were attacked by friends of the deceased, who killed one and wounded the other.

Bodysnatching is no longer a common occupation, but it is by no means extinct. In the late 1980s, two employees at the University of Pennsylvania Medical Center were suspended after allegedly selling human heads from cadavers to a local ear, nose, and throat specialist for $150 each. Even more recently, 18-year-old college student Kevin McQuain was charged with bodysnatching after he was discovered boiling a human head on a hot plate in his dorm room. The head belonged to a former mayor of the town who had died in 1886 and had been resurrected by McQuain in the hope that he could use it to improve his grade in sculpting class. The exhumation of bodies for other than legal reasons tends—historically and today—to fall into two categories: those who dig up the dead for profit and those who do it for fun. When the bottom dropped out of the black market in bodies in the nineteenth century, the spades of the resurrectionists were taken up by the ever-present graver-obbers in search of gold or saleable items. Of a less comprehensible nature are the rare human beings for whom unearthing the dead is not a means to an end, but an end in itself.

Necrophilia

Physical attraction to the dead has led to a number of indiscretions. In this quarter century, bodies have been hijacked by mortuary workers for personal pleasure. Historically, necrophilia has been suspected of Egyptian embalmers and amateur anatomists. While love of the dead may be nonsexual (gratified by mere proximity) or even accidental (as the result of the sudden death of a partner during sex), it is often the driving force behind serial murder. Serial killers make short work of murder to obtain a corpse they can then fondle and spend time with. Posthumous sex may be coupled with cannibalism or practiced on exhumed bodies. Some killers are so obsessed with the conjoined ideas of sex and death that they regard their own impending execution as the ultimate orgasm.

Some people are aroused by the *idea* of death. They may fantasize about their own death or about causing the deaths of others. Hungarian killer Sylvestre Matuschka experienced sexual excitement upon seeing (and later causing) dramatic and fatal train collisions. Cannibalistic murderer Albert Fish looked forward to his 1936 electrocution as the "supreme thrill" of his life, and prior to his execution by guillotine, serial killer Peter Kurten anticipated the sound of his own blood rushing out of his neck. Other people are excited by the trappings of death. Havelock Ellis wrote of a woman who became so sexually aroused at her husband's funeral that she had intercourse with the undertaker. Still others are stimulated by the corpse itself, the traditional form of necrophilia (also called necrophilism). While the idea of having sex with a dead body is repulsive to most of us, sex and death have in fact had a long marriage. Ancient dances in honor of the dead were often obscene, an imitation of the generation of life in hopes that the deceased would depart.[15] Necrophilia has been part of cultural ritual, for instance when a virgin died in northern Haiti and was penetrated vaginally with a wooden object to prevent her soul from wandering. It has been a religious rite in Renaissance and contemporary cults. But most often it has been a personal ritual embarked on by death care workers compelled to caress their clients and by killers raping their victims during or after death.

Those most often suspected of acts of necrophilia are those with easy (and private) access to the newly dead, including hospital orderlies, morgue attendants, and funeral home and cemetery workers. In past centuries, amateur anatomists were accused of engaging in "libertinage" with cadavers. The embalmers of ancient Egypt were not trusted with the bodies of highborn or particularly beautiful women until several days after death; female embalmers emerged as a further precaution. Even today state laws give families the right to request the presence of a representative during the embalming of a corpse. Although indiscretions are rarely reported, they do occur more frequently than most people imagine. A letter to columnist Ann Landers from a woman whose daughter married a mortician raised public consciousness as well as many eyebrows: "Her wedding night was a nightmare. Her husband asked her to take a very cold bath before coming to bed. He suggested that she stay in the tub for about half an hour. When she came to bed he asked her to close her eyes and lie perfectly still. Then he said, 'You may as well know that I am a necrophiliac as so many of my profession are. I can only make love to dead women or women who look as if they are.'"[16] That many necrophiles work in funeral homes is not to imply that the majority of people who work in funeral homes are necrophiles.

Karen Greenlee, however, is one. Notable for both her gender (90 percent of necrophiles are men) and her outspokenness, Greenlee—aged 23 at the time—admitted in Sacramento Superior Court to having sexual contact with between 20 and 40 male corpses before and during her employment at Sacramento Memorial Lawn mortuary as an apprentice embalmer. Because there is no law against necrophilia in California, she was charged with illegally driving a hearse and interfering with a burial. She had stolen the body of 33-year-old John Mercure in 1979 rather than delivering it to the cemetery and was discovered in the hearse with the dead man two days later in an adjacent county. Mercure's mother sued for severe emotional distress. She received $117,000, and Greenlee received 11 days in jail, a $255 fine, two years' probation, and a recommendation for medical treatment. In an interview, Greenlee made it clear that even necrophiles have discriminating taste: "Sure, I find the odor of death *very* erotic. There are death odors and there are death odors. Now you get your body that's been floating in the bay for two weeks, or a burn victim, that doesn't attract me much, but a freshly embalmed corpse is something else. There is also this attraction to blood. When you're on top of a body it tends to purge blood out of its mouth, while you're making passionate love.... You'd have to be there, I guess."[17] Obviously, most of us would rather not. But as gory as her testimony is, she does shed some light on this very hidden topic—that not all necrophiles are male, that necrophilia is not engaged in as a *substitute* for sex with a living partner but in preference to it, and that sex with the dead is as "natural" for some as it is unnatural for the rest of us.

"Everyone to his own taste," said Henri Blot during his nineteenth-century trial for disinterment and necrophilia. "Mine is for corpses."[18] And he was not alone. King Herod (d. 4 B.C.) supposedly had sex with his wife for seven years after her death. In 1849, Sergeant Bertrand of the French army was charged with breaking into cemeteries, cohabiting with the freshly buried bodies of young girls, and then mutilating the bodies to cover up his crimes. Earlier this century, Carl van Cassel of Key West, Florida, exhumed the body of a woman who had not responded to his advances and slept with it for seven years before being discovered.[19] Not all necrophiles are killers, but according to the FBI a number of killers are necrophiles. In their investigations of serial killers, 42 percent reported acts of necrophilia. For several serial killers, necrophilia is the motivation for, or a fringe benefit of, their crimes. Henry Lee Lucas had sex with the body of his girlfriend Becky Powell after stabbing her in a fit of rage and before dismembering her corpse. She was not his only posthumous partner, however, and when asked by an FBI agent why he only had sex with women after he killed them, Lucas replied, "I like peace and quiet."[20] John Reginald Halliday Christie copulated with the bodies of the prostitutes he killed because he was impotent with living women. Edmund Kemper cut the Achilles tendons of his female victims to facilitate his sexual acts with the body and to prevent the advance of rigor mortis. His predecessor, the "Thames nude murderer" of 1964, removed the teeth of his victims for the purposes of oral sex.

Some killers prefer to spend time with their victims after death. After killing her lover with a rifle earlier this century, Ginette Vidal spent the next three days with the corpse, talking to it, cooking for it, and fondling it as it decomposed. Dennis Nilsen parted with his male victims reluctantly: he kept as many as six beneath the floorboards of his living room and in the first few days brought them out, cleaned them up, and enjoyed their companionship before reinterring them. Ted Bundy transported the body of one of his victims to his apartment, where he redid her makeup and shampooed her hair. Jerome Brudos posed and photographed his murder victims nude and in varying outfits, with particular attention to their shoes. Killers have also contented themselves with only part of the body. Bundy was known to have returned to the site of a killing and sexually assaulted the severed body parts, for instance, ejaculating into the mouth of a disembodied head. Carl Drew of Massachusetts imprisoned several women and killed those who offended him, afterward raping their headless bodies in front of his other victims. Kemper found decapitation itself to be a sexual thrill: "You hear that little pop and pull their heads off and hold their heads up by the hair. Whipping their heads off, their body sitting there. That'd get me off."[21] To have the experience he wanted with a person, Kemper explained, he had to evict them from their bodies. "Bluebeard" of the fifteenth century, Gilles de Rais, evicted as many as 800 children from their bodies so that he could masturbate against their corpses.

"The grave's a fine and private place, / But none, I think, do there embrace," wrote Andrew Marvell in his poem "To His Coy Mistress." While the poem makes its point, the lines are untrue. Samuel Pepys bragged of kissing Henry V's queen, Catherine of Valois, during the two centuries that her remains were exposed after her death in 1437. When the crypt next to that of Marilyn Monroe was offered for sale for $50,000, author Herbert E. Nass lewdly suggested that "For that price, one can lie next to the immortal remains of the most illustrious sex goddess of our times for an eternity."[22] While the value of a person's celebrity or sex appeal may extend beyond the grave, for the true necrophiliac that is where the appeal begins. Unlike the average consumer of Ann Landers' advice, including panic-free instructions for dealing with the death of a partner during sex, the necrophile craves the corpse and goes to great lengths to obtain, borrow, or produce one. While only 17 percent of necrophiles can be classified as psychotic,[23] they are all clearly guilty of reversing the natural order of things by performing what is a life-giving act with a lifeless body or one that they have robbed of life for the purpose.

AFTERWORD

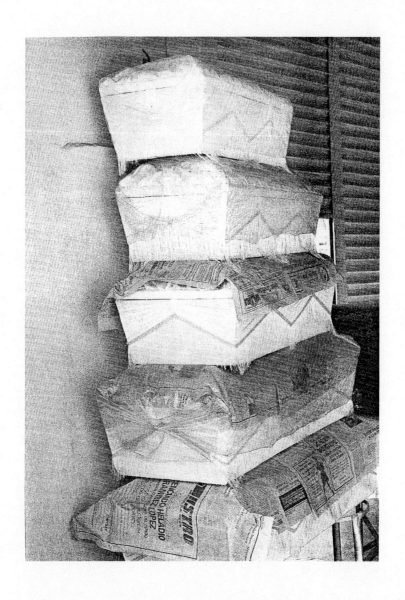

Caretakers of the Dead

19

He that toucheth the dead body of any man shall be
unclean seven days.
    —*Holy Bible* (Numbers XIX: 11)

Overview

Death care providers juggle a number of identities. In public, they are cordial to the family of the deceased and gentle toward the body. Behind the scenes, they may be casual, even callous. The aspects of their jobs that have traditionally been considered unclean make them unwelcome guests in social situations, yet they are sought out when needed by those very same hosts: "In America, those who deal with the dead have social identities that shift back and forth.... Sometimes they look like pariahs and deviants, sometimes like charlatans. Other times they look like heroes or even adepts, initiates, and priests."[1] The layperson knows the funeral director and pathologist has secret knowledge about the corpse and trusts him or her to keep that knowledge secret. The professionals turn to each other to "talk shop," but also for support and camaraderie. The gallows humor death professionals resort to in private contrasts with the ritualized and somber behavior that characterizes the public facets of their work. Both modes, in addition to repetition, facilitate dealing with the dead. It is when the corpse is that of a friend that it becomes a more potent symbol to those who are constant reminders of death to the rest of us.

Funeral Directors and Embalmers

Funeral directors are the obvious scapegoats for American attitudes toward death, which range from denial to disgust. Their expertise in carrying

Afterword title page: Stacked caskets. Photo by the author.

out a funeral is reduced to their manipulation of the dead body: "[The funeral director's] public efforts to be genteel in the presence of the dead body, his efforts to restore it to a somewhat lifelike appearance, his supposedly reverent treatment of it, and his vested interest in it, all make his relationship with the dead body somewhat unusual."[2] Funeral directors and embalmers disguise the dead with cosmetics, thus making some of the facts of death gentler to the bereaved, but they also draw attention to the body they have specially prepared. They take pride in their work, but they would be considered ghouls if they made much of it when talking to their clients. They downplay the activities in the embalming room, but then submit a substantial bill for them. Funeral directors are entrusted with the body of the deceased, but are not trusted to estimate correctly the value their work.

Funeral directors must also downplay their competitiveness. They must appear to be ready to assist when asked, rather than seeming to haggle over corpses. In an unseemly confrontation in Brazil in 1992, two morticians shot and killed each other vying for the privilege of conducting the funeral of one of the town's inhabitants. To a lesser extent and without the publicity, there is jealousy within the American trade. The man who prepared Andy Warhol's body remarked, "It was all the talk of the funeral trade about how I landed the Warhol body."[3] Purchasers of funeral services do not comparison shop or window shop, but rather base their decision on family tradition, location, or recommendation. Owners of funeral homes rely on their reputation for continued success. The desire to increase their business means that funeral directors—like the people in the organ-sharing network—are in the position of hoping for deaths to occur. But unlike the procurers of organs for transplant, funeral directors accept money for their dealings with the dead. This somehow makes their profession even more suspect, although it is common practice for people to pay someone to perform tasks that they do not wish to do themselves.

Because they do not wish to prepare and bury their own dead, many people wonder why anyone would. Funeral directing is assumed to be a family business and is still in large part a hereditary profession, with most practitioners having been acquainted with—and one third of them related to—someone in the field before they entered it. But funeral directing is wrongly assumed to require only a little "hands-on" experience: "To organize and direct a procession which must be profoundly ceremonial, which cannot be rehearsed or repeated, and in which mistakes are always magnified by a high level of emotional intensity, defines and fixes a responsibility which by conventional standards of occupational recognition elevates the funeral director's work beyond and above that of the craftsman, tradesman, or purveyor of petty personal services."[4] Today's mortuary schools teach the business and practical sides of the business, and some states require as much as three years of schooling, followed by an apprenticeship of one to three years. The work requires dedication and the understanding that they will be on call seven days a week, 24 hours a day, without complaint.

Despite the fact that they are professionals, funeral directors are overlooked or avoided by members of other professions. "Some people in the community won't shake hands with me... . They don't hate me but they won't shake hands with me," complains William B. Scott, a funeral director in Jeffersonville, Indiana.[5] Even others who regularly encounter corpses set funeral directors apart. "We handle death but we also deal with the living," says an emergency medical technician, "Clyde's world has only one dimension."[6] Funeral directors would disagree, pointing out that most of their time is spent with the living. And the living appreciate their attentiveness, if only on a case by case basis: "In fact, though funeral directors are the most publicly maligned of all death-related professionals, they continually score much higher in client satisfaction than doctors, nurses, or clergy."[7] And of course funeral directors are not friendless. In fact, it is the burial of their friends that drives home their own mortality. Some report the embalming of friends to be a very traumatic experience, and others choose early retirement when their peers begin to die.

Among their active colleagues, however, funeral directors maintain a sense of humor in the daily face of death. The owner of an Australian funeral home remarked that as drivers pass each other in their hearses, they hold up their fingers to indicate the number of funerals they have carried out that day—mindful that eventually one of those fingers will represent each of them in turn.[8] In *Death: The Trip of a Lifetime*, Greg Palmer defends the gallows humor necessary to all of the death professions: "Funeral home workers can become, if not callous, then certainly a bit larky about their work. We expect them to be as somber and reverential around death as we are, but really that's impossible, or they'd spend their whole lives looking like their clients."[9] An apprentice embalmer concurred, "A lot of people are under the misconception that morticians are very straight, very somber. If they ever went back into the prep room and heard all the jokes that are cracked, it would blow that theory right out the window."[10] Embalmers joke not only about the dead, but about the public's attitude toward death. Mortician Robert Yount began his career as a part-time, live-in worker in a funeral home. His mother had urged him to accept the job, later revealing she had done so because she knew that his girlfriends would refuse to walk through the mortuary to get to his apartment. "She was right," lamented Yount.[11]

Funeral home workers transform the body from an unsightly medical patient or accident victim into an approachable focus for grief, in addition to providing an adaptable setting for religious and secular rites. By taking the tasks of laying out and funeralizing the dead out of the home, funeral directors have allowed members of the public to dissociate themselves from death physically. Mentally, the family is insulated from death by being coached by

the funeral director, often in league with the clergy, through a series of ritualized events including the wake, the funeral itself, and the committal service. Death is made less painful through religion and less personal by being
acknowledged and arranged for in a public place rather than a private home.
The clothes in which the body will be buried may be chosen by the family,
but the corpse is dressed by the funeral director. The bereaved choose the
casket, but the corpse is laid inside by the staff. In the funeral home, death
and the dead are made presentable. In ways that are safe and acceptable,
funeral directors put a face on death. It is sometimes their own, but it is more
often the face of the loved one in the casket, a face that is restful, painless—
and familiar.

Doctors and Pathologists

Doctors and pathologists are often insulated from the discrimination of
the public by virtue of the fact that they perform their traditionally unclean
tasks for a greater good. Doctors-in-training cut open cadavers to learn about
the bodies of the living. Coroners, medical examiners, and hospital pathologists open the corpse to learn the cause of death, which often has a bearing
on the living. Relatives may have a hereditary condition that could be treated,
the public may be exposed to unnecessary health or safety risks that could be
eliminated, and both the family and society may seek justice when life has
been taken unlawfully. Doctors and pathologists are perceived as fighting
death, rather than relying on it like funeral directors. For the general practi-
tioner or specialist, the corpse represents failure. Surgeon William A. Nolen
explains the importance of each member in the team effort to preserve life:
"If he [the anesthesiologist] doesn't do his job properly, then it's possible to
wind up two hours of surgery with that horrible contradiction: a successful
operation and a dead patient."[12] Overworked hospital interns might momen-
tarily view such an outcome as providing them with one less patient to care
for, however. Speaking of his experience as a medical student, Joseph Sacco
confesses, "Sometimes I dreamed of my entire patient load dying simultaneously, and spending the rest of the day watching television."[13] While the
deaths of their charges necessitate unwelcome paperwork, corpses are unde-
manding patients. Students are said to choose the field of pathology because
it means working regular hours.

Work in the morgue soon becomes as routine as unwrapping the cadaver
at successive anatomy labs. Today's doctors and pathologists do not have to
defend their right to cut open the dead body in the midst of overwhelming
social, legal, and religious opposition. And their work is not often carried out
in the public eye. Except for the doctors who were responsible for their hospital care or the police officers who apprehended them—both of whom may

follow the case through to autopsy, the bodies that end up in the morgue are strangers. Because they were not known as living individuals, they are more easily pulled apart and reduced to their components—a diseased heart, a cancerous brain, a bullet wound. Yet they still occasionally prompt a reaction on an emotional level, as Max Salazar, a hospital registrar, noted: "I'm so grateful for my own good health. When I see people being moved in here on the stretcher with that pallid look and limp body, boy, it's a feeling that I'm so glad that I'm alive and I'm on this side of the counter."[14] Sigmund Freud proposed that it is impossible for a person to imagine his or her own death because by doing so he or she is present as a spectator. Medical examiners and those in the medical professions are perhaps most able to meditate on their own deaths, having corpses of all shapes, sizes, colors, and causes as raw material.

Executioners and Gravediggers

Unlike funeral directors, executioners have had a history spanning millennia during which they have been heavily discriminated against. Today in the United States, the identities of executioners are protected to keep them from being harmed or outcast. But when executions were public and frequent, the man who carried out the legal sentence was often scorned and disgraced. The modern gravedigger is also anonymous, and the job of opening and closing graves has been reduced from hours by hand to minutes with a backhoe. Modern executions and burials are both more antiseptic than those of the past, when their practitioners were intimately involved with blood and gore. Those who execute the living and bury the dead know the corpse, but are removed from it by curtained enclosure and casket. Because they are no longer in direct contact, they are not associated with the dead, but merely with death in general.

In France, executioners were often required to live in isolated locations and were sometimes forced to paint their houses red. At the market, merchants frequently refused to sell to them for fear of driving away other customers. Orders and messages were conveyed to them by throwing the paper to the ground so that the executioners would have to kneel to receive it. The discrimination also extended to their families. The daughters of executioners were forbidden to marry anyone outside the profession. In church, the family's pew was set apart from the other members of the congregation. Such prejudices only increased during the Revolution.[15] While executioners were once convicted felons given reprieve in exchange for their duties, today's executioners do not fit the traditional mold and are not singled out. While the person who flips the switch or pushes the button is hidden from public view, the members of the firing squad or the prison guards who escort the convict to the electric chair or gas chamber work as a well-rehearsed team and are therefore exempt from individual blame, in addition to sharing the emotional burden of putting a person to death.

Gravediggers also work in teams and are rarely the objects of public criticism. They are modern cemetery workers rather than churchyard sextons and inter boxes rather than bodies. The digging of graves used to put a person in direct contact with the dead. This has sometimes caused the public to associate the trade with the communication of disease. During the Black Death, gravediggers were sought out as the source of the scourge and were tortured and sometimes killed. Later, gravediggers were thought to be resistant to the diseases they carried, as J. F. E. Chardouillet wrote in 1881: "Gravediggers ... far from being more susceptible than other men to various maladies or occupational diseases, have always been reputed, rightly or wrongly, to enjoy a kind of immunity to infectious disease."[16] On the other hand, numerous stories exist of gravediggers being overcome by the fumes of the dead and losing their own lives while standing over the grave of another. Those who remained healthy kept their jobs for decades. Unlike the funeral director, who brags only to his colleagues, the gravedigger flaunted his prodigiousness. Hezekiah Briggs, a sexton in West Yorkshire for 43 years in the nineteenth century, was said to have buried 7,000 corpses in his parish, an average of one every two days. Sixty-one-year-old William "Tender" Russ said, "I've buried damn-near the whole of the village, every one of them."[17]

Like other members of death-encountering professions, including disaster identification and law enforcement, those who execute and bury the dead are confronted by example with their own demise. Those who uphold the law may consider themselves removed from the man strapped to the chair or the gang member killed in retaliation. Those who examine or exhume the dead may make the decision to have their bodies cremated. Certain causes of death and certain dispositions of the dead may be avoided, but the fact of death remains undeniable. As it is said, the hangman also dies, but he is not necessarily executed.

Conclusion

The ancient Hebrews regarded the corpse as unclean. All who touched the dead body were designated unclean in the Old Testament. The Koran, too, forbade touching the dead. Among the Maoris, anyone who handled a corpse, helped to convey it to the grave, or touched a dead person's bones was cut off from all communication with the living and was not allowed to touch food with the hand that had touched the dead.[18] In the Fiji Islands, a person who touches someone who died naturally is not allowed to touch food with his or her hands for several days, and a person who digs a chief's grave is considered unclean for a year.[19] In Japan and India, the people who handled dead bodies were outcast. They were ignored completely (even excluded from the census) in Japan. In India, they were required to brush their footprints away and forbidden from spitting on the ground.[20] In China, too, the person responsible for disposing of the dead was shunned. To overcome the taboos, Christians deemed the body sacred. By considering it a relic and by developing formal rituals for parting with it and disposing of it, they allowed the clergy and laity to touch and even kiss the dead without fear. The laying out of the dead by friends or family became an accepted practice that did not involve social disapproval. Over the centuries, however, the task was transferred to the funeral director and has remained with him or her ever since.

Funeral directors and other death care providers are therefore closer to death than most people, not only physically, but also mentally and emotionally. In order to continue in their chosen profession, they have had to come to terms with death and with their own mortality. This puts them at odds with much of society, which has what journalist Walter Werthmueller calls a schizophrenic relationship with death: eagerly reading about it in the newspaper and watching it on television, but sending their own dead away to be handled by professionals.[21] The most intimate knowledge about death is deposited with pathologists and embalmers. The layperson rarely attempts to learn the details. Those who have only marginal contact with the dead—even those in the medical professions—avoid this contact when possible, for instance, by allowing the following shift to "discover" the death of a patient. We all know that the corpse is, or soon becomes, a loathsome object. Andy Warhol regretted the fact that his body would have to be dealt with after death: "Dying is the most embarrassing thing that can ever happen to you, because someone's got to take care of all your details... . You'd like to help them, and most of all you'd like to do the whole thing yourself, but you're dead so you can't."[22] Somebody has to take the responsibility and in much of today's world, the family contracts with the funeral home to do so. Unfortunately, the work has a social price as well. The funeral director jokes about the corpse only behind closed doors, while his or her patrons snub him or her in private and in public.

The undeniable truth is that we will all—some sooner and some later—become corpses. Over that we have no control. Nor do we have posthumous control of our bodies if we die in dire circumstances: at the hands of a murderer (which may require autopsy or may result in a body which is never found), in times of war or political unrest (during which corpses may be mutilated or buried in mass graves), at the hands of the state (involving possible disfigurement and burial in the prison cemetery), or in an accident or disaster (after which the corpse may be used as food by starving survivors or hungry animals). We do have some control over whether our bodies will decay (by choosing cryonic preservation, cremation, or mummification), how our corpses will be used (by making anatomical gifts), and how much of a physical and financial imposition they will be on our survivors (by prearranging our funerals or cremations). But despite our careful planning, our bodies may still be victimized after death by those who hope to sell them, have sex with them, display them, or prevent their ghosts from haunting. That corpses are the most potent symbol of death in some measure protects them. In most circumstances, they are quickly given over to the professionals for investigation (if necessary), preparation, and disposal. Pathologists are trusted to perform the autopsy without excessive mutilation, funeral directors are asked to treat the dead with care and consideration, and gravediggers are expected to lay them gently to rest.

References

Introduction

1. Kim Long and Terry Reim, *Fatal Facts: A Lively Look at Common and Curious Ways People Have Died* (New York: Arlington House, 1985), 8.
2. James P. Sterba, "Aren't You Dying to Know If a Phorid Is in Your Future?" *The Wall Street Journal*, 25 April 1991, sec. A.
3. Sherwin B. Nuland, *How We Die: Reflections on Life's Final Chapter* (New York: Alfred A. Knopf, 1994), 122.
4. Eric W. Carlson, ed., *Introduction to Poe: A Thematic Reader* (Glenview, Ill.: Scott, Foresman, 1967), 221.
5. David Hunter, *Black Friday Coming Down* (New York: Berkley, 1992), 234.
6. Nuland, *How We Die*, 123.

Chapter 1

1. Philippe Ariès, *The Hour of Our Death*, trans. Helen Weaver (New York: Random House, 1982), 328.
2. Carl G. Jung, "Approaching the Unconscious," in *Man and His Symbols*, ed. Carl G. Jung (New York: Dell, 1964), 88.
3. John Pekkanen, *M.D.: Doctors Talk About Themselves* (New York: Delacorte, 1988), 11.
4. John Langone, *Vital Signs: The Way We Die in America* (Boston: Little, Brown, 1974), 68.
5. Troy Allen, *Disaster* (Chatsworth, California: Barclay House, 1974), 39.
6. Sherwin B. Nuland, *How We Die: Reflections on Life's Final Chapter* (New York: Alfred A. Knopf, 1994), 41.
7. Edna Buchanan, *Never Let Them See You Cry: More from Miami, America's Hottest Beat* (New York: Random House, 1992), 99.
8. Edna Buchanan, *The Corpse Had a Familiar Face* (New York: Charter, 1987), 332.
9. J. Bruce Long, "The Death That Ends Death in Hinduism and Buddhism" in *Death: The Final Stage of Growth*, ed. Elisabeth Kübler-Ross (Englewood Cliffs, N.J.: Prentice-Hall, 1975), 68-69.
10. Clarissa M. Silitch, ed., *Mad and Magnificent Yankees* (Dublin, N.H.: Yankee, 1973), 171.
11. John Hinton, *Dying* (Baltimore: Penguin, 1972), 21.

12. Michel Ragon, *The Space of Death: A Study of Funerary Architecture, Decoration, and Urbanism* (Charlottesville: University Press of Virginia, 1983), 16.

13. Warren Shibles, *Death: An Interdisciplinary Analysis* (Whitewater, Wis.: Language Press, 1974), 413.

Chapter 2

1. Luc Sante, *Evidence* (New York: Farrar, Strauss & Giroux, 1992), 60.

2. John Morley, *Death, Heaven and the Victorians* (Pittsburgh: University of Pittsburgh Press, 1971), 43-44.

3. Stanley B. Burns, *Sleeping Beauty: Memorial Photography in America* (Altadena, Calif.: Twelvetree, 1990).

4. Michael Lesy, *Wisconsin Death Trip* (New York: Random House, 1973).

5. Douglas Ubelaker and Henry Scammell, *Bones: A Forensic Detective's Casebook* (New York: Edward Burlingame, 1992), 264.

6. David Heilbroner, *Rough Justice: Days and Nights of a Young D.A.* (New York: Pantheon, 1990), 135-36.

7. Rudolf Schäfer, "Dead Faces," *Granta* 27 (Summer 1989): 193-209.

8. Luc Sante, *Evidence* (New York: Farrar, Strauss & Giroux, 1992).

9. Barbara P. Norfleet, *Looking at Death* (Boston: David R. Godine, 1993), 96.

10. Ibid, 13-14.

11. George Kirkham, *Signal Zero: The True Story of a Professor Who Became a Street Cop* (Philadelphia: J. B. Lippincott, 1976), 75.

12. Warren Shibles, *Death: An Interdisciplinary Analysis* (Whitewater, Wis.: Language Press, 413), 280.

13. Clifford L. Linedecker, *The Man Who Killed Boys* (New York: St. Martin's, 1980), 194.

14. S. Howard Bartley et al., eds., *Essentials of Life and Health* (New York: Random House, 1977), 324.

15. Yaffa Draznin, *How to Prepare for Death: A Practical Guide* (New York: Hawthorn, 1976), 113.

16. Philippe Ariès, *The Hour of Our Death*, trans. Helen Weaver (New York: Random House, 1982), 262.

17. Robert Wilkins, *The Bedside Book of Death: Macabre Tales of Our Final Passage* (New York: Citadel, 1990).

18. F. Gonzalez-Crussi, *The Day of the Dead and Other Mortal Reflections* (New York: Harcourt Brace, 1993), 17.

19. C. Hamilton and L. Ostendorf, *Lincoln in Photographs: An Album of Every Known Pose* (Norman, Okla.: University of Oklahoma Press, 1963), quoted in Richard Huntington and Peter Metcalf, *Celebrations of Death: The Anthropology of Mortuary Ritual* (Cambridge: Cambridge University Press, 1979), 206.

20. J. R. Francis, ed., *The Encyclopedia of Death and Life in the Spirit World* (1896; reprint, Amherst, Wis.: Amherst Press, n.d.), 383.

21. Gordon Burn, *Somebody's Husband, Somebody's Son* (New York: Penguin, 1986), 358.

22. Edna Buchanan, *Never Let Them See You Cry: More from Miami, America's Hottest Beat* (New York: Random House, 1992), 246.

23. Denis Brian, *Murderers Die* (New York: St. Martin's, 1986), 228.

24. Simone de Beauvoir, *A Very Easy Death*, trans. Patrick O'Brien (New York: Pantheon, 1964), 86.

25. Greg Palmer, *Death: The Trip of a Lifetime* (New York: HarperCollins, 1993), 159.

26. James L. Christensen, *The Complete Funeral Manual* (Westwood, N.J.: Fleming H. Revell, 1967), 26.

27. Howard C. Raether and Robert C. Slater, "The Funeral with the Body Present: An Experience of Value," in *Problems of Death: Opposing Viewpoints*, ed. David L. Bender (Anoka, Minn.: Greenhaven, 1974), 130.

Chapter 3

1. Richard Selzer, *Confessions of a Knife* (New York: Simon & Schuster, 1979), 64.

2. Elizabeth Beverly and Richard Wightman Fox, "Letting Sanji Die: How Cultures Understand Death and Loss," *Commonweal*, 20 May 1988, 299.

3. Adrian Jerome Kilker, *Extreme Unction: A Canonical Treatise* (St. Louis: B. Herder, 1927), 221.

4. James T. McHugh, ed., *Death, Dying and the Law* (Huntington, Ind.: Our Sunday Visitor, 1976), 79.

5. Joseph M. Champlin, *Together By Your Side: A Book for Comforting the Sick and Dying* (Notre Dame, Ind.: Ave Maria Press, 1984), 34.

6. Jorge Amado, *The Two Deaths of Quincas Wateryell*, trans. Barbara Shelby (New York: Avon, 1980), 75.

7. Irving Wallace, David Wallechinsky, and Amy Wallace, *The Book of Lists* (New York: E. P. Dutton, 1983), 52-53.

8. Robert W. Habenstein and William M. Lamers, *The History of American Funeral Directing* (Milwaukee: National Funeral Directors Assoc., 1955), 211.

9. David Dempsey, *The Way We Die: An Investigation of Death and Dying in America Today* (New York: McGraw-Hill, 1975), 176.

10. Michael A. Simpson, *The Facts of Death* (Englewood Cliffs, N. J.: Prentice-Hall, 1979), 122-23.

11. W. Lloyd Warner, *The Living and the Dead: A Study of the Symbolic Life of Americans* (New Haven: Yale University Press, 1959), 315.

12. Vanderlyn R. Pine, *Caretaker of the Dead: The American Funeral Director* (New York: Irvington, 1975), 115.

13. Bram Stoker, *Dracula* (London, 1897).

14. David E. Stannard, *The Puritan Way of Death: A Study in Religion, Culture, and Social Change* (New York: Oxford University Press, 1977), 188.

15. Barbara P. Norfleet, *Looking at Death* (Boston: David R. Godine, 1993), 96.

16. Jessica Mitford, *The American Way of Death* (New York: Simon & Schuster, 1963), 226.

17. Ken Englade, *A Family Business* (New York: St. Martin's Paperbacks, 1992), 27.

18. Barbara Jones, *Design for Death* (New York: Bobbs-Merrill, 1967), 25.

19. Kenneth Iserson, *Death to Dust: What Happens to Dead Bodies?* (Tucson: Galen, 1994), 223-24.

20. Greg Palmer, *Death: The Trip of a Lifetime* (New York: HarperCollins, 1993), 159.

21. Ibid., 157-58.

22. Philippe Ariès, "The Reversal of Death: Changes in Attitudes Toward Death in Western Societies," trans. Valerie M. Stannard, in *Death in America*, ed. David E. Stannard (Philadelphia: University of Pennsylvania Press, 1975), 155.

23. Edward C. Melissa and Gail Johnson, "The Man Who Embalmed Evita: Dr. Pedro Ara," *The Embalmer* 30:1, No. 1 (January–February 1987), 18.

24. Nicholas Fraser and Marysa Navarro, *Eva Perón* (New York: W. W. Norton, 1980), 169-70.

25. Peter Bushell, *London's Secret History* (London: Constable, 1983), 119.

26. Kim Long and Terry Reim, *Fatal Facts* (New York: Arlington House, 1985), 13.

Chapter 4

1. Robert Garland, *The Greek Way of Death* (Ithaca, N.Y.: Cornell University Press, 1985), xii.

2. Daniel David Cowell, "Funerals, Family and Forefathers," *Omega: Journal of Death and Dying* 16:1 (1985-86), 71.

3. Philippe Ariès, *Images of Man and Death*, trans. Janet Lloyd (Cambridge: Harvard University Press, 1985), 112.

4. Jane Burgess Kohn and Willard K. Kohn, *The Widow* (Boston: Beacon, 1978), 61.

5. Elisabeth Kübler-Ross, *Questions and Answers on Death and Dying* (New York: Macmillan, 1974), 101.

6. Edward W. Bauman, *Through Death to Life* (Arlington, Va.: Bauman Bible Telecasts, 1977), 103.

7. Robert W. Habenstein and William M. Lamers, *The History of American Funeral Directing* (Milwaukee, Wis.: National Funeral Directors Association, 1955), 41.

8. Victor W. Marshall, *Last Chapters: A Sociology of Aging and Dying* (Monterey, California: Brooks/Cole Publishing, 1980), 55.

9. Howard C. Raether and Robert C. Slater, "Immediate Postdeath Activities in the United States" in *New Meanings of Death*, ed. Herman Feifel (New York: McGraw-Hill, 1977), 244.

10. Kenneth V. Iserson, *Death to Dust: What Happens to Dead Bodies?* (Tuscon: Galen, 1994), 187.

11. Robert B. Dickerson, Jr., *Final Placement: A Guide to the Deaths, Funerals, and Burials of Notable Americans* (Algonac, Michigan: Reference Publications, 1982), 41.

12. Nicholas Fraser and Marysa Navarro, *Eva Perón* (New York: W. W. Norton, 1980), 165-66.

13. Malcolm Forbes with Jeff Bloch, *They Went That-a-Way...* (New York: Simon & Schuster, 1988), 247.

14. Peter Bushell, *London's Secret History* (London: Constable, 1983), 114.

15. John Morley, *Death, Heaven, and the Victorians* (Pittsburgh: University of Pittsburgh Press, 1971), 27.

16. Warren Shibles, *Death: An Interdisciplinary Analysis* (Whitewater, Wis.: Language Press, 1974), 234.

17. Howard C. Raether and Robert C. Slater, "Immediate Postdeath Activities in the United States," in *New Meanings of Death*, ed. Herman Feifel (New York: McGraw Hill, 1977), 237-41.

18. Garland, *Greek Way of Death*, 43.

19. Bauman, *Through Death to Life*, 96.

20. Shibles, *Death: An Interdisciplinary Analysis*, 401.

21. "Benevolent Clergyman" quoted in Edwin Chadwick, *Supplementary Report on the Results of a Special Inquiry into the Practice of Interment in Towns* (1843) in Morley, *Death, Heaven, and the Victorians*, 26.

22. Michael Lesy, *The Forbidden Zone* (New York: Farrar, Strauss & Giroux, 1987), 234.

23. Avery D. Weisman, *On Dying and Denying: A Psychiatric Study of Terminality* (New York: Behavioral Publications, 1972), 7.

24. Iserson, *Death to Dust*, 561.

25. *Four Days: The Historical Record of the Death of President Kennedy* (United Press International and American Heritage, 1964), 74.

26. Philippe Ariès, *The Hour of Our Death* (New York: Random House, 1982), 560.

Chapter 5

1. Greg Palmer, *Death: The Trip of a Lifetime* (New York: HarperCollins, 1993), 197.

2. Buchanan, Edna, *The Corpse Had a Familiar Face* (New York: Charter, 1987), 138.

3. Chuck Shepherd, John J. Kohut, and Roland Sweet, *News of the Weird* (New York: Penguin, 1989), 69-70.

4. Vanderlyn R. Pine, *Caretaker of the Dead: The American Funeral Director* (New York: Irvington, 1975), 111.

5. Michael Medved, *Hospital: The Hidden Lives of a Medical Center Staff* (New York: Pocket Books, 1982), 311.

6. Elisabeth Kübler-Ross, *Death: The Final Stage of Growth* (Englewood Cliffs, N.J.: Prentice-Hall, 1975), xv.

7. Tom Weil, *The Cemetery Book: Graveyards, Catacombs and Other Travel Haunts around the World* (New York: Hippocrene, 1992), 155.

8. Charles Panati, *Panati's Extraordinary Endings of Practically Everything and Everybody* (New York: Harper & Row, 1989), 33.

9. Philippe Ariès, *The Hour of Our Death*, trans. Helen Weaver (New York: Random House, 1982), 504-5.

10. Robert K. Ressler and Tom Shachtman, *Whoever Fights Monsters* (New York: St. Martin's, 1992), 136-37.

11. Robert Wilkins, ed., *The Doctor's Quotation Book: A Medical Miscellany* (New York: Barnes & Noble, 1991), 44.

12. Johannes Nohl, *The Black Death: A Chronicle of the Plague* (New York: Ballantine, 1960), 36.

13. Panati, *Extraordinary Endings*, 18.

14. Ariès, *Hour of Our Death*, 361.

15. Kenneth V. Iserson, *Death to Dust: What Happens to Dead Bodies?* (Tucson: Galen, 1994), 451.

16. F. Gonzalez-Crussi, *The Day of the Dead and Other Mortal Reflections* (New York: Harcourt Brace, 1993), 8.

17. *How to Interpret Your Dreams* (Pleasantville, N.Y.: Reader's Digest, 1979), 303.

18. Ange-Pierre Leca, *The Egyptian Way of Death: Mummies and the Cult of the Immortal*, trans. Louise Asmal (New York: Doubleday, 1981), 6.

19. Ronald Blythe, "In the Hour of Death," in *Akenfield: Portrait of an English Village* (New York: Delta, 1970), 314.

20. Ariès, *Hour of Our Death*, 58, 360.

21. Shibles, *Death: An Interdisciplinary Analysis*, 437.

22. Frances Toor, *A Treasury of Mexican Folkways* (New York: Bonanza, 1985), 167.

23. Michael A. Simpson, *The Facts of Death* (Englewood Cliffs, N.J.: Prentice-Hall, 1979), 126.

24. Dudley Wright, *The Book of Vampires* (New York: Dorset, 1987), 66-67.

25. Adolf Holl, *Death and the Devil*, trans. by Matthew J. O'Connell (New York: Seabury Press, 1973), 38.

26. Michael Lesy, *The Forbidden Zone* (New York: Farrar, Strauss & Giroux, 1987), 230.

27. Robert Wilkins, *The Bedside Book of Death* (New York: Citadel, 1990), 241.

28. Brian Bailey, *Churchyards of England and Wales* (London: Robert Hale, 1987), 130.

29. Shibles, *Death: An Interdisciplinary Analysis*, 401.

30. Weil, *Cemetery Book*, 319.

31. Robert J. Lifton and Eric Olson, *Living and Dying* (New York: Bantam, 1974), 20.

32. G. P. Kirsch, *The Catacombs of Rome* (Rome: Societa Amici Delle Catacombe, 1972), 14.

33. Michel Ragon, *The Space of Death* (Charlottesville: University Press of Virginia, 1983), 90.

34. Philippe Ariès, *Western Attitudes Toward Death: From the Middle Ages to the Present*, trans. Patricia M. Ranum (Baltimore: Johns Hopkins University Press, 1974), 72.

35. Wilkins, *Bedside Book of Death*, 155.

36. Weil, *Cemetery Book*, 53.

37. Ruth Richardson, *Death, Dissection and the Destitute* (London: Routledge and Kegan Paul, 1987), 273.

38. Michael Specter, "Hot Tombs," *New Republic*, 11 September 1989, 23-5.

39. Palmer, *Death: The Trip of a Lifetime*, 75-76.

40. Shepherd, Kohut, and Sweet, *News of the Weird*, 69.

41. Weil, *Cemetery Book*, 238-39.

42. Irving Wallace, David Wallechinsky, and Amy Wallace, *The Book of Lists* (New York: E. P. Dutton, 1983), 346.

43. Peter Potter, ed., *All About Death* (New Canaan, Conn.: William Mulvey, 1988), 195.

44. Ariès, *Hour of Our Death*, 554.

45. John Morley, *Death, Heaven, and the Victorians* (Pittsburgh, Pa.: University of Pittsburg Press, 1971), 37, 46, 100.

46. Blythe, "In the Hour of Death," 314.

47. Panati, *Extraordinary Endings*, 23.

48. Ariès, *Hour of Our Death*, 75.

49. Wilkins, *Bedside Book of Death*, 156.

50. Judi Culbertson and Tom Randall, *Permanent Parisians: An Illustrated Guide to the Cemeteries of Paris* (Chelsea, Vt.: Chelsea Green, 1986), 7.

51. Barbara Jones, *Design for Death* (New York: Bobbs-Merrill, 1967), 178.

52. Morley, *Death, Heaven, and the Victorians*, 35.

53. Ibid., 94.

54. Ragon, *Space of Death*, 258.

55. Ibid., 299.

56. Holl, *Death and the Devil*, 45.

57. Iserson, *Death to Dust*, 455, 471.

58. Weil, *Cemetery Book*, 393-94.

59. Peter Bushell, *London's Secret History* (London: Constable, 1983), 128.

60. Charles Kightly, *The Perpetual Almanack of Folklore* (London: Thames & Hudson, 1987), 20 May.

61. David Dempsey, *The Way We Die: An Investigation of Death and Dying in America Today* (New York: McGraw-Hill, 1975), 169.

62. Gyles Brandreth, *Famous Last Words and Tombstone Humor* (New York: Sterling, 1989), 89.

63. Frank H. Stauffer, *The Queer, the Quaint, the Quizzical: A Cabinet for the Curious* (1882; reprint, Detroit: Gale Research, 1968), 112.

64. Panati, *Extraordinary Endings*, 12.

65. Yaffa Draznin, *How to Prepare for Death* (New York: Hawthorn, 1976), 10.

66. Iserson, *Death to Dust*, 317.

67. James C. Whittaker, *We Thought We Heard the Angels Sing* (New York: Pocket Books, 1970), 78.

68. Kim Long and Terry Reim, *Fatal Facts: A Lively Look at Common and Curious Ways People Have Died* (New York: Arlington House, 1985), 87.

69. Iserson, *Death to Dust*, 237.

70. Sir Thomas Brown, "Urn Burial" in *The Oxford Book of Death*, ed. D. J. Enright (New York: Oxford University Press, 1987), 146.

71. Weil, *Cemetery Book*, 207.

72. Wilkins, *Bedside Book of Death*, 178-79.

73. Robert Jackson, *Francis Camps: Famous Case Histories of the Celebrated Pathologist* (London: Hart-Davis, MacGibbon, 1975), 151.

74. Geoffrey Grigson, *The Faber Book of Epigrams and Epitaphs* (London: Faber & Faber, 1977), 47.

75. Wilkins, *Bedside Book of Death*, 245.

76. President of the French Federation of Cremation quoted in Ruth Menahem, *La mort apprivoisée*, (1973) in Ragon, *Space of Death*, 271.

77. Carrie Dolan, "Burying Tradition, More People Opt for 'Fun' Funerals," *Wall Street Journal*, 20 May 1993, sec. A.

78. Draznin, *How to Prepare for Death*, 15.

79. Leon Weliczker Wells, *The Death Brigade (The Janowska Road)* (New York: Holocaust Library, 1963), 180.

80. *The Apparatus of Death* (Alexandria, Va.: Time-Life, 1990), 170.

81. Wilkins, *Bedside Book of Death*, 177.

82. Michael Marchal, *Parish Funerals* (Chicago: Liturgy Training Publications, 1987), 70.

83. Lesy, *Forbidden Zone*, 240.

Chapter 6

1. David Simon, *Homicide: A Year on the Killing Streets* (New York: Fawcett Columbine, 1992), 384.

2. E. R. Shushan, comp., *Grave Matters* (New York: Ballantine, 1990), 89.

3. Robert Graysmith, *The Sleeping Lady: The Trailside Murders Above the Golden Gate* (New York: Dutton, 1990), 315.

4. Joy Johnson, Marvin Johnson, and Adina Wroblenski, *Suicide of a Child* (Omaha: Centering Corp., 1984), 12.

5. Cherokee Paul McDonald, *Blue Truth: Walking the Thin Blue Line—One Cop's Story of Life in the Streets* (New York: St. Martin's Paperbacks, 1992), 80-82.

6. Tom Cullen, *The Mild Murderer: The True Story of the Dr. Crippen Case* (Boston: Houghton Mifflin, 1977), 161.

7. Chuck Shepherd, John J. Kohut, and Roland Sweet, *More News of the Weird* (New York: Penguin, 1990), 123.

8. David Loth, *Crime Lab: Science Turns Detective* (New York: Julian Messner, 1964), 144.

9. David Wallechinsky and Irving Wallace, *The People's Almanac* (Garden City, N.Y.: Doubleday, 1975), 1324.

10. Derek Humphry, *Let Me Die Before I Wake* (Los Angeles: Hemlock Society, 1984), 70.

11. Douglas Ubelaker and Henry Scammell, *Bones: A Forensic Detective's Casebook* (New York: Edward Burlingame, 1992), 153.

12. Anne Wingate, *Scene of the Crime: A Writer's Guide to Crime-Scene Investigations* (Cincinnati: Writer's Digest, 1992), 180-81.

13. Edna Buchanan, *Never Let Them See You Cry* (New York: Random House, 1992), 100.

14. Peter A. Micheels, *Heat: The Fire Investigators and Their War on Arson and Murder* (New York: St. Martin's, 1993), 213.

15. Simon, *Homicide*, 21.

16. Charles W. Sasser, *Homicide!* (New York: Pocket Books, 1990), 219.

17. Paul D. Shapiro, *Paramedic: The True Story of a New York Paramedic's Battles with Life and Death* (New York: Bantam, 1991), 64.

18. Sasser, *Homicide!* 241.

19. Eugene Richards, *The Knife and Gun Club: Scenes from an Emergency Room* (New York: Atlantic Monthly Press, 1989), 70.

20. Robert H. Adleman, *The Bloody Benders* (New York: Stein & Day, 1971), 17.

21. Terry Landau, *About Faces: The Evolution of the Human Face* (New York: Anchor, 1989), 33.

22. Simon, *Homicide*, 72.

23. Michael Lesy, *The Forbidden Zone* (New York: Farrar, Strauss & Giroux, 1987), 64.

24. Simon, *Homicide*, 231.

25. Edna Buchanan, *The Corpse Had a Familiar Face* (New York: Charter, 1987), 125.

26. F. Gonzalez-Crussi, *The Day of the Dead and Other Mortal Reflections* (New York: Harcourt Brace, 1993), 125-26.

27. Michael Medved, *Hospital* (New York: Pocket Books, 1982), 313-14.

28. Sherwin B. Nuland, *How We Die* (New York: Alfred A. Knopf, 1994), 192.

29. Gonzalez-Crussi, *Day of the Dead*, 129.

30. Edward E. Rosenbaum, *The Doctor* (New York: Ivy, 1988), 129.

31. Medved, *Hospital*, 313.

32. David Hellerstein, *Battles of Life and Death* (Boston: Houghton Mifflin, 1986), 124.

33. William A. Nolen, *The Making of a Surgeon* (New York: Random House, 1968), 124.

34. Edwin S. Shneidman, *Deaths of Man* (Baltimore: Penguin, 1974), 223.

35. Hellerstein, *Battles*, 123-24, 130.

36. Nuland, *How We Die*, 79.

37. David Hendin, *Death as a Fact of Life* (New York: W. W. Norton, 1984), 56.

38. Robert Kastenbaum and Beatrice Kastenbaum, *Encyclopedia of Death* (New York: Avon, 1989), 23.

39. Kastenbaum and Kastenbaum, *Encyclopedia of Death*, 20-22.

40. Michael Dibdin, "The Pathology Lesson," *Granta* 39 (Spring 1992): 100.

41. Medved, *Hospital*, 313.

42. Keith D. Wilson, *Cause of Death: A Writer's Guide to Death, Murder & Forensic Medicine* (Cincinnati: Writer's Digest, 1992), 60.

43. Kenneth Iserson, *Death to Dust* (Tucson: Galen, 1994), 136.

44. Loth, *Crime Lab*, 130.

45. Michael M. Baden with Judith Adler Hennessee, *Unnatural Death: Confessions of a Medical Examiner* (New York: Ivy, 1989), 53.

46. Douglas G. Browne and Tom Tullett, *Bernard Spilsbury: His Life and Cases* (1951; reprint, New York: Dorset, 1988), 374.

47. Dibdin, "Pathology Lesson," 95.

48. Simon, *Homicide*, 395.

49. Ibid., 391.

50. Iserson, *Death to Dust*, 152.

51. Baden, *Unnatural Death*, 33.

52. Loth, *Crime Lab*, 142.

53. Sir Sydney Smith, *Mostly Murder* (New York: David McKay, 1959), 194.

54. Keith Wilson, *Cause of Death*, 120-21.

55. Joel Norris, *Serial Killers* (New York: Doubleday, 1988), 88-90.

56. Ronald Markman and Dominick Bosco, *Alone with the Devil: Famous Cases of a Courtroom Psychiatrist* (New York: Doubleday, 1989), 34.

57. Michael Lesy, *The Forbidden Zone* (New York: Farrar, Strauss & Giroux, 1987), 64.

58. Browne and Tullett, *Bernard Spilsbury*, 196.

59. Simon, *Homicide*, 394.

60. Robert Jackson, *Francis Camps: Famous Case Histories of the Celebrated Pathologist* (London: Hart-Davis, MacGibbon, 1975), 28.

61. Milton Helpern with Bernard Knight, *Autopsy* (New York: New American Library, 1979), 220.

62. "D.C.'s Autopsy Technicians: Bearing the Constant Burden of Death," *Washington Post*, 3 Oct. 1993, sec. A.

63. Jackson, *Francis Camps*, 84.

64. Charles C. Thompson II and James P. Cole, *The Death of Elvis: What Really Happened* (New York: Delacorte, 1991), 8.

65. F. Gonzalez-Crussi, *Three Forms of Sudden Death and Other Reflections on the Grandeur and Misery of the Body* (London: Pan, 1986), 65.

66. Tom Philbin, *Murder U.S.A.: A True-Crime Travel Guide to the Most Notorious Killing Grounds in America* (New York: Warner, 1992), 197.

67. Malcolm W. Browne, "Scientist Tells Silent Victims' Tales of Terror: Old Bones Bear Witness to Murders, War Crimes and Government Terrorism," *New York Times*, 9 April 1991, sec. C.

68. Ubelaker and Scammell, *Bones*, 261.

69. Ibid., 185.

70. Loth, *Crime Lab*, 158.

71. Greg Palmer, *Death: The Trip of a Lifetime* (New York: HarperCollins, 1993), 232.

72. Ubelaker and Scammell, *Bones*, 76.

73. John K. Lattimer, *Kennedy and Lincoln: Medical and Ballistic Comparisons of Their Assassinations* (New York: Harcourt Brace Jovanovich, 1980), 69, 361.

74. Palmer, *Death: The Trip of a Lifetime*, 170.

75. H. J. Walls, *Forensic Science: An Introduction to Scientific Crime Detection* (New York: Praeger, 1974), 133.

76. Ubelaker and Scammell, *Bones*, 66.

77. Ibid., 160-63.

77. Ibid., 27.

78. Colin Wilson, *Clues! A History of Forensic Detection* (New York: Warner, 1991), 183-86.

79. Charles Earle Funk, *Thereby Hangs a Tale: Stories of Curious Word Origins* (New York: Harper & Row, 1950), 208.

80. Frank Gonzalez-Crussi, *Notes of an Anatomist* (New York: Harcourt Brace Jovanovich, 1986), 67.

81. Ubelaker and Scammell, *Bones*, 13.

82. Chuck Shepherd, John J. Kohut, and Roland Sweet, *News of the Weird* (New York: Penguin, 1989), 70.

83. Thomas G. Wheeler, *Who Lies Here? A New Inquiry Into Napoleon's Last Years* (G. P. Putnam's Sons, 1974), 150.

84. Ubelaker and Scammell, *Bones*, 159.

85. Keith Simpson, *Forty Years of Murder* (New York: Charles Scribner's Sons, 1978), 293.

86. Iserson, *Death to Dust*, 153-54.

87. Ibid., 155.

88. Richard Huntington and Peter Metcalf, *Celebrations of Death: The Anthropology of Mortuary Ritual* (Cambridge: Cambridge University Press, 1979), 94-95.

89. Judi Culbertson and Tom Randall, *Permanent Parisians: An Illustrated Guide to the Cemeteries of Paris* (Chelsea, Vt.: Chelsea Green, 1986), 118.

90. Huntington and Metcalf, *Celebrations of Death*, 195.

91. Hendin, *Death as a Fact of Life*, 217.

92. Philippe Ariès, *The Hour of Our Death* (New York: Random House, 1982), 499-500.

93. Medved, *Hospital*, 302.

94. R. F. Mould, *More of Mould's Medical Anecdotes* (Bristol, England: Adam Hilger, 1989), 215.

95. Harold Nicholson, *Byron: The Last Journey*, quoted in Mould, *More of Mould's Medical Anecdotes*, 216.

96. Tom Weil, *The Cemetery Book: Graveyards, Catacombs and Other Travel Haunts Around the World* (New York: Hippocrene, 1992), 43.

97. Ibid., 48.

98. Richard F. Mould, *Mould's Medical Anecdotes* (Bristol, England: Adam Hilger, 1984), 8-10.

99. Alex Heard, "Exhumed Innocent," *New Republic*, 5 August 1991, 12-14.

100. Paul G. Bahn, "The Face of Mozart," *Archaeology* (March–April 1991): 40-41.

101. Shepherd, Kohut, and Sweet, *More News of the Weird*, 142.

Chapter 7

1. Robert Jackson, *Francis Camps: Famous Case Histories of the Celebrated Pathologist* (London: Hart-Davis, MacGibbon, 1975), 77.

2. John Laurence, *A History of Capital Punishment* (New York: Citadel, 1960), xvii.

3. Richard Hammer, *Between Life and Death* (New York: Macmillan, 1969), 270-71.

4. George V. Bishop, *Executions: The Legal Ways of Death* (Los Angeles: Sherbourne, 1965), 169.

5. James Clarke, *Man Is the Prey* (New York: Stein & Day, 1969), 222.

6. Daniel P. Mannix, *The History of Torture* (New York: Dell, 1964), 158.

7. Judi Culbertson and Tom Randall, *Permanent Parisians: An Illustrated Guide to the Cemeteries of Paris* (Chelsea, Vt.: Chelsea Green, 1986), 195.

8. Laurence, *History of Capital Punishment*, 89.

9. Ann Hodgman, *True Tiny Tales of Terror* (New York: Perigee, 1982), 37.

10. Charles Duff, *A Handbook on Hanging* (Totowa, N.J.: Rowman & Littlefield, 1974), 119.

11. Ibid., 109.

12. Daniel P. Mannix, *The History of Torture* (New York: Dell, 1964), 109.

13. Denis Brian, *Murderers Die* (New York: St. Martin's, 1986), 54.

14. Sir Norman Birkett, *The Newgate Calendar* (London: Folio Society, 1951), 24-25.

15. Brian, *Murderers Die*, 225.

16. Lewis E. Lawes, *Life and Death in Sing Sing* (Garden City, N.Y.: Garden City Publishing, 1928), 161, 190.

17. Alister Kershaw, *A History of the Guillotine* (London: Tandem, 1965), 96.

18. Frank H. Stauffer, *The Queer, the Quaint, the Quizzical* (1882; reprint, Detroit: Gale Research, 1968), 204.

19. Kershaw, *History of the Guillotine*, 101-2.

20. Bishop, *Executions*, 41.

21. Charles Panati, *Panati's Extraordinary Endings of Practically Everything and Everybody* (New York: Harper & Row, 1989), 155.

22. Chuck Shepherd, John J. Kohut, and Roland Sweet, *News of the Weird* (New York: Penguin, 1989), 65.

23. George Orwell, "A Hanging," Adelphi (1931), quoted in Jonathan Glover, *Causing Death and Saving Lives* (New York: Penguin, 1977), 228.

24. Colin Wilson, *Clues! A History of Forensic Detection* (New York: Warner Books, 1991), 176.

25. Brian Masters, *Killing for Company: The Case of Dennis Nilsen* (New York: Stein & Day, 1985), 161.

26. Brian, *Murderers Die*, 220.

27. Jackson, *Francis Camps*, 83.

28. Ibid., 118.

29. Dudley Wright, *The Book of Vampires* (New York: Dorset, 1987), 21.

30. Paul D. Shapiro, *Paramedic: The True Story of a New York Paramedic's Battles with Life and Death* (New York: Bantam, 1991), 250.

31. Mark Baker, *Cops: Their Lives in Their Own Words* (New York: Pocket Books, 1985), 103.

32. Rachel Harding and Mary Dyson, eds., *A Book of Condolences from the Private Letters of Illustrious People* (New York: Continuum Publishing, 1981), 52.

33. Derek Humphry, *Let Me Die Before I Wake* (Los Angeles: Hemlock Society, 1984), 56.

34. Ibid., 59.

Chapter 8

1. Daniel Cohen, *The Black Death* (New York: Franklin Watts, 1974), 33.

2. Beverley Raphael, *When Disaster Strikes: How Individuals and Communities Cope with Catastrophe* (New York: Basic Books, 1986), 102.

3. Ibid., 242.

4. Stephen B. Seager, *Psychward* (New York: Berkley, 1992), 36-37.

5. Gyles Brandreth, *Famous Last Words and Tombstone Humor* (New York: Sterling, 1989), 100.

6. Upton Sinclair, *The Jungle* (New York: Bantam, 1981), 99.

7. Edna Buchanan, *The Corpse Had a Familiar Face* (New York: Charter Books, 1987), 339.

8. Kim Long and Terry Reim, *Fatal Facts: A Lively Look at Common and Curious Ways People Have Died* (New York: Arlington House, 1985), 9.

9. Charles W. Sasser and Michael W. Sasser, *Last American Heroes: Today's Firefighters* (New York: Pocket Books, 1994), 256-57.

10. H. David Baldridge, *Shark Attack* (New York: Berkley Medallion, 1974), 127.

11. Hal Scharp, *Shark Safari* (New York: Award Books, 1975), 41, 65.

12. Michael Jenkinson, *Beasts Beyond the Fire* (New York: E. P. Dutton, 1980), 16.

13. Raphael, *When Disaster Strikes*, 84.

14. John G. Fuller, *The Ghost of Flight 401* (New York: Berkley, 1976), 87.

15. Raphael, *When Disaster Strikes*, 236-37.

16. Michael E. Mulligan et al., "Radiologic Evaluation of Mass Casualty Victims: Lessons from the Gander, Newfoundland, Accident," *Radiology* 168, no. 1 (July 1988): 229-31.

17. Kenneth V. Iserson, *Death to Dust: What Happens to Dead Bodies?* (Tucson: Galen, 1994).

18. Paul D. Shapiro, *Paramedic: The True Story of a New York Paramedic's Battles with Life and Death* (New York: Bantam, 1991), 92.

19. William Dear, *The Dungeon Master: The Disappearance of James Dallas Egbert III* (Boston: Houghton Mifflin, 1984), 66.

20. Raphael, *When Disaster Strikes*, 235.

21. Hal Butler, *Inferno! 14 Fiery Tragedies of Our Time* (New York: Dorset, 1975), 78-79.

22. Douglas Myles, *The Great Waves: Tsunami* (New York: McGraw-Hill, 1985), 41-42.

23. David McCullough, *The Johnstown Flood* (New York: Touchstone, 1986), 185-86.

24. Willis Fletcher Johnson, *History of the Johnstown Flood* (n.p.: Edgewood, 1889), 137.

25. McCullough, *Johnstown Flood*, 200.

26. R. Hewitt, *From Earthquake, Fire and Flood* (New York: Charles Scribner's Sons, 1957), 87.

27. Troy Allen, *Disaster* (Chatsworth, Calif.: Barclay House, 1974), 148-49.

28. Ibid., 14.

29. Ibid., 36.

30. Peter S. Felknor, *The Tri-State Tornado: The Story of America's Greatest Tornado Disaster* (Ames: Iowa State University Press, 1992), 23.

31 Ibid., 48.

32. Hewitt, *From Earthquake, Fire and Flood*, 116-17.

33. Donald J. Sobol, *Disaster* (New York: Pocket Books, 1979), 2.

34. John Morley, *Death, Heaven and the Victorians* (Pittsburgh: University of Pittsburgh Press, 1971), 34.

35. Iserson, *Death to Dust*, 405.

36. Colin Wilson, *Clues! A History of Forensic Detection* (New York: Warner Books, 1991), 143.

37. Mark Baker, *Nam* (New York: Berkley, 1981), 75.

38. John Carey, ed., *Eyewitness to History* (New York: Avon, 1987), 120.

39. Raphael, *When Disaster Strikes*, 84.

40. Carey, *Eyewitness to History*, 611-12.

41. Ibid., 541.

42. *The Apparatus of Death* (Alexandria, Va.: Time-Life, 1990), 37.

43. David Louis, *2201 Fascinating Facts* (New York: Greenwich House, 1983), 179.

44. Baker, *Nam*, 65.

45. Peter Potter, ed., *All About Death* (New Canaan, Conn.: William Mulvey, 1988), 77.

46. Robert Garland, *The Greek Way of Death* (Ithaca, N.Y.: Cornell University Press, 1985), 92.

47. Michel Ragon, *The Space of Death* (Charlottesville: University Press of Virginia, 1983), 110-11.

48. Anne Wingate, *Scene of the Crime: A Writer's Guide to Crime-Scene Investigations* (Cincinnati: Writer's Digest Books, 1992), 134.

49. *The Apparatus of Death*, 102.

50. Ibid., 156, 170.

51. Leon Weliczker Wells, *The Death Brigade (The Janowska Road)* (New York: Holocaust Library, 1963), 150-51.

52. Ibid., 141-42.

53. Robert Payne, *Massacre: The Tragedy at Bangla Desh and the Phenomenon of Mass Slaughter Throughout History* (New York: Macmillan, 1973), 155-56.

Chapter 9

1. Joseph Sacco, *Morphine, Ice Cream, Tears: Tales of a City Hospital* (New York: Pinnacle, 1989), 119.

2. David E. Stannard, *The Puritan Way of Death* (New York: Oxford University Press, 1977), 131.

3. Anne Wahle as told to Roul Tunley, *Ordeal by Fire: An American Woman's Terror-Filled Trek through War-Torn Germany* (Cleveland: World, 1966), 23.

4. Eugene Richards, *The Knife and Gun Club* (New York: Atlantic Monthly Press, 1989), 79.

5. "Family Took Care of Mummy for Eight Years," *Washington Times*, 2 February 1988, 7.

6. Hal Morgan and Kerry Tucker, *Rumor!* (New York: Penguin, 1984), 103-5.

7. David Louis, *2201 Fascinating Facts* (New York: Greenwich House, 1983), 220.

8. Anne Wingate, *Scene of the Crime* (Cincinnati: Writer's Digest, 1992), 128.

9. Philippe Ariès, *The Hour of Our Death* (New York: Random House, 1982), 362-63.

10. Manuela Dunn Mascetti, *Vampire: The Complete Guide to the World of the Undead* (New York: Viking Studio, 1992), 69.

11. Theodore Malinin, *Processing and Storage of Viable Human Tissues* (Washington, D.C.: Dept. of Health, Education, and Welfare, 1966), 27.

12. Reginald Reynolds, *Beards: Their Social Standing, Religious Involvements, Decorative Possibilities and Value in Offence and Defence Through the Ages* (New York: Doubleday, 1949), 87.

13. John Langone, *Death Is a Noun: A View of the End of Life* (New York: Dell, 1972), 26.

14. George M. Gould and Walter L. Pyle, *Medical Curiosities* (n.p.: Hammond Publishing, 1982), 125.

15. Ibid., 125.

16. Irving Wallace, David Wallechinsky, and Amy Wallace, *The Book of Lists* (New York: E. P. Dutton, 1983), 267.

17. Irving Wallace, David Wallechinsky, and Amy Wallace, *The Book of Lists* 2 (New York: Bantam, 1981), 57-58.

18. *Ripley's Giant Book of Believe It or Not!* (New York: Warner, 1976).

19. Wallace Wallechinsky and Wallace, *The Book of Lists*, 464.

20. Chuck Shepherd, John J. Kohut, and Roland Sweet, *News of the Weird* (New York: Penguin, 1989), 70.

21. Ibid., 126.

22. Michael Medved, *Hospital: The Hidden Lives of a Medical Center Staff* (New York: Pocket, 1982), 311-12.

23. Langone, *Death Is a Noun*, 17-8.

24. E. T. Washburn in J. R. Francis, *The Encyclopedia of Death and Life in the Spirit World* (1896; reprint, Amherst, Wis.: Amherst Press, n.d.), 286-87.

25. Edward R. Ricciuti, *Killers of the Seas* (New York: Walker, 1973), 194.

26. Chuck Shepherd, John J. Kohut, and Roland Sweet, *More News of the Weird* (New York: Penguin, 1990), 188.

27. Robert Wilkins, *The Bedside Book of Death* (New York: Citadel Press, 1990), 48.

28. Medved, *Hospital*, 316.

29. Wilkins, *Bedside Book of Death*, 48.

30. Ibid., 21.

31. Ibid., 32.

32. Jim Holt, "Sunny Side Up," *The New Republic*, 21 February 1994, 24.

33. Wilkins, *Bedside Book of Death*, 25.

34. David Dempsey, *The Way We Die* (New York: McGraw-Hill, 1975), 26.

35. Wilkins, *Bedside Book of Death*, 22.

36. Ann Hodgman, *True Tiny Tales of Terror* (New York: Perigee, 1982), 27.

37. Ariès, *Hour of Our Death*, 399.

38. *Ripley's Giant Book of Believe It or Not!*

39. Richard F. Mould, *Mould's Medical Anecdotes* (Bristol, England: Adam Hilger, 1984), 78.

40. Charles Panati, *Panati's Extraordinary Endings of Practically Everything and Everybody* (New York: Harper & Row, 1989), 72.

41. Ibid., 251.

42. Ibid., 6.

43. Stannard, *Puritan Way of Death*, 37-8.

44. Elisabeth Kübler-Ross, *On Death and Dying* (New York: Macmillan, 1969), 53.

45. A. Alvarez, *The Savage God: A Study of Suicide* (New York: Bantam, 1971), 151.

46. Hodgman, *True Tiny Tales*, 28-9.

47. D. J. Enright, ed., *The Oxford Book of Death* (New York: Oxford University Press, 1987), 27.

48. Robert W. Habenstein and William M. Lamers, *The History of American Funeral Directing* (Milwaukee: National Funeral Directors Assoc., 1955), 199.

49. Warren Shibles, *Death: An Interdisciplinary Analysis* (Whitewater, Wis.: Language Press, 1974), 482.

50. Keith D. Wilson, *Cause of Death* (Cincinnati: Writer's Digest, 1992), 202.

51. Laurence D. Gadd, *The Second Book of the Strange* (New York: World Almanac Publications, 1981), 332.

52. Alice Morse Earle, *Curious Punishments of Bygone Days* (1896; reprint Port Townsend, Wash.: Loompanics Unlimited, 1986), 32.

53. Albert J. Hebert, *Raised from the Dead: True Stories of 400 Resurrection Miracles* (Rockford, Ill.: Tan Books, 1986), 69.

54. Ibid., 72-74.

55. Ibid., 282.

56. "Resurrection Song" in Geoffrey Grigson, *The Faber Book of Epigrams and Epitaphs* (London: Faber & Faber, 1977), 161.

Chapter 10

1. Samuel Gorowitz, *Drawing the Line: Life, Death, and Ethical Choices in an American Hospital* (New York: Oxford University Press, 1991), 48.

2. Andrew Kimbrell, *The Human Body Shop: The Engineering and Marketing of Life* (New York: HarperSan Francisco, 1993), 29.

3. John Pekkanen, *Donor: How One Girl's Death Gave Life to Others* (Boston: Little Brown, 1986), 119.

4. Lewis H. Lapham, Michael Pollan, and Eric Etheridge, *The Harper's Index Book* (New York: Henry Holt, 1986), 27.

5. David Hellerstein, *Battles of Life and Death* (Boston: Houghton Mifflin, 1986), 16.

6. David Dempsey, *The Way We Die: An Investigation of Death and Dying in America Today* (New York: McGraw Hill, 1975), 20.

7. Pekkanen, *Donor*, 11.

8. Michael Dibdin, "The Pathology Lesson," *Granta* 39 (Spring 1992): 97.

9. Perri Klass, *A Not Entirely Benign Procedure: Four Years as a Medical Student* (New York: G. P. Putnam's Sons, 1987), 17.

10. Charles LeBaron, *Gentle Vengeance: An Account of the First Year at Harvard Medical School* (New York: Penguin, 1981), 175-76.

11. Dempsey, *Way We Die*, 185.

12. Robert Wilkins, *The Bedside Book of Death: Macabre Tales of Our Final Passage* (New York: Citadel, 1990), 18.

13. Elizabeth Morgan, *The Making of a Woman Surgeon* (New York: Berkley, 1981), 22-23.

14. LeBaron, *Gentle Vengeance*, 169.

15. Ibid., 191.

16. Ibid., 40.

17. Ina Yalof, *Life and Death: The Story of a Hospital* (New York: Fawcett Crest, 1988), 331.

18. Shawna Vogel, "Science Behind the News," *Discover* 9, no. 4 (September 1988): 22.

19. Michael Brown, *Nurses: The Human Touch* (New York: Ivy, 1992), 203.

20. Michael A. Simpson, *The Facts of Death* (Englewood Cliffs, N.J.: Prentice-Hall, 1979), 26.

21. Chuck Shepherd, John J. Kohut, and Roland Sweet, *More News of the Weird* (New York: Penguin, 1990), 17.

22. Kenneth Iserson, *Death to Dust: What Happens to Dead Bodies?* (Tucson: Galen, 1994), 65.

23. George V. Bishop, *Executions* (Los Angeles: Sherbourne, 1965), 187.

24. James Moores Ball, *The Body Snatchers* (New York: Dorset, 1989), 60.

25. Wilkins, *Bedside Book of Death*, 31.

26. Josef Vincent Lombardo, *Michelangelo: The Pietà and Other Masterpieces* (New York: Pocket Books, 1965), 37.

27. Knut Haeger, *The Illustrated History of Surgery* (New York: Bell, 1988), 99.

28. Douglas Ubelaker and Henry Scammell, *Bones: A Forensic Detective's Casebook* (New York: Edward Burlingame, 1992), 108-13.

29. Keith Simpson, *Forty Years of Murder: An Autobiography* (New York: Charles Scribner's Sons, 1978), 273.

30. Iserson, *Death to Dust*, 99.

31. Ibid., 101.

32. Bishop, *Executions*, 47.

33. Robert K. Wilcox, *Shroud* (New York: Macmillan, 1977), 14-15.

34. Michael M. Baden with Judith Adler Hennessee, *Unnatural Death: Confessions of a Medical Examiner* (New York: Ivy, 1989), 175.

35. Colin Wilson, *Clues! A History of Forensic Detection* (New York: Warner, 1991), 271-72.

36. Robert Jackson, *Francis Camps: Famous Case Histories of the Celebrated Pathologist* (London: Hart-Davis, MacGibbon, 1975), 57.

Chapter 11

1. Edward E. Leslie, *Desperate Journeys, Abandoned Souls: True Stories of Castaways and Other Survivors* (Boston: Houghton Mifflin, 1988), 183.

2. Edward R. Ricciuti, *Killer Animals* (New York: Walker, 1976), 104.

3. Ibid., 82.

4. Jerome Agel and Walter D. Glanze, *Cleopatra's Nose: The Twinkie Defense & 1500 Other Verbal Shortcuts in Popular Parlance* (New York: Prentice Hall, 1990), 222.

5. Douglas Ubelaker and Henry Scammell, *Bones: A Forensic Detective's Casebook* (New York: Edward Burlingame, 1992), 123.

6. Lawrence H. Robbins, *Stones, Bones, and Ancient Cities: Great Discoveries in Archaeology and the Search for Human Origins* (New York: St. Martin's, 1989), 117.

7. Kenneth V. Iserson, *Death to Dust: What Happens to Dead Bodies?* (Tucson: Galen, 1994), 314.

8. Andrew Nikiforuk, *The Fourth Horseman: A Short History of Epidemics, Plagues, Famine and Other Scourges* (New York: M. Evans, 1991), 46.

9. Peter Hathaway Capstick, *Death in the Dark Continent* (New York: St. Martin's, 1983), 173.

10. Clarke, James, *Man Is the Prey* (New York: Stein & Day, 1969), 132-33.

11. Ubelaker and Scammell, *Bones*, 115.

12. Ibid., 115.

13. Hugh Wheeler, *Sweeney Todd: The Demon Barber of Fleet Street*, music and lyrics by Stephen Sondheim (New York: Dodd, Mead, 1979), 97-98.

14. Mel Heimer, *The Cannibal* (New York: Pinnacle, 1991), 54.

15. Reay Tannahill, *Flesh and Blood: A History of the Cannibal Complex* (New York: Dorset, 1975), 155.

16. Ibid., 35.

17. Peggy Reeves Sanday, *Divine Hunger: Cannibalism as a Cultural System* (New York: Cambridge University Press, 1986), 9.

18. Irving Wallace, David Wallechinsky, and Amy Wallace, *The Book of Lists*, 454.

19. George M. Gould and Walter L. Pyle, *Medical Curiosities* (n.p.: Hammond, 1982), 390.

20. Bronislaw Malinowski, *Magic, Science and Religion*, quoted in D. J. Enright, ed., *The Oxford Book of Death* (New York: Oxford University Press, 1987), 128-29.

21. Charles Panati, *Panati's Extraordinary Endings of Practically Everything and Everybody* (New York: Harper & Row, 1989), 9.

22. David Louis, *2201 Fascinating Facts* (New York: Greenwich House, 1983), 234.

23. Laurence D. Gadd, *The Second Book of the Strange* (New York: World Almanac Publications, 1981), 232.

24. Clarke, *Man Is the Prey*, 297.

25. Herman Feifel, *New Meanings of Death* (New York: McGraw-Hill, 1977), 342.

26. Nigel Davies, *Human Sacrifice in History and Today* (New York: William Morrow, 1981), 134.

27. Leslie, *Desperate Journies*, 219.

28. Ed Lucaire, *Phobophobia: The Fear of Fear Itself* (New York: Perigee, 1988), 61.

29. A. W. Brian Simpson, *Cannibalism and the Common Law: The Story of the Tragic Last Voyage of the Mignonette and the Strange Legal Proceedings to Which It Gave Rise* (Chicago: University of Chicago Press, 1984), 285.

30. Alexander McKee, *Death Raft: The Human Drama of the Medusa Shipwreck* (New York: Warner, 1975), 329.

31. F. Gonzalez-Crussi, *Three Forms of Sudden Death and Other Reflections on the Grandeur and Misery of the Body* (London: Pan, 1986), 95.

32. McKee, *Death Raft*, 123.

33. David Hellerstein, *Battles of Life and Death* (Boston: Houghton Mifflin, 1986), 38.

34. A. W. Brian Simpson, *Cannibalism*, 126-27.

35. Ibid., 139.

36. Ibid., 68.

37. Tannahill, *Flesh and Blood*, 46.

38. Charles Neider, ed., *Great Shipwrecks and Castaways: Authentic Accounts of Disasters at Sea* (New York: Dorset, 1990), 142.

39. Colin Wilson, *Clues! A History of Forensic Detection* (New York: Warner, 1991), 352.

40. Tom Philbin, *Murder U.S.A.* (New York: Warner, 1992), 29.

41. Ibid., 206.

42. Iserson, *Death to Dust*, 95.

43. Robert H. Gollmar, *Edward Gein: America's Most Bizarre Murderer* (New York: Pinnacle, 1981), 41.

44. Gonzalez-Crussi, *Three Forms of Sudden Death*, 100.

45. Ibid., 99.

46. Ibid., 104.

47. Ann Hodgman, *True Tiny Tales of Terror* (New York: Perigee Books, 1982), 62, 84.

48. Kim Long and Terry Reim, *Fatal Facts* (New York: Arlington House, 1985), 25.

49. Sanday, *Divine Hunger*, 104.

Chapter 12

1. Thorne Smith, *Skin and Bones* (New York: Sun Dial, 1939), 2.

2. Sir Sydney Smith, *Mostly Murder* (New York: David McKay, 1959), 115.

3. Chuck Shepherd, John J. Kohut, and Roland Sweet, *More News of the Weird* (New York: Penguin, 1990), 97.

4. Alexander McKee, *Death Raft: The Human Drama of the Medusa Shipwreck* (New York: Warner Books, 1975), 170.

5. *Annals of a Quiet Neighborhood*, quoted in Bergen Evans, *Dictionary of Quotations* (New York: Delacorte, 1986), 258.

6. Philippe Ariès, *The Hour of Our Death*, trans. Helen Weaver (New York: Random House, 1982),481.

7. Ibid., 482.

8. A. W. Brian Simpson, *Cannibalism and the Commonlaw: The Story of the Last Tragic Voyage of the Mignonette and the Strange Legal Proceedings to Which It Gave Rise* (Chicago: University of Chicago Press, 1984), 297-98.

9. Jim Schutze, *Cauldron of Blood: The Matamoros Cult Killings* (New York: Avon, 1989), 121.

10. F. Gonzalez-Crussi, *The Day of the Dead and Other Mortal Reflections* (New York: Harcourt Brace, 1993), 101.

11. Paul D. Shapiro, *Paramedic: The True Story of a New York Paramedic's Battles with Life and Death* (New York: Bantam, 1991), 79-80.

12. Robert J. Dvorchak and Lisa Holewa, *Milwaukee Massacre: Jeffrey Dahmer and the Milwaukee Murders* (New York: Dell, 1991), 18.

13. Philippe Ariès, *Images of Man and Death*, trans. Janet Lloyd (Cambridge: Harvard University Press, 1985), 103.

14. Charles Panati, *Panati's Extraordinary Endings of Practically Everything and Everybody* (New York: Harper & Row, 1989), 354.

15. Manuela Dunn Mascetti, *Vampire: The Complete Guide to the World of the Undead* (New York: Viking Studio Books, 1992), 70.

16. Robert Wilkins, *The Bedside Book of Death: Macabre Tales of Our Final Passage* (New York: Citadel, 1990), 45.

17. Douglas Ubelaker and Henry Scammell, *Bones: A Forensic Detective's Casebook* (New York: Edward Burlingame, 1992, 112.

18. Phil McArdle and Karen McArdle, *Fatal Fascination: Where Fact Meets Fiction in Police Work* (Boston: Houghton Mifflin, 1988), 119.

19. Jane McIntosh, *The Practical Archeologist: How We Know What We Know About the Past* (New York: Facts on File Publications, 1986), 92.

20. Anne Wingate, *Scene of the Crime: A Writer's Guide to Crime-Scene Investigations* (Cincinnati: Writer's Digest Books, 1992), 132.

21. Ambrose Bierce, *The Devil's Dictionary* (New York: Dover, 1958), 142.

22. Ronald Blythe, "In the Hour of Death," in *Akenfield: Portrait of an English Village* (New York: Delta, 1970), 317.

23. James P. Sterba, "Aren't You Dying to Know If a Phorid Is in Your Future?" *The Wall Street Journal,* 25 April 1991, sec. A.

24. *Is This Life All There Is?* (Brooklyn, N.Y.: Watchtower Bible and Tract Society, 1974), 171.

25. Blythe, *Hour of Death*, 315.

26. Edward Fitzgerald, ed., *Rubaiyat of Omar Khayyam* (London: Harrap, 1984), verse XIX.

27. John Hadfield, *A Chamber of Horrors* (Boston: Little, Brown, 1965), 304.

28. Georgess McHargue, *Mummies* (Philadelphia: J. B. Lippincott, 1972), 11.

29. Robert M. Goldwyn, *Beyond Appearance: Reflections of a Plastic Surgeon* (New York: Dodd, Mead, 1986), 228.

30. Loring M. Danforth, *The Death Rituals of Rural Greece* (Princeton, NJ: Princeton University Press, 1982), 50.

31. Reay Tannahill, *Flesh and Blood: A History of the Cannibal Complex* (New York: Corset, 1975), 133.

Chapter 13

1. Barbara Jones, *Design for Death* (New York: Bobbs-Merrill, 1967), 20.

2. Marc Fisher, "In California, They Have Seen the Future...and It Is Cold," *Washington Post Magazine,* 24 January 1988, 24.

3. David Hendin, *Death as a Fact of Life* (New York: W. W. Norton, 1984), 194-95.

4. Robert Wilkins, *The Bedside Book of Death* (New York: Citadel, 1990), 144.

5. Greg Palmer, *Death: The Trip of a Lifetime* (New York: HarperCollins, 1993), 122.

6. Joel Kurtzman and Phillip Gordon, *No More Dying: The Conquest of Aging and the Extension of Human Life* (Los Angeles: J. P. Tarcher, 1976), 113.

7. Kenneth Iserson, *Death to Dust* (Tucson: Galen, 1994), 301.

8. Palmer, *Death: The Trip of a Lifetime*, 9.

9. Hal Morgan and Kerry Tucker, *Rumor!* (New York: Penguin, 1984), 100.

10. P. V. Glob, *The Bog People: Iron-Age Man Preserved*, trans. Rupert Bruce-Mitford (Ithaca, N.Y.: Cornell University Press, 1988), 36.

11. Sergei I. Rudenko, *Frozen Tombs of Siberia: The Pazyryk Burials of Iron-Age Horsemen* (Berkeley: University of California Press, 1970), 279-81.

12. Aidan Cockburn and Eve Cockburn, eds., *Mummies, Disease, and Ancient Culture* (Cambridge: Cambridge University Press, 1980), 157.

13. Joan Carroll Cruz, *The Incorruptibles: A Study of the Incorruption of the Bodies of Various Catholic Saints and Beati* (Rockford, Ill.: Tan Books, 1977), 29.

14. Ange-Pierre Leca, *The Egyptian Way of Death* (New York: Doubleday, 1981), 173.

15. Ibid., 178.

16. Ibid., 136-39.

17. Georgess McHargue, *Mummies* (Philadelphia: J. B. Lippincott, 1972), 47-48.

18. Michel Ragon, *The Space of Death* (Charlottesville: University Press of Virginia, 1983), 275-76.

19. Frank H. Stauffer, *The Queer, the Quaint, the Quizzical* (1882; reprint, Detroit: Gale Research, 1968), 175.

20. James E. Harris and Kent R. Weeks, *X-Raying the Pharaohs* (New York: Charles Scribner's Sons, 1973), 92.

21. Leca, *Egyptian Way of Death*, 214-16.

22. John Carey, ed., *Eyewitness to History* (New York: Avon, 1987), 135-36.

23. G. Elliot Smith and Warren R. Dawson, *Egyptian Mummies* (1924; reprint London: Kegan Paul International, 1991), 5.

24. David Louis, *2201 Fascinating Facts* (New York: Greenwich House, 1983), 45.

25. Leca, *Egyptian Way of Death*, 12.

26. Peter A. Clayton, *The Rediscovery of Ancient Egypt: Artists and Travelers in the Nineteenth Century* (New York: Portland House, 1982), 132-33.

27. Iserson, *Death to Dust*, 222.

28. Leca, *Egyptian Way of Death*, 221.

29. Christina El Mahdy, *Mummies, Myth and Magic in Ancient Egypt* (London: Thames & Hudson, 1989), 11.

30. Ahmed Osman, *Stranger in the Valley of the Kings: Solving the Mystery of an Ancient Egyptian Mummy* (San Francisco: Harper & Row, 1987), 140.

31. El Mahdy, *Mummies, Myth and Magic*, 89.

32. Ibid., 75.

33. Carol Andrews, *Egyptian Mummies* (Cambridge: Harvard University Press, 1984), 64.

34. Leca, *Egyptian Way of Death*, 15.

35. Ibid., 241.

36. Charles Dana Gibson, *Sketches in Egypt* (New York: Doubleday & McClure, 1899), 92, 95.

Chapter 14

1. Charles Mackay, *Extraordinary Popular Delusions and the Madness of Crowds* (1841; reprint, New York: Farrar, Strauss & Giroux, 1932), 696.

2. Richard F. Mould, *Mould's Medical Anecdotes* (Bristol, England: Adam Hilger, 1984), 18-22.

3. Robert Wilkins, *The Bedside Book of Death: Macabre Tales of Our Final Passage* (New York: Citadel, 1990), 130.

4. Douglas Ubelaker and Henry Scammell, *Bones: A Forensic Detective's Casebook* (New York: Edward Burlingame, 1992), 253-54.

5. C. V. Wedgwood, *A Coffin for King Charles: The Trial and Execution of Charles I* (New York: Time, 1964), 183.

6. Mackay, *Extraordinary Popular Delusions*, 700.

7. Wade Davis, *Passage of Darkness: The Ethnobiology of the Haitian Zombie* (Chapel Hill: University of North Carolina Press, 1988), 109.

8. James Moores Ball, *The Body Snatchers* (New York: Dorset, 1989), xxviii.

9. Beverley Raphael, *When Disaster Strikes* (New York: Basic Books, 1986), 108.

10. Louis S. Schafer, *Best of Gravestone Humor* (New York: Sterling, 1990), 63.

11. Mackay, *Extraordinary Popular Delusions*, 695.

12. Tom Weil, *The Cemetery Book* (New York: Hippocrene, 1992), 248.

13. Ibid., 246.

14. C. E. Maine, *The Bizarre and the Bloody: A Clutch of Weird Crimes—Each Shockingly True!* (New York: Hart, 1967), 25-32.

15. Mould, *Mould's Medical Anecdotes*, 16-18.

16. Weil, *Cemetery Book*, 245.

17. Cruz, *The Incorruptibles*, 172-76.

18. Wilkins, *Bedside Book of Death*, 132.

19. Joan Carroll Cruz, *The Incorruptibles: A Study of the Incorruption of the Bodies of Various Catholic Saints and Beati* (Rockford, Ill.: Tan Books, 1977), 49-52.

20. Joan Carroll Cruz, *Relics* (Huntington, Ind.: Our Sunday Visitor, 1984), 230-31.

21. Weil, *Cemetery Book*, 252.

22. David Sox, *Relics and Shrines* (London: George Allen & Unwin, 1985), 7.

23. Michel Ragon, *The Space of Death: A Study of Funerary Architecture, Decoration, and Urbanism* (Charlottesville: University Press of Virginia, 1983), 223-24.

24. Weil, *Cemetery Book*, 259.

25. Ibid., 280.

26. Philippe Ariès, *The Hour of Our Death* (New York: Random House, 1982), 384.

27. Ragon, *Space of Death*, 50-1.

28. Weil, *Cemetery Book*, 264.

Chapter 15

1. John K. Lattimer, *Kennedy and Lincoln: Medical and Ballistic Comparisons of their Assassinations* (New York: Harcourt Brace Jovanovich, 1980), 38.

2. Kenneth V. Iserson, *Death to Dust: What Happens to Dead Bodies?* (Tucson: Galen, 1994), 88.

3. F. Gonzalez-Crussi, *The Day of the Dead and Other Mortal Reflections* (New York: Harcourt Brace, 1993), 84.

4. Richard F. Mould, *Mould's Medical Anecdotes*, (Bristol, England: Adam Hilger, 1984), 29.

5. Chuck Shepherd, John J. Kohut, and Roland Sweet, *More News of the Weird* (New York: Penguin, 1990), 123.

6. Richard Selzer, *Confessions of a Knife* (New York: Simon & Schuster, 1979), 182.

7. Iserson, *Death to Dust*, 507.

8. Douglas Ubelaker and Henry Scammell, *Bones: A Forensic Detective's Casebook* (New York: Edward Burlingame Books, 1992), 56.

9. Iserson, *Death to Dust*, 91.

10. Richard Selzer, *Mortal Lessons: Notes on the Art of Surgery* (New York: Simon & Schuster, 1976), 59.

11. John Carey, *Eyewitness to History* (New York: Avon, 1987), 557-58.

12. Edna Buchanan, *Never Let Them See You Cry* (New York: Random House, 1992), 110.

13. Shepherd, Kohut, and Sweet, *More News of the Weird* (New York: Penguin, 1990), 53.

14. Andrew Kimbrell, *The Human Body Shop* (New York: HarperSan Francisco, 1993), 63-64.

15. Ubelaker and Scammell, *Bones*, 260.

Chapter 16

1. Robert Wilkins, *The Bedside Book of Death* (New York: Citadel, 1990), 13-14.

2. Robert B. Dickerson, Jr., *Final Placement* (Algonac, Mich.: Reference Publications, 1982), 59.

3. Albert Hartshorne, *Hanging in Chains* (London: T. Fisher Unwin, 1891), 15.

4. John Laurence, *A History of Capital Punishment* (New York: Citadel, 1963), 60.

5. Bernard O'Donnell, *Should Women Hang?* (London: W. H. Allen, 1956), 104.

6. Kenneth Iserson, *Death to Dust* (Tucson: Galen, 1994), 515.

7. Greg Palmer, *Death: The Trip of a Lifetime* (New York: HarperCollins, 1993), 167.

Chapter 17

1. Greg Palmer, *Death: The Trip of a Lifetime* (New York: HarperCollins, 1993), 167.

2. Michael Medved, *Hospital* (New York: Pocket Books, 1982), 271-72.

3. Andrew Kimbrell, *The Human Body Shop* (New York: HarperSan Francisco, 1993), 298-99.

4. Marvin Harris, *Cannibals and Kings* (New York: Vintage, 1977), 275.

5. *Unite Notes* 6, no. 3 (Spring 1987): 2.

6. Saundra Shohen and Ann Loring, *Emergency!: Stories from the Emergency Department of a New York City Hospital* (New York: St. Martin's, 1989), 125-26.

7. John Morley, *Death, Heaven and the Victorians* (Pittsburgh: University of Pittsburgh Press, 1971), 35.

Chapter 18

1. Ruth Richardson, *Death, Dissection and the Destitute* (London: Routledge & Kegan Paul, 1987), 72.

2. Douglas Ubelaker and Henry Scammell, *Bones: A Forensic Detective's Casebook* (New York: Edward Burlingame, 1992), 254.

3. Kenneth V. Iserson, *Death to Dust: What Happens to Dead Bodies?* (Tucson: Galen, 1994), 357.

4. Glen W. Davidson, "The Human Remains Controversies," *Caduceus: A Museum Journal for the Health Sciences* 7, no. 1 (Spring 1991): 21.

5. Ibid., 25.

6. Richardson, *Death, Dissection, and the Destitute*, 54.

7. Robert Louis Stevenson, "The Body Snatchers."

8. William Bolitho, *Murder for Profit* (New York: Doubleday, 1961), 21.

9. Ibid., 12.

10. Iserson, *Death to Dust*, 345.

11. James Moores Ball, *The Body Snatchers* (New York: Dorset, 1989), 174-75.

12. Louis S. Schafer, *Best of Gravestone Humor* (New York: Sterling, 1990), 87.

13. Robert Wilkins, *The Bedside Book of Death: Macabre Tales of Our Final Passage* (New York: Citadel, 1990), 60-61.

14. Ball, *Body Snatchers*, 176-78.

15. Philip F. Waterman, *The Story of Superstition* (New York: AMS Press, 1970), 117.

16. Ann Landers, *The Ann Landers Encyclopedia A to Z* (New York: Ballantine, 1978), 712.

17. Jim Morton, "The Unrepentant Necrophile: An Interview with Karen Greenlee," in Adam Parfrey, ed., *Apocalypse Culture* (Los Angeles: Feral House, 1990), 29.

18. Harold Schechter, *Deviant: The Shocking True Story of the Original "Psycho"* (New York: Pocket Books, 1989), 106.

19. Iserson, *Death to Dust*, 403.

20. Tom Philbin, *Murder U.S.A.* (New York: Warner, 1992), 205.

21. Moira Martingale, *Cannibal Killers: The History of Impossible Murderers* (New York: Carroll & Graf, 1993), 170.

22. Herbert E. Nass, *Wills of the Rich and Famous: A Fascinating Look at the Rich, Often Surprising Legacies of Yesterday's Celebrities* (New York: Warner, 1991).

23. Iserson, *Death to Dust*, 400-401.

Chapter 19

1 Michael Lesy, *The Forbidden Zone* (New York: Farrar, Strauss & Giroux, 1987), 5.

2. Vanderlyn R. Pine, *Caretaker of the Dead* (New York: Irvington, 1975), 133.

3. Stephen M. Silverman, *Where There's A Will...Who Inherited What and Why* (New York: HarperCollins, 1991), 209.

4. Robert W. Habenstein and William M. Lamers, *The History of American Funeral Directing* (Milwaukee: National Funeral Directors Assoc., 1955), 256.

5. Ruth E. Messinger, "Burnout Taking Toll on Funeral Directors," *American Funeral Director* 110, no. 3 (March 1987): 34.

6. Pat Ivey, *EMT: Beyond the Lights and Sirens* (New York: Ivy, 1989), 156.

7. S. Howard Bartley et al., eds., *Essentials of Life and Health* (New York: Random House, 1977), 328.

8. Greg Palmer, *Death: The Trip of a Lifetime* (New York: HarperCollins, 1993), 180.

9. Palmer, *Death: The Trip of a Lifetime*, 176.

10. Jim Morton, "The Unrepentant Necrophile: An Interview with Karen Greenlee," in Adam Parfrey, ed., *Apocalypse Culture* (Los Angeles: Feral House, 1990), 33.

11. Palmer, *Death: The Trip of a Lifetime*, 153.

12. William A. Nolen, *The Making of a Surgeon* (New York: Random House, 1968), 235.

13. Joseph Sacco, *Morphine, Ice Cream, Tears* (New York: Pinnacle, 1989), 194.

14. Ina Yalof, *Life and Death* (New York: Fawcett Crest, 1988), 18.

15. Barbara Levy, *Legacy of Death: The Remarkable Saga of the Sanson Family, Who Served as Executioners of France for Seven Generations* (Englewood Cliffs, N.J.: Prentice-Hall, 1973), 10.

16. Philippe Ariès, *The Hour of Our Death* (New York: Random House, 1982), 540.

17. Ronald Blythe, "In the Hour of Death," in *Akenfield: Portrait of an English Village* (New York: Delta, 1970), 313.

18. Sir James G. Frazer, *The Golden Bough* (New York: Macmillan, 1951), 239.

19. Kenneth Iserson, *Death to Dust: What Happens to Dead Bodies?* (Tucson: Galen, 1994), 3.

20. Robert J. Lifton and Eric Olson, *Living and Dying* (New York: Bantam, 1974), 87.

21. Walter Werthmueller, "Stiffed: Travels with a City Medical Examiner," *New York Press* 8, no. 51 (22 December 1993), 19.

22. Silverman, *Where There's a Will*, 209.

Bibliography

Allen, Troy. *Disaster*. Chatsworth, Calif.: Barclay House, 1974.

Alvarez, A. *The Savage God: A Study of Suicide*. New York: Bantam, 1971.

Andrews, Carol. *Egyptian Mummies*. Cambridge: Harvard University Press, 1984.

Ariès, Philippe. *The Hour of Our Death*. Translated by Helen Weaver. New York: Random House, 1982.

_____. *Images of Man and Death*. Translated by Janet Lloyd. Cambridge: Harvard University Press, 1985.

Attwater, Donald. *The Penguin Dictionary of Saints*. New York: Viking Penguin, 1985.

Baden, Michael M., with Judith Adler Hennessee. *Unnatural Death: Confessions of a Medical Examiner*. New York: Ivy Books, 1989.

Baldridge, H. David. *Shark Attack*. New York: Berkley Medallion Books, 1974.

Ball, James Moores. *The Body Snatchers*. New York: Dorset, 1989.

Barber, Paul. *Vampires, Burial and Death: Folklore and Reality*. New Haven, Conn.: Yale University Press, 1988.

Beattie, Owen, and John Geiger. *Frozen in Time: Unlocking the Secrets of the Franklin Expedition*. New York: E. P. Dutton, 1987.

Bernard, Hugh Y. *The Law of Death and Disposal of the Dead*. Dobbs Ferry, N.Y.: Oceana Publications, 1966.

Birkett, Sir Norman. *The Newgate Calendar*, London: Folio Society, 1951.

Blair, Clay, Jr. *Survive!* New York: Berkley, 1973.

Bland, James. *The Common Hangman*. Essex, England: Ian Henry, 1984.

Bolitho, William. *Murder for Profit*. New York: Doubleday & Company, 1961.

Bowman, Leroy. *The American Funeral: A Way of Death*. New York: Paperback Library, 1959.

Brian, Denis. *Murderers Die*. New York: St. Martin's, 1986.

Brown, Frederick. *Père Lachaise: Elysium or Real Estate*. New York: Viking, 1973.

Brown, Walter R., and Norman D. Anderson. *Historical Catastrophes: Fires*. Reading, Mass.: Addison-Wesley, 1976.

Browne, Douglas G., and Tom Tullett. *Bernard Spilsbury: His Life and Cases*. New York: Dorset, 1988.

Buchanan, Edna. *The Corpse Had a Familiar Face*. New York: Charter Books, 1987.

_____. *Never Let Them See You Cry: More from Miami, America's Hottest Beat*. New York: Random House, 1992.

Burns, Stanley B. *Sleeping Beauty: Memorial Photography in America*. Altadena, Calif.: Twelvetree, 1990.

Bushell, Peter. *London's Secret History*. London: Constable, 1983.

Canning, John, ed. *50 True Tales of Terror.* New York: Bantam, 1972.

Carey, John, ed. *Eyewitness to History.* New York: Avon, 1987.

Chapman, Pauline. *The French Revolution as Seen by Madame Tussaud Witness Extraordinary.* London: Quiller, 1989.

Clarke, James. *Man Is the Prey.* New York: Stein & Day, 1969.

Cockburn, Aidan, and Eve Cockburn, eds. *Mummies, Disease, and Ancient Culture.* Cambridge: Cambridge University Press, 1980.

Cohen, Daniel. *The Black Death.* New York: Franklin Watts, 1974.

Copper, Basil. *The Vampire in Legend, Fact and Art.* New York: Citadel, 1973.

Cruz, Joan Carroll. *The Incorruptibles: A Study of the Incorruption of the Bodies of Various Catholic Saints and Beati.* Rockford, Ill.: Tan Books, 1977.

____. *Relics.* Huntington, Ind.: Our Sunday Visitor, 1984.

Culbertson, Judi, and Tom Randall. *Permanent Parisians: An Illustrated Guide to the Cemeteries of Paris.* Chelsea, Vt.: Chelsea Green, 1986.

Danforth, Loring M. *The Death Rituals of Rural Greece.* Princeton: Princeton University Press, 1982.

Davies, Nigel. *Human Sacrifice in History and Today.* New York: William Morrow, 1981.

Davis, Wade. *Passage of Darkness: The Ethnobiology of the Haitian Zombie.* Chapel Hill: University of North Carolina Press, 1988.

____. *The Serpent and the Rainbow.* New York: Warner Books, 1985.

Dempsey, David. *The Way We Die: An Investigation of Death and Dying in America Today.* New York: McGraw-Hill, 1975.

Dickerson, Robert B., Jr. *Final Placement: A Guide to the Deaths, Funerals, and Burials of Notable Americans.* Algonac, Mich.: Reference Publications, 1982.

Didier, Jean-Charles. *Death and the Christian.* Translated by P. J. Hepburne-Scott. New York: Hawthorn Books, 1961.

Donaldson, Norman, and Betty Donaldson. *How Did They Die?* New York: St. Martin's, 1989.

____. *How Did They Die?* Vol. 2. New York: St. Martin's, 1989.

Duff, Charles. *A Handbook on Hanging.* Totowa, N.J.: Rowman & Littlefield, 1974.

Dunand, Françoise, and Roger Lichtenberg. *Mummies: A Voyage Through Eternity.* New York: Harry N. Abrams, 1994.

Dyer, Gwynne. *War.* New York: Crown, 1985.

Edwards, Hugh. *Crocodile Attack.* New York: Harper & Row, 1989.

Eichenberg, Fritz. *Dance of Death: A Graphic Commentary on the Danse Macabre through the Centuries.* New York: Abbeville, 1983.

El Mahdy, Christina. *Mummies, Myth and Magic in Ancient Egypt,* London: Thames & Hudson, 1989.

Englade, Ken. *A Family Business.* New York: St. Martin's Paperbacks, 1992.

Enright, D. J., ed. *The Oxford Book of Death.* New York: Oxford University Press, 1987.

Etienne, Robert. *Pompeii: The Day a City Died.* New York: Harry N. Abrams, 1992.

Ettinger, Robert C. W. *The Prospect of Immortality.* Garden City, N.Y.: Doubleday & Company, 1964.

Felknor, Peter S. *The Tri-State Tornado: The Story of America's Greatest Tornado Disaster.* Ames: Iowa State University Press, 1992.

Fleming, Stuart, et al. *The Egyptian Mummy: Secrets and Science.* Philadelphia: University of Pennsylvania, 1980.

Forbes, Malcolm, with Jeff Bloch. *They Went That-a-Way....* New York: Simon & Schuster, 1988.

Forbes, Thomas Rogers. *Surgeons at the Bailey: English Forensic Medicine to 1878.* New Haven, Conn.: Yale University Press, 1985.

Four Days: The Historical Record of the Death of President Kennedy. United Press International and American Heritage, 1964.

Francis, J. R. *The Encyclopedia of Death and Life in the Spirit World.* Amherst, Wis.: Amherst Press, n.d. (facsimile of 1896 edition).

Fraser, Nicholas, and Marysa Navarro. *Eva Perón.* New York: W. W. Norton, 1980.

Frist, William H. *Transplant: A Heart Surgeon's Account of the Life-and-Death Dramas of the New Medicine.* New York: Atlantic Monthly Press, 1989.

Gantt, Paul H. *The Case of Alfred Packer the Man-Eater.* Denver, Colo.: University of Denver Press, 1952.

Gardner, Alexander. *Gardner's Photographic Sketch Book of the Civil War.* New York: Dover, 1959 (facsimile of 1866 edition).

Garland, Robert. *The Greek Way of Death.* Ithaca, N.Y.: Cornell University Press, 1985.

Glob, P. V. *The Bog People: Iron-Age Man Preserved.* Translated by Rupert Bruce-Mitford. Ithaca, N.Y.: Cornell University Press, 1988.

Gollmar, Robert H. *Edward Gein: America's Most Bizarre Murderer.* New York: Pinnacle Books, 1981.

Gonzalez-Crussi, F. *The Day of the Dead and Other Mortal Reflections.* New York: Harcourt, Brace & Company, 1993.

_____. *Notes of an Anatomist.* New York: Harcourt Brace Jovanovich, 1986.

_____. *Three Forms of Sudden Death and Other Reflections on the Grandeur and Misery of the Body.* London: Pan Books, 1986.

Gorer, Geoffrey. *Death, Grief, and Mourning.* New York: Anchor Books, 1967.

Goya, Francisco José de. *The Disasters of War: Eighty-Five Aquatint Etchings by Francisco de Goya.* New York: Doubleday, 1956.

Goya, Fred, and Mike Moriarty. *What a Way to Go! A Compendium of Bizarre Demises.* Secaucus, N.J.: Citadel, 1984.

Habenstein, Robert W., and William M. Lamers. *The History of American Funeral Directing.* Milwaukee, Wis.: National Funeral Directors Association, 1955.

Haeger, Knut. *The Illustrated History of Surgery.* New York: Bell, 1988.

Hansen, Jens Peter Hart, Jørgen Meldgaard, and Jørgen Nordqvist. *The Greenland Mummies.* Washington, D.C.: Smithsonian Institution Press, 1990.

Harmer, Ruth Mulvey. *The High Cost of Dying.* New York: Collier Books, 1963.

Harris, James E., and Kent R. Weeks. *X-Raying the Pharaohs.* New York: Charles Scribner's Sons, 1973.

Hartshorne, Albert. *Hanging in Chains,* London: T. Fisher Unwin, 1891.

Hatch, Robert T. *How to Embalm Your Mother-in-Law: All You Ever Wanted to Know About What Happens Between Your Last Breath and the First Spadeful.* New York: Citadel, 1993.

Haught, James A. *Holy Horrors: An Illustrated History of Religious Murder and Madness.* Buffalo, N.Y.: Prometheus Books, 1990.

Hebert, Albert J. *Raised from the Dead: True Stories of 400 Resurrection Miracles.* Rockford, Ill.: Tan Books, 1986.

Heimer, Mel. *The Cannibal.* New York: Pinnacle Books, 1991.

Helpern, Milton, with Bernard Knight. *Autopsy.* New York: New American Library, 1979.

Hewitt, R. *From Earthquake, Fire and Flood.* New York: Charles Scribner's Sons, 1957.

Hodgman, Ann. *True Tiny Tales of Terror.* New York: Perigee Books, 1982.

Holbein the Younger, Hans. *The Dance of Death.* New York: Dover, 1971 (facsimile of the 1538 edition).

Huntington, Richard, and Peter Metcalf. *Celebrations of Death: The Anthropology of Mortuary Ritual.* Cambridge: Cambridge University Press, 1979.

Ilse, Sherokee. *Empty Arms: Coping After Miscarriage, Stillbirth and Infant Death.* Maple Plain, Minn.: Wintergreen, 1990.

Iserson, Kenneth V. *Death to Dust: What Happens to Dead Bodies?* Tucson: Galen, 1994.

Jackson, Carlton. *The Dreadful Month.* Bowling Green, Ky.: Bowling Green State University Popular Press, 1982.

Jackson, Robert. *Francis Camps: Famous Case Histories of the Celebrated Pathologist.* London: Hart-Davis, MacGibbon, 1975.

Jenkinson, Michael. *Beasts Beyond the Fire.* New York: E. P. Dutton, 1980.

Jones, Barbara. *Design for Death.* New York: Bobbs-Merrill, 1967.

Joyce, Christopher, and Eric Stover. *Witnesses from the Grave: The Stories Bones Tell.* Boston: Little, Brown, 1991.

Kastenbaum, Robert, and Beatrice Kastenbaum. *Encyclopedia of Death.* New York: Avon Books, 1989.

Kershaw, Alister. *A History of the Guillotine.* London: Tandem Books, 1965.

Kimbrell, Andrew. *The Human Body Shop: The Engineering and Marketing of Life.* New York: HarperSan Francisco, 1993.

Krause, Charles A. *Guyana Massacre: The Eyewitness Account.* New York: Berkley Books, 1978.

Langone, John. *Vital Signs: The Way We Die in America.* Boston: Little, Brown, 1974.

Lattimer, John K. *Kennedy and Lincoln: Medical and Ballistic Comparisons of Their Assassinations.* New York: Harcourt Brace Jovanovich, 1980.

Laurence, John. *A History of Capital Punishment.* New York: Citadel, 1963.

Leslie, Edward E. *Desperate Journeys, Abandoned Souls: True Stories of Castaways and Other Survivors.* Boston: Houghton Mifflin, 1988.

Lesy, Michael. *The Forbidden Zone.* New York: Farrar, Strauss & Giroux, 1987.

Levy, Barbara. *Legacy of Death: The Remarkable Saga of the Sanson Family, Who Served as Executioners of France for Seven Generations.* Englewood Cliffs, N.J.: Prentice-Hall, 1973.

Lewis, Alfred Allen, with Herbert Leon MacDonnell. *The Evidence Never Lies: The Casebook of a Modern Sherlock Holmes.* New York: Dell, 1984.

Long, Kim, and Terry Reim. *Fatal Facts: A Lively Look at Common and Curious Ways People Have Died.* New York: Arlington House, 1985.

McArdle, Phil, and Karen McArdle. *Fatal Fascination: Where Fact Meets Fiction in Police Work.* Boston: Houghton Mifflin, 1988.

McCormick, Donald. *Blood on the Sea: The Terrible Story of the Yawl "Mignonette."* London: Frederick Muller, 1962.

McCullough, David. *The Johnstown Flood.* New York: Touchstone, 1986.

McHugh, James T., ed. *Death, Dying and the Law.* Huntington, Ind.: Our Sunday Visitor, 1976.

McKee, Alexander. *Death Raft: The Human Drama of the Medusa Shipwreck.* New York: Warner Books, 1975.

McNally, Raymond T., and Radu Florescu. *In Search of Dracula.* New York: Galahad Books, 1972.

Maine, C. E. *The Bizarre and the Bloody: A Clutch of Weird Crimes—Each Shockingly True!* New York: Hart, 1967.

Mancinelli, Fabrizio. *Catacombs and Basilicas: The Early Christians in Rome.* New York: Harper & Row, 1981.

Mannix, Daniel P. *The History of Torture.* New York: Dell, 1964.

_____. *Those About to Die.* New York: Ballantine, 1958.

Marriner, Brian. *On Death's Bloody Trail: Murder and the Art of Forensic Science.* New York: St. Martin's, 1991.

Martingale, Moira. *Cannibal Killers: The History of Impossible Murderers*. New York: Carroll & Graf, 1993.

Mascetti, Manuela Dunn. *Vampire: The Complete Guide to the World of the Undead*. New York: Viking Studio Books, 1992.

Masters, Brian. *Killing for Company: The Case of Dennis Nilsen*. New York: Stein & Day, 1985.

Mitford, Jessica. *The American Way of Death*. New York: Simon & Schuster, 1963.

Moore, Steve, ed. *The Fortean Times Book of Strange Deaths*. London: John Brown, 1994.

Morgan, Ernest. *Dealing Creatively with Death: A Manual of Death Education and Simple Burial*. Burnsville, N.C.: Celo, 1984.

Morley, John. *Death, Heaven and the Victorians*. Pittsburgh, Pa.: University of Pittsburgh Press, 1971.

Myles, Douglas. *The Great Waves: Tsunami*. New York: McGraw-Hill, 1985.

Neider, Charles, ed. *Great Shipwrecks and Castaways: Authentic Accounts of Disasters at Sea*. New York: Dorset, 1990.

Newton, Michael. *Serial Slaughter: What's Behind America's Murder Epidemic?* Port Townsend, Wash.: Loompanics Unlimited, 1992.

Nikiforuk, Andrew. *The Fourth Horseman: A Short History of Epidemics, Plagues, Famine and Other Scourges*. New York: M. Evans, 1991.

Nohl, Johannes. *The Black Death: A Chronicle of the Plague*. New York: Ballantine, 1960.

Norfleet, Barbara P. *Looking at Death*. Boston: David R. Godine, 1993.

Norris, Joel. *Henry Lee Lucas*. New York: Kensington, 1991.

_____. *Serial Killers*. New York: Doubleday, 1988.

Nuland, Sherwin B. *How We Die: Reflections on Life's Final Chapter*. New York: Alfred A. Knopf, 1994.

Nyiszli, Miklos. *Auschwitz: A Doctor's Eyewitness Account*. Translated by Tibere Kremer and Richard Seaver. New York: Fawcett Crest, 1960.

O'Suilleabhain, Sean. *Irish Wake Amusements*. Dublin, Ireland: Mercier Press, 1976.

Pace, Mildred Mastin. *Wrapped for Eternity: The Story of the Egyptian Mummy*. New York: Dell, 1974.

Packer, Vin. *Sudden Endings*. Greenwich, Conn.: Fawcett, 1964.

Palmer, Greg. *Death: The Trip of a Lifetime*. New York: HarperCollins, 1993.

Panati, Charles. *Panati's Extraordinary Endings of Practically Everything and Everybody*. New York: Harper & Row, 1989.

Payne, Robert. *Massacre: The Tragedy at Bangla Desh and the Phenomenon of Mass Slaughter Throughout History*. New York: Macmillan, 1973.

Pekkanen, John. *Donor: How One Girl's Death Gave Life to Others*. Boston: Little, Brown, 1986.

Pine, Vanderlyn R. *Caretaker of the Dead: The American Funeral Director*. New York: Irvington, 1975.

Poe, Edgar Allan. *The Narrative of Arthur Gordon Pym*. New York: Heritage, 1930.

Prideaux, Michael. *World Disasters*. London: Chartwell Books, 1976.

Ragon, Michel. *The Space of Death: A Study of Funerary Architecture, Decoration, and Urbanism*. Charlottesville: University Press of Virginia, 1983.

Randles, Jenny and Peter Hough. *Death by Supernatural Causes*. London: Grafton Books, 1988.

_____. *Spontaneous Human Combustion*. New York: Dorset, 1992.

Raphael, Beverley. *When Disaster Strikes: How Individuals and Communities Cope with Catastrophe*. New York: Basic Books, 1986.

Read, Piers Paul. *Alive: The Story of the Andes Survivors.* London: Pan Books, 1974.

Reed, Robert C. *Train Wrecks: A Pictorial History of Accidents on the Main Line.* New York: Bonanza Books, 1982.

Ressler, Robert K., and Tom Shachtman. *Whoever Fights Monsters.* New York: St. Martin's, 1992.

Ricciuti, Edward R. *Killer Animals.* New York: Walker, 1976.

Richardson, Ruth. *Death, Dissection and the Destitute.* London: Routledge & Kegan Paul, 1987.

Ripley, Robert. *Ripley's Believe It or Not! Tombstones and Graveyards.* New York: Pocket Books, 1966.

Ronan, Margaret, and Eve Ronan. *Death Around the World: Strange Rites and Weird Customs.* New York: Scholastic Book Services, 1978.

Rudenko, Sergei I. *Frozen Tombs of Siberia: The Pazyryk Burials of Iron-Age Horsemen.* Berkeley: University of California Press, 1970.

Sante, Luc. *Evidence.* New York: Farrar, Strauss & Giroux, 1992.

Savigny, J.-B. Henry, and Alexander Correard. *Narrative of a Voyage to Senegal in 1816.* Marlboro, Vt.: Marlboro Press, 1986 (facsimile of 1818 edition).

Scharp, Hal. *Shark Safari.* New York: Award Books, 1975.

Schechter, Harold. *Deviant: The Shocking True Story of the Original "Psycho."* New York: Pocket Books, 1989.

Schurmacher, Emile C. *True Tales of Terror.* New York: Paperback Library, 1972.

Selzer, Richard. *Confessions of a Knife.* New York: Simon & Schuster, 1979.

_____. *Mortal Lessons: Notes on the Art of Surgery.* New York: Simon & Schuster, 1976.

Shibles, Warren. *Death: An Interdisciplinary Analysis.* Whitewater, Wis.: Language Press, 1974.

Simpson, A. W. Brian. *Cannibalism and the Common Law: The Story of the Tragic Last Voyage of the Mignonette and the Strange Legal Proceedings to Which It Gave Rise.* Chicago: University of Chicago Press, 1984.

Simpson, Keith. *Forty Years of Murder: An Autobiography.* New York: Charles Scribner's Sons, 1978.

Simpson, Michael A. *The Facts of Death.* Englewood Cliffs, N.J.: Prentice-Hall, 1979.

Smith, G. Elliot, and Warren R. Dawson. *Egyptian Mummies.* London: Kegan Paul International, 1991.

Smith, Sir Sydney. *Mostly Murder.* New York: David McKay, 1959.

Sobol, Donald J. *Disaster.* New York: Pocket Books, 1979.

Spencer, A. J. *Death in Ancient Egypt.* New York: Penguin Books, 1982.

Stannard, David E., ed. *Death in America,* Philadelphia: University of Pennsylvania Press, 1975.

_____. *The Puritan Way of Death: A Study in Religion, Culture, and Social Change.* New York: Oxford University Press, 1977.

Stewart, George R. *Ordeal by Hunger: The Story of the Donner Party.* London: Michael Haag, 1986.

Taken: Photography and Death. Washington, D.C.: Tartt Gallery, 1989.

Tannahill, Reay. *Flesh and Blood: A History of the Cannibal Complex.* New York: Dorset, 1975.

Thomas, Gordon, and Max Morgan Witts. *The San Francisco Earthquake.* New York: Stein & Day, 1971.

Trombley, Stephen. *The Execution Protocol: Inside America's Capital Punishment Industry.* New York: Doubleday, 1992.

Ubelaker, Douglas, and Henry Scammell. *Bones: A Forensic Detective's Casebook.* New York: Edward Burlingame Books, 1992.

Van Der Zee, James, Owen Dodson, and Camille Billops. *The Harlem Book of the Dead*. Dobbs Ferry, N.Y.: Morgan & Morgan, 1978.

Vidic, Branislav, and Faustino R. Suarez. *Photographic Atlas of the Human Body*. St. Louis, Mo.: C. V. Mosby, 1984.

Walls, H. J. *Forensic Science: An Introduction to Scientific Crime Detection*. New York: Praeger, 1974.

Weider, Ben, and David Hapgood. *The Murder of Napoleon*. New York: Congdon & Lattes, 1982.

Weil, Tom. *The Cemetery Book: Graveyards, Catacombs and Other Travel Haunts Around the World*. New York: Hippocrene Books, 1992.

Wells, Leon Weliczker. *The Death Brigade (The Janowska Road)*. New York: Holocaust Library, 1963.

Wilkins, Robert. *The Bedside Book of Death: Macabre Tales of Our Final Passage*. New York: Citadel, 1990.

Willke, Dr. and Mrs. J. C. *Handbook on Abortion*. Cincinnati: Hiltz, 1971.

Wilson, Colin. *Clues! A History of Forensic Detection*. New York: Warner Books, 1991.

_____. *Written in Blood: Detectives and Detection*. New York: Warner Books, 1991.

Wilson, Keith D. *Cause of Death: A Writer's Guide to Death, Murder & Forensic Medicine*. Cincinnati: Writer's Digest Books, 1992.

Wingate, Anne. *Scene of the Crime: A Writer's Guide to Crime-Scene Investigations*. Cincinnati: Writer's Digest Books, 1992.

Wolf, Leonard. *A Dream of Dracula: In Search of the Living Dead*. New York: Popular Library, 1972.

Wolfenstein, Martha. *Disaster: A Psychological Essay*. Glencoe, Ill.: The Free Press, 1957.

Yadin, Yigael. *Masada: Herod's Fortress and the Zealots' Last Stand*. New York: Random House, 1966.

Zikmund, Miroslav, and Jiří Hanzelka. *Amazon Headhunters*. Translated by Olga Kuthanová. Prague: Artia Prague, 1963.

Zugibe, Frederick T. *The Cross and the Shroud: A Medical Inquiry into the Crucifixion*. New York: Paragon House, 1988.

Index

Abortion 3, 284–286; fetal tissue 285
Accident 12, 155–161, 212; airline 159–160, 210; automobile 38, 157–158, 206; industrial 157, 161; ship 159, 291; train 160; victims of 155, 288
Acilius 184
Adipocere 227, 270
Adrian, St. 261
Agatha, St. 259
Agesipolis 54
Agnes of Montepulciano, St. 192, 258
Agnes of Prague, Bl. 192
Ahmose–Nefertari, Queen 240
Alcor Life Extension Foundation 234
Aldritch, Willard 87
Alexander, Pope 119
Alexander the Great 54
Alphonsus, St. 260
Alyscamps Cemetery 85
Amasis, King 283
Ambrose, St. 192
Amenhotep I 245
Amenhotep II 246
Amenophis II 242
American Board of Funeral Service Education 3, 56
American Civil War 36, 54, 138, 171, 288; see also War
American Cryonics Society 233, 236
American Revolution 288; see also War
Amin, Idi 224
Amundsen, Roald 110
Anastasia, Albert 36
Anatomical gifts 179, 197–204; consent for 198, 200–202, 204, 206, 208; organs as 197, 201–202, 285–286;

procurement of 201; tissues as 198–200, 285–286, 291; transplant of 198; whole–body donation as 182
Andersen, Hans Christian 187
Anderson, Fanella 180
Andrée, Salomon August 110
Andrew, St. 260
Andrew Bobola, St. 262
Animals 158; scavenging by 32, 209–212
Ankhesenamun 246
Ann Catherine Emmerick, Venerable 261
Anne, St. 258–259
Anne of Denmark 66
Anointing 49–52, 210
Anthony, St. 263
Anthony, Susan B. 68
Anthony Bonfadini, Bl. 255
Anthony of Padua, St. 193, 258
Anthropological Research Facility 204
Antonio Vici, Bl. 255
Appel, George 146
Ara, Pedro 60
Aram, Eugene 250
Arcangela Girlani, Bl. 256
Aretino, Pietro 210
Ariès, Philippe 42
Arlington National Cemetery 94, 96, 288–289
Armed Forces Institute of Pathology 249
Armstrong, Louis 68
Ars Moriendi 30
Asklepios 181
Astor, John Jacob 159

345